GREEN GUIDE

Birds

OF BRITAIN AND EUROPE

GREEN GUIDE

Birds

OF BRITAIN AND EUROPE

jim flegg

ILLUSTRATED BY martin woodcock

NEW
HOLLAND

This edition first published in the UK in 2001 by
New Holland Publishers (UK) Ltd
Garfield House, 86-88 Edgware Road, London W2 2EA

www.newhollandpublishers.com

10

ISBN 1 85974 923 2

Phototypeset by AKM Associates (UK) Ltd
Reproduction by Scantrans Pte Ltd
Printed and bound in Singapore by
Kyodo Printing Co (Singapore) Pte Ltd

Contents

Introduction

The beauty of birdwatching is its simplicity – whether you are walking along the pavement or standing in a garden or park there will always be birds to watch. Birds are highly mobile, so there is always the chance of catching the unexpected – the brilliant streak of a Kingfisher darting along the riverbank or the muffled wingbeats of a group of swans flying low overhead. All you need is a keen eye, some basic equipment, and a guidebook such as this designed to help you identify the bird and understand something about its lifestyle and habitat.

The more that can be gleaned about how and where birds live, the more fascinating and rewarding this hobby will become. This guide will help you both to identify a bird correctly and to understand why and how such a bird was found at a particular time and place. It covers 150 of the species most likely to be seen in Britain and Europe, each with an individual illustration, easy-to-follow field notes to confirm identification and a map showing its main distribution.

The maps show the distribution for each species, using the following colour codes:
Blue   Winter visitors
Yellow   Summer visitors' breeding range
Green   All year-round presence

The symbols which appear on the illustrations indicate the sexes and plumage variations:

♂ Male
♀ Female
I Immature
S Summer plumage
W Winter plumage

How to Identify Birds

The shape of a bird is geared for flight and the basic body-plan of a bird differs little from species to species. The majority of birds are small, and the larger they are the more energy-saving their flight becomes.

The skeleton of a bird is made up of a strong central 'box' of backbone, ribs and breastbone. The vital organs are grouped within for protection and to form a centre of gravity between the wings that helps make flight much easier.

The wings, which are attached to this central box, are the most distinctive and identifiable feature of birds. The outline varies tremendously and is an invaluable aid to identification, especially when the outline of the bird may only be seen in flight. Game birds have rounded wings for quick take-off and short escape flights; birds of prey, on the other hand, have broad wings with heavily fingered tips to catch air thermals so they can glide effortlessly when searching for prey or during long migrations. Seabirds that habitually skim the rolling waves of the oceans, such as the Fulmar, have long, straight and narrow wings.

Feathers are unique to birds and are remarkable structures made of a protein called keratin. They are not just indispensable to successful flight, but also make the bird wind- and water-proof and provide thermal insulation. The colours and markings of feathers give birds excellent camouflage or dazzling display plumages for courtship – all of which adds another valuable clue to the identification of a particular species, and perhaps reveals its age or sex.

Tails vary as much as wings and are also a valuable marker for instant identification. They are essentially for steering, but are also

Introduction

used in courtship displays; and the way they are held, their colour and shape offer useful guides.

At the other end of the bird, the beak varies according to what the bird uses it for – the long decurved bill of the Curlew is for probing, while that of the Great Spotted Woodpecker is for chiselling, and that of the Goldfinch acts as a pair of tweezers. Beaks can be especially helpful in differentiating similar-looking species such as ducks, where one species may be a fish-eating 'sawbill' and another a broad-billed filter feeder.

Legs and feet are the last but by no means least valuable appendages to aid successful bird identification. As with beaks, the range of shapes reflects different lifestyles. Herons have long legs, ideally suited to wading, while the razor-sharp talons of raptors and owls are superbly designed to grab and kill prey; the webbed toes of divers and ducks are designed for efficient swimming.

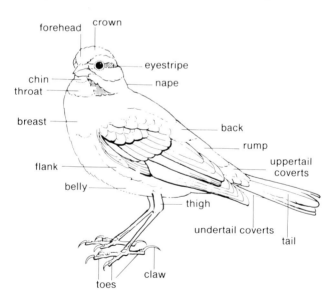

Bird Habitats

The power of flight has enabled birds to spread themselves over almost all the earth's surfaces. Insects may be more widely dispersed on land, but not many are found at sea. Birds, on the other hand, are found from the tropical oceans to the icy polar waters, above mountain-tops and in deep valleys.

Although birds can flit between habitats and turn up almost anywhere – particularly during the migration season or just after stormy weather when they may have been blown off course – it is essential to recognise the basic bird habitats just to anticipate what sort of bird you may wish to see, as well as to make identification easier.

Contrary to popular belief, if a particular species chooses to inhabitat a man-made landscape, this does not make it an uninteresting bird to watch. A number of quite surprising bird species have managed to penetrate human abodes such as villages, towns and even cities, and have adapted to them quite successfully. The hazards of traffic and domestic animals are outweighed by the abundance of cultivated food and scraps as well as the milder climate that urban conglomerations generate. Starlings and House Sparrows may predominate in such areas, but the odd Jackdaw, Greenfinch or Great Tit may also be spotted. If you have a garden and can put out a bird table, then a wider variety of species will be attracted – Robins, Song Thrushes and Blue Tits perhaps. The garden is a great magnet for birds, but municipal parks are good habitats for Woodpigeons and Tawny Owls, while city lakes will attract waterbirds such as Moorhens, Coot, Canada Geese, Mute Swans and several species of duck. Feral pigeons are ubiquitous and perhaps not welcome, but their relative, the Collared Dove, is a newcomer that has made an impressive move to farmland and cultivated surroundings from the Middle East over the past 50 years.

Further afield, farmland provides many species of birds with a diverse rural habitat, despite the trend towards prairie-type farming and the widespread use of pesticides and fertilisers. The combination of field, hedgerow and woodland edge that many farms provide, suits a great number of species including thrushes, finches and buntings, as well as seed-eating birds like the Linnet and the Yellowhammer and migrant warblers like the Whitethroat. Not many species favour the wide-open monoculture crop fields, with the notable exception of the Skylark. Farm buildings provide welcome nest sites for Spotted Flycatchers, Swallows, Wagtails and, if the buildings are old, the rapidly declining Barn Owl.

Introduction

As for the woodlands themselves, broadleaved trees such as oak, ash and beech attract owls as well as the Sparrowhawk. Neither is easy to find. The seasonal abundance of insects in the canopy will attract many year-round residents such as tits, but also migrants including the Turtle Dove and many warblers.

The more widely-spaced coniferous woodlands are good places to spot Coal Tits, Redstarts and Woodpeckers. The paucity of undergrowth does not deter the likes of Goldcrests and Chaffinches as well as Woodpigeons. Freshly planted or cleared forests attract the Tree Pipit and other unexpected birds.

Freshwater habitats or wetlands – from humble hill streams to mighty river estuaries as well as ponds, lakes, marshes and reservoirs – offer a wonderful variety of birdlife for the bird-watcher. On upland streams you may enjoy the sight of Common Sandpipers, Dippers and Grey Wagtails forever bobbing their tails or bodies on mid-stream boulders or pebbly banks scanning for food. The Kingfisher, too, may flash past. Waders such as the Redshank and Snipe will be seen in marshes and lowland rivers. Natural wetlands provide among the richest variety of bird species, but man-made reservoirs also make excellent, if not scenic, bird-watching sites with huge varieties of wintering waterfowl and the odd exotic migrant. Where the river finally joins the sea, the combination of brackish, sheltered, relatively warm water rich in nutrients is a magnet for wildfowl, gulls and waders in autumn, winter and spring. Many of these species are overwintering here before making their long-haul flights. Estuaries are essentially staging posts for such birds, so it makes sense to plan a field trip according to the seasonal migrations. Such an abundance of similar-looking species in close proximity can present a considerable problem when attempts are made to identify them.

From spectacular cliff faces and rock stacks facing the brunt of the Atlantic storms to the more sheltered low-lying mudflats, the coastline of Europe is very exposed and so attracts specific groups of birds such as auks and gulls. In the summer months the bird-watcher's rewards can be magnificent, especially where there are colonies of breeding seabirds like Gannets. Cliff-top walks or boat trip forays will afford spectacular aerial views and ample opportunity to watch differing plunge-dive techniques of fishing birds. This is also an excellent chance to study differing courtship and nesting techniques be it Puffins in cavities or Guillemots on flat ledges. In winter, waders and wildfowl predominate.

Scrub, heathland and moors are good spots to watch various warblers, pipits, shrikes and the Hoopoe. Bushes and brambles provide abundant nest sites for song and perching birds. Meadow Pipits are much in evidence in moorland as are the Golden Plover and Dunlin. With few trees, birds must nest on the ground and rely on camouflage against would-be predators such as foxes or stoats. Year-round moorland residents include Red Grouse.

The mountain areas of Europe are effectively ecological islands combining a mixture of Mediterranean and Arctic habitats suited to Buzzards and Golden Eagles swirling on upcurrents. The latter's home territory may cover some hundred square kilometres, as it ranges in search of prey to satisfy its food demands. Catching sight of such a bird is one of the true joys of birdwatching.

Practical Birdwatching and Conservation

Stealth – the ability to come up close to a bird without disturbing it – is probably the most useful attribute a would-be birdwatcher can hope to master. Birds have exceptionally keen eyesight and hearing (though fortunately their chances of picking up human scent in the wind are remote) and will disappear into a frustrating blur just as the watcher settles down for a good look. So the first rule of good fieldcraft is always to move quietly. In woodland, obviously, it is important to avoid crashing through undergrowth, snapping twigs underfoot.

Listening is almost as crucial as moving slowly. If you pause frequently to listen you will hear the various bird songs and calls that will give advance warning of what species to expect. Of course, much of this knowledge comes with experience, but tapes of bird calls, can be bought, or borrowed from a library, and the notes in this book contain the most common calls. Most birds are heard before they are seen, so learning to recognise the key repertoire of calls is a great asset.

Remember to walk slowly and take advantage of the natural cover provided by trees, bushes and other vegetation. When you reach a gap, pause to listen for a few moments, then look around. The birds will reveal themselves. It may sound obvious, but even experienced birdwatchers can forget where they are and suddenly pull out a handkerchief, scaring off any nearby birds.

Just as birds are well camouflaged in their natural habitats, so too the aspiring birdwatcher should wear dull browns or greens and certainly not ultrabright anoraks or loud rustling plastic kagouls. It is hard enough not drawing attention to yourself as you creep through the undergrowth so there is no point in advertising your presence by unsuitable outdoor clothing.

The *Concise Guide* will help you to plan a field trip, as it explains which species are likely to be seen in the type of habitat you have chosen to visit. A field note book is also indispensable for jotting down the essential characteristics of your sighting: size, colourings, markings, wing shape, tail shape, beak shape, plus any distinctive markings such as eyestripes or wingbars. Make a note of the bird call, using a phonetic spelling; also make a note of the habitat, time of day, month, and the species and numbers of each bird seen.

Birdwatching can be enjoyed without specialist equipment such as a telescope, tripod, single-lens reflex camera with telephoto lens and cassette recorder – but a pair of binoculars is an essential which will

literally open up a whole new avian world. A specialist camera/ binocular shop will advise on technical details such as the most suitable magnification.

The most important consideration when birdwatching is to put the birds' interests first: never disturb nesting birds or tired migrants. Kites and divers, for example, are suffering directly because of birdwatchers' activities during their breeding season. The need to get near to a bird does not mean that wild vegetation should be trampled underfoot or other wildlife scared off in the process. Wildlife habitats are precariously balanced these days and you should always be aware of not upsetting the delicate ecological balance in the pursuit of birdwatching. Any rubbish should be taken home for disposal – a casually discarded plastic wrapping can be a lethal time-bomb for an unsuspecting bird. It also goes without saying that you should be aware that birds and eggs are protected by law, and that effective prosecutions, leading to substantial fines, are now the routine.

You can help birds in a positive way by joining and giving financial support to one of the many bird clubs, societies and trusts that have become strong lobbying pressure groups. Bird societies also spend a large part of that financial support in setting up and maintaining a network of bird reserves that goes a long way to conserving both disappearing habitats and endangered species. Joining a local ornithological group will help conservation at grass-roots level. You can offer to collect data on local bird numbers and movements which is of great practical assistance to both the scientific study of birds and their conservation, locally *and* nationally.

Bird Classification and Characteristics

There is an accepted scientific naming system for birds (as for all animals and plants) which has the great advantage of being understood internationally, even if the bird's common name differs from country to country. For example, a British birdwatcher may call that popular songbird of our gardens with the red breast a 'Robin', but this would not mean much to a French bird spotter who knows it as *'Rouge-gorge'*. The scientific name *Erithacus rubecula*, however, is known worldwide, not just in Europe. To an American, on the other hand, the name 'Robin' means a different species altogether as clearly identified by its scientific name *Turdus migratorius*. But the classification system does more than this: it helps us identify bird species by placing them in a series of groupings. First there is the species; then closely-related species are grouped in the same genus. A genus that is related to another genus is then placed in a family grouping, and families in turn are combined into the largest grouping called orders.

The key to understanding these groups is to remember that they are partly based on structural similarities that generally speaking would be obvious to the birdwatcher in the field. So, for example, the large forward-looking eyes, disc-like face, hooked bill and sharp taloned feet of the owls place them in the order Strigiformes, and the families Tytonidae and Strigidae. Recognising such family likeness will certainly aid birdwatchers in the field. The species described in this book belong to the following groups.

Divers (order Gaviiformes, family Gaviidae)
As their name suggests, diving birds of the water with streamlined bodies, long necks, and dagger-shaped beaks. In flight their silhouette resembles a cigar and their rapidly beating wings are a good identification pointer.

Grebes (order Podicipediformes, family Podicipedidae)
Smaller and plumper diving waterbirds with rather shorter dagger-like beaks. They have stumpy, fluffy tails. Most of their body is submerged when swimming.

Tubenoses (order Procellariiformes)
Oceanic seabirds that get their name from the prominent paired tubular nostrils on the ridge of the beak that also looks segmented. Shearwaters and Fulmars glide low over the water on stiff wings, while Storm Petrels flutter low over the waves, dipping down to pick food off the surface.

Gannet and Cormorants (order Pelecaniformes)
Enormous waterbirds with huge feet. The spectacular black and white Gannet has slim pointed wings and plunge-dives into the sea from great heights. The dark and slim-bodied Cormorants are often seen standing on rocks with wings outstretched to dry.

Herons (order Ciconiiformes)
Wading birds with long legs, slender toes and long necks found along marshes and coasts. They stab at prey with their dagger beaks. Their wings are broad and heavily fingered and they fly with slow steady wingbeats at quite fast speeds.

Introduction

Waterfowl – swans, geese and ducks – (order Anseriformes)
All have webbed feet and three forward-pointing toes. The generally duck-like beaks are the other identifying feature. Swans are the largest in this order with their recognisable long necks and adult white plumage. Geese are somewhat smaller and are identifiable by their flying in 'V' formation and honking calls. Ducks have short necks with feet set well back on the body which gives their tell-tale waddling walk. The wings are fast beating and pointed at the tip. Ducks differ from other waterfowl in that the male and female have different plumages (the male is usually the more distinctive). The exception to this, and the short neck, is the Shelduck.

Birds of Prey (orders Accipitriformes and Falconiformes)
Often called raptors, they have powerful hooked beaks for tearing flesh, large eyes for locating prey and long legs with strong talons and sharp claws at the end for killing prey. All raptors have a fleshy pad called a cere, at the base of the beak, which contains the nostrils. As it takes several years to reach maturity, with irregular moults, there is a confusing variation of juvenile plumages. Females are generally larger than males.

Game Birds (order Galliformes)
Heavy set with small heads and chicken-like beaks. Their wings are round and fingered which gives them almost vertical take-off as well as their distinctive whirring flight.

Rails (order Gruiformes)
Dumpy wetland birds with long spidery toes that are often lifted well out of the water in their sedate walk. Most have a short, stout beak.

Waders, Shorebirds (part of order Charadriiformes)
The birds belonging to the order Charadriiformes are classified together because of anatomical features that are not obvious to the birdwatcher. Waders have long legs and horizontally-held bodies. Length and colour of legs and bills, and plumage details, especially wingbar, rump and tail patterns help to distinguish the species, as do their diverse feeding techniques.

Skuas (part of order Charadriiformes)
Gull-like seabirds characterised by the white flashes in the centre of the wings noticeable in flight. They have a faster dashing flight than gulls, and harry other seabirds for food.

Gulls (part of order Charadriiformes)
They have long legs with webbed feet and comparatively long wings. Male and female adults are usually white bodied with back and wings grey or black. Fine details of shape, size and plumage will assist identification of individual species.

Terns (part of order Charadriiformes)
Smaller than gulls with shorter necks, slimmer wings and shorter legs. Their name 'sea swallows' comes from their graceful flight. They often hover above the water before diving to plunge just beneath the surface for prey. Marsh terns, such as Black Terns, also hawk for insects over wetlands.

Auks (part of order Charadriiformes)
Stout strong-billed birds with webbed feet set far back on the body and small wings that whirr in low flight above the sea. They are superficially penguin-like when they stand erect.

Pigeons and Doves (order Columbiformes, family Columbidae)
Relatively heavy-bodied birds with small heads and beaks on longish necks. Their tails are long and wings pointed.

Owls (order Strigiformes, families Tytonidae and Strigidae)
They have large round heads, a distinctive facial disc with hooked beak and round eyes, and a characteristically neckless appearance. Body plumage tends to conceal their long legs but their feathered toes have strong sharp talons. Their eerie calls and generally nocturnal habits also single them out for identification.

Introduction

Cuckoos (order Cuculiformes, family Cucilidae)
Elusive medium-sized, long-tailed birds with short pointed wings giving them a flight silhouette like a falcon, but they can be distinguished by their small, weak, unhooked bills and their calls.

Kingfishers and Hoopoe (order Coraciiformes)
Brightly coloured birds whose individual plumage makes identification easy. Common features are scarce, except that they are hole-nesters.

Woodpeckers (order Piciformes, family Picidae)
Possess stout dagger-shaped beaks and climb trees in a head-uppermost position with long claws on their two-forward, two-back toes providing excellent grip. Plumage is generally a striking black, white and red, sometimes green and yellow. All are hole-nesters.

Swallows and Martins (order Passeriformes, family Hirundinidae)
All have relatively long curved wings with a recognisable forked tail. They will perch readily, which the similar Swift does not.

Swifts (order Apodiformes, family Apodidae)
Wings are distinctively long and sickle-shaped. Swifts live almost entirely on the wing. The dark body is shaped like a torpedo with a short tail and tiny legs.

Larks (order Passeriformes, family Alaudidae)
Well camouflaged, ground-nesting, mottled brown birds with long hind claws. They have a song-flight which aids identification. Beak shapes vary according to diet.

Pipits and Wagtails (order Passeriformes, family Motacillidae)
Spend much of their time running after insects. Wagtails are small and slim-bodied with a long white-bordered tail that they wag up and down continuously. They are boldly patterned while Pipits by contrast are generally brownish and well streaked but inconspicuous. Pipits have a distinctive song-flight. Song and habitat help to distinguish the species.

Accentors (order Passeriformes, family Prunellidae)
Small, shy inconspicuous birds with drab plumage. Knowing their habitat and song can aid correct identification.

Dipper (order Passeriformes, family Cinclidae)
Only one species, which has a large white bib and a habit of bobbing on boulders before plunging into rivers.

Wren (order Passeriformes, family Troglodytidae)
Only one species, with a tiny cocked tail, chestnut colours and a short-range whirring flight. The song is powerful and melodious.

Thrushes and Chats (order Passeriformes, family Turdidae)
Plump, strong-legged birds with medium-thick beaks for eating fruit, insects, snails and worms. Distinctive plumage helps distinguish the various members, which include Robins, redstarts, chats, wheatears and thrushes.

Introduction

Warblers and Crests (order Passeriformes, family Sylviidae)
All have finely pointed, often slim beaks for eating insects. Most are summer visitors. While some are melodious warblers, as their name implies, others produce a scratchy, metallic sound – so knowledge of song will help to differentiate the species.

Flycatchers (order Passeriformes, family Muscicapidae)
Summer visitors. They have slim beaks when viewed side-on, but broad-based when viewed from above or below. They have prominent bristles surrounding their gape. Their slim body has long wings and very short legs. They catch insects in flight, returning to a prominent perch. Plumage helps identification.

Tits (order Passeriformes, families Timaliidae, Aegithalidae, Paridae)
Three families, two of which are very distinctive. The true tits have stubby, sharply-pointed beaks and are tree dwellers. Their weak flight with bursts of fluttering wingbeats is a good field guide, as are their individual plumage markings and song. The Bearded Tit and Long-tailed Tit have plumages which are difficult to mistake.

Introduction

Treecreepers (order Passeriformes, family Certhiidae)
Move woodpecker-like on tree trunks, head-up with stiff tail acting as a prop. The beak is downcurved and finely pointed and the large eyes are set below a marked eyebrow. In flight the prominent wingbar pattern provides a good field guide.

Nuthatches (order Passeriformes, family Sittidae)
Resemble woodpeckers and have stout dagger-like beaks. They move with equal ease in a head-down or head-up pose. Toes are three forward, one back. The tail is soft and does not serve as a prop.

Shrikes (order Passeriformes, family Laniidae)
Have bold plumage with striking wingbars, long tails and hawk-like hooked beaks. Another characteristic is the habit of impaling prey temporarily on thorns or barbed wire.

Crows (order Passeriformes, family Corvidae)
Black or black and grey birds, usually with a metallic sheen. Their beaks are stout. They are prone to hopping about the ground when scavenging. Jays and Magpies are more strikingly plumaged members of this group.

Starlings (order Passeriformes, family Sturnidae)
Among the most ubiquitous of birds in urban and country habitats. Their glossy iridescent greens and purples, and direct flight on triangular wings, are useful guides to identification.

Finches (order Passeriformes, family Fringillidae)
Noticeable for their short triangular or wedge-shaped beaks, well adapted to crushing varying types of seed. Undulating flight and a forked tail in some species can also aid recognition.

Buntings (order Passeriformes, family Emberizidae)
Superficially resemble elongated and colourful Sparrows with thickish wedge-shaped beaks. The lower jaw is larger than the upper. Distinctive summer plumages and song help distinguish the males. The duller females and immatures are difficult to identify.

Sparrows (order Passeriformes, family Passeridae)
Small, stocky birds with robust wedge-shaped beaks for seed eating. Most have a drab plumage and undulating flight.

Divers/Grebes

Red-throated Diver *Gavia stellata* 55cm Smallest diver. Summer adult has grey-brown back, sparse, pale markings; underparts white. Head grey-brown. Neck white, dark brown streaks. Throat-patch dark red, appearing almost black. Beak pale; dagger-shaped, slightly upturned, held upwards. Winter adult greyish above, white flecking; white below. Immature resembles winter adult. In flight, slimmer and paler than other species, wingbeats more rapid and deeper. Cackling and barking calls during breeding season, silent in winter. Breeds beside moorland pools, occasionally by sea inlets. Occurs inshore along west European coast. Widespread, rarely numerous.

Little Grebe *Tachybaptus ruficollis* 25cm Smallest and dumpiest of the grebes. Short-necked and characteristically tail-less appearance. Summer adult dark brown, with chin and upper throat rich chestnut, and small yellow patch at base of beak. Winter adult drab brown above, paler below. Immature resembles winter adult. Far-carrying, shrill whinnying song. Found year-round on slow-moving rivers, canals, ditches, lakes and man-made waters, usually with ample marginal vegetation. Common and widespread.

Great Crested Grebe *Podiceps cristatus* 45cm Largest of the grebes. Summer adult grey-brown above, white below. Head conspicuously crested and tufted in chestnut and black. Neck white, long and slender. Beak orange, dagger-like. Winter adult generally greyer, with only slight indication of crest. Immature resembles winter adult. In flight appears hump-backed, and shows conspicuous white patches on whirring wings. Various guttural honks and croaks accompany display. Frequents larger reed-fringed fresh waters year-round; some winter on sheltered coastal waters. Widespread, fairly common.

Fulmar *Fulmarus glacialis* 45cm Heavy-bodied seabird, well streamlined. Adult and immature superficially gull-like in plumage, pale grey above shading to white below. Wings lack black tips. Beak yellowish, with tubular nostrils on ridge. Flies on short, straight wings, often held downcurved. Glides extensively, with few wingbeats except close to the cliffs. Various cackling and crooning calls on breeding ledges, silent elsewhere. Breeds colonially on coastal cliff ledges, on ground along remote coastlines, sometimes on buildings. Some remain in coastal waters all year, others disperse to mid-ocean in winter. Widespread, locally numerous.

23

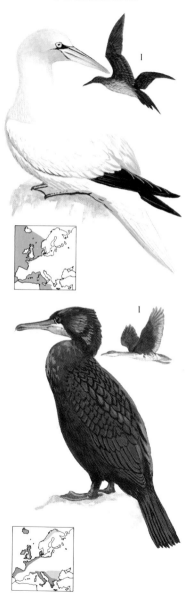

Gannet *Sula bassana* 90cm Huge seabird; long-necked, long-tailed, cigar-shaped body. Adult largely white above and below. Wings black tipped; long, straight, slender and sharply pointed. Head and neck tinged yellow. Beak steel-grey, long, dagger-shaped. Immature grey-brown flecked with white, gradually showing more white as adult plumage is acquired. In flight, characterised by slow, stiff wingbeats, with frequent glides. Plunges spectacularly when hunting fish. Raucous honks and grating calls on breeding grounds, silent elsewhere. Breeds in colonies on remote islands or headlands. Winters in coastal and offshore waters. Widespread, locally numerous.

Cormorant *Phalacrocorax carbo* 90cm Large, long-necked, broad-winged seabird. Adult blackish with metallic sheen. Face (and sometimes thighs) patched with white in summer. Southern European breeding birds may also have white head and neck. Facial skin yellow. Beak yellow and hooked. Winter adult lacks white patches. Immature dark brown above, paler on throat and underparts. Swims low in water, diving frequently. Deep guttural grunts when on breeding grounds. Breeds colonially on islands and cliffs beside shallow seas or estuaries, or in trees beside large inland fresh waters. Overwinters in same habitats. Widespread.

Shag *Phalacrocorax aristotelis*
75cm Large dark seabird,
similar to Cormorant but
smaller. Summer adult
blackish with green iridescent
sheen. Shags never show
white patches. Curled crest in
early spring, traces of which
persist into summer. Beak
yellow, slim and hooked at tip.
Immature brown above and
below, appreciably darker-
bellied than young Cormorant.
In flight, slighter build,
slimmer neck and smaller
head help separation from
Cormorant. Harsh croaks on
breeding grounds. Year-round
resident on rocky coasts and
nearby clear seas. Semi-
colonial or solitary breeding
bird. Locally common.

Little Egret *Egretta garzetta* 55cm
Slender, medium-sized heron.
Adult white, with long white
crest and fine plumes on back
in breeding season. Neck long
and slender, usually held
extended. Beak black, long and
dagger-shaped. Legs black and
long with striking and
characteristic golden feet.
Immature whitish, lacking
plumes and crest. Flies with
head withdrawn between
shoulders but legs extended.
Various harsh honks and
shrieks, usually confined to
breeding season. Inhabits
marshland of all types with
open water, rivers, saline
lagoons. Breeds colonially in
mixed 'egrettries' in trees.
Locally quite common.

Grey Heron *Ardea cinerea* 90cm
Huge waterside bird. Adult
blue-grey above; wings grey,
blackish primaries; white
below. Head white, black line
through eye. Neck white,
slender; throat dark-streaked.
Beak yellow, heavy, dagger-
shaped. Breeding adult has
black and white crest, silver-
grey plumes on back, pinkish
flush to beak. Legs yellowish,
long. Immature resembles
adult, lacks crest and plumes.
Flight stately on broad,
heavily-fingered wings, head
retracted, legs extended.
Harsh honks and shrieks,
especially 'fraank', mostly
during breeding season.
Frequents wetlands: ponds,
estuaries, sheltered sea coasts.
Breeds colonially in reedbeds
or trees. Widespread.

Mute Swan *Cygnus olor* 150cm
Huge and unmistakable. Adult
all-white year-round. Neck
long, carried in graceful 'S'
curve. Beak dark orange, with
black knob on forehead larger
in male than female. Adult
raises wings like sails high
over back in defence of
territory or young. Immature
pale grey-buff; beak pinkish-
grey. In flight, long, broad,
heavily-fingered wings creak
loudly. Rarely vocal, hisses or
grunts when annoyed.
Frequents all types of fresh
water larger than ponds,
including town park lakes.
Occasionally found on
sheltered seas. Widespread.

Bewick's Swan *Cygnus columbianus* 120cm Appreciably smaller than other swans. Adult all-white year round. Neck short, straight and goose-like. Beak short, wedge-shaped, largely black with irregularly shaped lemon-yellow patches at base, the pattern, varying between individuals. Immature pale grey, basal patches on beak greyish- or pinkish-yellow. In flight, more buoyant and with faster wingbeats than its larger relatives. Wingbeats silent. Musical goose-like honks and chatterings. Breeds on swampy tundra. Winters on sheltered seas, large freshwater areas and grazing marshes. Scarce, locally numerous on regular wintering grounds.

White-fronted Goose *Anser albifrons* 70cm Medium-sized grey goose. Adult grey-brown above and below, with white beneath the tail; heavy black barring across breast. Head and neck darker brown, with large white face-patch at base of beak. Beak pink (eastern or Russian race) or orange-yellow (western or Greenland race). Legs orange. Immature similar, but lacks white face and breast barring. Noisy, with a gabbling yapping call. Breeds on tundra. Winters on rough grassland, fresh and salt marshes, fields. Widespread, locally numerous.

Geese

Brent Goose *Branta bernicla*
60cm Small, dark, short-necked goose. Adult back blackish-brown, rump black. Tail white with black terminal band. Head and neck sooty black, with small white collar. Breast and belly grey (pale-bellied race *hrota*) or dark grey (dark-bellied race *bernicla*). Undertail white. Beak blackish, small. Legs blackish. Immature similar; pale barring across back, lacks white collar. Gregarious. In flight, white tail conspicuous. Wingbeats quick. Usually flies in irregular, loose flocks. Voice a soft low 'rruuk'. Breeds on Arctic tundra. In winter favours estuaries, sheltered bays and nearby marshes and fields. Widespread, locally numerous.

Canada Goose *Branta canadensis*
75cm Largest of the 'black' geese, almost swan-sized. Adult body dark brown above, paler below, with white patch below black tail. Head and long neck black; white face-patch on cheeks and under chin. Beak black. Legs dark grey. Immature similar to adult, duller. In flight, black rump and white-tail band conspicuous. Wingbeats powerful. Call a hoarse disyllabic 'aah-honk'. Vagrant North American birds winter with grey geese on coastal marshes. Most European birds are descendants of introduced stock; resident on large fresh waters, including park lakes, and nearby grassland. Widespread.

Shelduck *Tadorna tadorna* 60cm
Large, goose-like duck with striking pied plumage. Adult predominantly white. Back has two long black stripes, belly narrower central black stripe. Head bottle-green; neck has broad chestnut band round base. Beak scarlet, knob at base larger in male than female; female may have whitish patch at base. Legs pink. Immature has grey instead of green or black markings, lacks chestnut collar. Barking call 'ak-ak-ak' and deep nasal 'ark'. Seen year-round on estuaries and sheltered sandy or muddy coasts, occasionally on fresh waters. May breed far from water. Widespread, often numerous.

Wigeon *Anas penelope* 45cm
Medium-sized surface-feeding duck. Adult male has grey back, finely marked grey flanks and black undertail. Breast pink; head chestnut with gold crown stripe. Beak grey with black tip; stubby. In flight shows conspicuous white oval patch in wing. Female and immature similar, a mixture of cinnamon-browns flecked with darker markings, showing a greyish wing-patch in flight. Male produces a characteristic, plaintive whistle, female a low-pitched purr. Breeds on moorland and tundra close to water. Winters on lakes, estuaries and sheltered seas, and on nearby marshes and grassland. Widespread and often common.

Ducts

Mallard *Anas platyrhynchos* 58cm
One of the larger surface-feeding ducks; best-known duck in Europe. Adult male grey-brown above and below, with black above and below white tail. Rump has curled black feathers. Head bottle-green, separated from chestnut breast by narrow white neck-ring. Beak yellowish-green. Legs orange.

Female and immature speckled brown, buff and black; beak brownish-orange. In flight, all show broad purple speculum-patch between white bars on inner section of wing. Male gives quiet whistle, female harsh quacks. Frequents most waters year-round, from small ponds to open seas. Common, almost ubiquitous.

Teal *Anas crecca* 35cm One of the smallest surface-feeding ducks. Adult male predominantly greyish, flanks have conspicuous white stripe; undertail golden. Breast buff with fine grey barring. Head chestnut, with dark green patch around eye; may appear blackish at a distance. Female and immature similar,

speckled grey-brown. Flight fast and erratic. Male has distinctive low 'krit' call, and strange bell-like whistle; female harsh 'quack'. Breeds on boggy or marshy land with reed-fringed pools. Winters in similar habitats, often well inland, and on estuaries and sheltered coastal waters. Common, often numerous.

Pintail *Anas acuta* 70cm Large surface-feeding duck, slim build, longish neck. Adult male has grey-brown back, white belly, finely marked grey flanks. Tail black, long and pointed. Head and neck rich brown, distinctive white mark on side of neck. Beak and legs grey. Female and immature pale grey-brown marked with darker brown; short, pointed tail. In flight, slender, elongated silhouette; wings narrow, inconspicuous brown speculum on trailing edge. Rarely vocal; male has low whistle, female low quack and churring growl. Breeds on moors and freshwater marshes close to water. Winters on sheltered coastal waters; sometimes inland.

Shoveler *Anas clypeata* 50cm Medium-sized surface-feeding duck. Adult male brown above, white below; chestnut patches on flanks. Short neck and heavily-built head bottle-green. Beak dark grey; massive and spoon-shaped. Female and immature speckled brown, similarly massive beak brownish-orange. All swim low in water, head tilted down. In flight, rapid wingbeats and head-up, tail-down attitude are characteristic; pale grey forewing patches conspicuous. Male has low-pitched double quack 'tuk-tuk', female quiet quack. Breeds on marshland with reed-fringed pools or lakes, winters in similar areas, on reservoirs and sheltered coastal waters. Common.

Ducks

Pochard *Aythya ferina* 45cm
Medium-sized diving duck.
Adult male has grey back, and
is mostly white below; breast
and undertail black. Head dark
chestnut. Beak black with
grey band near the tip. Female
and immature dull rufous-
brown, paler on cheeks, throat
and belly. Both sexes have
steeply rising forehead; wings
greyish with an indistinct,
paler grey wingbar. Dives
frequently. Rarely vocal; male
has hoarse whistle, female
harsh growl. Breeds beside
large reed-fringed fresh
waters; winters on large fresh
waters including reservoirs,
occasionally along sheltered
coasts. Common and
widespread.

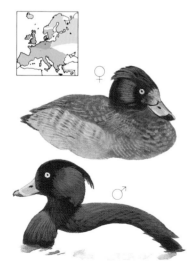

Tufted Duck *Aythya fuligula*
43cm Small, diving duck. Adult
male black above; breast black,
flanks and belly white;
undertail black. Head purplish,
crested during breeding
season. Female and immature
dark brown above, female
sometimes with rudimentary
crest in breeding season.
Older females may have white
patch at base of beak.
Underparts paler; belly grey-
buff. Eyes golden-yellow, beak
black-tipped lead-grey in both
sexes. In flight, wingbeats
rapid; white wingbar
conspicuous. Male has soft
whistle during breeding
season, female low-pitched
growl. Breeds beside ponds,
ditches, lakes; winters on
similar waters; occasionally on
sheltered coasts. Common.

Goldeneye *Bucephala clangula*
48cm Medium-sized sea duck.
Adult male predominantly
black above, white below.
Back black; closed wing has
row of white patches often
merging into bar. Head
greenish-black, crested and
angular; small circular white
patch below eye. Female and
immature brown above, flanks
paler, belly whitish. Head
chestnut, angular. Swims
buoyantly, in groups, diving
frequently. In flight, wing
feathers make rattling
whistle; white wing-patches
conspicuous. Rarely vocal;
male occasionally produces
disyllabic nasal call, female
harsh growl. Breeds near
water. Winters coastally or on
inland fresh waters. Regular,
rarely numerous.

Red-breasted Merganser
Mergus serrator 55cm Medium-
sized sawbill duck. Adult male
black above, flanks finely
marked grey, belly white.
Breast chestnut, dark brown
speckling. Head and bristling
crest bottle-green, throat
white, nape black. Beak
orange-red; long, narrow with
serrated edge. Female and
immature grey above, paler
below, belly white. Breast and
throat white, head and nape
chestnut-brown with spiky
crest. Swims low in water,
dives frequently. In flight
black and white wing-patches
conspicuous. Usually silent.
Breeds beside rivers and along
sheltered coasts. Winters
along coasts, also on large
fresh waters. Widespread,
regular, rarely numerous.

Raptors

Black Kite *Milvus migrans* 53cm
Large predominantly dark kite. Adult and immature various shades of dark brown; immature generally paler on breast. Tail long. Upright perching posture. In flight, wings appear long and relatively narrow, with fingered tips, usually showing pale mid-wing patch on underside; tail often fanned, showing very shallow fork, or twisted characteristically. Flight extremely agile. Social, often soaring or gathering at carrion in flocks. Call a Herring-gull-like mewing. Frequents forests, but also urban areas and especially refuse tips. Widespread, more numerous in warmer areas.

Marsh Harrier *Circus aeruginosus* 53cm Large broad-winged harrier. Adult male largely brown above, underparts chestnut. Wings strikingly patterned, patches of brown and grey contrasting with black flight feathers. Tail pale grey, long. Adult female largely rich dark brown, with much creamy-yellow on head. Immature predominantly brown with darker streaks, lacking yellow patches. Characteristic flight low and steady, with frequent extended glides on wings held stiffly in shallow 'V'. Voice rarely heard, disyllabic high-pitched 'kee-ya'. Characteristically inhabits marshland with extensive reed beds. Widespread, locally common.

Hen Harrier *Circus cyaneus*
48cm Medium-sized harrier.
Adult male pale grey on head,
back and tail, with white
rump-patch. Wings grey with
blackish flight feathers.
Female and immature rich
brown above and below, with
darker streaks; tail long and
brown with narrow dark bars;
large white rump-patch.
Sometimes collects in
communal winter roosts. In
flight and hunting technique
looks similar to Marsh
Harrier, but wings narrower.
Voice, not often heard, a
chattering 'kee-kee-kee'.
Frequents open country, from
moorland and forestry
plantations to farmland and
coastal or inland marshes,
especially in winter.
Widespread, rarely numerous.

Osprey *Pandion haliaetus* 58cm
Medium-sized fish-hunting
raptor. Adult and immature
upperparts brown; wings dark
above, generally pale below
with dark wingtips and 'wrist'
patch. Underparts largely
white; breast has band of
brown streaks. Head white
with large brown patch
through eye. Crown loosely
crested. Beak grey, relatively
small, hooked. Legs and large
feet with powerful long talons
grey. In flight, wings are
characteristically held in an
'M' and arched. Plunge dives
for fish. Voice rarely heard, a
brief whistle. Frequents lakes
and streams, saline lagoons
and man-made fresh waters.
Widespread but rarely
numerous.

Raptors

Buzzard *Buteo buteo* 53cm
Medium-large broad-winged raptor. Adult and immature variable in plumage, normally darkish brown above, whitish below with heavy darker streaking. Individuals may be pale buff above or dark brown below. Often perches in upright posture on poles or trees. In flight, usually dark 'wrist' patch contrasts with generally pale underwing. Soaring habits and flight silhouette are characteristic, with long, broad, heavily-fingered wings and short, dark, fanned tail. Voice a far-carrying, cat-like mewing. Inhabits open country, including farmland and moorland, with tracts of woodland. Widespread, locally common.

Kestrel *Falco tinnunculus* 35cm
Medium-sized falcon. Adult male has chestnut-brown back with heavy dark brown spots; tail grey with black terminal bar. Underparts buff, with darker spots. Head grey. Female and immature brown above, buffish below, with heavy brown spots and streaks. Long pointed wings may sometimes appear rounded. Hovers frequently and expertly. Call a shrill, repetitive 'kee-kee-kee'. Habitat widely varied, from towns and cities, farmland, marshes, to moors, mountains and sea coasts. Common.

Golden Eagle *Aquila chrysaetos*
83cm Huge typical and
majestic eagle. Adult
uniformly rich dark brown;
head and nape tinged golden.
Tail comparatively long and
broad. Beak massive and
hooked. Immature wings have
white patches; tail white with
broad, black terminal band.
White areas get smaller with
age, causing possible
confusion with other eagles.
In flight, wings impressively
long, broad and heavily
fingered, held slightly above
horizontal when soaring, but
with tips often curled
downwards. Voice rarely
heard, a barking 'kaah'.
Inhabits remote mountain and
forest areas, down to sea level
in places. Widespread, never
numerous.

Sparrowhawk *Accipiter nisus*
35cm Small dashing hawk.
Male dark grey above; tail
grey with darker bars, long.
Underparts distinctive: throat
white, breast and belly white
but closely barred with
chestnut, appear reddish at a
distance. Crown grey,
sometimes small white nape-
patch. No eyestripe. Female
much larger, grey-brown
above; underparts white,
barred with brown. Eyestripe
white, separating dark crown
and cheeks. Immature
plumage similar to female but
breast has brown streaks, not
barring. In flight, short,
rounded wings and long tail
confer good manoeuvrability.
Call a rapid 'kek-kek-kek'.
Inhabits forests and woodland.
Widespread, often common.

Game Birds

Red-legged Partridge *Alectoris rufa* 35cm Medium-sized game bird. Adult grey-brown above; buffish below, flanks boldly barred with black, white and chestnut. Head strikingly patterned with white chin and upper throat, surrounded by black border and black streaking extending onto breast. Beak and legs bright red. Immature sandy-brown, lacking distinctive head pattern. Flight low and direct on whirring wings. Voice 'chuck, chuck-arr.' Inhabits dry farmland, heath and scrub. Locally common.

Pheasant *Phasianus colchicus* 85cm Large long-tailed game bird. Adult male unmistakable: body iridescent bronze, beautifully marked; tail buff with dark brown bars, very long. Head glossy bottle-green with scarlet face-patches. Female and immature sandy-buff with darker streaks; tail shorter. Flight rapid, with long glides after bursts of flapping; take-off explosive. Male has a ringing 'cork-cork' call followed by loud wing-claps. Inhabits farmland, heath, scrub and open woodland. Widespread, numbers influenced by release of captive-reared birds.

Grey Partridge *Perdix perdix*
30cm Medium-sized game bird.
Adult has buff-streaked
brownish back; face and upper
throat rich chestnut; nape and
breast dove-grey, paling
towards the belly. Flanks have
bold chestnut barring. Dark
brown, inverted horseshoe
patch on belly larger in male
than female. Immature
streaked sandy-brown. Flight
low, direct and fast on
whirring wings, showing
chestnut sides to tail. Voice
'chirrick-chirrick'. Inhabits
arable fields, grassland, heaths
and scrub. Widespread, locally
common.

Red Grouse *Lagopus lagopus*
40cm Medium-sized, skulking
game bird. Adult male (in
Britain) mottled rich reddish-
chestnut above and below;
female drabber. Wings dark
brown in both sexes. Red
fleshy wattles over eyes. Beak
short and stubby. The
continental Willow Grouse
has white wings in summer, is
white with a black tail in
winter. Remains concealed
until threatened; takes off in
whirring flight, short,
downcurved wings beating
fast. Voice a loud 'go-back-
urr'. Inhabits heather
moorland, willow scrub and
tundra edges. Widespread,
locally common.

Crakes

Coot *Fulica atra* 38cm Medium-large crake. Adult uniformly dull velvety black. Forehead has fleshy patch, diagnostically white. Beak short. Legs and feet grey, with distinctive lobed webbing to toes. Immature dark grey-brown above, paler below. Swims buoyantly, diving frequently. Flies low over the water, revealing conspicuous white trailing edges to wings. Voice a single or repeated strident 'kowk'. Inhabits larger expanses of fresh or brackish water, including reservoirs in winter. Occasional on sheltered estuaries. Common.

Water Rail *Rallus aquaticus* 28cm Medium-sized, skulking crake. Adult has upperparts of rich buffish-brown, speckled and streaked with dark brown; predominantly leaden grey on face and underparts, with flanks boldly barred black and white and striking white undertail coverts. Beak reddish, long, slender and slightly downcurved. Legs and toes yellowish, long. Immature darker, more speckled above and barred below. Flies rarely, fluttering low with legs trailing. Various noisy, pig-like grunts and squeals. Inhabits dense reedbeds and heavily vegetated swamps. Widespread, rarely numerous. Difficult to see.

Moorhen *Gallinula chloropus*
33cm Medium-sized crake.
Adult velvety brownish-black;
flanks have characteristic
white streak. Undertail
coverts white, conspicuous
when tail is jerked while
swimming. Forehead scarlet,
fleshy. Beak red with yellow
tip. Legs and long toes green.

Immature drab grey-brown,
darker above than below.
Swims well, upends but does
not dive. Flies feebly and low
over water, legs trailing.
Several ringing calls, including
'whittuck'. Inhabits fresh
waters from the smallest pool
to the largest lake. Common.

Common Snipe *Gallinago
gallinago* 28cm Small, long-
beaked wader. Adult and
immature rich brown, barred
and streaked chestnut, buff
and black; crown has three
bold, yellowish-buff,
longitudinal stripes. Beak
brownish, straight, very long.
Legs greenish, comparatively
short. Flight a swift zig-zag
when flushed; wingbars and

striped back conspicuous; tail
rounded, showing dark band.
Display flight soaring and
diving, fanned tail produces
throbbing, bleating noise. Call
on taking flight, a harsh
'scarp'; in breeding season, a
clock-like 'tick-er, tick-er'.
Breeds on wetlands and
moorland. Winters in similar
habitats, salt marshes and
saline lagoons.

Waders

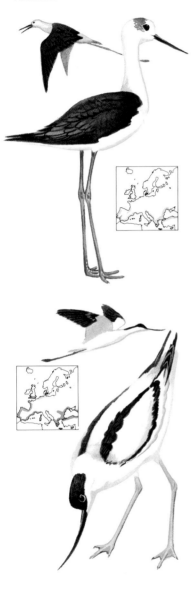

Black-winged Stilt *Himantopus himantopus* 38cm Medium-sized wader with extremely long legs. Adult has back and wings black, with head, neck and underparts white; nape shows varying amounts of grey or black. Beak black, long and very slender. Legs rich pink, almost ridiculously long, enabling it to wade and feed in deeper water than other waders. Immature browner above; legs greyish-pink. Flight feeble for a wader, showing dark undersides to wings but no wingbars, legs trailing conspicuously well beyond tail. Noisily vociferous with yelping 'kyip' call. Inhabits salt pans, coastal lagoons and marshes. Locally common.

Avocet *Recurvirostra avosetta* 43cm Medium-sized wader, with unmistakable pied plumage and upturned beak. Adult predominantly white above and below, crown and nape black; back and wings have black bars; wingtips black. Beak black; long and extremely slender towards tip, which is markedly upturned. Feeds by sweeping beak from side to side in shallow water. Legs grey, relatively long. Immature similarly patterned but browner. Vocal, with a 'kloo-oot' call varying from flute-like to strident if alarmed. Inhabits saline or brackish lagoons and pools. May overwinter on sheltered estuaries. Locally common. Breeds colonially, often winters in flocks.

Oystercatcher *Haematopus ostralegus* 43cm Conspicuously pied, medium-sized wader. Adult black backed; tail white, with black terminal band; underparts white. Head and neck black. Beak orange, long, fairly stout. Legs and feet pink, thick and fleshy. Winter adult and immature blackish on beak; white collar-mark on neck. In flight, usually in noisy flocks, black wings show conspicuous white wing-bars. Vociferous: various 'kleep' calls and pipings. Breeds on coastal marshes, grassy islands, sand dunes, and on inland damp grassland. Winters on coasts and estuaries. Widespread, often common, usually in flocks in winter.

Lapwing *Vanellus vanellus* 30cm Medium-large plover. Adult black above with purplish-green iridescent sheen; tail white with terminal black bar. Flanks and belly white, undertail coverts rich chestnut. Crown black with conspicuous long, slender, upturned crest. Cheeks greyish, throat and breast black. Beak black and stubby. Legs brown, long. Immature browner, with buff fringes to feathers giving scaly appearance to back. Gregarious. Flight floppy on rounded black and white wings. Voice a characteristic 'pee-wit'. Breeds on fields, moorland and marshes. Winters on arable land, grassland, estuaries. Common.

Waders

Ringed Plover *Charadrius hiaticula* 20cm Small, fast-running plover. Adult sandy-brown above, white below. Face patterned black and white; black collar. Beak stubby, yellowish with black tip. Legs yellow. Immature has brownish markings, not black, and an incomplete collar. Rarely seen in large flocks. In flight, white wingbar conspicuous. Voice a fluting 'too-lee'; trilling song. Inhabits sandy coasts and salt pans, occasionally found inland on river banks and excavations. Widespread, relatively common.

Knot *Calidris canutus* 25cm Medium-small, often nondescript wader. Summer adult brown above, with golden scaly markings; underparts distinctly rusty red. Winter adult and immature nondescript, flecked grey-brown above, whitish below. Beak dark, straight, medium length. Legs dark, medium length. Gregarious, often gathering in close-packed flocks, thousands strong. In flight, faint white wingbar visible. Rarely vocal, occasional grunting calls. Breeds on Arctic tundra, winters on extensive sand and mudflats of sheltered coastal bays and estuaries. Widespread, locally very numerous.

Golden Plover *Pluvialis apricaria*
28cm Medium-sized plover.
Summer adult striking, with
richly-flecked golden crown,
nape and back separated from
glossy black face, throat and
belly by broad white margin.
Beak stubby. Legs grey, long.
Winter adult and immature
flecked dull golden-buff
above; underparts buff
shading to white on belly,
with no black. Often
gregarious. In flight, no
wingbar visible. Call a fluting
whistle 'tloo-ee'. Breeds on
tundra and moorland; winters
on coastal marshes and inland
on damp fields and grassland.
Locally common, sometimes in
large flocks.

Grey Plover *Pluvialis squatarola*
28cm Medium-sized, often
solitary plover. Summer adult
strikingly handsome:
upperparts silver-grey, richly
black-flecked, separated from
black face, throat, breast and
belly by broad white margin.
Winter adult and immature
flecked grey-buff above, white
below. Beak black, stubby.
Legs black, long. In flight,
shows a faint wingbar and
characteristic bold black
patches in 'armpits' beneath
wings. Call a plaintive, fluting
'tee-too-ee'. Breeds on
northern tundra. Winters in
sheltered coastal bays and
estuaries. Widespread, though
rarely numerous.

Waders

Turnstone *Arenaria interpres*
23cm Small, dumpy, harlequin-like wader. Summer adult has rich pale chestnut back; underparts, head and neck white, all boldly patterned with black. Winter adult and immature retain pied parts of plumage, but chestnut is replaced with grey. Beak dark, short, flattened from top to bottom; used to overturn weeds and stones. Legs yellowish. Feeds among seaweeds on rocky shores and is well camouflaged. In flight, white wingbars and pied plumage unmistakable. Staccato chattering 'tuk-uk-tuk' call. Breeds on tundra and rocky Arctic coasts. Winters on rocky coasts, rare inland. Widespread, often common.

Common Sandpiper *Actitis hypoleucos* 20cm Small wader. Summer adult sandy-brown above, flecked with white. Underparts mostly white; brown streaking on throat and on sides of breast forms a half collar. Winter adult and immature duller, less spotted. Beak dark, short and straight. Legs greenish. Bobs incessantly. Flight low over surface and fast; rapid, shallow wingbeats with wings downcurved; shows white wingbar, brown rump, brown tail with brown-barred white outer feathers. Trilling 'twee-wee-wee. . . ' call. Song a high-pitched, rapid 'tittyweety-tittyweety'. Breeds beside lakes, rivers. Winters on marshes and coasts. Widespread, rarely numerous.

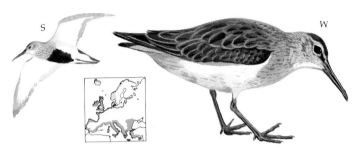

Dunlin *Calidris alpina* 18cm
Small wader. Summer adult
rich bronze with darker
rufous-brown speckling
above; breast pale, dark-
streaked; belly-patch black.
Winter adult and immature
dull speckled grey-brown or
buffish-brown above,
underparts paling to near-
white. Beak dark, relatively
long, slightly downcurved.
Legs dark, shortish.
Gregarious. In flight shows
pale wingbar and white
patches on each side of dark
rump and tail. Call a nasal
'treeer'; song a purring trill
delivered in flight. Breeds on
grassland, moorland and
tundra. At other times on
sheltered coastal bays,
estuaries, marshes and swamps.
Widespread, common.

Woodcock *Scolopax rusticola*
35cm Medium-large woodland
wader. Adult and immature
snipe-like, but heavier, with
bolder barring and finer
mottling on rich brown
plumage. Breast grey-buff,
barred. Head angular; *crosswise*
yellowish bands on rich brown
crown. Eyes large, bulging.
Beak yellowish-brown, long,
stout. Legs pinkish; short and
stout; squat stance. Rarely
flies until threatened. During
winter and spring displays
establishes 'roding' flight-
paths through woodland
glades. During display, voice a
frog-like 'orrrt-orrrt' with
high-pitched, sneezing 'swick'
calls, otherwise silent. Prefers
damp woodland; rare on fresh
or coastal marshes. Widespread
but difficult to see.

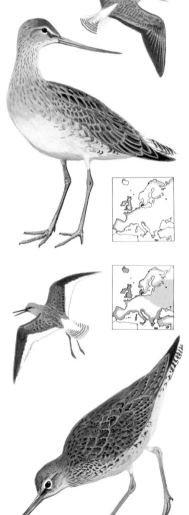

Bar-tailed Godwit *Limosa lapponica* 40cm Large, long-beaked wader. Summer adult richly marked brown on back; head, neck and breast rufous cinnamon-brown, belly chestnut. Winter adult and immature mottled grey to grey-brown above, shading to white below. Beak reddish, darker towards tip; very long, slightly upturned. Legs black and long. Gregarious, sometimes in large flocks. In flight shows dense, narrow, dark brown barring across white tail. Rarely vocal except in breeding season; usually a harsh 'kirrick'. Breeds on Arctic tundra. Winters on muddy or sandy estuaries or sheltered coastal bays. Common, locally numerous.

Redshank *Tringa totanus* 28cm Medium-sized wader. Summer adult rich brown above with pale flecks and fine dark brown streaks; buff below with heavy brown streaking; belly white. Winter adult and immature grey-brown above, grey-buff below, white on lower breast, belly and flanks. Beak reddish, slim, medium-long. Legs bright red, comparatively long. Occasionally gregarious. Wary. In flight, white wingbar, white rump and dark-barred white tail distinctive. Vocal; piping calls, usually variants of 'tu-lee-lee'. Breeds on marshes, wet meadows and moorland. Winters more often on salt marshes than fresh, and on estuaries and sandy bays.

Greenshank *Tringa nebularia*
30cm Medium-sized wader.
Summer adult grey-brown
above, richly flecked with
black and silver. Underparts
white. Winter adult and
immature paler and drabber
grey. Beak greenish, medium-
long, relatively stout, slightly
upturned. Legs green, long,
relatively stout. Rarely
gregarious. In flight, shows
all-dark wings and striking
white rump extending well up
back; tail white with dark
brown barring. Call a far-
carrying trisyllabic 'tu-tu-tu'.
Breeds on damp moorland,
marshes and tundra. On
migration and in winter
occasionally on fresh marshes,
more often on coastal lagoons
and sheltered sandy or muddy
estuaries and bays.

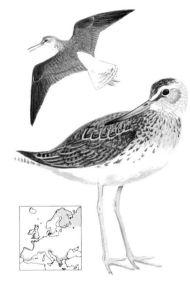

Curlew *Numenius arquata* 58cm
Very large wader. Adult and
immature sandy-buff above,
with whitish and brown flecks
and streaks. Underparts pale
buffish-fawn with darker
brown streaks, shading to
white on belly. Beak
brownish-black, exceptionally
long, markedly downcurved.
Legs blue-grey, relatively
long. Often gregarious in
winter. In flight, shows white
rump extending well up back,
and dark-barred buff tail.
Characteristic 'coor-lee' calls
at all times; in breeding season
has song flight with bubbling
trills. Breeds on moorland,
marshes and wet meadows.
Winters on sandy or muddy
coasts and estuaries.
Widespread, often common.

Arctic Skua *Stercorarius parasiticus* 45cm Medium-sized skua. Adults occur in two colour forms: dark phase uniformly chocolate-brown; pale phase sandy-brown above, cap blackish, neck, breast and belly buffish-white. Adult has slim elongated central tail feathers. Beak and legs greyish-brown, gull-like. Immature rich brown, heavily speckled and barred, lacks long tail feathers. In flight, shows white patches in long slender wings. Pursues other birds to steal food. Voice a yelping 'tuk-tuk', harsh 'eee-air'. Breeds colonially on moorland, remote islands, tundra. On migration in inshore waters. Regular; rarely numerous, except on breeding grounds.

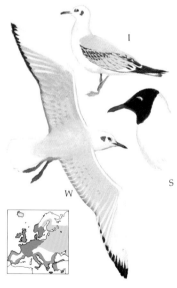

Black-headed Gull *Larus ridibundus* 35cm Medium-sized gull. Summer adult largely white, with chocolate hood. Wings pale silver-grey, black-tipped white flight feathers and white leading edge, characteristic in flight. Beak and legs blood-red. Winter adult lacks brown hood, has greyish nape and smudge through eye; beak and legs brownish. Immature wings have brownish bars on inner portion; black terminal band on white tail visible in flight. Gregarious. Various yelping 'keer' and drawn-out 'kwaar' calls. Breeds colonially on dunes, islands, marshes. In winter, almost ubiquitous coastally and inland, excluding mountainous regions. Common, often abundant.

Lesser Black-backed Gull
Larus fuscus 53cm Medium-large
gull. Adult predominantly
white; back and wings slate
grey; wingtips black with
small white markings. Beak
yellow, with red spot near tip.
Legs characteristically yellow.
Immature mottled brown and
white, whitish below, whitish below,
often impossible to distinguish
from young Herring.

Gregarious. Voice a powerful
'kay-ow', various laughing
'yah' calls and mewings.
Breeds (often in huge
colonies) on cliff tops, islands,
sand dunes and moorland
remote from human
disturbance. Migrates
southwards in winter to
coastal and inland habitats,
including urban areas.
Widespread, often common.

Herring Gull *Larus argentatus*
55cm Medium-sized gull.
Adult predominantly white;
back and wings silver-grey.
Wingtips black with white
markings. Beak yellow, with
red spot near tip. Legs pink;
yellow in southern and south-
western races. Immature
mottled brown and white
above, largely white below;
beak and legs brownish (*see*

Lesser Black-backed).
Gregarious. Vocal, with
various mewing cries, harsh
'kay-ow' and 'yah-yah-yah'
laughing calls. Breeds on
remote islands, moors, sand
dunes, cliffs and also
increasingly on buildings.
Winters in widespread
habitats from coasts to inland
and urban areas. Common,
often very numerous.

Gulls

Great Black-backed Gull *Larus marinus* 68cm Largest European gull. Adult largely white, jet black back and wings. Beak yellow with red spot near tip; large and strong. Legs pale pink. Immature speckled brown and white, tail white with broad black terminal bar. Takes four years to reach adult plumage. Flight powerful, wings showing conspicuous white trailing edge and white spots near tips of flight feathers. Voice a gruff 'kow-kow-kow'. Breeds on coastal islands and cliffs. The most maritime of large gulls, often wintering at sea, but also in coastal waters and inland, especially near refuse tips. Widespread.

Common Gull *Larus canus* 40cm Medium-sized gull. Adult predominantly white, occasionally with grey flecks around head and nape. Wings grey above; conspicuous black-and-white tips to flight feathers. Beak and legs greenish-yellow. Immature pale brown above, whitish below, with crown and nape streaked grey-brown; tail white with broad black terminal band; beak and legs dark brown. Gregarious. High-pitched 'kee-you' and 'gah-gah-gah' calls. Breeds on remote hillsides, islands, moorlands and tundra. Widespread on migration and in winter on farmland, grassland, urban areas, reservoirs and coasts of all types. Often common.

Kittiwake *Rissa tridactyla* 40cm
Medium-sized, slim-winged
gull. Adult largely white.
Wings pale grey; tips of flight
feathers black with no white
patches. Beak lemon yellow
with vermilion gape visible at
close range; small. Legs
distinctively black. Immature
similar, but with blackish
collar, black 'M' markings
across wings and black-tipped,
shallowly forked tail visible in
flight. Gregarious. Flight
buoyant and tern-like; wings
characteristically long and
slender. Very vocal at colony,
distinctive 'kitti-waaake' calls.
Breeds colonially on sea cliffs,
occasionally buildings. In
winter, most are well out to
sea, some remain in inshore
waters. Widespread, locally
numerous.

Black Tern *Chlidonias niger*
25cm Small, dark, marsh tern.
Summer adult largely dark
sooty-grey above and below;
tail dark grey, shallowly
forked. Head, breast and belly
jet black. Beak and legs black.
Winter adult grey above,
white below, with dark crown,
white forehead, and black
'half-collar' marks on
shoulders. Immature similar
to winter adult but browner.
Gregarious. Flight
characteristic, dipping down
to water surface to feed.
Rarely vocal, gives occasional
'krit' or 'kreek'. Breeds
colonially on swamps and
marshes. On migration seen
coastally and frequently
inland. Regular, locally
common.

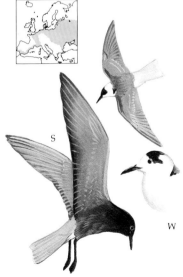

Terns

Common Tern *Sterna hirundo*
35cm Medium-sized sea tern.
Summer adult predominantly
white, with black cap. Wings
grey with appreciably darker
tips (*see* Arctic). Tail white,
deeply forked. Beak red with
black tip. Legs red. Winter
adult has white forehead.
Immature darker, with sandy-
grey markings on back and
wings. Gregarious. Voice a
harsh 'kee-aarh' with
emphasis on second syllable;
also hurried 'kirri-kirri-kirri'.
Breeds colonially on coastal
beaches and islands, and
increasingly often inland on
sand or gravel beside fresh
water. Feeds over coastal
lagoons, inshore waters and
various inland fresh waters
especially on migration.
Common.

Arctic Tern *Sterna paradisaea*
37cm Medium-sized sea tern.
Summer adult predominantly
white, with black cap. Wings
grey, distinctively pale and
translucent near tips. Tail
white, with long streamers.
Beak entirely red (*see*
Common). Legs red, very
short. Winter adult has white
forehead; beak and legs dark.
Immature similar, but with
sandy-brown back and wing
markings. Gregarious. Voice a
short, sharp 'keee-ah' with
emphasis on the first syllable.
Breeds colonially on remote
beaches, islands and grassy
areas near the sea. Feeds at
sea. On migration only
occasionally seen inland.
Widespread, locally common.

Auks

Guillemot *Uria aalge* 40cm
Medium-sized auk. Summer
adult chocolate-brown above
(northern birds almost black),
white below. Some ('bridled'
form), commoner in north,
have white eye-ring and stripe
behind eye. Beak long, dagger-
shaped. Legs grey. Winter
adult and immature similar
but grey, not brown. Long
and low-bodied while
swimming, stance upright on
cliffs. Dives frequently.
Gregarious. Whirring flight
low over sea, shows white
trailing edge to wing. Vocal
during breeding season with
various cooing and mooing
calls. Breeds colonially on sea
cliff ledges, winters in coastal
seas. Locally common.

Puffin *Fratercula arctica* 30cm
Medium-sized auk. Summer
adult unmistakable, black
above, white below, with large
white face-patch and huge
parrot-like beak striped grey-
blue, yellow and red. Legs and
feet bright orange-red. Winter
adult and immature drabber;
face-patch smoky-grey; beak
dark and much smaller.
Gregarious. Flight whirring
low over sea; characteristically
lacks white wingbar. Voice a
low growl in breeding season.
Breeds on sea coast cliffs,
screes and cliff-top grassland,
often in large colonies. Most
winter out at sea, some
remain inshore. Locally
common.

Pigeons

Woodpigeon *Columba palumbus* 40cm Large cumbersome pigeon. Adult and immature delicate grey-brown above, paler dove-grey below. Adult has metallic sheen on nape and conspicuous white collar-patches which are lacking in immature. Beak dark pink, short. Legs pinkish. Gregarious. In flight white crescentic wingbars are striking and diagnostic. Flight fast but clumsy. Voice a distinctive 'coo-*coo*-coo, coo-coo'. Breeds in woodland and scrub, feeds in woodland, on all types of farmland and in urban areas. Widespread, often common.

Stock Dove *Columba oenas* 33cm Medium-sized, farmland pigeon. Adult and immature uniformly dull leaden grey both above and below. Adults have a greenish metallic sheen on nape and pinkish flush to breast. Beak dark and short. Legs reddish. Gregarious. Flight swift and direct, showing distinctive black border to wing, two indistinct and irregular black wingbars, grey rump. Voice a booming 'coo-ooh', particularly in spring. Nests in holes on farmland and woodland, occasionally on coasts. Widespread, locally common.

Collared Dove *Streptopelia decaocto* 28cm Medium-small, sandy-coloured pigeon. Adult and immature sandy-brown on back and wings. Head, neck, breast and belly appreciably paler pinkish-buff. Collar-band a black and white continuous crescent, distinctive in adult, lacking in immature. Gregarious. In flight, wings show dark tips and conspicuous blue-grey forewing patches; brown tail with broad, white terminal band is striking. Voice a dry 'aaah' in flight; also strident 'coo-*coo*-coo'. Inhabits farmland, parks, urban areas. Widespread and common.

Turtle Dove *Streptopelia turtur* 28cm Medium-small pigeon. Adult rich bronze; back and wings mottled with brown and black. Underparts pinkish-buff shading to white on belly. Head and neck grey with chequered black and white collar-patches. Wings dark tipped; tail blackish with diagnostic narrow white border visible in flight (*see* Collared). Immature duller and browner, lacking collars. Gregarious. Flight swift and direct. Voice a distinctive and prolonged purring. Inhabits woodland, farmland with hedges, scrub. Widespread, fairly common.

Owls

Tawny Owl *Strix aluco* 38cm
Medium-sized, round-headed owl. Adult and immature brown above, quite frequently rich chestnut, occasionally almost grey, with fine black streaks and bold buff blotches. Underparts buffish-brown, finely marked with darker brown. Head large, conspicuously rounded. Facial disc roughly circular, grey-buff with narrow black border. Eyes all-dark, large. Nocturnal hunter; secretive during day when whereabouts are often revealed by flocks of agitated small birds. In flight, markedly round-winged. Voice the well-known, tremulous 'hoo-hoo-hoooo' and sharp 'kew-wit'. Inhabits woodland, farmland, urban areas. Widespread.

Little Owl *Athene noctua* 23cm
Small, bold owl, often seen in daylight. Adult and immature grey-brown above, with bold white spots and streaks. Underparts whitish or greyish-buff, heavily streaked with dark brown. Head comparatively large, flat-crowned. Facial disc oblong, greyish with paler margin; eyes bright yellow with dark pupils. Stance squat but upright, often perches on post and bobs occasionally if approached. Flight undulating on short, conspicuously rounded wings. Hunts during the evening and at night. Various puppy-like yelps, and a penetrating 'poo-oop'. Habitat widely varied. Widespread, locally fairly common.

Barn Owl *Tyto alba* 35cm Pale, medium-sized owl. Adult and immature pale sandy-brown above, delicately flecked with brown, grey and white. Underparts white in birds from north-western Europe, including Britain and Ireland, or rich buff, even chestnut, in birds from western and southern Europe. Facial disc white, heart-shaped. Eyes dark brown, large. Stance upright, legs long and 'knock-kneed'. Usually nocturnal, but in winter may hunt in daylight. In flight, relatively long wings appear very pale. Various snoring noises when roosting, occasional strident shriek at other times. Inhabits open woodland, farmland, heaths, villages. Widespread, nowhere numerous.

Cuckoo *Cuculus canorus* 33cm Slim and long-tailed, like a medium-sized falcon. Adult and immature dove-grey above; tail blackish, with white bars on underside visible at close range. Underparts white, finely barred grey. Head and neck grey. Beak black with yellow at base; short. Legs yellow, short. Rare rufous form (female and immature only) has rich brown upperparts. Voice a characteristic 'cuck-oo' and variants; female has bubbling trill and male rasping chuckle. Inhabits woodland, farmland, heath, scrub, moorland and marshes. Widespread, often numerous.

Kingfisher *Alcedo atthis* 17cm
Small but unmistakable. Adult
upperparts electric blue-green;
crown dark blue with paler
blue flecks. Cheeks chestnut
and white. Underparts bright
chestnut. Immature slightly
duller, with heavily flecked
crown. Beak all-black or
showing some red at base;
long, dagger-shaped. Legs and
feet bright scarlet and tiny.
Silhouette dumpy with
oversize beak and head. Flight
arrow-like on whirring wings
low over water. Voice a shrill
ringing 'cheet'. Inhabits lakes,
rivers and streams,
occasionally coasts in winter.
Widespread.

Hoopoe *Upupa epops* 28cm
Medium-sized, with fawn and
pied plumage. Adult and
immature have back and
wings boldly barred black and
white, tail black with white
bar. Head, neck and breast
unusual and characteristic
pinkish sandy-fawn; belly
white. Long, black-tipped, pale
ginger crest on head, erected
into fan when excited or
alarmed. Beak dark, long,
slender and downcurved. Legs
short. Flight characteristically
flopping. Voice a far-carrying
repetitive 'poo-poo-poo'.
Inhabits open country with
trees and scrub, orchards,
olive groves. Widespread, but
rarely numerous.

Great Spotted Woodpecker
Dendrocopos major 23cm Smallish
pied woodpecker. Adult
upperparts barred boldly in
black and white; underparts
whitish, with extensive area
of red beneath tail. Forehead
white; crown and neck black
(with scarlet nape-patch in
male only); white cheeks and
patches on sides of neck. Beak
black, short and stout.
Immature greyer; crown and
tail scarlet. Flight undulating,
showing bold barring across
back and striking white wing-
patches. Voice an explosive
'kek' or 'chack'. Drums often.
Inhabits all types of woodland,
urban parks and gardens,
farmland with large trees.
Widespread, often common.

Green Woodpecker *Picus viridis*
30cm Medium-sized
woodpecker. Adult strikingly
green and gold above,
greenish-grey below with
darker barring on flanks.
Crown and nape red in both
sexes, striking moustachial
streaks red and black in male,
black in female. Beak grey
with black tip, relatively long.
Immature paler; crown
reddish, upperparts heavily
buff-spotted; breast and
flanks barred. Often feeds on
ground. Flight deeply
undulating, gold rump
conspicuous. Voice a
characteristic ringing laugh,
'yah-yah-yah'; drums
relatively rarely. Inhabits open
dry grassland, heath, scrub
and deciduous woodland.
Widespread.

Swallow *Hirundo rustica* 20cm
Typical small hirundine. Adult
and immature dark glossy
blue-black over much of the
upperparts; underparts
predominantly white. Face-
patch dark chestnut. In flight,
shows slender curved wings,
slim silhouette and long,
deeply forked tail with narrow
streamers, longer in adults
than immatures and longer in
males than females; white
spots on tail conspicuous.
Flight swift, swooping; feeds
on the wing. Voice a
prolonged musical twittering,
call a sharp 'chirrup'. Breeds in
buildings on farmland and in
urban areas, feeds over most
habitats. Common.

House Martin *Delichon urbica*
12cm Tiny, pied hirundine.
Adult glossy blue-black on
upperparts, with rather duller,
blackish flight feathers and
diagnostic bold white rump-
patch. Tail blue-black,
shallowly forked. Underparts
white. Legs and toes white
and feathered, visible when
collecting mud for nest.
Immature greyer and lacking
iridescent sheen. Gregarious.
Voice an unmusical rattling
twitter. Nests colonially on
buildings, often in towns,
occasionally on cliffs; feeds
over open land and fresh
waters. Widespread, often
numerous.

Sand Martin *Riparia riparia*
12cm Tiny hirundine. Adult
and immature sandy-brown
above, whitish below with
characteristic brown band
across breast. Tail brown,
short, shallowly forked. Beak
and legs black, tiny. Eyes
relatively large. Immature has
pale feather fringes giving
scaly appearance. Gregarious.
Spends much of its time on
the wing. Voice a soft rattling
trill; sharp chirrup alarm call.
Breeds colonially in sandy
banks, often feeds by hawking
over nearby fresh waters.
Widespread, locally numerous.

Swift *Apus apus* 18cm Small,
with characteristic sickle-
shaped wings. Adult sooty-
black above and below, save
for greyish-white throat
visible at close range. Tail
short, shallowly forked. Beak
and legs tiny; eyes large and
dark. Immature dull grey,
with pale grey scaly markings.
Often gregarious. Flight fast
and characteristically
flickering; wings distinctively
long and narrow. Highly
mobile bird spending much of
its life on the wing. Shrill,
very high-pitched scream.
Breeds colonially in urban
areas, feeds over almost any
habitat. Widespread, locally
numerous.

Larks

Skylark *Alauda arvensis* 18cm
Typical lark. Adult and
immature buffish-brown
above, richer chestnut-brown
on wings and back, all
feathers with dark centres and
pale fringes; flight feathers
blackish. Underparts pale buff,
heavily streaked brown on
breast. Head pale buff, dark
brown streaks; short crest
raised when excited. Eyestripe
pale buff extending as pale
margin to cheek-patch. Beak
pale brown, stout. Legs
pinkish-brown. In flight,
white trailing edge to blackish
tail visible. Call a liquid
'chirrup'; song musical
produced in flight high above
ground. Inhabits open
farmland, marshes, moors,
heaths, mountains. Often
abundant.

Crested Lark *Galerida cristata*
17cm Typical lark with striking
crest. Adult and immature
rich fawn on upperparts,
tinged chestnut and with
brown streaking. Underparts
pale buffish-white; throat and
breast finely streaked with
dark brown. Crest on crown
brown, dark-streaked, long,
often held erect. Beak
brownish, relatively long.
Legs pale brown. In flight,
brown tail with striking,
sandy-chestnut outer feathers
is characteristic. Call 'doo-dee-
doo'; song similar to Skylark
but usually produced from
ground. Inhabits open land,
farms, roadside verges, often
near towns. Common,
though, strangely, extremely
rare in Britain and Ireland.

Meadow Pipit *Anthus pratensis*
15cm Small, nondescript pipit.
Adult and immature brownish
above (shade varying from
yellowish, through olive to
greenish) with abundant
darker streaks. Underparts
pale grey-buff, shading to
white on belly, with dark
streaks on breast and flanks.
Legs dark brown. Call a thin
'seep'; song (often produced in
parachuting song-flight) a
weak descending trill (see
Tree). Inhabits open
moorland, heath, farmland
and marshes. Widespread,
often common.

Tree Pipit *Anthus trivialis* 15cm
Predominantly woodland
pipit. Adult and immature
have upperparts of rich
yellow-brown with plentiful,
fine, darker brown streaks.
Breast buff, shading to white
on belly; conspicuous dark
brown streaks on breast and
flanks. Rather stockier in
build than Meadow, and with
pinkish legs. Call a distinctive
'tee-zee'; song, usually
produced in parachuting
display flight, a characteristic
descending trill ending in a
series of 'see-aah' notes.
Inhabits woodland clearings
and heathland with trees.
Widespread, locally common.

Pipits and Wagtails

Rock Pipit *Anthus petrosa* 17cm Largish, dark pipit. Adult and immature largely brownish-grey above, with plentiful darker streaks, and pale grey-buff below with heavy, dark brown markings. Tail long and dark, with characteristic smoky-grey outer tail feathers. Legs grey, relatively long. Continental Water Pipit is similar but paler. Call a strident 'zeep'; song a strong descending trill, often produced in a parachuting display flight. Frequents rocky coastlines. Widespread, but not numerous.

Yellow Wagtail *Motacilla flava flavissima* 17cm Comparatively short-tailed wagtail. Summer adult male has upperparts olive-green, some yellow on nape; underparts rich canary yellow. Eyestripe yellow, separating greenish crown from darker cheek-patch. Tail black, white edges. Summer female brownish-olive above, buff shading on breast and flanks; underparts paler yellow, throat and breast near white. Winter adults duller, resembling immature, which is grey-brown above, with whitish eyestripe over dark cheek-patch, pale buff below, only trace of yellow undertail. Often gregarious. Call a rich 'tseep'; song musical. Inhabits meadows, farmland and marshes. Locally common.

Grey Wagtail *Motacilla cinerea*
18cm Longest-tailed of the
European wagtails. Summer
adult male has upperparts
dove-grey, with bold white
eyestripe separating grey
crown from darker cheeks.
Tail black with white outer
feathers; long. Underparts
lemon-yellow, particularly
rich beneath tail. Summer
male has white moustachial
streaks and black bib absent in
winter. Female and immature
duller; breast whitish yellow
confined to undertail. Call a
high-pitched 'chee-seek'; song
resembles Blue Tit, 'tsee-tsee-
tsee' followed by trill.
Frequents fast-moving
watersides: streams, rapids,
sluices. Widespread.

White Wagtail *Motacilla alba
alba* 18cm Typical pied plumage
wagtail of continental Europe.
Summer adult male silvery-
grey on back; forehead white,
nape black. Cheeks white,
throat and breast black, rest
of underparts white. Summer
female similar but duller.
Winter adults and immature
have grey backs, smoky napes,
white faces and throats, grey
moustachial stripes and
indistinct blackish collar. Call
a soft disyllabic 'swee-eep';
twittering song. Inhabits open
grassland and waterside in
farmland and urban areas.
Common.

Dunnock *Prunella modularis*
15cm Small and drab. Adult
has dark brown upperparts
with prominent darker
markings. Head, nape and
breast are distinctive leaden
grey, belly buff. Immature
browner, lacking grey,
conspicuously pale-speckled
above. Spends much time on
ground, hopping under
vegetation, often flicking tail.
Call a shrill 'seek', often loud
in evening; song a brief,
suddenly-interrupted,
melodious warble. Inhabits
woodland of all types,
farmland, scrub, town parks
and gardens. Widespread,
locally common.

Dipper *Cinclus cinclus* 17cm
Dumpy, like a thrush-sized
Wren. Adult has rich, dark
brown upperparts. Throat and
breast strikingly white; belly
rich chestnut (Britain and
Ireland) or blackish (rest of
Europe). Immature scaly grey,
darker above than below.
Characteristically stands,
bobbing, on rocks before
plunging into river. Flight
fast, whirring and low over
water. Call a loud 'zit'; song a
fragmented warbling.
Frequents fast-flowing clear
rivers in hilly country,
occasionally lakes or sheltered
coasts. Locally common.

Wren *Troglodytes troglodytes* 10cm
One of the smallest European
birds. Adult and immature
rich chestnut-brown above,
barred with dark brown;
underparts rather paler with
less barring. Tail
characteristically narrow and
carried cocked upright. Spends
much time on ground under
dense vegetation. Flight low
and direct on short, rounded
whirring wings. Call a
scolding 'churr'; song musical,
extended and astonishingly
loud. Well vegetated habitats
of all types, also cliffs and
mountain screes. Widespread,
often common.

Robin *Erithacus rubecula* 13cm
Small but well known. Adult
predominantly sandy-brown
above; face, throat and breast
orange-red, broadly edged
with dark grey. Grey on lower
breast is extensive, shading to
white on belly. Wingbars buff,
narrow; conspicuous in
perched bird, not striking in
flight. Tail sandy-brown,
unmarked. Immature darker
brown above, pale buff below,
copiously speckled and barred.
Call a sharp 'tick'; song a high-
pitched warble. Inhabits
woods, parks and urban
gardens, usually with plentiful
undergrowth. Widespread and
common.

Thrushes and Chats

Black Redstart *Phoenicurus ochruros* 15cm Small, very dark chat. Summer adult male dark ash-grey above. Rump and tail (often flicked) conspicuously chestnut-red. White wingbar striking, especially in older birds. Face and breast sooty-black, belly white. Winter plumage duller, retains chestnut tail. Female uniformly drab, dark grey-brown, but tail characteristic chestnut-red. Immature dark brown with copious paler spots, tail chestnut. Call a sharp 'tick'; song a rapid, but brief, rattling warble. Inhabits mountain screes and towns, including large factory sites. Widespread, locally common.

Redstart *Phoenicurus phoenicurus* 15cm Small, red-tailed chat. Summer adult male unmistakable, upperparts strikingly pale blue-grey, forehead white, tail chestnut. Face and throat black, breast bright chestnut, belly white. Plumage altogether browner and less well-marked in winter. Female brown above, fawn below, tail chestnut. Immature brown, paler below, copiously buff-flecked like immature Robin but tail chestnut, paler and shorter than tail of immature Nightingale. Call a melodious 'tu-eet'; song a brief melodious warble ending in a dry rattle. Inhabits woodlands of all descriptions, sometimes scrub. Widespread, locally common.

Stonechat *Saxicola torquata* 13cm
Small, upright and noisy chat.
Summer adult male has dark
brown back, white rump and
black tail. Head and throat
black; neck patches white.
Breast orange-buff, shading
towards white on belly.
Winter plumage similar, but
obscured by pale feather
fringes. Female similarly
patterned, browner and
heavily streaked; lacking
white rump. Immature brown
above, paler below, copiously
buff speckled. Frequently
perches on bushes, wings and
tail flicking. Call a sharp
'tcchack'; song a high-pitched
scratchy warble, often
produced in song flight.
Inhabits heath and scrub,
inland or coastal. Widespread,
locally common.

Whinchat *Saxicola rubetra* 13cm
Small, upright chat. Summer
adult male speckled brown
and fawn above, with bold
white eyestripe separating
crown from characteristic
dark cheek-patch. Tail dark
brown with distinctive white
markings at base visible in
flight. Underparts pale
orange. Winter plumage
appreciably duller. Female
paler and duller than male.
Immature paler and duller;
underparts heavily streaked.
Often perches on low bushes
or tufts of grass. Wings and
tail constantly flicked. Call a
harsh 'teck'; song a short,
high-pitched warble, often
produced in song-flight.
Inhabits open grassland, heath
and scrub. Widespread but
only locally numerous.

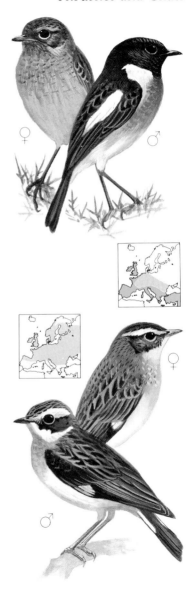

Thrushes and Chats

Bluethroat *Luscinia svecica* 15cm
Small, secretive thrush.
Summer adult male brown
above; characteristic chestnut
patches on each side of base of
tail often striking as it dives
for cover. Throat and breast
bright blue fringed with black
and chestnut, with white
central spot (southern race) or
red (northern race). Breast
colours duller but still
distinctive at other seasons.
Female has white throat
fringed with black. Immature
resembles slim, immature
Robin but has chestnut tail
markings. Call a sharp 'tack';
song an extended high-pitched
melodious warble. Inhabits
northern swampy scrub or
heathland. Locally fairly
common.

Black-eared Wheatear
Oenanthe hispanica 15cm Small,
terrestrial chat. Adult male
pale cinnamon brown above
and below; wings black. Two
forms occur: one with a large
black patch through the eye,
the other with a complete
black face and throat. Winter
plumage appreciably duller.
Female and immature similar
to Wheatear, but with darker
cheeks and wings. In flight,
characteristic white inverted
'V' marking on rump and tail
prominent. Call a harsh
'tchack'; song a high-pitched,
scratchy warble. Inhabits dry,
open, often stony areas with
mostly low-growing
vegetation. Locally common.

Wheatear *Oenanthe oenanthe*
15cm Small, pale chat.
Summer adult male pale grey
above; underparts apricot-
buff. Wings blackish; tail
black, white inverted 'V' mark
on rump and base of tail
conspicuous in flight. Eye-
patch black. Winter plumage
browner. Female grey-brown
above, buff below; eye-patch
brown. Immature similar, but
buff-speckled. Both show
distinctive tail and rump
pattern. Largely terrestrial,
running in short bursts, then
pausing, tail cocked. Call a
harsh 'tack'; song a brief,
scratchy warble, often
produced in song flight.
Inhabits open areas of heath,
grassland or moorland, often
with scanty vegetation.
Widespread, locally common.

Blackbird *Turdus merula* 25cm
Familiar and comparatively
long tailed. Male plumage
unmistakable, entirely glossy
velvet black; beak and eye-
ring contrasting orange.
Female dark brown above,
paler below, throat whitish
with dark border; beak dark
with trace of yellow at base.

Immature rather more ginger-
brown than female, heavily
buff-spotted. Call a loud
'chink' or 'chack', often
persistent; song fluting,
varied, extended and
melodious. Inhabits farmland,
woodland, heaths and urban
areas. Widespread, often
abundant.

Thrushes and Chats

Mistle Thrush *Turdus viscivorus*
27cm Largish, pale and
relatively long-tailed thrush.
Adult pale grey-brown above;
underparts whitish, heavily
spotted with brown. Wings
dark brown. Tail long, dark
with pale grey-buff outer
feathers. Immature greyer,
appears much paler because of
copious, pale scaly feather
margins on upperparts. In
flight, characteristic white
underwing conspicuous. Call
an angry extended rattle; song
simple and slow but tuneful,
often produced early in spring
and usually delivered from a
prominent perch. Inhabits
woodland, parks, gardens and
well-treed farmland; often on
open grassland in winter.
Widespread.

Song Thrush *Turdus philomelos*
23cm Smallish, short-tailed,
upright thrush. Adult olive or
sandy-brown above, tinged
yellowish-buff, with pale
eyestripe above darker brown
cheek-patch. Wings and tail
chestnut-brown. Underparts
greyish-white, tinged
cinnamon, heavily streaked
with dark brown. Immature
similar, but with copious
yellow-buff speckling on
upperparts. In flight,
underwings are pale sandy-
brown (*see* Redwing, Mistle).
Call a thin 'seep'; song (often
from a prominent perch) a
series of musical notes, each
repeated two or three times.
Inhabits woods, parks,
gardens and farmland with
plentiful trees. Widespread,
often common.

Fieldfare *Turdus pilaris* 25cm
Comparatively long-tailed
thrush. Adult has back,
mantle and wings rich golden
russet-brown. Breast golden-
buff shading to white on belly,
heavily speckled. Crown, nape
and rump dove-grey,
contrasting with black tail.
Immature is browner above,
fawn below, heavily speckled.
Often gregarious. Call a very
characteristic series of
laughing 'chacks'; song a
scratchy warble. Breeds in
northern forests, parks and
gardens, winters on open
farmland and open woodland.
Widespread, often common.

Redwing *Turdus iliacus* 20cm
Smallish dark, short-tailed
thrush. Adult is dark russet-
brown above, with
conspicuous buffish eyestripe
and moustachial streak on
either edge of dark cheek-
patch. Underparts whitish,
streaked dark brown, with
conspicuous reddish flanks.
Immature similar but duller,
with copious sandy speckling
on back. In flight,
characteristic red underwing
is prominent. Often
gregarious. Call an extended
'see-eep'; song a low series of
fluting notes. Breeds in
northern forests, parks and
gardens, winters in woodland
and on open farmland,
occasionally in parks and
gardens. Widespread, often
numerous.

Nightingale *Luscinia megarhynchos* 17cm Small, drab thrush but an incomparable songster. Adult olive-brown above, with striking, long, round-ended rufous tail. Underparts pale buff, almost white on belly, always unmarked. Immature sandy-brown above, paler below, copiously spotted but with long rufous tail. Legs relatively long and strong, suited to terrestrial habits. Call a soft 'hoo-eet'; song long, loud and melodious, richly varied and containing some mimicry of other birds, often produced night and day. Inhabits dense woodland undergrowth and swampy thickets. Widespread, locally common.

Reed Warbler *Acrocephalus scirpaceus* 13cm Tiny, unstreaked warbler. Adult and immature have rich reddish-brown upperparts lacking darker streaks; tail reddish-brown, relatively long and tapered towards tip. Eyestripe faint buffish. Underparts whitish, shading to buff on flanks. Legs normally dark brown. Alarm call 'churr'; song prolonged and repetitive, with spells of chirruping, more musical and less twangy than Sedge, with some mimicry. Normally inhabits reedbeds, sometimes other heavily vegetated fresh water margins. Widespread, often common.

Cetti's Warbler *Cettia cetti* 15cm
Small, unstreaked warbler.
Adult and immature have
entire upperparts rich
reddish-brown, shading to
buff on sides of breast and
flanks, and to white on belly.
Tail rich brown, relatively
long, and conspicuously
rounded at the tip. Secretive,
normally flying only short
distance between clumps of
vegetation. Call a sharp 'teck';
song an explosive burst of
metallic 'cher-chink' notes.
Inhabits damp, heavily
vegetated marshes, ditches,
swamps and scrub. Non-
migratory. Widespread, locally
common.

Sedge Warbler *Acrocephalus
schoenobaenus* 13cm Tiny,
heavily-streaked warbler.
Adult and immature have
olive-brown back, heavily
streaked with blackish-brown;
tail brown, tinged chestnut.
Underparts whitish, tinged
buff on flanks. Crown brown,
with narrow blackish stripes,
separated by clear whitish
eyestripe from grey-brown
cheeks. Inquisitive, but rarely
flies far in the open. Call an
explosive 'tuck' of alarm; song
(often produced in short,
vertical song-flight) a rapid,
repetitive, metallic jingle,
often loud and interspersed
with chattering notes.
Inhabits reedbeds and adjacent
shrubby swamps. Widespread,
often common.

Warblers

Whitethroat *Sylvia communis*
14cm Small active warbler.
Adult male grey above, wings
characteristic pale chestnut,
tail dull brown with white
edge. Throat strikingly white,
rest of underparts whitish,
tinged pinkish-buff. Legs
brownish. Female and
immature browner and paler,
but with chestnut wings still
evident. Active but fairly
secretive, except in song. Call
a rasping 'tschack'; song a
rapid, scratchy warble, usually
produced in song-flight.
Inhabits heath, scrubby
hillsides, maquis and
woodland clearings.
Widespread, locally common.

Garden Warbler *Sylvia borin*
15cm Small warbler, lacking
distinctive features. Adult
characteristically drab
greyish-olive on upperparts;
underparts whitish shaded
grey or buff, especially on the
flanks. Head rounded, with
comparatively heavy beak.
Eyestripe faint and pale. Legs
bluish. Immature paler,
yellowish-buff. Secretive. Call
a sharp 'tack'; song an
extended, liquid, melodious
warbling, usually produced in
deep cover. Inhabits well-
grown, thick scrub or dense
woodland undergrowth; tall
trees seem unnecessary
(unlike Blackcap). Widespread,
occasionally quite common.

Blackcap *Sylvia atricapilla* 15cm
Small warbler. Adult male is
greyish-olive above, with
characteristic black crown;
underparts pale grey. Legs
bluish. Female and immature
have grey plumage with
browner tinge; cap brown in
female, ginger-chestnut in
immature. Call a sharp 'tack';
song a melodious warble,
similar to but briefer than
Garden Warbler, usually
ending in a rising note.
Inhabits parks, gardens and
woodland with both well-
developed undergrowth and
tall trees. Widespread, locally
quite common.

Wood Warbler *Phylloscopus
sibilatrix* 13cm Small, but one of
the larger leaf warblers. Adult
and immature have yellowish-
olive upperparts. Wings
brown, with yellowish feather
fringes but lacking wingbars.
Eyestripe yellowish, distinct;
face, throat and breast rich
yellow. Rest of underparts
strikingly white. Legs pale
pinkish-brown. Call a liquid
'dee-you'; song a characteristic
trill based on an accelerating
repetition of 'sip' notes, often
produced in song-flight.
Inhabits mature deciduous
woodland, often with
comparatively little
undergrowth. Widespread,
locally common.

Warblers

Willow Warbler *Phylloscopus trochilus* 10cm Tiny leaf warbler. Adult and immature have pale olive-green upperparts, with a clear whitish eyestripe. Underparts are whitish, strongly tinged with yellow in immature, especially on the flanks. Legs usually brown (*see* Chiffchaff).

Call a plaintive 'too-eet'; song a characteristic, melodious and silvery descending warble with a final flourish. Inhabits woodlands with dense undergrowth, heath, parkland and, in the far north, scrub without trees. Widespread and common.

Chiffchaff *Phylloscopus collybita* 10cm Tiny, drab leaf warbler. Adult and immature have drab brownish-olive upperparts; wings brown lacking wingbars; tail brown. Eyestripe pale yellow. Underparts whitish, shaded buff on flanks, often yellow-tinged in immature. Legs

usually blackish. Call a plaintive 'hoo-eet'; song striking and diagnostic, a monotonous series of 'chiff' 'chaff' notes. Favours mature woodlands with both tall trees and well-developed undergrowth; rarely in scrub except on migration. Widespread, often common.

Firecrest *Regulus ignicapillus* 9cm
Smallest European bird. Adult
and immature have olive
green upperparts, tinged
golden-bronze on the mantle
in adults; wings brownish
with double white wingbars;
tail brown, short. Underparts
whitish. Head pattern (lacking
in immature) striking and
diagnostic, with crown stripe
orange (flame in male) edged
in black and contrasting with
bold white stripe over eye.
Call a rasping high-pitched
'tsee'; song a monotonous
accelerating repetition of 'tsee'
notes lacking final flourish of
Goldcrest. Inhabits woodland
of all types. Widespread,
locally common.

Goldcrest *Regulus regulus* 9cm
Tiny, one of the smallest
European birds. Adult and
immature have olive-green
upperparts; wings brownish
with double white wingbar;
tail brown, short. Underparts
whitish. Head pattern
characteristic, with crown-
stripe flame coloured in male,
yellowish-gold in female,
broadly edged in black; diffuse
white eye-ring. Beak dark,
short and finely pointed. Legs
dark brown. Immature lacks
head pattern. Call a very high-
pitched 'tsee'; song also high-
pitched, a descending series of
'tsee-tsee' notes terminating
in flourishing trill. Inhabits
woodland of all types,
occasionally parks and
gardens. Widespread and
common.

Flycatchers

Pied Flycatcher *Ficedula hypoleuca* 13cm Small flycatcher with pied plumage. Summer adult male has black upperparts (year-old birds may have brownish wings and tail); wingbars bold white; forehead has white patch. Tail black with white edges, frequently flicked. Underparts white. Winter male, female and immature brown above, white below with grey-buff shading. Call a sharp 'wit'; song an unmelodious rattle of notes. Inhabits mature woodland, usually deciduous, with scant undergrowth. Locally common.

Spotted Flycatcher *Muscicapa striata* 15cm Small, elongated flycatcher. Adult and immature have drab brown upperparts with dark brown, closely-spaced streaks on crown. Underparts buff shading to white on belly; breast has brown streaking. Immature has scaly pale markings on back when freshly fledged. Flight characteristic, dashing out from prominent perch to catch insect prey, usually returning to same perch; shows relatively long wings and tail. Call a sharp 'zit'; song a brief sequence of squeaky notes. Inhabits woodland clearings, scrub, farmland, parks and gardens with plentiful trees. Widespread.

Long-tailed Tit *Aegithalos caudatus* 15cm Tiny but long-tailed. Adult and immature have fluffy body; upperparts largely white and brown, tinged pink; tail black, white edged. Underparts white, tinged pale buffish-pink on belly and flanks. Head white with dark stripes over eyes (head all-white in northern race); reddish, fleshy wattles over eyes. Beak black, short and stubby. Tends to move in noisy flocks. Flight feeble on short, rounded wings. Calls a repeated thin 'see', or a low 'tupp'; song (rarely heard) varied 'see' and 'tsew' notes. Inhabits woodland undergrowth, scrub, heathland and farmland hedges. Widespread, often common.

Bearded Tit *Panurus biarmicus* 15cm Small and long-tailed. Adult male predominantly chestnut-brown above. Tail long and relatively broad. Head distinctive dove-grey. Throat white, with characteristic, broad black moustachial streaks; rest of underparts pale buff. Female and immature brown above, cap darker; underparts grey-buff. Tends to move in flocks. Flight feeble on short, rounded wings. Call a distinctive 'ping'; song a twittering rattle. Inhabits wetlands with extensive *Phragmites* reed beds. Locally common.

Tits

Great Tit *Parus major* 15cm
Largest of the tits. Adult back
greenish; wings blue-grey
with white wingbars; tail
blackish with conspicuous
white edges. Crown and nape
glossy black, with striking
white cheeks and indistinct
whitish nape-patch. Breast
and belly yellow, with central
black stripe broader in male
than female. Immature duller
and greener, with grey-green
rather than black markings.
Feeds more often on ground
than other tits. Calls varied,
but 'tchink' common; song a
repetitive, ringing 'tea-cher,
tea-cher'. Inhabits woodland
of all types, farmland, parks
and gardens. Widespread,
often numerous.

Coal Tit *Parus ater* 12cm Tiny,
agile tit. Adult and immature
have olive-grey upperparts
(bluer in Continental birds).
Underparts pale buff, with
richer cinnamon tones on
flanks. Head and bib glossy
black (duller in immature)
relieved by contrasting white
patches on cheeks and nape.
Call a high-pitched, plaintive
'tseet'; song a repetitive, high-
pitched 'wheat-see, wheat-
see'. Inhabits woodland of all
types, but favours conifers;
also found in gardens and
parks. Widespread, often
common.

Blue Tit *Parus caeruleus* 12cm
Tiny tit. Adult has greenish
back; wings and tail
characteristic bright blue.
Underparts yellow. Head
white, with bright blue crown,
black line through eye and
black bib. Male shows brighter
blues than female. Immature
less well-marked, with
greenish upperparts and
lacking blue crown until
autumn. Varied calls, but
'tsee-tsee-tsee-sit' often used;
song a fast trill opening with a
series of 'tsee' notes. Habitat
ranges from woodland of all
types to urban gardens,
farmland and even marshland
in winter. Widespread, often
numerous.

Marsh Tit *Parus palustris* 13cm
Small, sombre brownish tit.
Adult and immature have
upperparts of uniform brown;
wings and tail slightly darker
brown. Crown and nape
glossy black, contrasting with
whitish cheeks. Underparts
largely greyish-buff, with
small black bib on throat. Call
a diagnostic, explosive 'pit-
chew'; song a bell-like note
repeated several times, or
sometimes 'pitchaweeoo'
variants of the call. Inhabits
woodland, usually deciduous
or mixed with abundant
undergrowth; scrub, park and
garden shrubberies.
Widespread but rarely
numerous.

Treecreeper *Certhia familiaris*
12cm Woodpecker-like but
tiny. Adult and immature
have dark brown upperparts,
densely streaked with white,
more conspicuously so in
immature. Tail brown, long,
central feathers pointed.
Underparts whitish, often
stained with green or brown
from tree trunks. Long
whitish eyestripe over darker
brown cheek-patch; eye large
and dark. Beak long and fairly
pointed, downcurved. Creeps
mouse-like, head-up on bark.
Flight deeply undulating,
showing multiple wingbars.
Call a shrill 'tseeu'; song a
high-pitched descending series
of notes with final flourish.
Inhabits mature woodland,
especially conifers. Widespread
but rarely numerous.

Nuthatch *Sitta europaea* 15cm
Small and woodpecker-like.
Adult and immature have
distinctive blue-grey
upperparts; wings dark grey;
tail feathers white-tipped,
dove-grey. Eyestripe broad
and black. Throat white, rest
of underparts pale buff,
shading to rich chestnut on
flanks of male, cinnamon on
female. Northern race almost
completely white below. Beak
relatively long and dagger-
like. Moves actively on tree
trunks and branches, both
head-up and head-down,
unlike woodpeckers. Call a
distinctive, far-carrying,
ringing 'chwit'; song a
repetitive 'toowee toowee'.
Inhabits mature deciduous
woodland and parkland.
Widespread, locally common.

Red-backed Shrike *Lanius collurio* 18cm Small, colourful shrike. Adult male has a chestnut-brown back; crown and nape dove-grey; rump grey and tail black with white edges. Black patch through eye. Throat white, rest of underparts white, tinged pinkish-buff. Female dull brown above with dark brown eyepatch, whitish below with fine bars. Beak dark, large and conspicuously hooked. Immature resembles female, but with heavy scaly markings. Call a harsh 'chack'; song a melodious warble. Inhabits dryish open country with bushes or scrub, heathland. Widespread.

Jay *Garrulus glandarius* 35cm Medium-sized, brightly-coloured crow. Adult and immature have rich pinkish-buff upperparts with chestnut shading; rump white, tail black. Wings blackish, with bold white wingbar and bright blue patch conspicuous at 'wrist'. Underparts pale pinkish-buff. Crown pinkish with black flecks, raised as short crest if excited. Black moustachial stripes. Eye pale pink. Beak dark grey, stout. Flight floppy on erratically beating, rounded, fingered wings. Noisy: call a harsh 'skaark'; song a subdued mixture of cackling notes, rarely heard. Inhabits woods, farmland and parkland with plentiful trees. Widespread, often quite common.

Crows

Rook *Corvus frugilegus* 45cm
Medium-large crow. Adult male and female have whole plumage glossy black with iridescent sheen. Upper leg (thigh) feathers loose and rough, giving 'baggy-trousered' appearance (*see* Carrion Crow). Beak pale, running to whitish cheek-patches; long, dagger-shaped. Immature has duller sooty-black plumage; beak blackish; lacks cheek-patches. Colonial when breeding and gregarious feeding, often with Jackdaws. Noisy: call a raucous 'carr'. Inhabits arable farmland with adjacent woodland or plenty of tall trees. Widespread, often common.

Jackdaw *Corvus monedula* 33cm
One of the smaller crows. Adult and immature have most of head and body dull sooty black; crown, nape and upper breast have variable amount of grey. Eye startlingly white. Beak relatively short but stout. Gregarious: often in large flocks with Rooks. Flight usually direct, with quicker wingbeats than other crows, and lacking fingered wingtips. Vocal: call a metallic 'jack'. Inhabits open woodland, parkland, farmland and urban areas, often nesting colonially in old trees or ruined buildings. Widespread, often common.

Magpie *Pica pica* 45cm Long-tailed, pied crow. Adult and immature have black back and upper breast; belly white; wings black and white; tail black with purple and green iridescence, long and tapered. Head and nape glossy black. Immature when freshly fledged is duller and with rather shorter tail. Flight direct but on fluttering, rounded wings. Call a harsh chatter; song a surprisingly musical, quiet collection of piping notes, not often heard. Inhabits woodland, parkland, farmland, heath and scrub, mature gardens, even city-centre parks. Widespread, locally numerous.

Carrion Crow *Corvus corone* 45cm One of the larger crows. Adult and immature wholly black. Upper leg (thigh) feathers neatly close-fitting (*see* Rook). Beak black; stout with convex upper mandible; black feathers at base (*see* Rook). Only occasionally gregarious. Voice a deep, harsh 'caw' or 'corr'. Inhabits open countryside of all types with suitable tall trees for nesting, also urban areas, even city centres. Widespread but rarely very numerous.

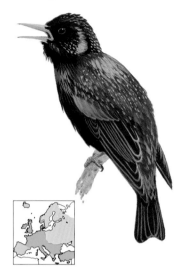

Starling *Sturnus vulgaris* 22cm
Small. Summer adult plumage
blackish, glossily iridescent at
close range; back has bright
buffish flecks. Beak yellow
with blue base in male, pink in
female. Legs pinkish-brown.
Winter adult lacks much of
the iridescence; heavily
spotted with white. Immature
uniformly drab brown.
Gregarious, often in huge
flocks. Flight swift and direct,
characteristic triangular wing
silhouette. Noisy: calls include
harsh shrieks and scolding
chattering; song extended and
varied, including much expert
mimicry of other birds, often
accompanied by wing-flapping
display on perch. Habitat
widely varied. Mostly
abundant. Common.

Greenfinch *Carduelis chloris*
15cm Small finch with robust
beak. Summer adult male
olive-green above, grey on
nape and cheeks. Wings
brown with bold yellow
patches conspicuous in flight;
tail brown with yellow patch
on either side of base.
Underparts largely rich
yellow. Beak pale,
comparatively large,
triangular. Winter male and
female brownish-olive, less
dramatic yellow patches in
wings and tail. Immature
similar, but with narrow
brown streaks on back and
flanks. Call a drawling 'dwee-
ee'; song an extended purring
trill, often given in display
flight. Inhabits woodland,
farmland, parks and gardens.
Widespread, often numerous.

Chaffinch *Fringilla coelebs* 15cm
Small finch. Adult male
rufous-brown on back; wings
dark brown, with two white
wingbars; tail blackish
showing white outer feathers.
Underparts rich pink, shading
to white on lower belly. Head
and nape grey, forehead black.
Winter plumage subdued.
Beak grey, comparatively
long. Female and immature
brown above, pale fawn
below; wings brownish
showing wingbars; tail dark
brown, white-edged. Often
gregarious in winter. Flight
deeply undulating, wingbars
conspicuous. Call a ringing
'pink'; song a descending
cascade ending in flourish.
Inhabits woodland, farmland,
parks and gardens.
Widespread, common.

Brambling *Fringilla
montifringilla* 15cm Small,
colourful finch. Summer adult
male largely glossy black on
head and back; wings dark
brown, with orange forewing
and white wingbar; tail
blackish. Throat and breast
bright orange, shading to
white on belly. Winter male
plumage obscured by buff
scaly markings. Female and
immature mottled brown and
blackish above, pale orange-
brown below. Often
gregarious in winter. In flight,
wingbar and white rump-
patch conspicuous. Call a
flourishing 'tchway', often
given in flight; song a series of
'twee' notes. Inhabits
woodland, farmland and parks
in winter. Widespread;
variable numbers.

Finches

Linnet *Carduelis cannabina* 13cm
Small brown finch. Summer
adult male has rich chestnut
back; wings brown, with
poorly defined white patch;
rump whitish; tail black with
white edge. Head and
underparts pale fawn, with
variable areas of glossy pink
on crown and breast. Winter
male, female and immature
dull brown, paler below than
on back, with brown streaks
and lacking pink patches. Beak
blackish, stubby. Gregarious.
Flight deeply undulating. Call
a penetrating 'tsweet'; song a
musical and varied twittering
often given from prominent
perch. Inhabits heath, scrub
and farmland, occasionally
parks and gardens.
Widespread, locally common.

Siskin *Carduelis spinus* 12cm
Tiny dark finch. Adult male
greenish on upperparts, often
heavily streaked with black.
Wings dark brown; double
yellowish wingbars. Crown
and small bib black,
underparts yellowish shading
to white on belly, flanks
streaked with brown. Female
and immature duller and
browner; brown streaking
above and below. Beak dark,
relatively long, pointed at tip.
In flight, yellow rump and
yellow patches beside base of
dark, deeply forked tail
conspicuous. Call, often given
in flight, a wheezy 'chwee-oo';
song a prolonged twittering.
Inhabits woodland, parks,
occasionally gardens.
Widespread, sometimes
common.

Goldfinch *Carduelis carduelis*
13cm Small colourful finch.
Adult male and female
unmistakable, with harlequin
plumage. Crown and nape
black, face red and white.
Wings black; broad gold
wingbars are distinctive in
flight, as is white rump
contrasting with black tail.
Beak whitish with dark tip,
relatively long and pointed for
a finch. Immature is paler and
buffer, with plain buff head.
Call a distinctive 'dee-dee-lit';
song a prolonged, liquid
warbling twitter. Inhabits
open woodland, heath, scrub,
farmland, parks and gardens.
Widespread, locally common.

Redpoll *Carduelis flammea* 12cm
Small dark finch. Adult male
and female have brown
upperparts with blackish
streaking; underparts buffish,
paling to white on belly. Small
black bib. Forehead and crown
have characteristic small red
patch. Summer male may
have pinkish flush on breast.
Immature duller, lacking bib
and red 'poll'. Several
geographical races occur:
northern birds tend to be
paler and slightly larger than
southern ones. Call 'chee-
chee-chit'; song a distinctive,
high-pitched, purring trill,
often delivered in circling
song-flight high above
woodland. Inhabits mixed
woodland (favouring birch),
farmland and well-treed
scrub. Fairly common.

Bullfinch *Pyrrhula pyrrhula*
15cm Small heavy-headed
finch. Adult male has bold
black cap, dove-grey mantle
and back, striking white rump
contrasting with black tail.
Wings black; bold white
wingbar. Underparts rich pink
to crimson, shading to white
on belly. Beak black, rounded.
Female has black cap, grey-
brown mantle and back; wing
and rump patterns as male.
Underparts soft fawn.
Immature similar to female,
lacking black cap. Flight
hesitant, deeply undulating.
Call a distinctive whistle
'peeu'; song a rarely-heard,
quiet creaking warble.
Inhabits woodland, scrub,
parks, farmland and gardens.
Widespread, but rarely
numerous.

Yellowhammer *Emberiza
citrinella* 18cm Small bunting.
Summer male has back, rump
and wings rich chestnut,
streaked with black and
brown. Tail dark with whitish
outer feathers; relatively long.
Head and neck bright yellow;
variable black markings on
head. Breast and belly canary
yellow, tinged chestnut on
breast and flanks. Winter male
much browner. Female and
immature streaked brown
above chestnut rump. Head
yellowish, with dark streaking;
underparts pale yellow, white
on belly, streaked brown on
flanks and breast. Call a sharp
'twick'; song a series of 'zit'
notes, ending in wheezy
'zeee'. Inhabits heath, scrub
and farmland. Widespread,
often common.

Reed Bunting *Emberiza schoeniclus* 15cm Small bunting. Summer male has rich brown back with darker streaks; grey-brown rump; blackish tail with white outer feathers. Crown and face black; white collar running into white moustachial streaks and whitish underparts; throat and upper breast black. Winter plumage obscured by buff feather fringes. Female and immature brown above, buff below; dark streaks on back and flanks. Crown rich brown, separated from dark cheek-patch by buffish eyestripe; adjacent whitish and black moustachial streaks. Call 'tsee-you'; song short harsh, discordant. Inhabits marshes, scrub and farmland. Widespread, often common.

Corn Bunting *Miliaria calandra* 18cm One of the larger, and certainly most nondescript, European buntings. Adult and immature relatively plump; dark sandy-brown above, paler sandy-brown below, paling to white on the belly, with copious brown streaks. Tail dark brown, lacking white outer feathers. Call a short 'tsrip' or disyllabic 'tsip-ip'; song characteristic, an unmistakable harsh, metallic jangling, delivered from prominent song-post. Inhabits open, dry farmland, heath and scrub. Widespread but with large local variations in numbers.

Sparrows

House Sparrow *Passer domesticus*
15cm Small, with triangular
beak. Adult male has rich
brown back with darker
brown streaks. Wings brown
with double white wingbar.
Rump dark grey-buff; tail
blackish. Crown grey and
nape rich dark chestnut;
cheeks whitish; throat and
upper breast black, rest of
underparts whitish. Female
and immature sandy-brown
above, with darker brown
markings and clear buff
eyestripe. Underparts pale
grey-buff. Beak relatively
long, blackish in male,
brownish in female.
Gregarious. Call a clear
'chirrup'; song a monotonous
chirruping. Frequents human
habitats. Widespread, often
numerous.

Tree Sparrow *Passer montanus*
13cm Small, with triangular
beak. Adult male and female
similar. Upperparts rich
brown mottled with black
streaks. Crown and nape pale
chestnut; characteristic white
cheeks with central black spot.
Small black bib, with rest of
underparts off-white. Beak
black and stubby. Immature
drabber, less clearly marked.
Gregarious, but not to same
extent as House. Calls include
short metallic 'chip' and 'chop',
and a repeated 'chit-tchup'.
Distinctive liquid flight-call,
'tek, tek', is difficult to
describe but diagnostic once
learnt. Frequents woodland,
well-treed farmland and
scrub, usually distant from
habitation. Widespread.

Further Reading

There is an enormous number of bird books available, of which the following is a useful selection.

Campbell, B. and Lack, E. (Eds), *A Dictionary of Birds*. T.& A.D. Poyser, Calton, 1985.

Cramp, S. and Simmons, K.E.L. (Eds), *Handbook of the Birds of Europe, the Middle East and Africa* (vols. I-V published to date). Oxford University Press, Oxford, 1977.

Fisher, J. and Flegg, J., *Watching Birds*. Penguin Books, Harmondsworth, 1978.

Flegg, J., *In Search of Birds; Their Haunts and Habitats*. Blandford Press, Poole, 1983.

Flegg, J., *Birdlife*. Pelham Books, London, 1986.

Harrison, P., *Seabirds – An Identification Guide*. Croom Helm, London, 1985.

Hayman, P., Marchant, J. and Prater, T., *Shorebirds – An Identification Guide*. Croom Helm, London, 1986.

Jellis, R., *Bird Sounds and Their Meaning*. BBC Publications, London, 1977.

Madge, S., *Wildfowl: An Identification Guide to the Ducks, Geese and Swans of the World*. Christopher Helm, London, 1988.

Mead, C., *Bird Migration*. Country Life Books, London, 1983.

Ogilvie, M., *The Wildfowl of Britain and Europe*. Oxford University Press, Oxford, 1982.

Useful Addresses

British Ornithologists' Union (BOU)
c/o Zoological Society of London, Regent's Park, London NW1 4RY.

British Trust for Ornithology (BTO)
Beech Grove, Station Road, Tring, Herts HP23 5NR.

British Waterfowl Association
6 Caldicott Close, Over, Windsford, Cheshire CW7 1LW.

Hawk Trust
c/o Birds of Prey Section, Zoological Society of London, Regent's Park, London NW1 4RY.

National Trust
36 Queen Anne's Gate, London SW1H 9AS.

National Trust for Scotland
5 Charlotte Square, Edinburgh EH2 4DU.

Royal Society for the Protection of Birds (RSPB)
The Lodge, Sandy, Beds SG19 2DL.

Scottish Ornithologists' Club
21 Regent Terrace, Edinburgh EH7 5BT.

Wildfowl and Wetland Trust
Gatehouse, Slimbridge, Glos GL2 7BT.

In Britain, most counties have a County Naturalists' Trust, which is responsible for the management of various reserves (though not all of them are for birds), and an ornithological society. Addresses of such organisations can be obtained from local libraries.

Index

Index

Index

Index

Index

SPANISH   Made Simple

Eugene Jackson and
Antonio Rubio, PhD

Advisory editor

Irene Hart, LeL, MSc, DIC, PhD, FIL

MADE SIMPLE
B O O K S

HEINEMANN : London

© 1981 William Heinemann Ltd

Made and printed in Great Britain
by Richard Clay Ltd, Bungay, Suffolk
for the publishers William Heinemann Ltd,
10 Upper Grosvenor Street, London W1X 9PA

First edition 1969
Reprinted 1972
Reprinted 1973
Reprinted 1975
Second edition (completely revised) 1977
Reprinted 1979
Reprinted 1981
Reprinted 1982
Reprinted 1984
Reprinted 1985
Reprinted 1986

British Library Cataloguing in Publication Data

Jackson, Eugene
    Spanish made simple.—2nd ed., completely
    revised.—(Made simple books, ISBN 0265–0541)
    1. Spanish language—Text-books for
    foreign speakers
    I. Title   II. Rubio, Antonio
    III. Hart, Irene   IV. Series
    468.2′4   PC4112

ISBN 0 434 98451 5

Spanish holds a key position amongst the world's languages today. It is spoken not only in Spain but also in Central and South America (with the exception of Brazil, where Portuguese is spoken), in Cuba and the Dominican Republic, and it is one of the three official languages of the Philippines. With English, French, Russian and Chinese it is also an official language at the United Nations. It is a language of prime importance to businessmen, and its varied and rich literature provides its readers with infinite enjoyment.

Whatever his reasons for learning the language, the beginner will find *Spanish Made Simple*, with its bilingual dialogues, numerous illustrative drills, exercises and answer keys, the ideal book for self-instruction. The essential grammatical facts of Spanish grow naturally out of the conversations and reading texts. The facts are clearly explained. Non-essentials are omitted. This book is equally suitable for use as an introductory course in evening institutes and schools. The book's frequent well-laid-out revision lessons and reading passages will also be of especial help to those who wish to consolidate their already acquired notion of the language.

Spanish pronunciation is not difficult. As a guide to pronunciation the symbols of the widely accepted International Phonetic Alphabet are used. Once known, these symbols will also help the student in his study of other languages.

The student who conscientiously works through this book will have at his command the basic structures of the language and a vocabulary of some 1,500 words. He will have laid a solid foundation for further study of the language to GCE O-level and beyond, and for the enjoyment of reading Spanish and Hispanic–American literature, newspapers and magazines in the original. The text will also be invaluable to businessmen and business studies students who wish to learn the language for practical purposes, and some of the chapters are in fact set in the business context.

Those who want to know about the countries where Spanish is spoken (19 in all, with Spain) will find that Hispanic America offers a vast and varied production in the literary field. Its novels, essays, short stories and poetry provide insights into the way the inhabitants of nearly a fifth of the world's land surface think, feel and react in their everyday lives.

When the learner visits Spain or any of the Spanish-speaking countries of America he or she will be greatly rewarded for the effort by the warm-hearted hospitality that one usually meets in Spain—and the Canary and Balearic Islands—if one can converse in Spanish. The same is true if one travels further afield—to Mexico or South America. There is a cultural, historical, and ethnic affinity among the Hispanic peoples, as there is among the English-speaking peoples, which outsiders notice perhaps more than 'insiders'. Spanish in America has developed variations of pronunciation as English has in the U.S.A., Australia and elsewhere. It has absorbed many indigenous words—which it has often passed to other languages, e.g. *tomato, chocolate, tobacco, marijuana*. Many elegant Spanish expressions have been retained in Hispanic America that have been lost in Spain, and some find the pronunciation of, say, Mexican or Colombian Castilian, or *castellano* as Hispanic Americans prefer to call Spanish, more pleasant and clearer than the language in the old country.

The aim of *Spanish Made Simple* is to open new perspectives to this vast area of mankind and to enable the student to converse in the second most extended European language after English with the people who speak that language: Spanish.

Although the author and publishers endeavour to keep this book up to date in consecutive reprints, slight inaccuracies of fact in the text are almost inevitable because of the immense political and social changes in Spain in recent years. Rapidly rising incomes and a widespread desire by Spaniards to share in the material benefits of their emergent industrial society are bringing corresponding changes in lifestyles. Rural people have flocked to the towns; old ways are changing fast. Women and girls go about freely, and both smoke and drink. Censorship is a thing of the past, as is the stereotype of the well-mannered Spanish 'caballero' (gentleman). 'Cortesía' (old-fashioned courtesy) has almost disappeared, especially in the young. Material things, of which Spaniards were deprived for so long, have become increasingly important and enjoyable to the majority of the nation.

The constitution of 1978 re-established government by universal suffrage under the monarchy. With the rapid industrial and technological development and the growing desire to be 'European', Spain has taken a definite turn in her history. 'España es diferente'—Spain is different—is a thing of the past. In January 1986 Spain joined the European Community and Spanish is now one of the languages of the European Community. Therefore, because of the increasingly important role Spain plays, and will play in Europe, a command of Spanish is a prerequisite for practical purposes such as in business deals, intellectual pursuits, and for a true understanding of the country and her people to make a holiday visit fully enjoyable.

Table of Contents

and tin wares—Raw materials—Present of **volver, volver a hablar**—
Use of **acabar de.**—Two ways of saying *and* and two ways of saying *or*.

participles of some familiar verbs—Irregular past participles—Use of **haber** and **tener.**

CHAPTER 30

Tickets—Passports—Present and present perfect of **dormir, despedirse.** —Past participles used as adjectives.

REVISION 7

Vocabulary revision—Vocabulary and Grammar Exercises—Dialogue: **En el aeropuerto.** Reading Selection: **Un programa extraordinario en el cine.**

CHAPTER 31

Words indicating past time, yesterday, last year, etc.—Preterite tense of regular verbs—Preterite of **leer, creer, caer, oír.**

CHAPTER 32

La merienda—Irregular preterite with **i**-Stems—Preterite of stem-changing verbs like **pedir.**

CHAPTER 33

The Gran Vía, the Prado Museum, the Botanical Garden, the Retiro Park, etc.—Irregular preterites with **u**-Stems—Preterite of **dar, ser, ir**—The personal **a.**

CHAPTER 34

Ordinary things and luxury articles—Fruit, flowers, baskets, clothing —Imperfect tense—Imperfect of **ver, ser, ir**—Imperfect and preterite of **hay.**

CHAPTER 35

Craft shops, Museum of Decorative Arts—Possessive pronouns— The definite article used as a pronoun.

REVISION 8

CHAPTER 36

CHAPTER 37

CHAPTER 38

CHAPTER 39

CHAPTER 40

REVISION 9

CHAPTER 41

REGIONAL ACCENTS

There is a great variety of regional accents in Spanish and different language speeds in Spain, let alone the dialectical forms and three altogether different languages—Basque, Catalan and Galician, which will not be dealt with in this book. But it is worth mentioning the fact because the foreigner who knows a fairly good amount of Spanish may be baffled when visiting certain regions, such as Majorca, to hear a language so different from the one he studies or to hear Spanish spoken with an unfamiliar accent. Therefore, as a guide, the student should bear in mind the following linguistic regions drawn in very broad and conventional terms (see also map on page 354):

(see also map on page 354)

Region I   *Castilian* (Standard Spanish: best spoken in Old Castile) Castile, León, Asturias, Navarra.

Region II   *Marked regional accents* plus a variety of dialectical forms Aragón, Levante (in Valencia, Spanish plus a dialect of Catalan), Andalucía.

Region III   *The Islands*
  (i) Balearic: Majorca, Minorca, Ibiza, etc.
      Dialect of Catalan plus Spanish.
  (ii) Canaries
      Spanish with an accent reminiscent of Spanish-speaking America.
      No sound z, c (th).

Region IV   *Catalonia* (NE) Catalan (related to French) plus Spanish as a second language.

Region V   *Galicia* (NW) Slow Spanish with a very distinct accent and intonation plus Galician (similar to Portuguese).

Region VI   *The Basque Country*, or *Euskadi* in Basque (N Centre, border with France)
      Spanish, good and clear accent and Basque or Euskera (a very difficult language of unknown origin so far).

CHAPTER 1

MEET THE SPANISH LANGUAGE

1 *Spanish is not a complete stranger*

On your introduction to the Spanish language you will be glad to learn that you already know or can guess the meaning of many Spanish words.

actor	**piano**	**canal**	**principal**
hotel	**gratis**	**auto**	**hospital**
error	**animal**	**conductor**	**director**
doctor			

Then there are many Spanish words whose spelling is only a bit different from like words in English, and whose meaning is easily recognized. Thus:

aire	**centro**	**mula**	**conversación**
air	*centre*	*mule*	*conversation*
arte	**barbero**	**profesor**	**color**
art	*barber*	*professor*	*colour*

Many Spanish verbs differ from corresponding English verbs only in the matter of ending. Thus:

declarar	**admirar**	**informar**	**dividir**
declare	*admire*	*inform*	*divide*
adorar	**usar**	**defender**	
adore	*use*	*defend*	

English has borrowed words directly from the Spanish with or without changes in spelling. Thus:

adobe	**fiesta**	**patio**	**siesta**
adobe	*fiesta*	*patio*	*siesta*
rodeo	**lazo**	**tomate**	**rancho**
rodeo	*lasso*	*tomato*	*ranch*

Spanish has borrowed words directly from the English. This is especially true in the field of sports. You will recognize these words even in their strange spellings.

rosbif	**pudín**	**fútbol**
roastbeef	*pudding*	*football*
mitin	**tenis**	**golf**
meeting	*tennis*	*golf*

1

The similarities between the Spanish and English vocabularies will be a great help to you in learning Spanish. However, you must bear in mind that words of the same or similar spelling in the two languages are pronounced differently. Also you must be on the lookout for some Spanish words which are alike or similar in spelling to English words, but different in meaning.

2 *Spanish is not difficult to pronounce and spell*

Spanish is a phonetic language. This means that words are spelled as they are pronounced. There are no silent letters in Spanish except **h,** which is always silent, and **u,** which is silent under certain circumstances. How much simpler this is than English, where such words as *height, knight, cough, rough, rogue, weigh, dough,* and a host of others, give so much difficulty to the foreigner learning English.

When you see the letter **a** in Spanish words like **Ana, mapa, sala,** you know it is pronounced like *a* in *father*, because Spanish **a** is always like *a* in *father*. It is never like *a* in *cat, all,* or *fame*. Like **a,** the other letters of the Spanish alphabet are an accurate guide to the pronunciation of the words.

In Chapter 2, the pronunciation of the Spanish sounds and their spelling is explained in detail. Most of the Spanish sounds have like sounds in English, or sounds so similar that they are easy to learn. The description of the sounds should enable you to pronounce them quite well. If possible you should get some Spanish-speaking person to help you with your pronunciation, for it is important for you to hear the sounds correctly spoken and to have your own pronunciation checked.

You can improve your pronunciation and understanding of the spoken word by listening to Spanish recordings and radio broadcasts, and watching Spanish films and courses on television.

CHAPTER 2

SPANISH PRONUNCIATION

This chapter contains many useful words and expressions. If you follow the instructions for pronunciation practice carefully, you will acquire many of these without difficulty. It is not necessary to try to memorize all of them at this point as they will appear again in later chapters when you will have the opportunity to learn them thoroughly. However, it is desirable to memorize at once the numbers and the days of the week as these serve to illustrate most of the Spanish sounds.

PRIMERA PARTE (FIRST PART)
THE SOUNDS OF SPANISH

The pronunciation of Spanish sounds given here is that of most educated Spaniards. There are, however, some variations in pronunciation in different parts of Spain and in Central and South America. Follow carefully the instructions given here and learn to distinguish between the different phonetic symbols, and you will have a very acceptable pronunciation. To perfect your pronunciation you should try to get a Spaniard to help you with all the sounds and to converse with you in Spanish.

The Vowels

Spanish words are pure, that is they are not diphthongs as they often are in English, where, for example, the *a* in *face* often sounds like the *eigh* in *weight*, or the *o* in *go* like the *ow* in *bow-tie*. Pay especial attention to these sounds described in table form on page 4.

Stress is marked in the phonetic pronunciation by the sign ' placed before the syllable to be stressed (see also Part Four of this chapter). There are only five vowel sounds in Spanish.

3

Spanish letter	Phonetic symbol	Description of Sound	Example	Phonetic transcription
a	(a)	like the *a* in father, even in unstressed positions (NEVER like the *a* in *face*, or *sofa*)	**cuatro** (four) **una** (one, fem.)	('kwa-tro) ('u-na)
e	(e)	a pure vowel, not a diphthong, like the *e* in *café* (NEVER like the *e* in *scene*, and NEVER silent)	**siete** (seven) **nueve** (nine)	('sje-te) ('nwe-ve) *or* ('nwe-βe)
i, y	(i)	like the *i* in *machine* (NEVER like the *i* in *fine*, or the *y* in *try*)	**cinco** (five) **muy** (very) **y** (and)	('θiŋ-ko) (mwi) (i)
o	(o)	a pure vowel, not a diphthong, like the *o* in *tom* (NEVER like the *o* in *won*)	**dos** (two) **ocho** (eight)	(ðos) ('o-tʃo)
u	(u)	a pure vowel, like the *u* in *rule* (NEVER like the *u* in *tune* or *up*)	**uno** (one, masc.) **(lunes)** (Monday)	('u-no) ('lu-nes)

The Semivowels

i, y and **u** are also semivowels when they occur in diphthongs

i, y	(j)	like *y* in *you* (Be careful not to confuse the phonetic symbol (j) with the Spanish letter **j**, which is a different sound, and is dealt with below.)	**seis** (six) **siete** (seven) **rey** (king) **yo** (I)	(sejs) ('sje-te) (rrej) (jo)
u	(w)	like *w* in *wife*	**cuatro** (four) **caudillo** (leader)	('kwa-tro) (kaw-'ði-ʎo)

The Consonants

Take especial care with those consonants that resemble familiar English ones, but whose pronunciation is different.

b	(b)	at the beginning of a word if this word is the first word in a sentence or is spoken after a pause, like the English *b* also when preceded by **m** or **n**	**bien** (well) **boca** (mouth) **hombre** (man)	(bjen) ('bo-ka) ('om-bre)

Spanish letter	Phonetic symbol	Description of sound	Example	Phonetic transcription
b	(β)	like an English *b* pronounced with the lips slightly open, in all other positions and when it is the first letter of a word with no pause before it	**sábado** (Saturday) **febrero** (February) **la boca** (the mouth)	('sa-βa-ðo) (fe-'βre-ro) (la'βo-ka)

(If in doubt, pronounce both these sounds like the English *b*. Many Spaniards do not distinguish between **v** and **b** in pronunciation (see below).)

(c)	(θ)	like English *th* in *thin* before e or i (In some parts of Spain and in Central and S. America it is pronounced like the *c* in *centre*.)	**catorce** (fourteen) **cinco** (five)	(ka-'tor-θe) ('θiŋ-ko)
	(k)	like the *c* in *can* before any other letter	**octubre** (October) **cuatro** (four)	(ok-'tu-βre) ('kwa-tro)
ch	(tʃ)	like *ch* in *chin*. NB **ch** is a separate letter in Spanish and comes after **c** in a dictionary	**ocho** (eight) **coche** (car)	('otʃo) ('ko-tʃe)
d	(d)	after **n** it is similar to an English *d*, but it is pronounced with the tip of the tongue against the upper teeth	**cuando** (when) **con dolor** (with pain)	('kwan-do) (kon do'lor)
	(ð)	like a mild (d). In some regions like *th* in 'thing'	**Madrid** **después** (after)	(ma-'ðrið) (ðes-'pwes)
f	(f)	as English *f*	**febrero** (February)	(fe-'βre-ro)
g	(g)	in initial position, after **n** or a pause or before **a, o** or **u**, like *g* in *go*	**grande** (big) **ponga** (put, imperative) **gusto** (pleasure)	('gran-de) ('poŋ-ga) ('gus-to)
	(ɣ)	between two vowels or when it is the first letter of a word with no pause before it, like an English *g* pronounced with the lips slightly open, so that it is scarcely audible	**pago** (I pay) **la gota** (the drop)	('pa-ɣo) (la'ɣo-ta)
	(x)	before e or i, very close to the *ch* in *loch* or *bach*	**gigante** (giant) **general** (general)	(xi-'ɣan-te) (xe-ne-'ral)

(Do not confuse the phonetic symbol (x) with the Spanish letter **x**, which is a different sound and is dealt with below.)

Spanish letter	Phonetic symbol	Description of sound	Example	Phonetic transcription
h	—	always silent	**hombre** (man) **hoy** (today)	('om-bre) (oj)
j	(x)	as *ch* in *loch* or *bach* (Do not confuse the Spanish letter **j** with the phonetic symbol (j) (see above), they represent two different sounds.)	**garaje** (garage) **jamón** (ham)	(ɣa-'ra-xe) (xa-'mon)
k	(k)	as in English, it occurs in a few words only and is not a true Spanish letter	**kilo** (kilogramme) **kilómetro** (kilometre)	('ki-lo) (ki-'lo-me-tro)
l	(l)	as in English	**lana** (wool)	('la-na)
ll	(ʎ)	as *lli* in *million* (in some parts of Spain and in other Spanish-speaking countries it is pronounced like the *y* in *you*) NB **ll** is a separate letter in Spanish, and comes after *l* in dictionaries	**calle** (street) **llamar** (to call)	('ka-ʎe) (ʎa-'mar)
m	(m)	as in English	**madre** (mother)	('ma-ðre)
n	(n)	similar to English *n*, but pronounced with the tip of the tongue touching the upper teeth	**cuando** (when)	('kwan-do)
	(ŋ)	like the *n* in *ink* before the sounds (k), (g) and (x)	**cinco** (five) **ángel** (angel) **pongo** (I put)	('θiŋ-ko) ('aŋ-xel) ('poŋ-go)
	(m)	before the sounds (b) and (v)	**invitación** (invitation) **buen viaje** (happy journey)	(im-bi-ta-'jon) ('bwem 'bja-xe)
ñ	(nj)	as *ni* in *onion* NB this is a separate letter in Spanish, and comes after **n** in a dictionary	**mañana** (tomorrow)	(ma-'nja-na)
p	(p)	similar to the English *p*, but without the little puff of breath that follows the sound in English	**padre** (father)	('pa-ðre)

Spanish letter	Phonetic symbol	Description of sound	Example	Phonetic transcription
qu	(k)	as English *k*	**quince** (fifteen)	('kin-θe)
r	(r)	slightly trilled, except at the beginning of a word when this word begins a sentence or is spoken after a pause	**sombrero** (hat) **la ropa** (the clothing)	(som-'bre-ro) (la 'ro-pa)
	(rr)	similar to the *rr* in the exclamation of cold *brr!*, it is very strongly trilled when **r** is the first letter of a word when this word begins a sentence or when it is spoken after a pause, see example	**Roberto dijo: soy Roberto** (Robert said: I am Robert)	(rro-'βer-to 'ði-xo soj ro-'βerto)
rr	(rr)	the same sound as above NB the letter **rr** never begins a word; it is a separate letter, and comes after **r** in dictionaries	**error** (error) **jarro** (jug)	(e-'rror) ('xa-rro)
s	(s)	like the English *s* in *sat*	**blusas** (blouses) **sastre** (tailor)	('blu-sas) ('sas-tre)
	(z)	before **b, d, m** and sometimes **l**, like the *z* in *zoo*	**las blusas** (the blouses) **desde** (since)	(laz 'blu-sas) ('ðez-ðe)
t	(t)	similar to the English *t* but with the tip of the tongue against the upper teeth	**tostada** (toast)	(tos-'ta-ða)
v	(v)	similar to the English *v*, but many Spaniards do not make any distinction between this sound and (b) and (β); both pronunciations will be indicated in the phonetic transcriptions in this book	**vivo** (I live) **viaje** (journey)	('vi-vo) ('vja-xe) you will also hear: ('bi-βo) and ('bja-xe)
x	(ks) (s)	as *x* in *extra* between vowels as *s* in *sit*, in the prefix **ex-** followed by a consonant (Do not confuse the Spanish letter **x** with the phonetic symbol (x), they represent two entirely different sounds.)	**examen** (exam) **excepto** (except) **explicar** (to explain)	(ek-'sa-men) (es-'θep-to) (es-pli-'kar)
z	(θ)	as *th* in *think* (In some parts of Spain and in other Spanish-speaking countries it is pronounced like the *s* in *sit*.)	**diez** (ten) **zumo** (juice)	(ðjeθ) ('θu-mo)

SEGUNDA PARTE (SECOND PART)

The Numbers 1–21—The Days of the Week

Among the most important words in any language are the numbers. Let us start by learning the Spanish numbers 1–21. These numbers illustrate many of the Spanish sounds.

Pronounce each number aloud five times. Stress (emphasize) the syllable preceded by the mark ¹.

1 **uno** ('u-no) *masculine*	12 **doce** ('ðo-θe)
una ('u-na) *feminine*	13 **trece** ('tre-θe)
2 **dos** (ðos)	14 **catorce** (ka-'tor-θe)
3 **tres** (tres)	15 **quince** ('kin-θe)
4 **cuatro** ('kwa-tro)	16 **diez y seis** (ðjeθ i sejs)
5 **cinco** ('θiŋ-ko)	17 **diez y siete** (ðjeθ i 'sje-te)
6 **seis** (sejs)	18 **diez y ocho** (ðjeθ i 'o-tʃo)
7 **siete** ('sje-te)	19 **diez y nueve** (ðjeθ i 'nwe-ve) or
8 **ocho** ('o-tʃo)	(ðjeθ i 'nwe-βe)
9 **nueve** ('nwe-ve) or ('nwe-βe)	20 **veinte** ('vejn-te) or ('bejn-te)
10 **diez** (ðjeθ)	21 **veinte y uno** ('vejn-te i 'u-no) or
11 **once** ('on-θe)	('bejn-te i 'u-no)

(The numerals from 16 to 19 and 21 to 29 may also be written in one word: **dieciséis, diecisiete, dieciocho, diecinueve, veintiuno, veintidós, veintitrés, veinticuatro, veinticinco, veintiséis, veintisiete, veintiocho, veintinueve.** Note: the change into **c** of the **z** in **diez**; **veinte** loses its final *e*; as these combinations make one word each, the *-dós*, *-tres* and *-séis* are written with an accent to emphasize the stress on the last syllable—otherwise the stress would, according to the rules, be on the next-to-the-last syllable.)

Days of the Week and Months of the Year

Practise aloud and memorize

domingo (ðo-'miŋ-go)	Sunday
lunes ('lu-nes)	Monday
martes ('mar-tes)	Tuesday
miércoles ('mjer-ko-les)	Wednesday
jueves ('xwe-ves) or ('xwe-βes)	Thursday
viernes ('vjer-nes) or ('bjer-nes)	Friday
sábado ('sa-βa-ðo)	Saturday
enero (e-'ne-ro)	January
febrero (fe-'βre-ro)	February
marzo ('mar-θo)	March

Note: **lunes,** Monday, is the first day of the week in Spain.

abril (a-'βril)	April
mayo ('ma-jo)	May
junio ('xu-njo)	June
julio ('u-ljo)	July
agosto (a-'ɣos-to)	August
septiembre (sep-'tjem-bre)	September
octubre (ok-'tu-βre)	October
noviembre (no-'vjem-bre)	
or (no-'βjem-bre)	November
diciembre (ði-'θjem-bre)	December

TERCERA PARTE (THIRD PART)

Useful Expressions for the Traveller

Here are some key words which every traveller needs:

1 **por favor** (por fa-'vor) or (por fa-'βor) please. This is most handy for introducing a question or request.

2 **señor** (se-'njor) Mr., sir; **señora** (se-'njo-ra) Mrs., madam'; **señorita** (se-njo-'ri'ta) Miss. It's polite to follow your **por favor** with one of these. **Por favor, señor, etc.**

3 **¿Cuánto cuesta?** ('kwan-to 'kwes-ta) How much does it cost? For short, **¿Cuánto?** will do.

In this connection the following words are handy: **Es caro** (es 'ka-ro) It is dear. **Más barato** (maz βa-'ra-to) cheaper.

NOTE: Spanish questions begin with an inverted question mark.

4 **¿Dónde está —?** ('ðon-de es-'ta) Where is — ?

5 **Quiero** ('kje-ro) I want. **Deseo** (ðe-'se-o) I want. If you begin with **Por favor,** you won't sound too abrupt.

6 **¿A qué hora?** (a ke 'o-ra) At what time? The Spanish says: At what hour?

REMEMBER: **h** in Spanish is always silent.

7 **Muchas gracias** ('mu-tʃaz 'ɣra-θjas) Many thanks. Thank you very much.

8 **De nada** (ðe 'na-ða) or **No hay de qué** (no aj ðe ke). Don't mention it or you're welcome. You'll hear either of these in reply to your **gracias.**

9 **¿Cómo se llama usted?** ('ko-mo se 'ʎa-ma us-'teð) What's your name? The Spanish says: What do you call yourself?

10 **Me llamo ...** (me 'ʎa-mo) My name is ... The Spanish says: I call myself ...

NOTE: 1. It does not quite correspond with the English meaning. Often it is a matter of age rather than status. Legally a woman in Spain never loses her maiden name. Socially she may use it after her own preceding de. E.g. **Sra. María Pérez de Ruiz** (husband's).

Some Useful Words

Repeat aloud, three times, the words listed under each heading. Then repeat each word with the heading under which it is listed. Thus:

¿Cuánto cuesta la alfombra? etc.　　¿Dónde está la Calle A? etc.

¿Cuánto cuesta . . .?

1 **la alfombra** (al-ˈfom-bra) rug
2 **el echarpe** (e-ˈtʃar-pe) shawl
3 **el sombrero** (som-ˈbre-ro) hat
4 **la blusa** (ˈblu-sa) blouse
5 **la camisa** (ka-ˈmi-sa) shirt
6 **el vestido** (ves-ˈti-ðo) or (bes-ˈti-ðo) clothing

7 **la cesta** (ˈθes-ta) basket
8 **el plato** (ˈpla-to) plate
9 **el jarro** (ˈxa-rro) pitcher, jug
10 **el coche** (ˈko-tʃe) car

¿Dónde está . . .?

1 **la Calle de Goya** (ˈka-ʎe ðe ˈyo-ja) Goya Street
2 **la Avenida de José Antonio** (a-ve-ˈni-ða ðe xo-ˈse an-ˈto-njo) Jose Antonio Avenue
3 **el hotel** (o-ˈtel) hotel
4 **los servicios de señores** (ser-ˈvi-θjos) or (ser-ˈβi-θjos) men's toilet, also **el lavabo de caballeros**

5 **los servicios (el lavabo) de señoras** ladies' toilet
6 **el correo** (ko-ˈrre-o) post office
7 **el museo** (mu-ˈse-o) museum
8 **el agente** (a-ˈxen-te) agent
9 **la oficina** (o-fi-ˈθi-na) office
10 **el garaje** (ya-ˈra-xe) garage

NOTE: g, before e or i, is pronounced like Spanish j. Before any other letter it is hard as in *goat*.

Quiero . . . Deseo . . .

1 **un cuarto con baño** (ˈkwar-to kom ˈba-njo) a room with bath
2 **agua caliente** (ˈa-ywa ka-ˈljen-te) hot water
3 **el jabón** (xa-ˈβon) soap
4 **toallas** (to-ˈa-ʎas) towels
5 **el menú** (me-ˈnu) menu
6 **la cuenta** (ˈkwen-ta) bill

7 **la revista** (rre-ˈvis-ta) or (rre-ˈβis-ta) magazine
8 **el periódico** (pe-ˈrjo-ði-ko) newspaper
9 **telefonear** (te-le-fo-ne-ˈar) to telephone
10 **cambiar dinero** (kam-ˈbjar ði-ˈne-ro) to change money

Me llamo . . .

1 **el señor Gómez** (ˈyo-meθ) Mr. Gómez
2 **la señora Gómez** Mrs. Gómez
3 **Pablo** (ˈpa-βlo) Paul
4 **Felipe** (fe-ˈli-pe) Philip
5 **Roberto** (rro-ˈβer-to) Robert

6 **José** (xo-ˈse) Joseph
7 **Juan** (xwan) John
8 **Isabel** (i-sa-ˈβel) Isabelle
9 **Ana** (ˈa-na) Anna
10 **María** (ma-ˈri-a) Mary

The Numbers 21 to 100

Practise aloud:

20	**veinte** ('vejn-te) ('βejn-te)	66	**sesenta y seis**
22	**veinte y dos**	70	**setenta** (se-'ten-ta)
30	**treinta** ('trejn-ta)	77	**setenta y siete**
33	**treinta y tres**	80	**ochenta** (o-'tʃen-ta)
40	**cuarenta** (kwa-'ren-ta)	88	**ochenta y ocho**
44	**cuarenta y cuatro**	90	**noventa** (no-'ven-ta) or
50	**cincuenta** (θiŋ-'kwen-ta)		(no-'βen-ta)
55	**cincuenta y cinco**	99	**noventa y nueve**
60	**sesenta** (se-'sen-ta)	100	**ciento** ('θjen-to), **cien** (θjen)

NOTE: **veinte y dos** can be made into one word **veintidós,** as can the numerals 23–29. Higher numerals cannot be thus contracted.

Practise aloud:

10	**diez alfombras**	60	**sesenta vestidos**
20	**veinte echarpes**	70	**setenta cestas**
30	**treinta sombreros**	80	**ochenta platos**
40	**cuarenta blusas**	90	**noventa jarros**
50	**cincuenta camisas**	100	**cien garajes**

NOTE: **cien** is used instead of **ciento** before a noun.

CUARTA PARTE (FOURTH PART)

The Stress in Spanish Words

The stressed syllable of a word is the syllable which is emphasized. In the word *father*, the syllable *fa-* gets the stress; in *alone*, *-lone* gets the stress; in *education*, the stressed syllable is *-ca-*. There are no good rules for stress in English.

In Spanish there are three simple rules by means of which you can tell which syllable of a word is stressed. They are:

RULE 1. If a word ends in **a o u e i n** or **s,** the next-to-the-last syllable is stressed.

som-**bre**-ro a-ve-**ni**-da **sie**-te **quin**-ce **lu**-nes se-**ño**-ra
e-**char**-pe **en**-tran

RULE 2. If a word ends in any consonant except **n** or **s,** the last syllable is stressed.

se-**ñor** ho-**tel** fa-**vor** I-sa-**bel** us-**ted** cam-**biar**
te-le-fo-ne-**ar**

RULE 3. If the stress does not follow Rules 1 or 2, an accent mark shows which syllable is stressed.

sá-ba-do **miér**-co-les **Gó**-mez ja-**bón** Jo-**sé** mi-**llón**

Dialogues for Pronunciation Practice

Directions for study of Dialogues.

1 Read the Spanish text silently, sentence by sentence, using the English translation to get the meaning.

2 Practise aloud the words which follow the text under the heading 'Practise These Words'.

3 Finally read the whole Spanish text aloud several times.

Diálogo 1 ('ðja-lo-ɣo)
¿Cómo está usted?

1 Buenos días, señor López. ¿Cómo está usted?
2 Muy bien, gracias. ¿Y usted?
3 Muy bien, gracias. ¿Y cómo está la señora López?
4 Muy bien, gracias. ¿Y cómo están su padre y su madre?
5 Muy bien, gracias. Hasta la vista, señor López.
6 Hasta mañana, Felipe.

How Are You?

1 Good day, Mr. López. How are you?
2 Very well, thank you. And you?
3 Very well, thank you. And how is Mrs. López?
4 Very well, thank you. And how are your father and mother?
5 Very well, thank you. Good-bye, Mr. López.
6 Until tomorrow, Philip.

Practise these Words

1 **Buenos días** ('bwe-noz 'ði-as). In this case pronounce the **s** of **buenos** like the English *z* instead of like the usual **s** sound.
2 **muy bien** (mwi βjen) **gracias** ('ɣra-θjas)
3 **cómo** ('ko-mo) **están** (es-'tan)
4 **padre** ('pa-ðre) **madre** ('ma-ðre)
5 **hasta la vista** ('as-ta la 'vis-ta)
6 **usted** (us-'teð)
7 **hasta** ('as-ta)

Diálogo 2
Los días de la semana   The Days of the Week

1 ¡Oiga, Jaime! ¿Cuántos días hay en una semana?
2 En una semana hay siete días.
3 Bueno. Dígame, los siete días, por favor.

4 Los siete días de la semana son lunes, martes, miércoles, jueves, viernes, sábado y domingo.
5 Muy bien. ¡Oiga, Jorge! ¿Qué día es hoy?
6 Hoy es lunes. Mañana, martes.
7 Carlos, ¿sabe usted los números desde el uno hasta el doce?
8 Sí, señor, los números son uno, dos, tres, cuatro, cinco, seis, siete, ocho, nueve, diez, once, doce.
9 Muy bien, Carlos.

1 Listen, James. How many days are there in one week?
2 There are seven days in one week.
3 Good. Tell me, please, the seven days.
4 The seven days of the week are Monday, Tuesday, Wednesday, Thursday, Friday, Saturday and Sunday.
5 Very good. Listen, George. What day is today?
6 Today is Monday. Tomorrow, Tuesday.
7 Charles, do you know the numbers from one to twelve?
8 Yes, sir, the numbers are one, two, three, four, five, six, seven, eight, nine, ten, eleven, twelve.
9 Very good, Charles.

Practise these Words

1 **Oiga** ('oj-ɣa) **oi** in Spanish is like *oi* in *oil*.
2 **hoy** (oj) **oy** is like Spanish **oi**
3 **hay** (aj) and **ai** are like *ai* in *aisle*.
4 **semana** (se-'ma-na)
5 **dígame** ('ði-ɣa-me)
6 **Jorge** ('xor-xe)
7 **sabe** ('sa-βe)
8 **desde** ('ðez-ðe)

Diálogo 3
¿Habla usted español?   Do You Speak Spanish?

1 ¿Habla usted español, Claudio?
2 Sí, señor, yo[1] hablo español.
3 ¿Habla Pancho español?
4 Sí, señor, él habla español bien.
5 ¿Habla Paulina español?
6 Sí, señor, ella habla español bien.
7 ¿Habla ella inglés también?
8 No, señor, ella no habla inglés.
9 ¿Es Pablo español?
10 Sí, señor, él es español.

1 Do you speak Spanish, Claude?
2 Yes, sir, I speak Spanish.
3 Does Frank speak Spanish?

4 Yes, sir, he speaks Spanish well.
5 Does Pauline speak Spanish?
6 Yes, sir, she speaks Spanish well.
7 Does she speak English also?
8 No, sir, she does not speak English.
9 Is Paul Spanish?
10 Yes, sir, he is Spanish.

NOTE: 1. The subject pronouns **yo** I, **él** he, **ella** she, are usually omitted in Spanish. They are used here for emphasis. You will learn more about this later.

Practise these Words

1 **español** (es-pa-ˈnjol)
2 **hablo** (ˈa-βlo), **habla** (ˈa-βla)

3 **yo** (jo), **él** (el), **ella** (ˈe-ʎa), **usted** (us-ˈteð) or (us-ˈte)
4 **Paulina** (paw-ˈli-na)

NOTE: **el** (without the accent) = the (masc. sing.); **él** (with the accent) = he.

Diálogo 4
¿Cómo se llama Ud.? What Is Your Name?

1 **¿Cómo se llama Ud., joven?**
2 **Me llamo Pablo Rivera.**
3 **¿Dónde vive Ud.?**
4 **Vivo en la calle de Jorge.**
5 **¿Cuántas personas hay en su familia?**
6 **Hay cinco personas, mi padre, mi madre, mi hermano Carlos, mi hermana Ana, y yo.**
7 **Ud. habla bien el español. ¿Estudia Ud. la lengua en la escuela?**
8 **Sí, señor. Además hablamos español en casa. Mis padres son españoles**
9 **Adiós, Pablo.**
10 **Adiós, señor.**

1 What is your name, young man?
2 My name is Paul Rivera.
3 Where do you live?
4 I live in George Street.
5 How many persons are there in your family?
6 There are five persons, my father, my mother, my brother Charles, my sister Anna, and I.
7 You speak Spanish well. Are you studying the language in school?
8 Yes, sir. Besides, we speak Spanish at home. My parents are Spanish.

9 Good-bye, Paul.
10 Good-bye, sir.

NOTE: **Ud.** is the normal written abbreviation of **usted**. This word is a contraction of **vuestra merced** = your honour.

Practise these Words

1 **llama** (ˈʎa-ma) **calle** (ˈka-ʎe)
2 **joven** (ˈxo-ven) or (ˈxo-βen)
  Rivera (rri-ˈve-ra) or (rri-ˈβe-ra)
3 **vive** (ˈvi-ve) or (ˈbi-βe)
  vivo (ˈvi-vo) or (ˈbi-βo)
4 **personas** (per-ˈso-nas) **familia** (fa-ˈmi-lja)
5 **padre** (ˈpa-ðre) **madre** (ˈma-ðre)
6 **mi hermana** (mi er-ˈma-na)
7 **estudia** (es-ˈtu-ðja) **lengua** (ˈleŋ-gwa)
8 **en la escuela** (en la es-ˈkwe-la)
9 **hablamos** (a-ˈβla-mos)
10 **además** (a-ðe-ˈmas)
11 **españoles** (es-pa-ˈnjo-les)
12 **adiós** (a-ˈðjos)

LANGUAGE CASSETTE RECORDINGS
BASED ON THIS BOOK
SPANISH MADE SIMPLE

Two excellent cassette recordings have been produced, based on all the conversation and dialogue passages which appear at the beginning of each chapter in this book and are highly recommended for all who want to hear everyday spoken Spanish at its best.

These Made Simple recordings by experienced Spanish linguists bring all the conversation passages to life, providing not only an enjoyable listening experience but an invaluable expert guide to help *you* speak Spanish with self-confidence and conviction.

Whilst you listen you learn—naturally and in your own time, at your own pace—and remember you can replay the sections you want over and over again until you feel confident to progress to the next passage.

The two **Spanish Made Simple** cassettes (Reference **WH/9** & **WH/10**) cost £15 for the set of two, fully inclusive, in the UK. Overseas £18 per set inclusive of airmail postage.

Please send your order and remittance direct to:

STUDENTS RECORDINGS LIMITED

The Audio Visual Centre
88 Queen Street
NEWTON ABBOT
Devon
ENGLAND

CHAPTER 3

¿QUIÉN ES LA SEÑORA ADAMS?

You now have a good working knowledge of Spanish pronunciation and are ready for a more intimate study of the language. However, pronunciation must at no time be neglected. Practise conscientiously the pronunciation aids after each conversational text and follow all directions for reading aloud and speaking. Remember: the only way you can learn to speak a language is by speaking it.

This chapter will introduce you to Mrs. Adams, a London business-woman who is eager to learn Spanish. You will also meet her teacher, Señor López, a Spaniard living in London. As he teaches Mrs. Adams he will also teach you in a pleasant and interesting way.

So **Buena Suerte** (Good Luck) and **Buen Viaje** (Happy Voyage) as you accompany Mrs. Adams on the road which leads to a practical knowledge of the Spanish language.

PRIMERA PARTE

¿Quién es la señora Adams?   Who is Mrs. Adams?
Instrucciones para estudiar   Instructions for study

1 Read the Spanish text silently, referring to the English only when necessary to get the meaning.
2 Cover up the English text and read the Spanish text silently.
3 Study the Pronunciation and Spelling Aids which follow the text. Then read the Spanish text aloud, pronouncing carefully.
4 Study the section 'Building Vocabulary'.
5 Do the exercise 'Completion of Test'.
6 Proceed to Segunda Parte (Second Part).
7 Follow these instructions with the conversational texts in succeeding chapters.

1 La señora Adams es una comerciante de Londres. Es inglesa.

2 Vive con su familia en una de las zonas residenciales de la ciudad.

3 En la familia Adams hay seis personas: el padre, el señor Adams; la madre, la señora Adams; dos hijos, y dos hijas. El señor Adams es un hombre de cuarenta años de edad. La señora Adams es una mujer de treinta y cinco años.

4 Los hijos se llaman Felipe y Guillermo. Las hijas se llaman Rosita y Anita.

16

5 La casa de la señora Adams tiene diez habitaciones[1]: el comedor, la sala, la cocina, cinco dormitorios y dos cuartos de baño. Hay también un vestíbulo. Tiene un jardín y un garaje.

6 Es una casa particular, y todos los habitaciones están en un piso.

7 La oficina de la señora Adams está en la calle de Oxford.

8 Está en el quinto piso de un edificio muy grande.

9 El lunes, el martes, el miércoles, el jueves, y el viernes, la señora Adams va en tren a su oficina en la ciudad.

10 Allí trabaja activamente todo el día.

1 Mrs. Adams is a businesswoman of London. She is English.[1]

2 She lives with her family in one of the suburbs of the city.

3 In the Adams family there are six persons: the father, Mr. Adams; the mother, Mrs. Adams; two sons, and two daughters. Mr. Adams is a man of forty years of age. Mrs. Adams is a woman of thirty-five years.

4 The sons are named Philip and William. The daughters are named Rosie and Annie.[2]

5 The house of Mrs. Adams has ten rooms: the dining-room, the living-room, the kitchen, five bedrooms, and two bathrooms. There is also a hall. It has a garden and a garage.

6 It is a private house and all the rooms are on one floor.

7 The office of Mrs. Adams is in Oxford Street.

8 It is on the fifth floor of a very big building.

9 On Monday, Tuesday, Wednesday, Thursday and Friday, Mrs. Adams goes by train to her office in the city.

10 There she works diligently all day.

NOTE: 1. *England* is **Inglaterra**, *English* = **inglés** (masculine singular), **inglesa** (feminine singular), **ingleses** (m. plural), **inglesas** (f. plural), *Scotland, Scottish* = **Escocia; escocés, escocesa**. *Ireland, Irish* = **Irlanda; irlandés, irlandesa**. *Wales, Welsh* = **el País de Gales; galés, galesa**. *Great Britain* = **Gran Bretaña**. 2. Literally (word for word): The sons call themselves Philip and William. The daughters call themselves Rosie and Annie. *Lit.* will be used hereafter as an abbreviation for literally.

Pronunciation Aids

1 Practise aloud:

instrucciones (in-struk-'θjo-nes)
comerciante (co-mer-'θjan-te)
familia (fa-'mi-lja)
inglesa (iŋ-'gle-sa)
comedor (ko-me-'ðor)
dormitorio (ðor-mi-'to-rjo)

Guillermo (ɣi-'ʎer-mo)
particular (par-ti-cu-'lar)
oficina (o-fi-'θi-na)
calle ('ka-ʎe)
vestíbulo (ves-'ti-βu-lo) or (bes-'ti-βu-lo)

2 The **u** in **gui** (Gui-ller-mo) is silent. Its purpose is to show that the **g** is hard as in *gold*. Without silent **u**, it would be like **g** in **gente** ('xen-te). Remember: **g** before **e** or **i** is pronounced like Spanish **j**.

Building Vocabulary

A. La Familia   The Family

el padre	the father	**el hermano**	the brother
la madre	the mother	**la hermana**	the sister
el hijo	the son	**el tío**	the uncle
la hija	the daughter	**la tía**	the aunt
el niño	the child (little boy)	**el señor**	the gentleman, Mr.
la niña	the child (little girl)	**la señora**	the lady, Mrs.
el muchacho	the boy (teenage)	**el hombre**	the man
la muchacha	the girl (teenage)	**la mujer**	the woman, wife

B. Los Cuartos de la Casa   The Rooms of the House

el comedor	the dining-room	**el dormitorio**	the bedroom
la sala	the living-room	**el cuarto de baño**	the bathroom
la cocina	the kitchen	**el vestíbulo**	the hall
el cuarto	the room		

Expresiones Importantes   Important Expressions

en tren   by train   **todo el día**   all day

Exercise No. 1—Completion of Text

For maximum benefit follow these instructions carefully in all 'Completion of Test' exercises.

1 Complete each sentence by putting the English words into Spanish. Where you can, do this from memory.

2 If you do not remember the words refer to the Spanish text. There you will find the words in the order of their appearance in the sentences. You have only to re-read the text to find them easily.

3 When you have completed the sentence with the needed words, read the complete sentence aloud in Spanish.

4 It will be a great help to your memory if you write each completed sentence. This is true for all exercises.

5 The correct Spanish words for the 'Completion of Text' exercises are in the Answer Section of this book, along with the answers to all other exercises. Check all your answers.

WARNING: Never refer to the English text when you do the 'Completion of Text' exercise.

Ejemplo (Example): **1. La señora Adams es una comerciante de Londres.**

1 **La señora Adams es una** (businesswoman) **de Londres.**
2 ¿(Who) **es la señora Adams?**
3 **Vive** (with) **su familia.**
4 **El señor Adams es el** (father).
5 **La señora Adams es la** (mother).
6 (There are) **seis personas.**
7 **Los hijos** (are called) **Felipe y Guillermo.**
8 **En** (her) **familia hay seis personas.**
9 **Es una casa** (private).
10 (All the rooms) **están en un piso.**
11 **La oficina está en el quinto** (floor).
12 **Está en la** (street) **de Oxford.**
13 **El edificio es** (big).
14 (There) **trabaja la señora Adams** (all day).
15 **Su oficina está en la** (city).

SEGUNDA PARTE

Grammar Notes

1 *The Definite Article*. Note the four forms of the definite article.

	masculine		feminine	
Singular:	**el** padre	*the* father	**la** madre	*the* mother
Plural:	**los** padres	*the* fathers	**las** madres	*the* mothers

The definite article has four forms. These agree with their nouns in number and gender.

2 *The Gender of Nouns*

(a) Nouns are either masculine or feminine in gender. This is true for thing-nouns as well as person-nouns. Thus:

el señor	**el hijo**	**el cuarto**	**el piso**	**el comedor**
la señora	**la hija**	**la sala**	**la calle**	**la casa**

(b) Nouns ending in **-o** are usually masculine. Nouns ending in **-a** are usually feminine.

(c) The definite article must be repeated before each noun to which it refers. Thus: **el** padre y **la** madre *the* father and mother.

(d) Many nouns for persons have a masculine form in **-o** and a feminine form in **-a**. Thus: **el hermano** the brother, **la hermana** the sister; **el muchacho** the boy, **la muchacha** the girl; **el tío** the uncle, **la tía** the aunt; **el esposo (marido)** the husband, **la esposa (mujer)** the wife.

3 *The Plural of Nouns.* Note the singular and plural of the following nouns.

el padre	el hermano	la casa	la mujer
los padres[1]	los hermanos	las casas	las mujeres
el señor	la ciudad		
los señores	las ciudades		

To form the plural of nouns add -s if the nouns end in a vowel. Add -es if the nouns end in a consonant.

NOTE: 1. **los padres** means either *the fathers,* or *the parents*; **los hermanos** *the brothers,* or *brother(s) and sister(s)*; **los hijos** *the sons, son(s) and daughter(s),* or *children.* In such words the plural masculine may include both genders.

4 *The Indefinite Article.* Note the four forms of the indefinite article.

un cuarto	*a* room	**una** casa	*a* house
unos cuartos	*some* rooms	**unas** casas	*some* houses

un *a* or *one,* is used before a masculine noun; **una** *a* or *one,* before a feminine noun; **unos** *some,* before a masculine plural; **unas** *some,* before a feminine plural.

5 *Some Common Verbs*

es	(he, she, it) is	vive	(he, she, it) lives
está	(he, she, it) is (located)	tiene	(he, she, it) has
están	(they) are (located)	se llaman	they are named, or their
hay	there is, there are		names are (*Lit.* they call themselves)

NOTE. 1. The subject pronouns corresponding to *he, she, it* and *they,* are usually omitted in Spanish, since the ending of the verb indicates the subject pronoun quite clearly. 2. **es** indicates an intrinsic, permanent quality of a person or thing: **es inglés, es simpático,** etc. **Está,** as well as indicating location, also shows a temporary quality or state: **está en Londres, está cansado** = he is tired (but he will not always be tired).

TERCERA PARTE

Ejercicios (Exercises) No. 2A–2B–2C

2A. Replace the English articles by the correct Spanish articles.

Ejemplo: (La) familia[1] Adams vive en Londres.

1 (The) **familia Adams vive en Londres.**

2 **Londres es** (a) **ciudad grande.**

3 (The) **casa está en** (the) **la zona residencial.**

4 (The) **padre es el señor Adams;** (the) **madre es la señora Adams.**

5 Anita es (a) **hija;** Felipe es (a) **hijo.**
6 (The) **dormitorio es grande.**
7 (The) **cuartos están en** (one) **piso.**
8 (Some) **muchachos están en** (the) **sala;** (some) **muchachas están en** (the) **cocina.**
9 (The) **niños están en** (the) **calle.**
10 (The) **hermanos y** (the) **hermanas están en** (the) **ciudad.**

NOTE: 1. **Familia** involves not only wife and children but grandparents, cousins etc. So single people always have '**familia**'.

2B. Change the following nouns into the plural.

1 la calle	5 el dormitorio	9 la sala	13 la mujer
2 el comedor	6 la cocina	10 la hija	14 el hombre
3 el cuarto	7 la madre	11 la ciudad	15 el tío
4 el señor	8 el padre	12 el año	

2C. Translate into Spanish:

1 Mrs. Adams is English.
2 She lives in London.
3 There are six persons in the family.
4 The house has six rooms.
5 It is a private house.
6 Mrs. Adams is the mother.
7 Mr. Adams is the father.
8 The office is in Oxford Street.
9 She goes by train to the city.
10 There she works all day.

Exercise No. 3

Preguntas Questions **Respuestas** Answers

Study and read aloud the questions and answers. Note. (a) the question words; (b) the inverted question mark which begins all Spanish questions; (c) the omission of subject pronouns in Spanish.

1 ¿Quién es la señora Adams?
  Es una comerciante de Londres.
2 ¿Es inglesa?
  Sí, señor, es inglesa.
3 ¿Dónde vive la señora Adams?
  Vive en la zona residencial de la ciudad.
4 ¿Cuántas personas hay en su familia?
  Hay seis personas en su familia.
5 ¿Cómo se llaman sus hijos?
  Se llaman Felipe y Guillermo.
6 ¿Cómo se llaman sus hijas?
  Se llaman Rosita y Anita.

7 ¿Cuántos cuartos tiene la casa de la señora Adams?
Tiene diez habitaciones.

8 ¿Dónde están todos los cuartos?
Están en un piso.

9 ¿En qué calle está la oficina de la señora Adams?
Está en la calle de Oxford.

10 ¿Es grande el edificio?
Sí, señor, es muy grande.

1 Who is Mrs. Adams?
She is a businesswoman of London.

2 Is she English?
Yes, sir, she is English.

3 Where does Mrs. Adams live?
She lives in the suburbs of the city.

4 How many persons are there in her family?
There are six persons in her family.

5 What are the names of her sons?
They are named Philip and William.

6 What are the names of her daughters?
They are named Rosie and Annie.

7 How many rooms has the house of Mrs. Adams?
It has ten rooms.

8 Where are all the rooms?
They are on one floor.

9 In what street is the office of Mrs. Adams?
It is in Oxford Street.

10 Is the building big?
Yes, sir, it is very big.

CHAPTER 4

¿POR QUÉ ESTUDIA EL ESPAÑOL?

PRIMERA PARTE

Instrucciones para estudiar. (See Chapter 3)

1 La Sra. Adams es importadora.

2 Importa objetos de arte y otros artículos de España.

3 En primavera la Sra. Adams va a hacer un viaje a España. Desea visitar a sus agentes en Madrid y en México. Desea hablar con ellos en español.

4 También desea ver unos lugares de interés en España. Espera además ir a Tenerife, y tal vez a las otras Islas Canarias y las Baleares.

5 La Sra. Adams sabe leer el español un poco. Pero no habla español. Por eso estudia el idioma.

6 Su profesor es el Sr. López.

7 El Sr. López, amigo del Sr. y de la Sra. Adams, es español pero su madre es mexicana. Es un hombre de cuarenta y cinco años de edad.

8 Los martes y los jueves la Sra. Adams y el Sr. López tienen una cita, casi siempre en la casa de la Sra. Adams, Allí hablan español.

9 El Sr. López es un buen profesor.

10 La Sra. Adams es muy inteligente y aprende rápidamente.

11 En la primera conversación aprende de memoria este diálogo:

12 Buenos días, Sr. López. ¿Cómo está Ud?
Muy bien, gracias. ¿Y Ud?
Muy bien, gracias.

13 La Sra. Adams aprende también unos saludos y unas despedidas.

14 Buenos días. Buenas tardes. Buenas noches.

15 Adiós. Hasta la vista. Hasta luego. Hasta mañana.

1 Mrs. Adams is an importer.

2 She imports art objects and other articles from Spain.

3 In the spring Mrs. Adams is going to make a trip to Spain. She wants to visit her agents in Madrid and in Mexico. She wants to speak with them in Spanish.

4 She also wants to see some places of interest in Spain. She expects, moreover, to go to Tenerife, and perhaps to the other Canary Islands and the Balearic Islands.

5 Mrs. Adams knows how to read Spanish a little. But she does not speak Spanish. Therefore she is studying the language.

6 Her teacher is Mr. López.

23

7 Mr. López, a friend of Mr. and Mrs. Adams, is Spanish but his mother is Mexican. He is a man of forty-five.

8 On Tuesdays and Thursdays Mrs. Adams and Mr. López have an appointment, almost always in the house of Mrs. Adams. There they speak Spanish.

9 Mr. López is a good teacher.

10 Mrs. Adams is very intelligent and learns rapidly.

11 In the first lesson she learns this dialogue by heart.

12 Good day, Mr. López. How are you?
Very well, thank you. And you?
Very well, thank you.

13 Mrs. Adams also learns some salutations and farewells.

14 Good day. Good afternoon. Good night.

15 Good-bye. Until we meet again. So long. Until tomorrow.

NOTE: All the expressions in sentence 15 are ways of saying '*Goodbye*'.

Pronunciation and Spelling Aids

1 Practise:

importador (im-por-ta-ˈðor)
importa (im-ˈpor-ta)
artículos (ar-ˈti-cu-los)
Tenerife (te-ne-ˈri-fe)
Islas Canarias (ˈis-las ka-ˈna-rjas)
ciudad (θju-ˈðað)
profesor (pro-fe-ˈsor)
rápidamente (ˈrra-pi-ða-ˈmen-te)
desea (ðe-ˈse-a)
estudia (es-ˈtu-ðja)

espera (es-ˈpe-ra)
primavera (pri-ma-ˈve-ra) or
 (pri-ma-ˈβe-ra)
allí (a-ˈʎi)
inteligente (in-te-li-ˈxen-te)
saludos (sa-ˈlu-ðos)
despedidas (ðes-pe-ˈði-ðas)
además (a-ðe-ˈmas)
agente (a-ˈxen-te)
luego (ˈlwe-ɣo)

2 **el** = the **él** = he or him.

3 The names of countries are written with capital letters. The names of nationalities, languages (**español** Spanish), days of the week, and months are written with small letters.

Building Vocabulary

A. Synonyms (Words of the Same Meaning)

1 **el negociante** = **el comerciante** = **el hombre de negocios** businessman
la negociante = **la comerciante** = **la mujer de negocios** businesswoman

2 **también** = **además** also, moreover

3 **el maestro**[1] = **el profesor** teacher (*m*) **la maestra**[2] = **la profesora** teacher (*f*)

NOTE: 1. and 2. For infant and primary schools.

B. Antonyms (Words of Opposite Meaning)

1 **grande** big **pequeño** small
2 **bueno** good **malo** bad
3 **allí** there **aquí** here

4 **importador** (*m*) **importadora** (*f*) importer **exportador** (*m*) **exportadora** (*f*) exporter
5 **el saludo** greeting **la despedida** farewell

C. Lenguas o Idiomas (Languages)

1 **el español, el castellano** Spanish
2 **el inglés** English
3 **el francés** French

4 **el portugués** Portuguese
5 **el alemán** German
6 **el italiano** Italian

Expresiones Importantes

1 **Buenos días** Good morning (day)
2 **Buenas tardes** Good afternoon
3 **Buenas noches** Good evening (night)
4 **adiós** good-bye
5 **hasta la vista** until we meet again
6 **hasta luego** so long
7 **hasta mañana** until tomorrow
8 **de memoria** by heart
9 **por eso** therefore
10 **tal vez** perhaps

Exercise No. 4—Completion of Text

Follow carefully the instructions given in Exercise No. 1.

1 ¿(Who) **es la Sra. Adams?**
2 **Es** (a businesswoman of London).
3 (Her office) **está en Londres.**
4 **Importa objetos de arte y** (other) **artículos.**
5 **En primavera** (she is going) **a hacer un viaje.**
6 (She wants) **visitar Madrid.**
7 **Espera** (moreover) **ir a Tenerife.**
8 (But) **no habla español.**
9 (She is studying) **el idioma.**
10 **Los** (Tuesdays) **y los** (Thursdays) **tienen una cita.**
11 **La Sra. Adams aprende** (rapidly).
12 **Es** (very intelligent).
13 **El Sr. López es** (Spanish).
14 **Es** (a good teacher).
15 **La Sra. Adams aprende un diálogo** (in the first conversation).

SEGUNDA PARTE

Grammar Notes

1 The use of **es** and **está**.

In Spanish there are two words for *to be*, **ser** and **estar**. The form **es** comes from **ser**. The form **está** comes from **estar**. Both mean *he, she,* or *it is*.

(a) The form **es** and other forms of **ser** are used in such questions and answers as:

¿Quién es la Sra. Adams?	Who is Mrs. Adams?
Es una comerciante de Londres.	She is a London businesswoman.
¿Qué es el Sr. López?	What is Mr. López?
Es un profesor de español.	He is a Spanish teacher.

(b) The form **está,** and other forms of **estar,** are used in questions and answers that have to do with place. They really mean *is* or *are located*. Thus:

¿Dónde está la Sra. Adams?	Where is Mrs. Adams?
Está en casa.	She is at home.

Later you will learn more about the uses of **ser** and **estar**.

2 Some Common Verbs

habla	(he, she, it) speaks	aprende	(he, she, it) learns
hablan	they speak	sabe	(he, she, it) knows how
no habla	(he, she, it) does not speak	hablar	to speak
		visitar	to visit
importa	(he, she, it) imports	leer	to read
estudia	(he, she, it) studies	ver	to see
desea	(he, she, it) wants	ir	to go
espera	(he, she, it) expects	va a hacer	he is going to make

NOTE: The verb endings -a and -e mean *he, she,* or *it*. The verb endings -ar, -er and -ir mean *to*.

3 Special uses of the Definite Article

(a) Use the definite article before titles when speaking about a person. Omit it when speaking to a person.

La Sra. Adams va a España.	Mrs. Adams is going to Spain.
Buenos días, Sra. Adams.	Good day, Mrs. Adams.

(b) Use the definite article before a language. Omit it generally if the language is used after the verb **hablar** or after **en.**

El francés es la lengua de Francia.	French is the language of France.
La Sra. Adams no habla francés.	Mrs. Adams does not speak French.
en español en francés en inglés	in Spanish in French in English

TERCERA PARTE
Ejercicios (Exercises) No. 5A–5B–5C

5A. Complete the sentences with **es** or **está** as the sense requires.

Ejemplo: 1. La Sra. Adams es importadora.

1 La Sra. Adams —— impor-
tadora.
2 ¿Dónde —— su oficina?
3 ¿Qué —— el Sr. López?
4 La familia —— en la sala.
5 ¿Quién —— inglés?

6 ¿—— Carlos español?
7 Su agente —— en España.
8 La ciudad de Londres no —— en
España.
9 ¿Qué —— la Sra. Adams?
10 Carlos —— inglés.

5B. Select from Column II the word groups that best complete the sentences begun in Column 1.

Ejemplo: (1 d) La Sra. Adams desea hablar con su agente en español.

I	II
1 La Sra. Adams desea hablar	(a) aprende **rápidamente.**
2 La Sra. Adams sabe leer	(b) de España.
3 Es muy inteligente y por eso	(c) en la casa de la Sra. Adams.
4 Importa objetos de arte	(d) con su agente en español.
5 La Sra. Adams y el Sr. López tienen una cita	(e) de cuarenta y cinco años de edad.
6 El Sr. López es un hombre	(f) el español un poco.

5C. Find the corresponding Spanish words in the text or in 'Building Vocabulary' and write them.

1 and
2 in
3 with
4 also
5 to
6 perhaps
7 but
8 therefore
9 there
10 here
11 almost
12 always
13 How are you?
14 very well
15 thank you
16 big
17 small
18 good
19 bad
20 rapidly

Exercise No. 6—Preguntas y Respuestas

Study and read aloud the questions and answers. Note: (a) the word order; (b) the omission of subject pronouns; (c) that all question words have an accent mark.

1 ¿Quién es el profesor?
El Sr. López es el profesor.
2 ¿Habla español?
Sí, señor, habla español.
3 ¿Quién es la comerciante?
La Sra. Adams es la comerciante.

4 ¿Habla español?
No, señor, no habla español.
5 ¿Dónde está la oficina de la Sra. Adams?
Está en la calle de Oxford.
6 ¿Importa coches?
No importa coches.
7 ¿Aprende rápidamente?
Sí, señor, aprende rápidamente.
8 ¿Cuándo tienen una cita?
Los martes y los jueves tienen una cita.
9 ¿Es inteligente la Sra. Adams?
Es muy inteligente.
10 ¿Por qué[1] estudia el español?
Porque desea hacer un viaje a España.

1 Who is the teacher?
Mr. López is the teacher.
2 Does he speak Spanish?
Yes, sir, he speaks Spanish.
3 Who is the merchant?
Mrs. Adams is the merchant.
4 Does she speak Spanish?
No, sir, she does not speak Spanish.
5 Where is the office of Mrs. Adams?
It is in Oxford Street.
6 Does she import cars?
She does not import cars.
7 Does she learn rapidly?
Yes, sir, she learns rapidly.
8 When have they an appointment?
On Tuesdays and Thursdays they have an appointment.
9 Is Mrs. Adams intelligent?
She is very intelligent.
10 Why is she studying Spanish?
Because she wants to make a trip to Spain.

NOTE: 1. **por qué** means *why*. **porque** means *because*.

CHAPTER 5

EN LA SALA DE LA SEÑORA ADAMS

PRIMERA PARTE

1 Es viernes, 2 (dos) denero de 1987.[1]

2 Son las 8 (ocho) de la tarde.

3 La señora Adams está sentada en la sala de su casa. El señor López está sentado cerca de ella.

4 El señor López dice a la señora Adams—Alrededor de nosotros hay muchas cosas; en la casa, en la calle, en la oficina, en el parque, en la ciudad y en el campo.

5 En Gran Bretaña y en los Estados Unidos es necesario saber los nombres de las cosas en inglés. En España y en Hispano-América es necesario saber los nombres de las cosas en español.

6 Estamos en la sala de su casa. Dígame, por favor ¿Qué es esto?

7 Es un piano. Mi esposo toca bien el piano.

8 Muy bien. ¿Y qué hay encima del piano?

9 Una lámpara y un libro de música.

10 ¿Y qué hay en la pared, sobre el piano?

11 El retrato de mi esposo.

12 Excelente. Dígame, por favor, los nombres de otros objetos en la sala y dónde están.

13 Con mucho gusto.

14 La estantería está delante de una ventana. El escritorio está cerca de la puerta. Una silla está cerca del escritorio. Encima del escritorio hay un lápiz, un bolígrafo, unos papeles, y unas cartas. Unos libros están en la mesita.

15 Bueno. Basta por hoy. Hasta la vista, señora Adams.

16 Hasta el jueves, señor López.

1 It is January 2, 1987.

2 It is eight o'clock in the evening.

3 Mrs. Adams is seated in the living-room of her house. Mr. López is seated near her.

4 Mr. López says to Mrs. Adams, 'Around us there are many things: in the house, in the street, in the office, in the park, in the city and in the country.'

5 In Great Britain and in the United States it is necessary to know the names of things in English. In Spain and in Spanish America it is necessary to know the names of things in Spanish.

29

6 We are in the living-room of your house. Tell me, please, what is this?

7 It is a piano. My husband plays the piano well.

8 Good (*lit.* very well). And what is on the piano?

9 A lamp and a music book (*lit.* a book of music).

10 And what is on the wall over the piano?

11 The picture of my husband.

12 Excellent. Tell me, please, the names of other objects in the living-room and where they are.

13 With pleasure.

14 The bookcase is in front of a window. The desk is near the door. A chair is near the desk. On the desk are a pencil, a ballpoint pen, some papers, and some letters. Some books are on the little table.

15 Good. Enough for today. Good-bye, Mrs. Adams.

16 Until Thursday, Mr. López.

NOTE: 1, 1986 = **mil novecientos ochenta y seis.**

Pronunciation Aids

1 Pronounce carefully:

alrededor (al-re-ðe-'ðor)	**estamos** (es-'ta-mos)
escritorio (es-kri-'to-rjo)	**estantería** (es-tan-te-'ri-a)
lápiz ('la-piθ)	**dígame** ('ði-ɣa-me)
aquí (a-'ki)	**Hispano-América** (is-'pa-no a-'me-ri-ka)
necesario (ne-θe-'sa-rjo)	
viaje ('vja-xe) or ('bja-xe)	**Estados Unidos** (es-'ta-ðos u-'ni-ðos)
bolígrafo (bo-'li-ɣra-fo)	**Gran Bretaña** (ɣram bre-'ta-nja)
excelente (es-θe-'len-te)	**España** (es-'pa-nja)

2 All question words in Spanish have an accent mark.

quién (sing.)	who	**cómo**	how
quiénes (plur.)	who	**cuánto**	how much
dónde	where	**cuántos**	how many
cuándo	when	**por qué**	why
qué	what		

Building Vocabulary

A. **En la Sala** In the Living-Room

la carta	letter	**la pared**	wall
el escritorio	desk	**el bolígrafo**	ballpoint pen
la estantería	bookcase	**la pluma**	(fountain) pen
la lámpara	lamp	**la puerta**	door
el libro	book	**el retrato**	portrait
el lápiz	pencil	**la silla**	chair

la mesa	table	el sillón	armchair
la mesita	little table	la ventana	window
el papel	paper	el sofá	sofa

B. Some Common Prepositions

a	to, at	detrás de	behind
de	of, from	encima de	on top of
alrededor de	around	con	with
cerca de	near	en	in, on, at
debajo de	under	entre	between
delante de	in front of	sobre	over, above

Expresiones Importantes

1	**está sentado** (*m*)	is seated	5	**con mucho gusto**	with pleasure
	está sentada (*f*)		6	**basta por hoy**	enough for
2	**es necesario**	it is necessary			today
3	**por favor**	please	7	**son las ocho**	it's 8 o'clock
4	**dígame**	tell me	8	**dos de enero**	January 2

Exercise No. 7—Completion of Text

1 **El señor** (is seated) **en la sala.**
2 (There are) **muchas cosas en la calle.**
3 **Es necesario** (to know) **los nombres.**
4 (Tell me) — **¿Qué es esto?**
5 (My husband) **toca bien el piano.**
6 **El retrato está** (over the piano).
7 **En el escritorio hay** (a pencil, a ballpoint pen, and some papers).
8 **Unos libros** (are on the little table).
9 (Enough) **por hoy.**
10 (Until Thursday) **Sr. López.**

SEGUNDA PARTE

Grammar Notes

1 The Contractions **del** and **al**

(a) The preposition **de** (*of, from*) contracts with **el** and forms **del** (*of, from the*)

¿Dónde está la oficina *del*	Where is the office *of the*
comerciante?	merchant?

(b) The preposition **a** (*to*) contracts with **el,** and forms **al** (*to the*).

El profesor habla *al*	The teacher speaks *to the*
comerciante.	merchant.

(c) The other forms of the definite article do not contract with **de** or **a.**

El padre *de los* niños está aquí.	The father *of the* children is here.
Los niños van *a la* escuela.	The children go *to* school.

2 Possession

(a) Possession is indicated by a phrase with **de,** never by means of an apostrophe.

la casa **del profesor**	the house *of the teacher*	the teacher's house
el tío **de María**	the uncle *of Mary*	Mary's uncle

(b) **de quién, de quiénes** whose, of whom

¿De quién es la oficina?	Whose office is it?
Es la oficina de la Sra. Adams.	It is Mrs. Adams's office.
¿De quiénes son estos libros?	Whose are these books?
Son los libros de los alumnos.	They are the students' books.

3 Omission of the Indefinite Article

Omit the indefinite article with words indicating professions and occupations after the verb **ser** *to be.* If such words are modified, the indefinite article is not omitted.

La Sra. Adams es negociante.	Mrs. Adams is a businesswoman.
Es una buena negociante.	She is a good businesswoman.

TERCERA PARTE

Ejercicios (Exercises) No. 8A–8B–8C–8D

8A. Write the singular, plural, and meaning of the following nouns. Use the definite article.

Ejemplo: el edificio, los edificios building

1 calle	3 pared	5 señor	7 papel	9 estantería
2 oficina	4 silla	6 mesa	8 puerta	10 ventana

8B. Complete in Spanish. First revise 'Building Vocabulary B'.

Ejemplo: 1. El lápiz está debajo de los papeles.

1 **El lápiz está** (under) **los papeles.**
2 **Un parque está** (near) **la casa.**
3 (On top of the) **escritorio hay muchas cartas.**
4 **Un retrato está** (above) **el piano.**
5 **Un sillón está** (between) **las ventanas.**
6 **Un coche está** (in front of the) **edificio.**
7 **Las sillas están** (around) **la mesa.**
8 **¿Qué hay** (behind) **la puerta?**
9 **¿Qué hay** (under) **la mesa?**
10 **¿Qué está** (near the) **escritorio?**

8C. Use **del, de la, de los, de las, al, a la, a los,** or **a las** as required. First revise 'Grammar Notes 1'.

Ejemplo: 1. La sala de la casa es grande.

1 **La sala** (of the) **casa es grande.**
2 **María habla** (to the) **maestro.**
3 **La señora Gómez es la maestra** (of the) **muchachas.**
4 **El Sr. López es un amigo** (of the) **negociante.**
5 **Los señores van** (to the) **puerta.**
6 **Felipe es un amigo** (of the) **niños.**
7 **El maestro habla** (to the) **alumnos.**
8 **El negociante va en tren** (to the) **ciudad.**
9 **¿Quién habla** (to the) **padre?**
10 **¿Quién habla** (to the) **alumnas?**

8D. Practise the Spanish aloud.

1 **¿De quién es este sombrero?**   1 Whose is this hat?
   Es el sombrero de Juan.   It is John's hat.
2 **¿Es este escritorio de Carlos o**   2 Is this desk Charles's or
   de María?   Mary's?
   Es de María.   It is Mary's.
3 **¿Es esta pluma de él o de ella?**   3 Is this fountain pen his or hers?
   Es de ella.   (*Lit.* of him or of her)
     It is hers. (*Lit.* of her)
4 **¿De quién es el retrato?**   4 Whose portrait is it?
   Es el retrato del señor Adams.   It is Mr. Adams's portrait.
5 **¿De quiénes son estos papeles?**   5 Whose are these papers?
   Son los papeles de los maestros.   They are the teachers' papers.

Exercise No. 9—Preguntas

Answer in complete Spanish sentences. Consult the text for your answers. The correct answers to these questions and those in all later lessons are given in the Answer Section of the Appendix. Check all your answers.

1 **¿Dónde está sentada la Sra. Adams?**
2 **¿Quién está sentado cerca de ella?**
3 **¿Hay muchas cosas alrededor de nosotros?**
4 **¿Hay muchas cosas en la calle?**
5 **¿Quién toca bien el piano?**
6 **¿Dónde está el libro de música?**
7 **¿Dónde está el retrato del Sr. Adams?**
8 **¿Qué está delante de una ventana?**
9 **¿Dónde está el escritorio?**
10 **¿Qué está cerca del escritorio?**
11 **¿Dónde están las cartas?**
12 **¿Dónde están los libros?**

REVISION 1

CHAPTERS 1–5 PRIMERA PARTE

Each Revision Chapter will begin with a summary of the most important words and expressions that have occurred in the chapters revised. Check yourself as follows:

1. Cover up the English words. Read one Spanish word at a time aloud and give the English meaning. Uncover the English word of the same number in order to check.

2 Cover up the Spanish words. Say aloud, one at a time, the Spanish for each English word. Uncover the Spanish word to check.

3 Write the words you have difficulty in remembering, three or four times.

Repaso de Palabras (Word Revision)

NOUNS

1 la alfombra	19 la familia	37 el objeto
2 el alumno	20 el hermano	38 el ordenador
3 la alumna	21 la hermana	39 el padre
4 el amigo	22 el hijo	40 el papel
5 el bolígrafo	23 la hija	41 la pluma
6 la calle	24 el hombre	42 el profesor
7 la casa	25 el lápiz	43 la puerta
8 el campo	26 el idioma	44 la sala
9 la carta	27 el lugar	45 el señor
10 la ciudad	28 el libro	46 la señora
11 el comedor	29 la madre	47 la silla
12 el coche	30 la mesa	48 el tío
13 la cosa	31 la mujer	49 la tía
14 el cuarto	32 el maestro	50 el tren
15 el día	33 el muchacho	51 la ventana
16 el edificio	34 la muchacha	52 el viaje
17 el escritorio	35 el niño	
18 la esposa	36 la niña	

1 rug	12 car	23 daughter
2 student (*m*)	13 thing	24 man
3 student (*f*)	14 room	25 pencil
4 friend (*m*)	15 day	26 language
5 ballpoint pen	16 building	27 place
6 street	17 desk	28 book
7 house	18 wife	29 mother
8 country	19 family	30 table
9 letter	20 brother	31 woman
10 city	21 sister	32 teacher (*m*)
11 dining-room	22 son	33 boy

34 girl	41 fountain pen	48 uncle
35 child (*m*)	42 teacher	49 aunt
36 child (*f*)	43 door	50 train
37 object	44 living-room	51 window
38 computer	45 Mr.	52 trip
39 father	46 Mrs.	
40 paper	47 chair	

VERBS

1 es	9 aprende	17 saber
2 está	10 sabe	18 ver
3 estamos	11 tiene	19 ir
4 están	12 vive	20 pedir
5 espera	13 hablar	21 hay
6 estudia	14 visitar	22 dígame
7 habla	15 hacer	
8 va	16 leer	

1 he (is)	9 he learns	17 to know
2 he is (place)	10 he knows (how)	18 to see
3 we are (place)	11 he has	19 to go
4 they are (place)	12 he lives	20 to ask for
5 he expects	13 to speak	21 there is
6 he studies	14 to visit	22 tell me
7 he speaks	15 to make (do)	
8 he goes	16 to read	

NOTE: The same form of the verb is good for *he, she, it,* and *you (usted)*. Thus: **es** = *he, she, it* is, *you* are   **espera** = *he, she, it* expects, *you* expect.

ADJECTIVES

1 bueno	6 mi	11 sentado
2 excelente	7 mucho	12 su
3 grande	8 necesario	13 todos
4 importante	9 otro	14 un poco
5 malo	10 pequeño	

1 good	6 my	11 seated
2 excellent	7 much	12 his, her, its
3 great, big	8 necessary	13 all
4 important	9 other	14 a little
5 bad	10 small	

ADVERBS

1 allí	6 diligentemente	11 además
2 aquí	7 muy	12 si
3 basta	8 rápidamente	13 sí
4 bien	9 siempre	14 ya
5 casi	10 también	

1 there	6 diligently	11 moreover
2 here	7 very	12 if
3 enough	8 rapidly	13 yes
4 well	9 always	14 now, already
5 almost	10 also	

PREPOSITIONS

1 a	6 del	11 delante de
2 al	7 sobre	12 detrás de
3 con	8 alrededor de	13 encima de
4 en	9 cerca de	14 por
5 de	10 debajo de	

1 to, at	6 of the	11 in front of
2 to the	7 above	12 behind
3 with	8 around	13 on top of
4 in, on	9 near	14 for, by,
5 of, from	10 under	through

QUESTION WORDS

1 cómo	4 dónde	6 cuánto
2 qué	5 quién	7 cuántos (as)
3 por qué		

1 how	4 where	6 how much
2 what, which	5 who	7 how many
3 why		

CONJUNCTIONS

1 o	2 pero	3 porque	4 y

1 or	2 but	3 because	4 and

IMPORTANT EXPRESSIONS

1 basta	11 en casa
2 por hoy	12 es necesario
3 Buenos días	13 hasta luego
4 Buenas noches	14 hasta mañana
5 Buenas tardes	15 hasta la vista
6 Adiós	16 por eso
7 ¿Cómo está Ud?	17 por favor
8 con mucho gusto	18 ¿Qué es esto?
9 muy bien	19 todo el día
10 gracias	20 tal vez

1 enough	11 at home
2 for today	12 it is necessary
3 Good day	13 so long
4 Good night	14 until tomorrow
5 Good afternoon,	15 so long
Good evening	16 therefore
6 Good-bye	17 please
7 How are you?	18 What is this?
8 with pleasure	19 all day
9 very well	20 perhaps
10 thanks	

SEGUNDA PARTE

Ejercicio 10   From Group II select the antonym (opposite) for each word in Group I.

I

1 bueno	5 encima de	9 buenos días
2 sí	6 padre	10 el muchacho
3 allí	7 mucho	11 la ciudad
4 pequeño	8 detrás de	12 la mujer

II

(a) delante de	(e) no	(i) aquí
(b) el campo	(f) el hombre	(j) debajo de
(c) la muchacha	(g) malo	(k) poco
(d) buenas noches	(h) grande	(l) madre

Ejercicio 11 Complete the following sentences in Spanish.

1 Trabajo (all day).
2 Dígame (please).
3 (Perhaps) está en la oficina.
4 (Good-afternoon) señor.
5 Aprende los saludos (with pleasure).
6 (Therefore) estudia el español.
7 ¿(How) está Ud?
8 ¿(Where) vive el señor?
9 ¿(What) es esto?
10 ¿(Who) es negociante?

Ejercicio 12 Select the group of words in Column II which best completes each sentence begun in Column I.

Ejemplo: (1 d) En la familia Adams hay seis personas.

I

1 En la familia Adams
2 La casa de la Sra. Adams
3 La Sra. Adams va en tren
4 Estudia el español
5 Trabaja todo el día
6 Sabe leer el español
7 Aprende rápidamente
8 Los martes y los jueves
9 En la primera conversación
10 El esposo de la Sra. Adams
11 La Sra. Adams va a hacer

II

(a) aprende los saludos y las despedidas.
(b) toca bien el piano.
(c) porque es muy inteligente.
(d) hay seis personas.
(e) un viaje a España.
(f) está en los suburbios.
(g) pero no habla el idioma.
(h) en su oficina.
(i) a la ciudad.
(j) tienen una cita.
(k) porque desea hablar el idioma.

Ejercicio 13 Complete these sentences in Spanish.

1 **El coche está** (in front of the house).
2 **Las sillas están** (near the door).
3 **Las zonas residenciales están** (around the city).
4 **El Sr. Adams está sentado** (behind the desk).
5 **Las lámparas están** (on top of the piano).
6 (The boy's books = the books of the boy) **están en la mesa.**
7 (The girls' mother = the mother of the girls) **está en casa.**
8 (Philip's brother) **es médico.**
9 (Mary's father) **es profesor.**
10 (The children's teacher) **es español.**

TERCERA PARTE

Practise all Spanish dialogues aloud:

Diálogo 1

¿Dónde está la Calle de Atocha?

1 **Por favor, señor, ¿Dónde está la calle de Atocha**	1 Please sir, where is Atocha Street?
2 **Siga adelante, señorita.**	2 Continue straight ahead, Miss.
3 **¿Cuántas manzanas?**	3 How many blocks?
4 **Cinco manzanas, señorita.**	4 Five blocks, Miss.
5 **Muchas gracias.**	5 Many thanks.
6 **De nada.**	6 Don't mention it (you're welcome).

Diálogo 2

¿Dónde para el autobús?

1 **Dígame, por favor, señor — ¿Dónde para el autobús?**	1 Please tell me, sir, where does the bus stop?
2 **Para en aquella esquina, señorita.**	2 It stops at that corner, Miss.
3 **Muchas gracias, señor.**	3 Many thanks, sir.
4 **No hay de qué.**	4 Don't mention it (you're welcome).

LECTURA (READING SELECTION)

Exercise No. 14 — How to Read the Lecturas

1 Read the passage silently from beginning to end to get the meaning as a whole.

2 Re-read the passage looking up any words you may have forgotten, in the Spanish–English vocabulary at the end of this book. There are few new words in the Lecturas of the Revision Chapters and the meaning of these is given in parentheses.

3 Read the passage silently a third time. Then translate it and check your translation with that given in the answer section of the appendix.

4 Follow this procedure in all succeeding Lecturas.

Exercise No. 14A—La señora Adams, comerciante de Londres

La señora Adams es una comerciante inglesa que (who) importa objetos de arte de España. Por eso desea hacer un viaje a España en la primavera. Desea hablar con su agente y visitar algunos lugares de interés en España. Pero no sabe hablar español.

La señora Adams tiene un buen profesor. Es un español que vive en Londres y se llama señor López. Los martes y los jueves el profesor va en tren a la casa de su estudiante. Allí hablan un poco en español. La señora Adams es muy inteligente y aprende rápidamente. Por ejemplo (for example), en la primera conversación aprende de memoria los saludos y las despedidas. Ya (already) sabe decir (to say) — Buenos días, — ¿Cómo está Ud? — Hasta la vista — y — Hasta mañana. Ya sabe decir en español los nombres de muchas cosas que (which) están en su sala, y sabe contestar (to answer) bien a las preguntas — ¿Qué es esto? — y — ¿Dónde está . . . ?

El señor López está muy satisfecho (satisfied) con el progreso de su estudiante y dice (says), — Bueno. Basta por hoy. Hasta luego.

CHAPTER 6

PRIMERA PARTE

LOS VERBOS SON IMPORTANTES

1 La Sra. Adams y el Sr. López están sentados en la sala de la señora Adams. El Sr. López comienza a hablar. La señora Adams le escucha con atención.[1]

2 Ya sabe Ud. que los nombres de las cosas y de las personas son importantes. Pero los verbos son importantes también. No es posible formar una frase sin verbos. Tampoco es posible conversar sin verbos.

3 Vamos a practicar unos verbos corrientes. Voy a hacer unas preguntas. Yo pregunto y Ud. contesta. Si Ud. no sabe la respuesta, diga, por favor — No sé.

4 Bueno, dice la señora Adams. Voy a decir — No sé, si no sé la respuesta.

5 ¿Es Ud. comerciante?

6 Sí, señor López, soy comerciante, importadora de objetos de arte y otros artículos de varios países y sobre todo de España.

7 ¿Y por qué estudia Ud. el español?

8 Estudio el español porque deseo hacer un viaje a España para visitar a mi agente allí. Deseo hablar con él en español. Él no habla inglés.

9 ¿Espera Ud. visitar otras partes de España además de la Península?

10 Espero ir además a Tenerife, y tal vez a las otras Islas Canarias.

11 ¿Cuándo sale Ud. de Londres para España?

12 Salgo el 31 (treinta y uno) de mayo.

13 ¿Viaja Ud. en tren, en barco o en avión?

14 Viajo por avión porque es el modo más rápido.

15 ¿Cuánto cuesta el vuelo?

16 No sé. Mañana voy a pedir información y una reserva.

17 Excelente, Sra. Adams. Ud. aprende el español muy rápidamente.

18 Gracias. Es favor que Ud. me hace.

19 No es favor. Es verdad. Bueno, basta por hoy. Hasta luego.

20 Hasta el próximo jueves.

1 Mrs. Adams and Mr. López are seated in the living-room of Mrs. Adams. Mr. López begins to speak. Mrs. Adams listens to him attentively.

2 You already know that the names of things and of persons are important. But verbs are important, too. It is not possible to make a sentence without verbs. Neither is it possible to converse without verbs.

3 We are going to practise some common verbs. I am going to ask some questions. I ask and you answer. If you do not know the answer, please say 'I do not know.'

4 'Good,' says Mrs. Adams. 'I will say "I don't know," if I don't know the answer.'

5 Are you a businesswoman?

6 Yes, Mr. López, I am a businesswoman, importer of art objects and other things from various countries and especially from Spain.

7 And why are you studying Spanish?

8 I am studying Spanish because I want to make a trip to Spain to visit my agent there. I want to speak with him in Spanish. He does not speak English.

9 Do you expect to visit other parts of Spain besides the Peninsula?

10 I expect to go besides to Tenerife, and perhaps the other Canary Islands.

11 When do you leave London for Spain?

12 I am leaving on May 31.

13 Are you travelling by train, by boat or by plane?

14 I am travelling by plane because it is the quickest way.

15 How much does the flight cost?

16 I do not know. Tomorrow I am going to ask for information and a reservation.

17 Excellent, Mrs. Adams. You are learning Spanish very quickly.

18 Thank you. You are very kind.[2]

19 It is not kindness. It is the truth. Well, enough for today. Goodbye.

20 Until next Thursday.

NOTE: 1. **le** *him* or *to him*. It is an object pronoun. Object pronouns usually precede the verb. 2. *Lit.* It is a favour that you are doing me.

Pronunciation Aids

1. Practise:

atención (a-ten-'θjon)

reserva (rre-'ser-va) or (rre-'ser-βa)

conversar (kon-ver-'sar) or (kom-ber-'sar)

visitar (vi-si-tar) or (bi-si-tar)

hacer (a-'θer)

practicar (prak-ti-'kar)

decir (ðe-'θir)

preguntar (pre-ɣun-'tar)

estudio (es-'tu-ðjo)

deseo (ðe-'se-o)

espero (es-'pe-ro)

salgo ('sal-ɣo)

viajo ('vja-xo) or ('bja-xo)

estudia (es-'tu-ðja)

espera (es-'pe-ra)

dice ('ði-θe)

aprende (a-'pren-de)

corrientes (ko-'rrjen-tes)

viaja ('vja-xa) or ('bja-xa)

2. **pa-í-ses** (pa-ˈi-ses). The accent mark over the **í** shows that the **í** is a separate syllable. Otherwise **ai** would be pronounced like *ai* in the English word *aisle* and in the Spanish word **aire** (ˈaj-re).

Building Vocabulary

A. **Algunos Países de Europa** (ew-ˈro-pa)   Some Countries of Europe

1 **Inglaterra** England		5 **Italia** Italy
2 **Gran Bretaña** Great Britain		6 **España** Spain
3 **Francia** France		7 **Portugal** Portugal
4 **Alemania** Germany		

B. **Los Países de Norte América**   The Countries of North America

1 **Los Estados Unidos**   The United States
2 **México**   Mexico
3 **El Canadá**   Canada

C. **Los Países de América del Sur**

1 **La Argentina**	5 **El Ecuador**	8 **El Uruguay**
2 **Bolivia**	6 **El Paraguay**	9 **Venezuela**
3 **Colombia**	7 **El Perú**	10 **El Brasil**
4 **Chile**		

Los habitantes (inhabitants) **del Brasil hablan portugués. Los habitantes de los otros países de América del Sur hablan español.**

Expresiones Importantes

1 **Es favor que Ud. me hace**	You are very kind.
2 **hacer preguntas**	to ask questions
3 **hacer un viaje**	to take a trip
4 **en avión (tren, barco)**	by plane (train, boat)
5 **sobre todo**	above all, especially

Exercise No. 15—Completion of Text

Complete the following sentences based on the text.

1 **Los verbos** (are important).
2 **Vamos a practicar** (some common verbs).
3 ¿(Why) **estudia Ud. el español?**
4 (Because) **deseo visitar a** (my) **agente.**
5 **Deseo hablar** (with him in Spanish).
6 **Espero ir** (to other countries).
7 ¿**Viaja Ud.** (by train.or by plane)?
8 ¿(How much) **cuesta el vuelo?**
9 **Ud. aprende** (very rapidly).
10 Enough for today.

SEGUNDA PARTE (SECOND PART)

Grammar Notes

1 About Verb Endings

The infinitive is the base form of the verb. In English it is expressed by *to*. Thus: *to* speak, *to* learn, *to* live, etc.

In Spanish there are infinitive endings which mean *to*. Thus:

<blockquote>hablar to speak   aprender to learn   vivir to live</blockquote>

The infinitives of all Spanish verbs end in -ar, -er or -ir. That part of the verb which is left after the endings is removed is called the stem. Thus **habl-, aprend-, viv-** are the stems of **hablar, aprender** and **vivir**.

The infinitive endings of the verb are dropped and other endings added to the stem as the verb is used in various persons and tenses.

Let us see how the endings change, and what they mean, in the present tense of the verb **hablar**.

2 Present Tense of **hablar**. Model Regular -ar Verb.

(yo)	**habl-o**	I speak
(tú)	**habl-as**	you speak (fam.)
usted⎫	**habl-a**	you speak
(él) ⎬	**habl-a**	he, it speaks
(ella)⎭	**habl-a**	she, it speaks
(nosotros)	**habl-amos**	we speak
(vosotros)	**habl-áis**	you speak (fam.)
ustedes⎫	**habl-an**	you speak
(ellos) ⎬	**habl-an**	they (*m.*) speak
(ellas) ⎭	**habl-an**	they (*f.*) speak

(a) The endings of a regular -ar verb in the present tense are:

<blockquote>singular -o, -as, -a   plural amos, -áis, -an</blockquote>

NOTE: The verb ending -a is used with **usted, él** and **ella**. The verb ending -an is used with **ustedes, ellos** and **ellas**.

(b) Since the ending indicates the subject pronoun quite clearly, subject pronouns, except usted (**Ud.**) and **ustedes** (**Uds.**) are usually omitted. They may be used for emphasis or to make the meaning clear.

Yo hablo inglés. **Ella** habla francés.

I speak English. She speaks French.

(c) The present tense may be translated: I speak, I do speak, I am speaking, etc.

(d) **nosotros** and **vosotros** have feminine forms **nosotras, vosotras**.

3 Polite and Familiar *you*.

(a) **usted** (*you, sing.*) and **ustedes** (*you, plur.*) are the polite forms of address. They are used extensively in Mexico and all the other countries of Spanish-speaking America.

¿Habla Ud. francés, Sr. Muñoz?	Do you speak French, Mr. Muñoz?
Uds. hablan muy bien, señoras.	You speak very well, ladies.

(b) **tú** (*you, sing.*) and **vosotros(as)** (*you, plur.*) are the familiar forms of address. They are used with members of the family, with good friends, and with children; and generally they have become more commonly used now in Spain.

¿Hablas (tú) inglés, papá?	Do you speak English, daddy?
(Vosotros) habláis demasiado alto, niños.	You speak too loudly, children.

4 The Negative and Interrogative.

(a) To form the negative, put the word **no** (*not*) directly before the verb.

No hablamos portugués.	We do not speak Portuguese.

(b) To form a question, place the subject after the verb. If the subject is not expressed, the double question mark is sufficient.

¿Charlan los alumnos?	Are the students chatting?
¿No van a hacer un viaje?	Are they not going to make a trip?

TERCERA PARTE

Ejercicios (Exercises) No. 16A–16B–16C–16D

16A. Translate the following **-ar** verbs. They take the same endings as the model **-ar** verb, **hablar.**

1 escuchar	7 practicar	12 estudiar
2 desear	8 viajar	13 importar
3 comenzar[1]	9 preguntar	14 tocar (an
4 formar	10 contestar	instrument)
5 esperar	11 empezar[1] (*also*	15 visitar
6 conversar	*means* to begin)	

NOTE 1: **comenzar** and **empezar** are two verbs of a type which, although the endings are the same as the model **-ar** verb, undergo certain changes in the present tense. The **-e-** of the stem becomes **-ie-** in the following cases: **comienzo, empiezo; comienzas, empiezas; comienza, empieza; comienzan, empiezan.** In the forms **comenzamos, empezamos; comenzáis, empezáis,** the **-e-** of the stem does not change. Verbs of this type will be studied in greater detail later.

16B. Practise aloud the following brief dialogues. Translate them.

1 ¿Habla Ud. español?
Sí, hablo español.
¿Qué lenguas habla su profesor?
Habla inglés, español y francés.

2 ¿Quién toca el piano?
María toca el piano.
¿No tocas tú el piano, Rosita?
No, no toco el piano.

3 ¿Estudian los alumnos la lección?
No, no estudian la lección.
¿Hablan en español?
Sí, hablan en español.

4 ¿Escuchan Uds. con atención
cuando el profesor habla?
Sí, escuchamos con atención
cuando el profesor habla.

16C. Copy each sentence, filling in the correct verb endings.

Ejemplo: La Sra. Adams no habla español.

1 La Sra. Adams no habl —— español.
2 Nosotros estudi —— la lección.
3 ¿Quién import —— objetos de arte?
4 ¿Dese —— Ud. aprender a hablar español?
5 Yo esper —— ir a Cuba.
6 Uds. charl —— mucho.
7 Juan y Carlos (= ellos) practic —— la pronunciación.
8 ¿Viaj —— el señor en tren o por avión?
9 Pablo y yo (= nosotros) esper —— salir mañana.
10 Eva y Ana (= ellas) empiez —— a estudiar.

16D. Complete with the form of the verb that fits the pronoun.

Ejemplo: yo empiezo

1 yo (empezar)
2 él no (escuchar)
3 tú (formar)
4 ella (conversar)

5 ellos (practicar)
6 ¿(preguntar) Ud?
7 ellas (contestar)
8 ¿(estudiar) nosotros?

9 Uds. (desear)
10 yo no (visitar)
11 yo (viajar)
12 ¿(esperar) Ud?

Exercise No. 17—Preguntas

Answer in complete Spanish sentences.

1 ¿Dónde están sentados los señores?
2 ¿Quién empieza a hablar?
3 ¿Quién escucha con atención?
4 ¿Quién pregunta?
5 ¿Quién contesta?
6 ¿Son importantes los verbos?
7 ¿Es comerciante la Sra. Adams?
8 ¿Habla (ella) español?
9 ¿Por qué desea hablar español?
10 ¿Qué países espera visitar?
11 ¿Viaja en tren, en avión, o en barco?
12 ¿Aprende la Sra. Adams rápidamente o despacio (slowly)?

CHAPTER 7

PRIMERA PARTE

LA FAMILIA DE LA SEÑORA ADAMS

1 Es jueves, 8 de enero, a las 8 (ocho) de la tarde.

2 El señor López toca el timbre de la casa Adams. La criada abre la puerta y dice — Pase Ud. a la sala, por favor.

3 En la sala la señora Adams espera al señor López, y cuando éste entra, dice — Buenas tardes. ¿Cómo está Ud.?

4 Regular. ¿Y cómo está Ud.? ¿Y su familia?

5 Yo estoy muy bien, gracias. Pero mi hija Anita está enferma. Tiene catarro.

6 Lo siento mucho. ¿Tiene Ud. otros hijos?

7 Sí. Tengo cuatro hijos, dos muchachos y dos muchachas. Somos una familia de seis personas.

8 ¿Y cómo se llaman sus hijos?

9 Se llaman Felipe, Guillermo, Rosita y Anita.

10 ¿Cuántos años tienen?

11 Felipe tiene diez años. Es el mayor. Guillermo tiene ocho años. Rosita tiene seis años. Anita es la menor. Tiene cuatro años.

12 Todos menos Anita van a la escuela.

13 Hablan un rato más. Luego la señora Adams invita al señor López a visitar su oficina el lunes próximo, a las doce y media de la tarde. Éste acepta la invitación con mucho gusto.

14 A las nueve el señor López dice — Hasta la vista.

15 La señora Adams responde — Hasta el lunes a las doce y media.

1 It is Thursday, January 8, at 8 o'clock in the evening.

2 Mr. López rings the bell of the Adams house. The maid opens the door and says, 'Go to the living-room, please.'

3 In the living-room Mrs. Adams is awaiting Mr. López, and when the latter enters, she says: 'Good evening. How are you?'

4 So so. And how are you and your family?

5 I am very well, thank you. But my child Annie is ill. She has a cold (*lit*. catarrh).

6 I'm very sorry. Have you other children?

7 Yes. I have four children, two boys and two girls. We are a family of six people.

8 And what are the names of your children?

9 Their names are Philip, William, Rosie and Annie.
10 How old are they?
11 Philip is ten years old. He is the oldest. William is eight years old. Rosie is six years old. Annie is the youngest. She is four years old.
12 All except Annie go to school.
13 They talk a while longer. Then Mrs. Adams invites Mr. López to visit her office the following Monday at 12.30 p.m. The latter accepts the invitation with much pleasure.
14 At nine o'clock Mr. López says, 'Good-bye.'
15 Mrs. Adams answers, 'Till Monday at 12.30.'

Pronunciation Aids

1 Practise

jueves ('xwe-ves) or ('xwe-βes)
familia (fa-'mi-lja)
catarro (ka-'ta-rrɵ)
enferma (en-'fer-ma)
siento ('sjen-to)
Guillermo (ɣi-'ʎer-mo)
invitar (in-vi-'tar) or (im-bi-'tar)

invitación (in-vi-ta-'θjon) or (im-bi-ta-'θjon)
responde (rres-'pon-de)
aceptar (a-θep-'tar)
tienen ('tje-nen)
seguramente (se-ɣu-ra-'men-te)
luego ('lwe-ɣo)
llaman ('ʎa-man)

Building Vocabulary

A. Most Spanish words ending in **-ción** have corresponding English words ending in *-tion*. Words ending in **-ción** are feminine.

1 la invitación	4 continuación	7 aplicación	10 solución
2 pronunciación	5 atención	8 invención	11 revolución
3 elección	6 dirección	9 prevención	12 nación

B. The ending **-mente** is equal to the ending *-ly* in English.

1 **seguramente**, surely	4 **ciertamente**, certainly
2 **rápidamente**, rapidly	5 **atentamente**, attentively
3 **generalmente**, generally	6 **probablemente**, probably

Important Expressions

1 **¿Cómo se llama Ud.?**	1 What is your name?
2 **Me llamo Felipe.**	2 My name is Philip.
3 **¿Cómo se llama su amigo?**	3 What is your friend's name?
4 **Mi amigo se llama Pablo.**	4 My friend's name is Paul.
5 **¿Cuántos años tiene Ud?**[1]	5 How old are you?
6 **Tengo 13 (trece) años.**[1]	6 I am thirteen years old.

7 ¿Cuántos años tiene Pablo?　　7 How old is Paul?
8 Tiene 15 (quince) años.　　8 He is fifteen years old.

NOTE: 1. *Lit.* How many years have you? I have 13 years.

Exercise No. 18—Completion of Text

Complete the following sentences based on the text.

1 **La criada** (opens) **la puerta.**
2 **Dice-**(Pass) **a la sala, por favor.**
3 (Good evening). **¿Cómo está** (your) **familia?**
4 **Ella tiene** (a cold).
5 **¿Tiene Ud.** (other) **hijos?**
6 (I have) **cuatro hijos.**
7 (We are) **una familia de seis personas.**
8 **¿Cuántos** (years) **tienen sus hijos?**
9 **Anita es** (the youngest).
10 **Felipe es** (the oldest).
11 **Hablan** (a while longer).
12 **La Sra. Adams invita** (Mr. López).

SEGUNDA PARTE

Grammar Notes

1 Present Tense of **ser** to be, **estar** to be, **ir** to go.

	Singular		Plural
soy	I am	**somos**	we are
eres	you are (fam.)	**sois**	you are (fam.)
Ud. **es**⎱	you are	Uds. **son**⎱	you are
es⎰	he, she, it is	**son**⎰	they are
estoy	I am	**estamos**	we are
estás	you are (fam.)	**estáis**	you are (fam.)
Ud. **está**⎱	you are	Uds. **están**⎱	you are
está⎰	he, she, it is	**están**⎰	they are
voy	I go	**vamos**	we go
vas	you go (fam.)	**vais**	you go (fam.)
Ud. **va**⎱	you go	Uds. **van**⎱	you go
va⎰	he, she, it goes	**van**⎰	they go

NOTE: All forms of **estar** except **estamos** are stressed on the last syllable.

2 Use of **ir** to indicate Future Time

(a) **Voy a hacer un viaje a Colombia.**　　I am going to take a trip to Colombia.
¿Van Uds. a aprender el francés?　　Are you going to learn French?

(b) **Vamos** may be translated: *Let us,* or *We are going to*—whichever makes best sense.

Vamos a empezar. Vamos a ver.	Let us begin. Let's see.
Vamos a visitar a nuestro amigo.	We are going to visit our friend.

Note that the verb **ir** is followed by **a** in such constructions.

3 The Personal **a.** This is placed before the direct object, if the direct object is a person or proper name. The personal **a** is not translated. **a quién** and **a quiénes** equal *whom.*

¿A quién espera Ud.?	Whom are you expecting?
Espero a Juan.	I am expecting John.
¿Van Uds. a visitar México?	Are you going to visit Mexico?

4 The Possessive Adjectives **mi** and **su.** Observe the forms and meanings of **mi** and **su:**

(a) *Mi* **niña está enferma.**	*My* child is ill.
(b) *Mis* **niños van a la escuela.**	*My* children go to school.
(c) **Ana, ¿dónde está** *su* **madre?**	Anna, where is *your* mother?
(d) **Juan, ¿dónde están** *sus* **libros?**	John, where are *your* books?
(e) **Maria está aquí.** *Su* **amiga está ausente.**	Marie is here. *Her* friend is absent.
(f) **Felipe está aquí.** *Su* **amigo está ausente.**	Philip is here. *His* friend is absent.
(g) **Los alumnos están aquí.** *Su* **profesor está ausente.**	The pupils are here. *Their* teacher is absent.

mi (*my*) is used with a sing. noun; **mis** (*my*) with a plur. noun.
su (*his, her, its, their, your*) is used with a sing. noun.
sus (*his, her, its, their, your*) is used with a plur. noun.

The sense of the sentence determines which meaning of **su (sus)** applies.

Ejercicios (Exercises) No. 19A–19B–19C

19A. Fill in the correct forms of **ser** and **estar.**

Remember: **ser** is used to express *Who is?* or *What is?* **estar** is used to express *place where* or *health.*

1 ¿Quién (is) **el señor López?** (He is) **profesor.**
2 ¿Cómo (are) **Ud.?** (I am) **muy bien.**
3 ¿Dónde (are) **Uds.?** (We are) **en la sala.**
4 ¿(Are) **Ud. negociante?** Sí, (I am) **negociante.**
5 ¿(Is) **enferma su hija?** Sí, mi hija (is) **enferma.**

6 ¿Cómo (are) **Uds.?** (We are) **muy bien, gracias.**
7 ¿Dónde (are) **los libros?** (They are) **en la estantería.**
8 ¿(Are) **Uds. españoles? No,** (we are) **ingleses.**
9 ¿Quiénes (are) **en la sala? Los dos señores** (are) **allí.**
10 ¿(Are) **Uds. amigos del profesor? Sí,** (we are) **sus amigos.**

19B. Complete the following sentences with the words in parenthesis, using the personal **a** whenever necessary.

Ejemplo: Hoy invitamos *al* señor Adams.

1 Hoy invitamos (el señor Adams).
2 No voy a visitar (la escuela).
3 Carlos espera (su amigo) Pablo.
4 Estudian (la lección).
5 Vamos a visitar (la señora López).
6 ¿Esperan Uds. (el tren)?
7 No, esperamos (Isabel).
8 La Sra. Adams desea ver (su agente).
9 Ellos no visitan (el parque).
10 Hoy visitamos (José).

19C. Translate into Spanish.

1 How are you?
2 So so, thank you.
3 My daughter is ill.
4 I am very sorry.
5 You are a family of six people.
6 Do your children go to school?
7 Do you speak Spanish?
8 No, I do not speak Spanish.
9 I invite Charles to visit my house.
10 We are going to chat a while.
11 Let's begin.
12 I want to study Spanish.

TERCERA PARTE

Exercise No. 20—Preguntas

1 ¿Quién abre la puerta?
2 ¿Quién toca el timbre?
3 ¿Dónde espera la Sra. Adams al Sr. López?
4 ¿Quién está enferma?
5 ¿Qué tiene ella?
6 ¿Cuántos hijos tiene la comerciante?
7 ¿Cuántas personas hay en su familia?
8 ¿Cómo se llaman sus hijos?
9 ¿Cuántos años tiene Felipe?
10 ¿Hablan un rato más?
11 ¿A quién (whom) invita la negociante a visitar su oficina?
12 ¿Acepta el profesor la invitación?

CHAPTER 8

EN LA OFICINA DE LA SEÑORA ADAMS

PRIMERA PARTE

1 La oficina de la señora Adams está en el quinto piso de un edificio alto. No es grande, pero es muy cómoda. Hay dos ventanas grandes que dan a la calle. En las paredes grises hay algunos carteles de España en colores vivos y un mapa de España.

2 En el escritorio de la señora Adams hay muchos papeles. Cerca de la puerta hay un escritorio pequeño con una máquina de escribir, un ordenador y una calculadora. Entre las dos ventanas hay una mesa larga. En la mesa hay periódicos y revistas y un bonito cenicero.

3 La señora Adams, que está sentada detrás de su escritorio cuando el señor López entra en la oficina, se levanta y va a saludarle.

4 Buenas tardes, señor López. Mucho gusto en verle.

5 El gusto es mío. ¿Cómo está Ud.?

6 Muy bien, gracias.

7 Su oficina es hermosa. Me gustan muchísimo este mapa de España y estos carteles. ¡Qué colores tan bonitos! A propósito, Sra. Adams, ¿Qué ve Ud. en ese cartel?

8 Veo el cielo y el sol, unas montañas, un tren y casas blancas con tejados rojos.

9 ¿De qué color es el sol?

10 Es amarillo y muy grande.

11 ¿De qué colores son las montañas, el cielo y el tren?

12 El tren es negro. El cielo es azul. Las montañas son verdes. ¡Dios mío! Es la una. Basta de colores. Tengo hambre. ¿No tiene Ud. hambre?

13 Sí. También yo tengo hambre.

14 Bueno. No lejos de aquí hay un buen restaurante.

15 Pues, ¡vámonos!

1 The office of Mrs. Adams is on the fifth floor of a tall building. It is not large, but it is very comfortable. There are two large windows that face the street. On the grey walls there are some posters of Spain in bright colours and a map of Spain.

2 On the desk of Mrs. Adams there are many papers. Near the door is a small desk with a typewriter, a computer and a calculator. Between the two windows there is a long table. On the table there are newspapers and magazines and a pretty ashtray.

3 Mrs. Adams, who is seated behind her desk when Mr. López enters the office, gets up and goes to greet him.
4 Good afternoon, Mr. López. I am very glad to see you.
5 The pleasure is mine. How are you?
6 Very well, thank you.
7 Your office is beautiful. I like this map of Spain and these posters very much. What pretty colours! By the way, Mrs. Adams, what do you see on that poster?
8 I see the sky and the sun, some mountains, a train and white houses with red roofs.
9 What colour is the sun?
10 It is yellow and very large.
11 What colours are the mountains, the sky and the train?
12 The train is black. The sky is blue. The mountains are green. My goodness! It's one o'clock. Enough of colours. I am hungry. Aren't you hungry?
13 Yes, I am also hungry.
14 Not far from here there is a good restaurant.
15 Well, let's go!

Pronunciation Aids

1 Practise:

edificio (e-ði-'fi-θjo)
periódicos (pe-'rjo-ði-kos)
revistas (rre-'vis-tas) or
  (rre-'βis-tas)
muchísimo (mu-'tʃi-si-mo)

propósito (pro-'po-si-to)
amarillo (a-ma-'ri-ʎo)
basta ('bas-ta)
cenicero (θe-ni-'θe-ro)
máquina ('ma-ki-na)

2 **qué, cuándo** and other question words drop the accent mark when they are not used as question words. Thus: **La Sra. Adams, que está sentada cuando el Sr. López entra en la sala, se levanta.**

Building Vocabulary

A. Common Descriptive Adjectives

amarillo	yellow	**simpático**	nice
azul	blue	**alto**	high, tall
blanco	white	**bajo**	low
negro	black	**grande**	big
gris	grey	**pequeño**	little
rojo	red	**corto**	short
verde	green	**largo**	long
vivo	lively	**pobre**	poor
enfermo	ill	**rico**	rich

bueno	good	fácil	easy
malo	bad	difícil	hard, difficult
barato	cheap	cómodo	comfortable
caro	dear	inteligente	intelligent
bonito	pretty	importante	important
hermoso	beautiful	interesante	interesting

B. **-ísimo** This ending means *very*. Thus:

1 muchísimo	very much	4 hermosísimo	very beautiful
2 altísimo	very high	5 larguísimo	very long
3 pobrísimo	very poor	6 bonísimo	very good

Expresiones Importantes

1 **dan a la calle** they face the street. The usual meaning of **dan** is *they give*.

2 **¿Tiene Ud. hambre?** Are you hungry? (*Lit.* Have you hunger?) **Tengo hambre.** I am hungry. (*Lit.* I have hunger.)

3 **a propósito** by the way.

4 **¿De qué color es el papel?** What colour (*Lit.* of what colour) is the paper?

5 Expressions of Liking. In Spanish the idea of liking is expressed by means of the verb **gustar** *to be pleasing to*. The person *to whom* something is pleasing, begins the sentence. The thing which is pleasing follows the verb. Thus: **Me gusta el libro.** I like the book. (*Lit. To me* is pleasing the book.) **Me gustan los carteles.** I like the posters. (*Lit. To me* are pleasing the posters.)

Exercise No. 21—Completion of Text

1 **Dos ventanas** (face the street).

2 **En la mesa hay** (newspapers).

3 **La Sra. Adams está sentada** (behind her desk).

4 **El Sr. López** (enters the office).

5 (I'm very glad to see you).

6 (The pleasure is mine).

7 (I like = to me is pleasing) **este mapa.**

8 (By the way), **¿ve Ud. ese cartel?**

9 (I see) **el cielo y el sol.**

10 **¿**(What colour) **es el sol?**

11 **¿**(What colours) **son las montañas?**

12 (My goodness!) **Es la una.**

13 (I am hungry).

14 (Not far from here) **hay un restaurante.**

15 (Let's go!)

SEGUNDA PARTE

Grammar Notes

1 Agreement of Adjectives

Observe the position of the adjectives in the following examples and how they agree with the nouns they modify.

el hombre **bueno**	the good man
la mujer **buena**	the good woman
los hombres **buenos**	the good men
las mujeres **buenas**	the good women
el libro **azul**	the blue book
la casa **azul**	the blue house
los libros **azules**	the blue books
las casas **azules**	the blue houses

El edificio es **grande y hermoso.**	The building is large and beautiful.
La ciudad es **grande y hermosa.**	The city is large and beautiful.
Los edificios son **grandes y hermosos.**	The buildings are large and beautiful.
Las ciudades son **grandes y hermosas.**	The cities are large and beautiful.

(a) Adjectives agree with the nouns they modify in number and gender.

(b) Adjectives ending in -o change to -a in the feminine. (**bueno buena; hermoso hermosa**)

(c) Adjectives not ending in -o do not change in the feminine. (**grande grande; azul azul**)

(d) Adjectives, like nouns, form their plurals by adding -s if they end in a vowel (**bueno buenos; verde verdes**); and by adding -es if they end in a consonant. (**azul azules; gris grises**)

(e) Descriptive adjectives usually follow the noun. Adjectives of quantity precede it.

una mesa larga   a long table   **muchas hijas**   many daughters

2 More about the uses of **ser** and **estar.**

(a) You have learned:

ser is used in answer to such questions as *Who is? What is?*
¿Quién es el profesor? El Sr. López es el profesor.
¿Qué es esto? Es el retrato de mi esposo.
estar is used in expressions of place and health.
¿Dónde está la oficina? Está en la Calle de Oxford.
¿Cómo está su niño? Mi niño está enfermo.

(b) Study the following sentences and note:

ser is used with adjectives which indicate *lasting qualities*, that is, qualities not likely to change, such as colour, size, shape, personal characteristics.

estar is used with adjectives which indicate *non-lasting qualities*, that is, qualities quite subject to change. Among these are adjectives of health.

Adjectives with **ser** (*Lasting Qualities*)	Adjectives with **estar** (*Non-lasting Qualities*)
1 **La oficina es pequeña.**	1 **La cocina está caliente** (*hot*).
2 **Los libros son azules.**	2 **La sala está fría** (*cold*).
3 **La lección es fácil.**	3 **Estamos listos** (*ready*).
4 **Mis amigos son inteligentes.**	4 **¿Están Uds. contentos** (*happy*)?
5 **Las cestas son baratas.**	5 **Las ventanas están limpias** (*clean*).
6 **María es simpática.**	6 **El jarro está lleno** (*full*).
7 **El niño es bueno.**	7 **Estoy bueno (bien)** (*well*).
8 **Los cuartos no son malos.**	8 **Jorge está malo** (*ill*).

NOTE: **bueno** and **malo** go with **ser** when they mean *good* and *bad*.

NOTE: **bueno** and **malo** go with **estar** when they mean *well* and *sick*.

(c) **estar** is also used with adjectives indicating a finished action, like sentado seated; **escrito** written.

Los señores están sentados. La carta está escrita.

TERCERA PARTE

Ejercicios (Exercises) No. 22A–22B–22C

22A. Fill in the correct form of the adjective in parenthesis.

Ejemplo: Los colores de los carteles son *vivos*.

1 **Los colores de los carteles son** (lively).
2 **La oficina es** (comfortable).
3 **Veo las casas con tejados** (red).
4 **¿Dónde están las montañas** (green)?
5 **Los edificios de mi ciudad son muy** (high).
6 **Hay** (many) **carteles en la pared.**
7 **Las casas son** (white).
8 (Many) **ventanas dan a la calle.**
9 **El cielo es** (blue).
10 **Es una señorita muy** (nice).

22B. Fill in the correct form of **ser** or **estar** as needed.

1 **Los niños —— simpáticos.**
2 **Un coche —— en la esquina.**
3 **El color de los tejados —— rojo.**
4 **¿Cómo —— Ud.?**
5 **—— muy bien.**
6 **Mis niños —— enfermos.**
7 **Nosotros —— sentados en el comedor.**
8 **Nosotros —— los amigos de Felipe.**
9 **Los alumnos —— muy inteligentes.**
10 **¿—— muy altos los edificios?**

22C. Translate:

1 The office of Mrs. Adams is very nice.
2 The windows of the office are large.
3 Many papers are on the floor (**suelo**).
4 The roofs of the houses are red.
5 The sky is blue.
6 The mountains are green.
7 The building is very high.
8 How are you, Mrs. Adams?
9 I am very well, thank you.
10 The posters are beautiful.

Exercise No. 23—Preguntas

Answer in complete Spanish sentences.

1 ¿Dónde está la oficina de la Sra. Adams?
2 ¿Es grande la oficina?
3 ¿Es cómoda la oficina?
4 ¿Dónde hay algunos carteles de España?
5 ¿Dónde están muchos papeles?
6 ¿Dónde está el escritorio pequeño?
7 ¿Qué hay entre las dos ventanas?
8 ¿Quién está sentado?
9 ¿De qué color es el sol en el cartel?
10 ¿De qué color es el tren?
11 ¿De qué color son las montañas?
12 ¿Es azul el cielo?
13 ¿De qué color son las casas?
14 ¿Son rojos los tejados?
15 ¿De quién (whose) es la oficina?

CHAPTER 9

UN AMIGO VISITA LA OFICINA DE LA SEÑORA ADAMS

PRIMERA PARTE

1 El señor Gómez, amigo de la señora Adams, es un habitante de Londres. Sin embargo habla bien el español, porque sus padres son españoles. Es un caballero de treinta y cinco años de edad.

2 Sabe que su amiga la Sra. Adams aprende el español. Desea saber cómo adelanta su amiga. Por eso entra un día en la oficina de la señora Adams y le saluda en español. Sigue la conversación.

3 ¿Qué tal, Juana?

4 Muy bien, gracias. ¿Y Ud.?

5 Así, así. A propósito, ¿Ud. aprende el español, verdad?

6 ¿Cómo no? Aprendo a hablar, a leer y a escribir el español.

7 ¿Es difícil el español?

8 Pues no, no es difícil. Me gusta la lengua y estudio mucho.

9 ¿Quién es su profesor de español?

10 El señor López. Es un maestro muy bueno, y día por día hablo, leo y escribo mejor. Aprendo las palabras y las expresiones de la vida diaria. Yo comprendo al señor López cuando él habla español, y él me[1] comprende cuando yo hablo la lengua. Me gusta mucho el español.

11 Amiga mía, Ud. habla estupendamente bien.

12 Es favor que Ud. me hace.

13 No es favor. Es verdad. Mis amigos me dicen que Ud. va a hacer un viaje a España el verano que viene.[2]

14 Espero ir en primavera, el 31 de mayo. Voy a viajar por avión. Quiero llegar a España cuanto antes.

15 ¡Buen viaje! ¡Y buena suerte! Hasta luego, amiga mía.

16 Hasta la vista.

1 Mr. Gómez, a friend of Mrs. Adams, is an inhabitant of London. Nevertheless he speaks Spanish well because his parents are Spanish. He is a gentleman of thirty-five.

2 He knows that his friend Mrs. Adams is learning Spanish. He wants to find out how his friend is progressing. Therefore he enters the office of Mrs. Adams one day and greets her in Spanish. The conversation follows.

3 How are things, Jane?

4 Very well, thank you. And you?

5 So, so. By the way, you are learning Spanish, aren't you?

6 Of course! I am learning to speak, read and write Spanish.

7 Is Spanish difficult?

8 Well no, it's not difficult. I like the language and I study very hard.

9 Who is your Spanish teacher?

10 Mr. López. He is a very good teacher and day by day I speak, read and write better. I learn the words and expressions of daily life. I understand Mr. López when he speaks Spanish, and he understands me when I speak it. I like Spanish very much.

11 My friend, you speak wonderfully well.

12 You are very kind.

13 Not at all. It is the truth. My friends tell me that you are going to take a trip to Spain this coming summer.

14 I hope to go in the Spring, on the 31st of May. I am going to travel by plane. I want to arrive in Spain as soon as possible.

15 Happy voyage! And good luck! Good-bye, friend.

16 So long.

NOTE: 1. **me** *me*. Object pronouns usually precede the verb. 2. *Lit*. The summer which is coming.

Pronunciation Aids

habitante (a-βi-ˈtan-te)
adelanta (a-ðe-ˈlan-ta)
conversación (kon-ver-sa-ˈθjon)
  or (kom-ber-sa-ˈθjon)
diligentemente
  (ði-li-ˈxen-te-ˈmen-te)
expresiones (es-pre-ˈsjo-nes)

estupendamente
  (es-tu-ˈpen-da-ˈmen-te)
fácil (ˈfa-θil)
difícil (ði-ˈfi-θil)
buena (ˈbwe-na)
suerte (ˈswer-te)
buen viaje (ˈbwem ˈbja-xe)

Building Vocabulary

A. Palabras Relacionadas (Related Words)

1 **habitar**	to inhabit	**el habitante**	the inhabitant
2 **conversar**	to converse	**la conversación**	the conversation
3 **estudiar**	to study	**el estudiante**	the student
		el estudio	the study
4 **comprender**	to comprehend	**la comprensión**	the comprehension
5 **viajar**	to travel	**el viaje**	the voyage
		el viajero	the traveller

B. More Adverbs ending in -mente

1 **diligentemente**	diligently	4 **seguramente**	surely
2 **estupendamente**	wonderfully	5 **ciertamente**	certainly
3 **rápidamente**	rapidly	6 **posiblemente**	possibly

Expresiones Importantes

1	**sin embargo**	nevertheless	4 **¿cómo no?**	of course, why not?
2	**por eso**	therefore	5 **día por día**	day by day
3	**¿qué tal?**	how goes it?	6 **cuanto antes**	as soon as possible

7 **¿verdad?, ¿no es verdad?** is it not true? Translated in various ways, such as: Isn't he, she, it? Aren't you? etc.

8 **el verano que viene** the coming summer (*Lit.* the summer which is coming).

Exercise No. 24—Completion of Text

1 (His parents) **son españoles.**
2 **Su amigo** (is progressing).
3 **Cuando el Sr. Gómez entra, dice — ¿** (How goes it?)?
4 (By the way), **Ud. aprende el español,** ¿(aren't you)?
5 (Of course).
6 (I am learning) **a hablar, a leer y a escribir el español.**
7 **Es** (easy). **No es** (difficult).
8 (I am studying) **diligentemente, porque** (I want) **ir a España.**
9 **Cuando él habla, yo** (understand).
10 **¿Aprende Ud. las** (words) **de la vida** (daily)?
11 **Sí, y aprendo también las** (expressions).
12 (I like = to me is pleasing) **la lengua.**

SEGUNDA PARTE

Grammar Notes

1 Present Tense of **aprender** and **vivir.** Model **-er** and **-ir** Verbs.

Singular		Plural	
aprend-o	I learn	**aprend-emos**	we learn
aprend-es	you learn (*fam.*)	**aprend-éis**	you learn (*fam.*)
Ud. aprend-e	you learn	**Uds. aprend-en**	you learn
aprend-e	he, she, it learns	**aprend-en**	they learn
viv-o	I live	**viv-imos**	we live
viv-es	you live (*fam.*)	**viv-is**	you live (*fam.*)
Ud. viv-e	you live	**Uds. viv-en**	you live
viv-e	he, she, it lives	**viv-en**	they live

(a) The endings of **aprender** are like the endings of **hablar,** except that the letter **-e** replaces the letter **-a.**

The endings of **aprender** are the same as those of **vivir,** except in the **nosotros** (*we*) and **vosotros** (*you, fam.*) forms.

(b) Some common -er and -ir verbs like **aprender** and **vivir.**

beber	to drink	**abrir**	to open
comer	to eat	**escribir**	to write
comprender	to understand	**dividir**	to divide
leer	to read	**recibir**	to receive
responder	to answer	**permitir**	to permit
ver[1]	to see	**prohibir**	to prohibit

NOTE: The present tense of **ver**: Sing. **veo, ves, ve.** Plur. **vemos, veis, ven.**

2 Verbs followed by an Infinitive with **a.**

Va a hacer un viaje.	He is going to make a trip.
Aprende a leer.	He learns to read.
Empieza a hablar.	He begins to speak.
Comenzamos a comer.	We begin to eat.

After the verbs **ir, aprender, comenzar,** and **principiar,** a complementary infinitive must be preceded by **a.**

TERCERA PARTE (THIRD PART)

Ejercicios (Exercises) No. 25A–25B

25A. Practise these short dialogues aloud. They will give you a 'feeling' for the correct use of verbs in the present tense.

1 ¿Aprenden Uds. el español?
Sí, aprendemos el español.
¿Aprende Carlos el español?
No aprende el español.
2 ¿Escribe Ud. una carta?
No escribo una carta.
¿Qué escribe Ud.?
Escribo los ejercicios.
3 ¿Qué lee Ud.?
Leo el periódico.
¿Qué lee Ana?
Ella lee una revista.

4 ¿Quién abre la puerta?
La criada abre la puerta.
¿Quién entra en la casa?
El Sr. López entra en la casa.
5 ¿Qué ve Ud.?
Veo el mapa.
¿Ve Ud. los carteles?
No veo los carteles.
6 ¿Dónde viven Uds.?
Vivimos en Londres.
¿Dónde viven los españoles?
Viven en España.

25B. Fill in the missing endings. -ar, -er and -ir verbs are included in this exercise.

Ejemplo: Aprendo el español.

1 (Yo) aprend— el español.
2 El señor López toc— el timbre.
3 (Nosotros) estudi— diligentemente.
4 (Ellos) no comprend— al maestro.
5 ¿Le— Uds. los periódicos?
6 Los niños beb— leche.

7 ¿Escrib— Ud. los ejercicios?   11 (Ellas) no viaj— en la prima-
8 ¿Viv— (ella) en la ciudad?   vera.
9 Niño, ¿por qué no beb— la leche? 12 La criada abr— la puerta.
10 Papa, ¿quier— (tú) la revista?

Exercise No. 26—Preguntas

1 ¿Quién es un habitante de Londres?
2 ¿Habla el Sr. Gómez bien el español?
3 ¿Son sus padres ingleses?
4 ¿Qué sabe el señor Gómez?
5 ¿En dónde entra un día?
6 ¿A quién saluda el Sr. Gómez en español?
7 ¿Quién aprende a hablar, a leer y a escribir el español?
8 ¿Cómo estudia la Sra. Adams?
9 ¿Quién es su profesor de español?
10 ¿Es un buen profesor?
11 ¿Comprende la señora Adams cuando el profesor habla español?
12 ¿Qué clase de (what kind of) palabras aprende la señora Adams?
13 ¿Quién va a hacer un viaje a España?
14 ¿Cuándo espera ir a España?
15 ¿Quién dice — Buen viaje y buena suerte?

REVISION 2

CHAPTERS 6–9 PRIMERA PARTE

Repaso de Palabras

NOUNS

1 el año	11 la manera	21 el restaurante
2 el avión	12 el mapa	22 la revista
3 el caballero	13 la montaña	23 el sol
4 el cartel	14 la noche	24 la suerte
5 la criada	15 el país	25 la tarde
6 el cielo	16 el parque	26 el tejado
7 la escuela	17 el periódico	27 la verdad
8 el estudiante	18 la plaza	28 el viaje
9 el habitante	19 la pregunta	29 la vida
10 la lección	20 la respuesta	30 el vuelo

1 year	11 manner	21 restaurant
2 aeroplane	12 map	22 magazine
3 gentleman	13 mountain	23 sun
4 poster	14 night	24 luck
5 servant (*f*)	15 country	25 afternoon, evening
6 sky	16 park	26 roof
7 school	17 newspaper	27 truth
8 student	18 square	28 voyage
9 inhabitant	19 question	29 life
10 lesson	20 answer	30 flight

VERBS

1 aceptar	14 pasar	27 responder
2 adelantar	15 practicar	28 tener
3 comenzar	16 preguntar	29 saber
4 contestar	17 saludar	30 ver
5 desear	18 tocar	31 abrir
6 empezar	19 trabajar	32 escribir
7 entrar(en)	20 viajar	33 ir
8 escuchar	21 visitar	34 pedir
9 esperar	22 aprender	35 seguir
10 estudiar	23 beber	36 salir (de)
11 hablar	24 comprender	37 salgo
12 invitar	25 hacer	38 no sé
13 llegar	26 leer	39 voy a

1 to accept	8 to listen	15 to practice
2 to progress	9 to expect	16 to ask
3 to begin	10 to study	17 to greet
4 to answer	11 to speak	18 to play (instrument)
5 to want	12 to invite	19 to work
6 to begin	13 to arrive	20 to travel
7 to enter	14 to pass	21 to visit

22 to learn	28 to have	34 to ask for
23 to drink	29 to know	35 to follow
24 to understand	30 to see	36 to leave, go out of
25 to make	31 to open	37 I leave
26 to read	32 to write	38 I do not know
27 to answer	33 to go	39 I am going to

ADJECTIVES

1 alto	10 difícil	19 listo
2 amarillo	11 enfermo	20 limpio
3 azul	12 fácil	21 lleno
4 bajo	13 frío	22 próximo
5 barato	14 gris	23 rápido
6 caro	15 hermoso	24 rico
7 caliente	16 importante	25 rojo
8 cómodo	17 inteligente	26 sucio
9 corriente	18 largo	27 verde

1 high	10 difficult	19 ready
2 yellow	11 ill	20 clean
3 blue	12 easy	21 full
4 low	13 cold	22 next
5 cheap	14 grey	23 rapid
6 dear	15 beautiful	24 rich
7 hot	16 important	25 red
8 comfortable	17 intelligent	26 dirty
9 common	18 long	27 green

ADVERBS

| 1 alto | 3 hoy | 5 tampoco |
| 2 despacio | 4 tan | 6 demasiado |

| 1 loudly | 3 today | 5 neither |
| 2 slowly | 4 such, so | 6 too much |

PREPOSITIONS

| 1 para | 3 lejos de | 5 menos |
| 2 sin | 4 por | 6 cerca de |

| 1 for, in order to | 3 far from | 5 except |
| 2 without | 4 for, by, through | 6 near |

NOTE: The uses of **por** and **para** offer some difficulty in Spanish. You can best get a feeling for their correct use by memorizing **por** and **para** phrases as you meet them. Thus: **por favor; basta por hoy; para visitar** (in order to visit). **Sale para España.** He leaves for Spain.

In general **para** is used to indicate *purpose, destination*, **por** is used to indicate *price* (**por peso**); *duration of time* (**por dos meses**); *through* (**por la calle**).

QUESTION WORDS

| 1 quién | 3 a quién | 5 de quién |
| 2 cuál | 4 cuáles | 6 cuándo |

| 1 who | 3 whom, to whom | 5 of whom, whose |
| 2 which (one) | 4 which (ones) | 6 when |

CONJUNCTIONS

1 pues	2 si	3 cuando	4 porque
1 well	2 if	3 when	4 because

IMPORTANT EXPRESSIONS

1 Buena suerte	14 mucho gusto en verle
2 Buen viaje	15 lo siento mucho
3 a propósito	16 pedir información
4 ¿cómo no?	17 en tren
5 con su permiso	18 en barco
6 con mucho gusto	19 en avión
7 ¿Cuánto cuesta?	20 ¿qué tal?
8 ¿Cuántos años tiene Ud.?	21 tengo hambre
9 Tengo quince (15) años	22 sin embargo
10 ¿de qué color?	23 sobre todo
11 ¿(no es) verdad?	24 vámonos
12 hacer un viaje	25 un rato más
13 hacer preguntas	

1 good luck	14 very glad to see you
2 Happy voyage	15 I am very sorry
3 by the way	16 to ask for information
4 of course, why not?	17 by train
5 if you please, with your permission	18 by boat
6 with great pleasure	19 by aeroplane
7 How much does it cost?	20 how are things?
8 How old are you?	21 I am hungry
9 I am 15 years old	22 nevertheless
10 what colour?	23 especially
11 isn't it so?	24 let's go
12 to take a trip	25 a while longer
13 to ask questions	

SEGUNDA PARTE

Ejercicio 27   Give the Spanish words that correspond to these English words. The ending *-tion* becomes *-ción*.

Ejemplo: prevention prevención

1 civilization	4 exception	7 invitation	9 invention
2 reservation	5 revolution	8 election	10 solution
3 instruction	6 observation		

Ejercicio 28   Answer each of the following questions in complete sentences, using the suggested words in the answer.

Ejemplo: ¿De qué color es el jarro? (azul.) El jarro es azul, or Es azul.

1 ¿De qué color es el cielo? (azul)
2 ¿Qué lengua hablan los españoles? (español)
3 ¿Quién tiene hambre? (La Sra. Adams)

4 ¿De qué color es la revista? (blanc- y negr-)
5 ¿Dónde vive Ud.? (en Gran Bretaña)
6 ¿De qué color son los tejidos? (roj-)
7 ¿Qué beben los niños? (leche)
8 ¿A quién saluda la Sra. Adams? (a su amigo)
9 ¿Cuántos años tiene Ud.? (treinta años)
10 ¿Cómo se llama Ud.? (your own name)

Ejercicio 29 Select the words in Column II which best complete the sentence begun in Column I.

I

1 No comprendo bien al profesor
2 El señor dice — Con su permiso —
3 Si Ud. no sabe la respuesta
4 El profesor dice — Lo siento mucho
5 Vamos por avión porque
6 Si estudiamos mucho
7 Cuando tengo hambre
8 Las ventanas de la oficina
9 El amigo saluda a la señora Adams y dice —
10 No sé cuánto cuesta

II

(a) diga — no sé.
(b) es el modo más rápido.
(c) voy al restaurante.
(d) dan a la calle.
(e) cuando habla rápidamente.
(f) el vuelo a España.
(g) cuando pasa delante de una persona.
(h) vamos a adelantar día por día.
(i) porque la niña está enferma.
(j) Mucho gusto en verle.

Ejercicio 30 Complete each verb with the correct ending.

1 nosotros trabaj ——
2 ellos aprend ——
3 él empiez ——
4 Ud. sab ——
5 Uds. escrib ——
6 tú abr ——
7 yo permit ——
8 Ud. beb ——
9 nosotros adelant ——
10 yo ve ——

Ejercicio 31 Answer each of the following questions in the affirmative:

Ejemplo: ¿Habla Ud. inglés? Sí, hablo inglés.

1 ¿Aprende Ud. el español?
2 ¿Estudia Ud. la lección?
3 ¿Trabaja Ud. diligentemente?
4 ¿Espera Ud. viajar?

5 ¿Ve Ud. los carteles?
6 ¿Lee Ud. el periódico?
7 ¿Comprende Ud. la pregunta?

8 ¿Acepta Ud. la invitación?
9 ¿Visita Ud. al maestro?

Ejercicio 32 Complete with the correct forms of **ser** or **estar**. (See grammar notes 2a, b, c, page 54.)

1 El padre (is) **profesor.**
2 ¿Cómo (are) **Ud.?**
3 (I am) **enfermo.**
4 (We are) **contentos.**
5 La casa (is) **blanca.**
6 (He is) **sentado.**
7 Los niños (are) **listos.**
8 Ella (is) **inteligente.**

9 Los muchachos (are) **simpáticos.**
10 La sala (is) **fría.**
11 (They are) **importantes.**
12 Tú (are) **bonito, niño.**
13 Ud. (are) **alto.**
14 Uds. no (are) **ricos.**
15 (I am) **bien.**

TERCERA PARTE

Diálogo 1

Practise the Spanish aloud:

¿Quién es Ud.?

1 ¿Cómo se llama Ud.?
2 Me llamo Carlos Sánchez.
3 ¿Cuántos años tiene Ud.?
4 Tengo veinte años.
5 ¿Dónde vive Ud.?
6 Vivo en la Calle de Toledo 50.
7 ¿Dónde trabaja Ud.?
8 Trabajo en la casa Velarde y Cía (Compañía).

Who are You?

1 What is your name?
2 My name is Charles Sánchez.
3 How old are you?
4 I am 20 years old.
5 Where do you live?
6 I live at 50 Toledo St.
7 Where do you work?
8 I work for the firm, Velarde and Co.

Diálogo 2

¿Qué autobús tomo?

1 Ud. perdone, senõr, ¿qué autobús tomo para la Plaza de Colón (para el parque) (para el centro)? etc.
2 Tome Ud. este autobús. Para aquí mismo en la esquina.
3 Muchas gracias, señor.
4 De nada.

What Bus Do I Take?

1 Excuse me, sir, what bus do I take for Columbus Square (for the park) (for the centre)? etc.
2 Take this bus. It stops right here on the corner.
3 Thank you very much, sir.
4 You're welcome.

Diálogo 3
¿Qué autobús va a . . . ?

1 Dispénseme or Perdone señor, ¿me hace el favor de decirme qué autobús va al museo del Prado (al Palacio Real) (a la Plaza Mayor)? etc.
2 No sé, señor. Pero aquel policía en la esquina puede decirle, estoy seguro.
3 Muchas gracias, señor. Voy a preguntarle.

What bus Goes to . . .?

1 Excuse me, sir, would you please tell me, what bus goes to the Prado Museum (to the Royal Palace) (to the Main Square)?
2 I do not know, sir. But that policeman on the corner can tell you, I am sure.
3 Thank you very much, sir. I am going to ask him.

LECTURA 1
Follow the instructions given in Exercise No. 14.

Exercise No. 33—Dos amigos de la señora Adams

La señora Adams ya sabe los nombres de todos los objetos de su casa. Ahora empieza a estudiar los verbos porque desea aprender a leer, a escribir y a conversar en español. También desea saber los números en español. Siendo (being) una comerciante que espera visitar a su agente en España, necesita (she needs) la práctica de charlar (chatting) con españoles o hispanoamericanos. Afortunadamente (Luckily) tiene dos amigos que son de España y que trabajan cerca de su oficina en la calle de Oxford.

Un día la señora Adams va a visitar a estos (these) españoles. Los dos señores escuchan con atención a la señora Adams mientras (while) habla con ellos en español. Después de (After) diez minutos de conversación, los españoles hacen muchas preguntas a su (their) amiga y están muy contentos (pleased) de sus (her) respuestas.

Exercise No. 34—La Sra. Adams se pone enferma (falls ill)

El jueves, diez y ocho de abril, a las nueve de la mañana, llega (arrives) el señor López[1] a la casa de su alumna, la señora Adams. El hijo mayor, un muchacho de diez años, abre la puerta y saluda al profesor. Entran en la sala donde la señora Adams generalmente espera a su profesor.

Pero esta (this) tarde no está en la sala. Tampoco (Neither) está allí el señor Adams. El señor López está muy sorprendido (surprised) y pregunta al muchacho — ¿Dónde está tu mamá? El hijo responde tristemente, — Mi mamá está enferma y no puede (cannot) salir de su dormitorio. Está en cama (bed) porque tiene un fuerte (severe) catarro. También tiene dolor de cabeza (headache).

El profesor se pone (becomes) muy triste y dice, — ¡Qué lástima! (What a pity!) Hoy no es posible dar la clase, pero la semana próxima vamos a estudiar dos horas. Hasta el martes próximo.

NOTE: 1. Quite frequently the subject is placed after the verb in Spanish, even when the sentence is not a question. Thus: **llega la Sra. Adams = la Sra. Adams llega.** Watch out for this inverted word order.

CHAPTER 10

EN EL COMEDOR

PRIMERA PARTE

1 La señora Adams y el señor López están sentados en el comedor de la casa Adams. Toman café y pastas.

2 Dice la señora Adams — ¿Le gustan estas tazas y estos platillos?

3 — ¡Qué bonitos son! — contesta el señor López. — Son de México, ¿verdad?

4 — Sí, contesta la señora Adams. Esta taza blanca con dibujos azules es de Talavera. Este tipo de cerámica se llama Talavera de la Reina. Es conocida en todas partes. Es interesante ver que cada distrito tiene su propio estilo de cerámica.

5 ¿De dónde es ese jarro verde y blanco?

6 Este jarro para crema es de México. Mire Ud. los dibujos de pájaros y flores. Ese otro para agua es de Michoacán.[1]

7 Ya sabe Ud., señora Adams, que los indios de México son verdaderos artistas. Trabajan despacio. Como cualquier artista, no tienen prisa.

8 Sí, quiero importar estos objetos de arte, pero es difícil hoy día obtener un surtido adecuado para el mercado británico.

9 — Pobre artista, — dice el señor López. — Para aquel mercado lejano tiene que trabajar de prisa. Así no es fácil mantener la calidad artística.

10 — Es verdad, — responde la señora Adams. — Pero de todos modos veo mucha cerámica de interés artístico.

11 — ¡Ya lo creo! — contesta el señor López. — Me gustan mucho aquellos platos fruteros en el aparador. ¡Qué finos son los dibujos amarillos y azules sobre el fondo blanco!

12 Tengo también ejemplares de cerámica corriente. Es muy sencilla. Como ese plato cerca de Ud., muchas veces es de color café.

13 — Es para usarlo, — dice el señor López. — Pero también tiene dibujos.

14 ¿Quiere Ud. más café? ¿No quiere Ud. también esa torta?

15 — Gracias. Todo está muy sabroso, — contesta el señor López.

1 Mrs. Adams and Mr. López are seated in the dining-room of the Adams' house. They are having coffee and cakes.

2 Mrs. Adams says: 'Do you like these cups and saucers?'

3 'How pretty they are!' answers Mr. López. 'They are from Mexico, aren't they?'

4 'Yes,' replies Mrs. Adams. 'This white cup with the blue designs is from Talavera. This kind of pottery is called Talavera de la Reina. It is known everywhere. It is interesting to see that each district has its own style of pottery.'

5 Where does that green and white jug come from?

6 This cream jug is from Mexico. Look at the designs of birds and flowers. That other one for water is from Michoacán.[1]

7 You already know, Mrs. Adams, that the Indians of Mexico are true artists. They work slowly. Like any artist, they are not in a hurry.

8 Yes, I want to import these art objects, but it is hard nowadays to obtain an adequate assortment for the British market.

9 'Poor artist,' says Mr. López. 'For that distant market he has to work fast. Thus it is not easy to maintain artistic quality.'

10 'It is true,' answers Mrs. Adams. 'But anyway, I see a lot of pottery of artistic interest.'

11 'I should say so!' answers Mr. López. 'I very much like those fruit dishes on the sideboard. How fine the yellow and blue designs are on the white background!'

12 I also have samples of ordinary pottery. It is very simple. Like that plate near you, it is often brown.

13 'It is for use,' says Mr. López. 'But it also has designs.'

14 Do you want more coffee? Do you not want that cake, too?

15 'Thank you. Everything is very tasty,' answers Mr. López.

NOTE: 1. These are names of Indian origin, hence the exceptional pronunciation.

Pronunciation Aids

1 Practise:

platillo (pla-'ti-ʎo)   aparador (a-pa-ra-'ðor)
dibujo (ði-'βu-xo)   cucharita (ku:tʃa-'ri-ta)
cerámica (θe-'ra-mi-ka)   lejano (le-'xa-no)
conocido (ko-no-'θi-ðo)   sencillo (sen-'θi-ʎo)
pájaro ('pa-xa-ro)   Michoacán[1] (Mi-tʃwa-'kan)
azucarero (a-θu-ka-'re-ro)   Oaxaca[1] (wa-'xa-ka)
artesano (ar-te-'sa-no)

2 Exclamations begin with a reversed exclamation mark.

¡Qué finos son los dibujos!   How fine the designs are!

3 When a feminine noun begins with a stressed **a** the masculine article **el** is used for the sake of the sound. Thus: **el** agua, but **las** aguas; **el** arte, **las** artes

Building Vocabulary

A. En el Comedor   In the Dining-Room

el aparador	buffet	**el jarro para crema**	cream jug
el azucarero	sugar-bowl	**el jarro para agua**	water jug
la cuchara	spoon	**el plato**	plate
la cucharita	teaspoon	**el platillo**	saucer
el cuchillo	knife	**el sillón**	armchair
la mesa	table	**el vaso**	glass

B. The endings -ito, -ita, -illo, -illa, added to a noun, have the meaning *small*. They are also used to indicate affection, friendliness, sympathy, or informality. The Spaniards are very fond of these endings and use them even on adjectives and adverbs.

cuchara	spoon	**Ana**	Anna
cucharita	little (tea)spoon	**Anita**	Annie
plato	plate	**Juan**	John
platillo	saucer	**Juanito**	Johnny, Jack
hijo (a)	son, daughter		
hijito (a)	sonny, little girl		

Expresiones Importantes

1	**cada artista**	each artist
2	**de todos modos**	anyway
3	**hoy día**	nowadays
4	**muchas veces**	many times, often
5	**por todas partes**	everywhere
6	**tener que**	to have to
7	**tiene que trabajar**	he has to work
8	**tener prisa**	to be in a hurry
9	**tengo prisa**	I am in a hurry
10	**¡Ya lo creo!**	Of course! I should say so!

Exercise No. 35—Completion of Text

1 (They are having) **café y pastas.**
2 **¡Qué bonitos son estos** (designs)!
3 **Este tipo de cerámica es conocido** (everywhere).
4 (Each) **distrito tiene su** (own) **estilo.**
5 **Este jarro es** (for cream).
6 **Ese otro es** (for water).
7 **Cualquier artista trabaja** (slowly).
8 (He has to) **trabajar de prisa.**
9 **Pero** (anyway) **veo mucha cerámica.**

10 (I have) **ejemplares de cerámica corriente.**
11 **Ese plato es** (very simple).
12 (Often) **es de color café.**
13 **Es** (for use), **pero tiene dibujos.**
14 ¿(Do you wish) **más café?**
15 ¿(Do you not wish) **esta torta?**

SEGUNDA PARTE

Grammar Notes

1 The Demonstrative Adjectives. Note the forms and meanings of **este, ese,** and **aquel** in the following sentences.

Este jarro es de Puebla, México.	*This* jug is from Puebla, Mexico.
Esta taza es de Oaxaca, México.	*This* cup is from Oaxaca, Mexico.
Este jarro es de Puebla.	*These* jugs are from Puebla.
Esta taza es de Oaxaca.	*These* cups are from Oaxaca.
Ese plato es de Granada.	*That* plate is from Granada.
Esa cuchara es de Toledo.	*That* spoon is from Toledo.
Esos platos son de Granada.	*Those* plates are from Granada.
Esas cucharas son de Toledo.	*Those* spoons are from Toledo.
Mire Vd. **aquel** tejado rojo.	Look at *that* roof.
Mire Vd. **aquella** montaña alta.	Look at *that* high mountain.
Mire Vd. **aquellos** tejados rojos.	Look at *those* red roofs.
Mire Vd. **aquellas** montañas altas.	Look at *those* high mountains.

(a) Demonstrative adjectives agree in number and gender with the nouns they modify.

(b) **ese, esa, esos, esas** (*that, those*) are used to point out persons or things near the persons spoken to. **aquel, aquella, aquellos, aquellas** (*that, those*) are used to point out distant persons or things.

2 Present Tense of **tener** to have, **venir** to come.

	Singular			Plural	
	tengo	I have		**tenemos**	we have
	tienes (*fam.*)	you have		**tenéis**	you have (*fam.*)
Ud.	**tiene**⎱	you have	Uds.	**tienen**⎱	you have
	tiene⎰	he, she, it has		**tienen**⎰	they have
	vengo	I come		**venimos**	we come
	vienes	you come (*fam.*)		**venís**	you come (*fam.*)
Ud.	**viene**⎱	you come	Uds.	**vienen**⎱	you come
	viene⎰	he, she, it comes		**vienen**⎰	they come

Memorize the proverb (**el refrán**): **Quién primero viene primero tiene.**
First come first served. (*Lit.* He who comes first, has first.)

TERCERA PARTE

Ejercicios (Exercises) No. 36A–36B–36C

36A. Complete with the correct form of **este, ese, aquel.** The abbreviation, *dist.* (*distant*) after *that* and *those*, means use the correct form of **aquel,** not of **ese.**

Ejemplo: **¿Ven Uds. aquellas montañas verdes?**

1 **¿Ven Uds.** (those-*dist.*) **montañas verdes?**
2 (This) **taza es de Puebla.**
3 (These) **señores toman café.**
4 (These) **sillas son nuevas.**
5 (Those) **revistas son muy interesantes.**
6 (Those) **dibujos son muy finos.**
7 (That-*dist.*) **casa es gris.**
8 (This) **retrato es de mi esposa.**
9 **Vamos a visitar** (those-*dist.*) **ciudades.**
10 (This) **camisa es de Juan.**
11 (That) **blusa es de María.**
12 **Me gustan** (these) **dibujos.**

36B. Read each question and answer aloud several times.

1 **¿Tiene Ud. que escribir una carta?**
Sí, tengo que escribir una carta.
2 **¿Tienen Uds. que hacer un viaje?**
No, no tenemos que hacer un viaje.
3 **¿Tienes hambre, hijito?**
Sí, tengo hambre.
4 **¿Tienes prisa, Carlitos?**
No, no tengo prisa.
5 **¿De dónde viene Ud.?**
Vengo del cine.
6 **¿De dónde vienen Uds.?**
Venimos del parque.

36C. Translate into Spanish:

1 These gentlemen are seated in the dining-room.
2 These cups are from Puebla.
3 I like **(me gustan)** these designs.
4 Those plates are from Oaxaca.
5 Do those (*dist.*) artists work slowly?
6 Has this family five-children?
7 Are you hungry, sonny?
8 No, I am not hungry.
9 Do you have to write a letter, Mrs. Adams?
10 Yes, I have to write a letter.

CUARTA PARTE

Exercise No. 37—Preguntas

Answer in complete Spanish sentences.

1 ¿Dónde están sentados la señora Adams y el señor López?
2 ¿Qué toman?
3 ¿Qué dice la Sra. Adams?
4 ¿De dónde es la taza blanca con dibujos azules?
5 ¿Tiene cada distrito su propio estilo?
6 ¿De dónde es el jarro para crema?
7 ¿De dónde es el jarro para agua?
8 ¿Son verdaderos artistas los indios?
9 ¿Cómo trabajan los artesanos indios, despacio o de prisa?
10 ¿Tienen prisa los artistas?
11 ¿Para qué mercado es difícil obtener un surtido adecuado?
12 ¿Quién ve mucha cerámica de interés artístico?
13 ¿Dónde están los platos fruteros?
14 ¿De qué color son los dibujos en los platos fruteros?
15 ¿Tiene la Sra. Adams ejemplares de cerámica corriente?

CHAPTER 11

NÚMEROS, NÚMEROS, SIEMPRE NÚMEROS

PRIMERA PARTE

1 Ya sabe Ud. que los nombres de cosas y de personas son importantes. Ya sabe Ud. que no es posible construir una frase sin verbos.

2 Es verdad, Sr. López.

3 Pues bien, hay palabras, Sra. Adams, que son tan importantes como los nombres y los verbos. En efecto, no es posible imaginar nuestra civilización moderna sin estas palabras. ¿Puede Ud. adivinar en qué pienso?

4 Creo que sí. Ud. quiere decir[1] los números, las cifras.

5 Tiene razón. ¿Puede Ud. enumerar algunas ocasiones en la vida moderna en que se necesitan números?

6 Naturalmente. Nada es más fácil. Necesitamos números para comprar y vender.

7 Una comerciante piensa primero en comprar y vender. Pero sin dinero no valen mucho los números ¿no es verdad?

8 Es verdad, necesitamos números para indicar la fecha, las horas del día, la temperatura; para expresar medidas y cantidades; para telefonear; para la radio; para la televisión; para todas las ciencias, y para mil cosas más.

9 Números, números, siempre números. Sí, Sra. Adams, no es posible pasar sin números. Pero una cosa es saber los números. Otra cosa es usarlos[2] y comprenderlos rápidamente y correctamente en la vida diaria.

10 Tiene Ud. razón. Yo voy a hacer todo lo posible para comprenderlos y usarlos perfectamente.

11 Entretanto quiero decirle que día por día adelanta Ud. mucho.

12 Es favor que Ud. me hace, señor López.

13 No es favor. Es verdad. Pues basta por hoy. Hasta luego.

14 Hasta el jueves próximo, señora Adams.

1 You already know that the names of things and of persons are important. You already know that it is not possible to build a sentence without verbs.

2 It's true, Mr. López.

3 Well, there are words, Mrs. Adams, that are as important as nouns and verbs. In fact, it is not possible to imagine our modern civilization without these words. Can you guess what I am thinking of?

4 I think so. You mean numbers, figures.

5 You are right. Can you enumerate some occasions in modern life that require numbers?

6 Certainly. Nothing is easier. We need numbers for buying and selling.

7 A businesswoman thinks first of buying and selling. But without money numbers are not worth much, are they?

8 That's true. Well, we need numbers to indicate the date, the time of day, the temperature; to express measures and quantities; to telephone; for the radio; for the television; for all the sciences, and for a thousand more things.

9 Numbers, numbers, always numbers. Yes, Mrs. Adams, it is not possible to do without numbers. But it is one thing to know numbers. It is another thing to use them and understand them rapidly and correctly in daily life.

10 You are right. I am going to do everything possible to understand them and use them perfectly.

11 Meanwhile I want to say that day by day you are making much progress.

12 You flatter me, Mr. López.

13 Not at all. It is the truth. Well, enough for today. Good-bye.

14 Until next Thursday, Mrs. Adams.

NOTE: 1. *Lit.* you wish to say. 2. **los** *them.* Pronouns which are objects of infinitives *follow* the verb and are attached to it.

Pronunciation Aids

1 Practise:

civilización (θi-vi-li-θa-'θjon) or
(θi-βi-li-θa-'θjon)
enumerar (e-nu-me-'rar)
necesitar (ne-θe-si-'tar)
adivinar (a-ði-vi-'nar) or
(a-ði-βi-'nar)

seguramente (se-ɣu-ra-'men-te)
temperatura (tem-pe-ra-tu-ra)
entretanto (en-tre-'tan-to)
ciencias ('θjen-θjas)
cantidades (kan-ti-'ða-ðes)
perfectamente (per-'fek-ta-'men-te)

Building Vocabulary

A. Palabras Relacionadas

1 **necesitar**	to need	**necesario**	necessary
		la necesidad	necessity
2 **enumerar**	to enumerate	**el número**	the number
		la enumeración	enumeration
3 **civilizar**	to civilize	**la civilización**	civilization
4 **indicar**	to indicate	**la indicación**	indication

B. **El día** and **el mapa** are exceptions to the rule that nouns ending in **a** are feminine.

Important Expressions

1	**basta por hoy**	enough for today
2	**Creo que sí**	I think so
3	**Creo que no**	I think not
4	**Tiene razón**	You are right
5	**en efecto**	in fact
6	**pensar en**	to think of
7	**pasar sin números**	to do without numbers
8	**no valen mucho**	are not worth much
9	**en la vida diaria**	in daily life
10	**todo lo posible**	everything possible

Exercise No. 38—Completion of Text

1 ¿(Do you know) **los números?**
2 **Hay palabras que son** (as important as) **los verbos.**
3 (Our civilization) **no es posible sin números.**
4 (You are right.)
5 ¿(Can you) **enumerar unas ocasiones en** (that) **se necesitan números?**
6 **Los números sin dinero** (are not worth) **mucho.**
7 (We need) **números para indicar** (the date).
8 **No es posible** (to get along) **sin números.**
9 (In the meantime) **quiero decir** (that) **adelanta Ud. mucho.**
10 ¿(What is the meaning of) **esta palabra?**

SEGUNDA PARTE

Grammar Notes

1 Verbs with Stem Changes—**pensar** to think, **querer** to wish, **contar** to count, **poder** to be able.

The stem of a verb is that part which remains after the infinitive ending -ar, -er or -ir has been removed. Note the stem changes in the following verbs. The endings are regular.

I think, etc.	I wish, etc.	I count, etc.	I am able, etc.
pienso	**quiero**	**cuento**	**puedo**
piensas	**quieres**	**cuentas**	**puedes**
piensa	**quiere**	**cuenta**	**puede**
pensamos	**queremos**	**contamos**	**podemos**
pensáis	**queréis**	**contáis**	**podéis**
piensan	**quieren**	**cuentan**	**pueden**

Many verbs have stem changes from e to ie, like **pensar** and **querer**. Many verbs have stem changes from o to ue, like **contar** and **poder**. They will be indicated in the vocabulary as follows: **pensar(ie), querer(ie), poder(ue), contar(ue)**.

NOTE: The stem changes do not occur in the **nosotros-as** (*we*) and the **vosotros-as** (*you, fam.*) forms.

2 Los Números Desde **uno (1) Hasta ciento (100)**

0	**cero**	23	**veinte y tres (veintitrés)**
1	**uno**	24	**veinte y cuatro (veinticuatro)**
2	**dos**	25	**veinte y cinco (veinticinco)**
3	**tres**	26	**veinte y seis (veintiséis)**
4	**cuatro**	27	**veinte y siete (veintisiete)**
5	**cinco**	28	**veinte y ocho (veintiocho)**
6	**seis**	29	**veinte y nueve (veintinueve)**
7	**siete**	30	**treinta**
8	**ocho**	31	**treinta y uno**
9	**nueve**	32	**treinta y dos**
10	**diez**	40	**cuarenta**
11	**once**	43	**cuarenta y tres**
12	**doce**	50	**cincuenta**
13	**trece**	54	**cincuenta y cuatro**
14	**catorce**	60	**sesenta**
15	**quince**	65	**sesenta y cinco**
16	**diez y seis (dieciséis)**	70	**setenta**
17	**diez y siete (diecisiete)**	76	**setenta y seis**
18	**diez y ocho (dieciocho)**	80	**ochenta**
19	**diez y nueve (diecinueve)**	87	**ochenta y siete**
20	**veinte**	90	**noventa**
21	**veinte y uno (veintiuno)**	99	**noventa y nueve**
22	**veinte y dos (veintidós)**	100	**ciento**
			cien (before a noun)

(a) Before a masculine noun **uno** becomes **un**. Before a feminine noun **uno** becomes **una**.

> **un** amigo **una** amiga veinte y **un** amigos, **veintiún** amigos
> veinte y **una** amigas

(b) Like any other adjective, **cuánto** (sing. *how much*, plur. *how many*) must agree with the noun it modifies: **cuánto dinero, cuánta tinta** (ink), **cuántos niños, cuántas niñas**.

TERCERA PARTE

Ejercicios (Exercises) No. 39A–39B–39C–39D

39A. Read aloud, saying the numbers in Spanish:

Ejemplo: treinta palabras españolas

1 30 palabras españolas	7 17 casas blancas
2 10 lecciones fáciles	8 15 niños bonitos
3 50 personas buenas	9 62 papeles verdes
4 49 carteles mexicanos	10 97 libros azules
5 16 colores vivos	11 84 ciudades grandes
6 78 señoritas inteligentes	12 13 plumas negras

39B. Read aloud and write in Spanish:

$2 + 6 = 8$ dos más seis son ocho
$10 - 7 = 3$ diez menos siete son tres
$5 \times 4 = 20$ cinco por cuatro son veinte
$12 : 4 = 3$ doce dividido por cuatro son tres

$4 + 9 = 13$ $19 - 8 = 11$
$8 + 7 = 15$ $16 - 3 = 13$
$7 \times 8 = 56$ $50 : 10 = 5$
$8 \times 3 = 24$ $80 : 20 = 4$

39C. Read questions and answers aloud, saying all numbers in Spanish:

Ejemplo: ¿Cuántos días hay en enero? (31) treinta y un días.

1 ¿Cuántos días hay en junio? (30 días)
2 ¿Cuántos meses hay en el año? (12 meses)
3 ¿Cuántos días hay en la semana? (7 días)
4 ¿Cuántas horas tiene un día? (24 horas)
5 ¿Cuántos minutos hay en una hora? (60 minutos)
6 ¿Cuántos segundos tiene un minuto? (60 segundos)
7 ¿Cuántos libros hay en la estantería? (75 libros)
8 ¿Cuántos alumnos hay en la clase? (36 alumnos)
9 ¿Cuántos años tiene Ud? Tengo (35) años
10 ¿Cuántos años tiene Carlos? Tiene (16) años.

39D. Substitute the correct form of the verb for the infinitive in parenthesis:

Ejemplo: 1. Yo quiero aprender los números.

1 Yo (querer) aprender los números.
2 Yo no (poder) ir a casa.
3 Nosotros (pensar) en los números.
4 ¿(Pensar) Ud. en su profesor?
5 ¿Qué (querer) decir esta palabra?[1]
6 Rosa no (querer) ir a la escuela.

7 ¿(Querer) Uds. hablar español?

8 Ellos no (poder) comprar el coche.

9 ¿(Poder) tú adivinar la respuesta?

10 Ellas (pensar) en comprar y vender.

11 Esta radio (valer) mucho.

12 Yo (contar) en español.

13 Tú (contar) en inglés.

14 ¿(Contar) ella bien?

NOTE: 1. What does this word mean? (*Lit.* What does this word wish to say?)

Exercise No. 40—Preguntas

Answer each question in a complete Spanish sentence.

1 ¿Son importantes los números?

2 ¿Son los números tan importantes como los nombres?

3 ¿Qué necesitamos para comprar y vender?

4 ¿En qué piensa primero el negociante?

5 ¿Valen mucho los números sin dinero?

6 ¿Es posible comprar y vender sin dinero?

7 ¿Vende y compra un comerciante?

8 ¿Es un comerciante comprador y vendedor?

9 ¿Quién adelanta día por día?

10 Dígame estos números en español: 10, 20, 30, 40, 50, 100.

CHAPTER 12

EL SISTEMA MONETARIO DE ESPAÑA

PRIMERA PARTE

1 En nuestra última conversación hemos dicho que no es posible imaginar nuestra civilización moderna sin números, es decir sin matemáticas. Igualmente no es posible imaginar un viaje sin matemáticas.

2 ¿Sabe Ud. cuántas veces se usan las matemáticas en un viaje?

3 Creo que sí. Se usan para cambiar dinero, para comprar billetes y comida, para pesar maletas, para medir distancias y tamaños, para ir de compras en tiendas, mercados y almacenes y para manejar las calculadores.

4 ¿Conoce Ud. el sistema monetario de España?

5 ¡Desde luego! Ciertamente lo[1] conozco. Yo soy una negociante que importa artículos españoles. La peseta es la 'libra' de España. En el momento actual la libra vale 200 pesetas pero el cambio fluctúa constantemente.

6 Si quiere Ud. cambiar en pesetas 10 (diez) libras ¿cuántas pesetas va Ud. a recibir?

7 Voy a recibir 2.000[2] (mil quinientas) pesatas.

8 Si quiere Ud. cambiar en pesetas 50 (cincuenta) libras ¿cuántas pesetas va Ud. a recibir?

9 Voy a recibir 10.000[2] pesetas.

10 ¡Exacto! Ud. va a la estación de ferrocarril. Quiere comprar dos billetes para Guadalajara. Cada billete cuesta 145 (ciento cuarenta y cinco) pesetas y Ud. da al taquillero 500 (quinientas) pesetas. ¿Cuánto recibe Ud. de cambio?

11 Recibo 210 (doscientas diez) pesetas de cambio.

12 Muy bien. En nuestra próxima conversación vamos a continuar con este importante tema. El ejercicio hace al maestro.

1 In our last conversation we said that it is not possible to imagine our modern civilization without numbers, that is to say, without mathematics. Likewise, it is not possible to imagine a trip without mathematics.

2 Do you know how many times one uses mathematics on a trip?

3 I think so. One uses it in order to change money, buy tickets and food, to weigh suitcases, to measure distances and sizes and to make purchases in shops, markets and department stores.

4 Do you know the monetary system of Spain?

5 What an idea! I certainly do know it. I am a businesswoman who imports Spanish things, am I not? The peseta is the 'pound' of Spain. At present the pound is worth 200 pesetas but the rate changes constantly.

6 If you want to change £10 into pesetas, how many pesetas will you receive?

7 I shall receive 2,000 pesetas.

8 If you want to change £50 into pesetas, how many pesetas will you receive?

9 I shall receive 10,000 pesetas.

10 Right! You go to the railway station. You want to buy two tickets for Guadalajara. Each ticket costs 145 pesetas and you give the booking clerk 500 pesetas. How much do you receive in change?

11 I receive 210 pesetas change.

12 Very well. In our next conversation let us continue this important topic. Practice makes perfect. (*Lit.* Practice makes the master.)

NOTE: 1. **lo** (*m*) it. Object pronouns usually precede the verb. 2. When writing figures in thousands, Spanish uses a full stop where English uses a comma. For writing dates Spanish usage is the same as English. The decimal point is indicated by a comma (,); e.g. 2.50 will be 2,50.

Pronunciation and Spelling Aids

1 Practise:

igualmente (i-ɣwal-ˈmen-te)   **estación de ferrocarril**   (es-ta-ˈθjon
distancias (ðis-ˈtan-θjas)   de fe-rro-ka-ˈrril)
Guadalajara (ɣwa-ða-la-ˈxa-ra)   **continuar** (kon-ti-ˈnwar)

2 **Una vez, dos veces.** Since the letter z is unusual before e or i, words ending in z change z to c in the plural. Other examples are: el lápiz (pencil) **los lápices; la voz** (voice) **las voces; la actriz** (actress) **las actrices.**

Building Vocabulary

A. 1 **la maleta** suitcase   2 **el equipaje** baggage   3 **el baúl** trunk

B. **El sistema monetario de España.**

The monetary system of Spain is based on pesetas and céntimos. There are 100 céntimos in a peseta. At the time of going to press the rate of exchange is approximately £1 = 200 pesetas.

Expresiones Importantes

1 **es decir** that is to say   4 **ir de compras** to go shopping
2 **¡Qué cosa!** The idea!   5 **El ejercicio hace** Practice makes
3 **de cambio** in change   **al maestro**   perfect

Exercise No. 41—Completion of Text

1 Nuestra civilización no es posible sin números, (that is to say) sin matemáticas.
2 ¿(How many times) usa Ud. las matemáticas en un día?
3 Compro (tickets and meals).
4 Ud. no puede pesar (suitcases) y saber los (sizes) y las (distances).
5 (The monetary system) de España no es difícil.
6 (Each) libra esterlina vale 200 pesetas.
7 En cada peseta hay cien (cents).
8 (That's correct). Ud. va a recibir ocho pesetas (in change).
9 Dos billetes para Guadalajara cuestan (two hundred and ninety) pesetas.
10 En nuestra (next) conversación vamos a continuar con (this) tema.

SEGUNDA PARTE

Grammar Notes

1 Present tense of **dar** to give, and **saber** to know, to know how.

I give, etc.		I know, etc.	
doy	damos	sé	sabemos
das	dais	sabes	sabéis
da	dan	sabe	saben

NOTE: Spanish verbs in the **yo** (*I*) form, present tense, end in **-o.** There are only five exceptions: **soy, estoy, voy, doy** and **sé.**

2 The Numbers 100 to 1,000.

100	ciento (cien)	500	quinientos (as)
101	ciento uno (un, una)	600	seiscientos (as)
102	ciento dos	700	setecientos (as)
200	doscientos (as)	800	ochocientos (as)
300	trescientos (as)	900	novecientos (as)
400	cuatrocientos (as)	1.000	mil

(a) Before a noun **ciento** becomes **cien.** Thus: **cien libros, cien plumas,** etc.

(b) **y** is never used between the hundreds and tens. Thus: 342 (**trescientos cuarenta y dos**)

(c) Note the formation of numbers over one thousand:

1.954 **mil novecientos cincuenta y cuatro**
2.662 **dos mil seiscientos sesenta y dos**
1968 (the year) **mil novecientos sesenta y ocho**

(d) The hundreds agree in gender with the nouns they modify. Thus:
trescientos libros, trescientas plumas, quinientas pesetas

3 More about Object Pronouns.

(a) **lo** (*it*), direct object pronoun, stands for a thing in the masculine gender.

(b) **la** (*it*), direct object pronoun, stands for a thing in the feminine gender.

¿**Conoce Ud. el sistema monetario?**	Do you know the monetary system?
Lo conozco.	I know it.
¿**Conoce Ud. la respuesta? La sé.**	Do you know the answer? I know it.

Ejercicios (Exercises) No. 41A–41B

41A. Write out the numbers in Spanish.

Ejemplo: 250 **doscientos cincuenta**

1	400	3	525	5	627	7	560	9	200
2	350	4	860	6	490	8	780	10	970

41B. Translate:

1 I know the numbers.
2 Do you (**Ud.**) know where he lives?
3 We know what (**qué**) he wants.
4 We do not give the money.
5 Do they give the tickets?

6 What does John give?
7 She does not know the answer.
8 We are not giving our books.
9 Do you (**tú**) know the questions?
10 They do not know who (**quién**) lives here.

Exercise No. 42—Preguntas

Answer each question giving the numbers in full in Spanish.

Ejemplo: Recibo cuarenta pesetas de cambio.

1 Si una cosa cuesta 100 pesetas y Ud. da un billete de 500 pesetas, ¿cuánto recibe Ud. de cambio?

2 Si un billete cuesta 25 pesetas, ¿cuánto da Ud. por tres billetes?

3 Si una revista cuesta 15 pesetas, ¿cuánto da Ud. por dos revistas?

4 Si un diario cuesta una peseta y Ud. le[1] da al vendedor un duro[2], ¿cuánto recibe Ud. de cambio?

5 Si Ud. tiene un billete de cincuenta pesetas, dos billetes de cien pesetas, y veinte duros, ¿cuánto dinero tiene Ud. en el bolsillo (pocket)?

6 Si un hombre tiene un millón de pesetas, ¿es millonario?

7 ¿Qué vale más, £50 (cincuenta libras) o 5000 (cinco mil) pesetas?

8 ¿Sabe Ud. cuánto dinero hay en el Banco de España?

9 ¿Conoce Ud. el sistema monetario de España?

10 ¿Cuándo vamos a continuar con este tema?

NOTE: 1. **le** = *to him*. Do not translate it. The Spanish often uses a pronoun object, even when the noun object (in this case **al vendedor**) is expressed. 2. The five-peseta coin is often called **un duro** (but it is becoming obsolete).

CHAPTER 13

PROBLEMAS DE ARITMÉTICA. EN EL RESTAURANTE. EN LA ESTACIÓN. EN LA TIENDA

PRIMERA PARTE

1 Vamos a continuar nuestro estudio de los usos de las matemáticas en un viaje.

2 En el restaurante cenamos. Somos cuatro. Las cenas cuestan 130 (ciento treinta) pesetas, 90 (noventa) pesetas, 145 (ciento cuarenta y cinco) pesetas y 105 (ciento cinco) pesetas.[1] Damos al camarero una propina de diez por ciento. ¿Cuánto es la cuenta? ¿La propina?

3 La cuenta es 470 (cuatrocientas setenta) pesetas. La propina es de 47 (cuarenta y siete) pesetas.

4 Está bien. En la estación de ferrocarril tengo una maleta muy pesada. Pongo la maleta en la balanza. Pesa 30 kilos. ¿Qué hago para saber cuánto pesa la maleta en libras?

5 No es difícil. En un kilo hay aproximadamente 2,2 (dos y dos décimos) libras. Ud. multiplica 30 (treinta) por 2,2. La maleta pesa 66 (sesenta y seis) libras.

6 Correcto. En España y en los otros países de Europa no se usan[2] millas, sino kilómetros para medir las distancias. ¿Sabe Ud. cambiar kilómetros en millas?

7 Cierto. Divido por ocho y multiplico por cinco. De este modo ochenta kilómetros son iguales a cincuenta millas. Es fácil, ¿verdad?

8 Ud. calcula muy aprisa. Solamente un problema más. En una tienda Ud. compra dos echarpes a 90 (noventa) pesetas, tres corbatas a 75 (setenta y cinco) pesetas, un sombrero a 200 (doscientas) pesetas y tres cestas a 50 (cincuenta) pesetas. ¿Cuál es el precio total?

9 755 (setecientas cincuenta y cinco) pesetas. Y si doy al comerciante 1.000 (mil) pesetas, voy a recibir 245 (doscientas cuarenta y cinco) pesetas de cambio.

10 Bueno. Basta de matemáticas por hoy. El jueves vamos a hablar sobre la hora. Es un tema de inmensa importancia.

11 Seguramente. Espero una conversación interesante.

12 A propósito, Sra. Adams, el próximo jueves no puedo llegar antes de las ocho y media de la tarde.

13 Bien. Más vale tarde que nunca.

14 Bien dicho. Hasta la vista, Sra. Adams.

15 Hasta el jueves, Sr. López.

1 Let us continue our study of the uses of mathematics on a trip.

2 In the restaurant we have dinner. We are four. The dinners cost 130 pesetas, 90 pesetas, 145 pesetas and 105 pesetas.[1] We give the waiter a ten per cent tip. How much is the bill? The tip?

3 The bill is 470 pesetas. The tip is 47 pesetas.

4 That is correct. In the railway station I have a very heavy suitcase. I put the suitcase on the scales. It weighs 30 kilos. What do I do to find out how much the suitcase weighs in pounds?

5 It is not difficult. In one kilo there are approximately 2.2 pounds. You multiply 30 by 2.2. The suitcase weighs 66 pounds.

6 Correct. In Spain and in the other countries of Europe, not miles but kilometres are used[2] to measure distances. Do you know how to change kilometres into miles?

7 Certainly. I divide by eight and multiply by five. Thus eighty kilometres are equal to fifty miles. It's easy, isn't it?

8 You calculate very quickly. Only one more problem. In a shop you buy two shawls at 90 pesetas, three ties at 75 pesetas, one hat for 200 pesetas and three baskets at 50 pesetas. What is the total price?

9 755 pesetas. And if I give the merchant 1,000 pesetas, I will receive 245 pesetas in change.

10 Good. Enough mathematics for today. On Thursday we are going to talk about the time of day. It is a topic of great importance.

11 Indeed. I am expecting an interesting conversation.

12 By the way Mrs. Adams, next Thursday I cannot arrive before 8.30 p.m.

13. That's all right. Better late than never.

14 Well said. Good-bye, Mrs. Adams.

15 Until Thursday, Mr. López.

NOTE: 1. Due to inflation and other factors, the cost of living has risen considerably in Spain and the above prices would now be at least quadruple.

NOTE: 2. The reflexive verb is often used in Spanish to express the passive. Thus: **Se venden echarpes.** Shawls are sold. *Lit.* Shawls sell themselves.

Pronunciation Aids

1 Practise:

restaurante (rres-taw-'ran-te)   **comerciante** (ko-mer-'θjan-te)
multiplicar (mul-ti-pli'kar)   **países** (pa-'i-ses)
multiplico (mul-ti-'pli-ko)

2 **kilómetro.** A few foreign words borrowed by Spanish are spelled with **k.**

Building Vocabulary

A. el día, el mapa, el sistema, el problema, el tema, are masculine.
Remember: Most nouns ending in **-a** are feminine.

B Synonyms (words of about the same meaning)

1 **aprisa**	**rápidamente**	rapidly
2 **el negociante**	**el comerciante**	the businessman
3 **despacio**	**lentamente**	slowly
4 **de este modo**	**de esta manera**	in this way

C. Antonyms (opposites)

1 **rápidamente**	rapidly	**despacio**	slowly
2 **comprador**	buyer	**vendedor**	seller
3 **dar**	to give	**recibir**	to receive
4 **multiplicar**	to multiply	**dividir**	to divide

Expresiones Importantes

1 **por ciento**	per cent.
2 **de este modo**	thus, in this way
3 **nada más**	nothing more, that's all
4 **kilómetro**	kilometre, about $\frac{5}{8}$ mile
5 **por cierto**	certainly, surely
6 **Tomamos la cena**	We have dinner
7 **¿Cuánto es la cuenta?**	How much is the bill?
8 **Está bien**	Good, that's right
9 **Refrán** (proverb):	
Más vale tarde que nunca.	Better late than never.

SEGUNDA PARTE

Grammar Notes

1 The present Tense of **hacer** to make, to do; **decir** to say; **poner** to put.

I make, etc.		I say, etc.		I put, etc.	
hago	**hacemos**	**digo**	**decimos**	**pongo**	**ponemos**
haces	**hacéis**	**dices**	**decís**	**pones**	**ponéis**
hace	**hacen**	**dice**	**dicen**	**pone**	**ponen**

(a) **salir** to leave, **valer** to be worth, **traer** to bring, and **caer** to fall, have a **g** in the first person, but are regular in the other forms of the present tense.

Singular			Plural		
salgo	sales	sale	salimos	salís	salen
valgo	vales	vale	valemos	valéis	valen
traigo	traes	trae	traemos	traéis	traen
caigo	caes	cae	caemos	caéis	caen

2. Possessive Adjectives. Summary. You are familiar with the possessive adjective **mi (mis)** and **su (sus)**. Learn the meaning and forms of all the possessive adjectives.

Singular

	masc.	fem.
(my)	mi hijo	mi hija
(your—*fam.*)	tu hijo	tu hija
(your, his, her)	su hijo	su hija
(its, their)		
(our)	nuestro hijo	nuestra hija
(your—*fam.*)	vuestro hijo	vuestra hija

Plural

	masc.	fem.
(my)	mis hijos	mis hijas
(your—*fam.*)	tus hijos	tus hijas
(your, his, her)	sus hijos	sus hijas
(its, their)		
(our)	nuestros hijos	nuestras hijas
(your—*fam.*)	vuestros hijos	vuestras hijas

(a) Possessive adjectives agree with the nouns they modify in number and gender.

(b) **tu (tus)** *your* is used to show possession when one person is addressed familiarly. **tú** (*you*) has an accent mark, **tu** (*your*) has not.

Tú no tienes tu libro, hijita.   You haven't your book, little girl.

(c) **Vuestro, (-a, -os, -as)** (*your*) is used to show possession when more than one person is addressed familiarly.

Vosotros no tenéis vuestros   You haven't your books, children.
libros, niños.

(d) **su (sus)** means *your*, *his*, *her*, *its*, *their*, according to the sense of the sentence. In cases where the meaning would be in doubt the definite article is used before the noun, and the phrase **de Ud., de él, de ella, de Uds., de ellos,** or **de ellas** after the noun.

el padre de él	his father	la familia de ellos	their family
la madre de ella	her mother	la clase de ellas	their class
la casa de Ud.	your house	los hijos de Uds.	your sons

3 **pero** and **sino**. After a negative, **sino** is used instead of **pero** in the sense of 'but on the contrary', 'but rather'.

No es rico *sino* pobre.	He is not rich, *but* poor.
No se usan libras *sino* kilos.	Not pounds, *but* kilos are used.

However, **pero** must be used if the subject changes.

El no es rico, *pero* su tío es rico.	He is not rich, *but* his uncle is rich.

Ejercicios (Exercises) No. 43A–43B–43C–43D

43A. Complete the following sentences, substituting the correct form of **mi, tu, su** or **nuestro** for the words in parentheses.

Ejemplo: No tenemos nuestros billetes

1 No tenemos (our) billetes.
2 ¿Cuánto cuesta (your) cena, señor?
3 ¿Son muy pesadas (your) maletas, señorita?
4 No, (my) maletas no son muy pesadas.
5 ¿Es muy interesante (their) conversación?
6 ¿Hay cien pesetas en (his) escritorio?
7 (Our) equipaje está en la estación.
8 ¿Dónde está (your) madre, niño?
9 (My) amigos están en el restaurante.
10 (Our) civilización no es posible sin números.

43B. Read the following, giving the numbers in Spanish.

Ejemplo: Diez kilos son iguales a veinte y dos libras.

1 **10 kilos = 22 libras**	6 **16 kilómetros** = 10 miles
2 **20 kilos = 44 libras**	7 **32 kilómetros** = 20 miles
3 **30 kilos = 66 libras**	8 **48 kilómetros** = 30 miles
4 **40 kilos = 88 libras**	9 **64 kilómetros** = 40 miles
5 **50 kilos = 110 libras**	10 **80 kilómetros** = 50 miles

43C. Translate into Spanish:

1 I say	9 do you (**Ud.**) make?
2 I do	10 do you (**Uds.**) go out?
3 I am going out	11 do you (**Uds.**) say?
4 I have	12 you (**tú**) make
5 we say	13 do you (**Ud.**) put?
6 we do not put	14 I put
7 they make	15 it is worth
8 they put	

43D. Complete the following sentences with **pero** or **sino** as the sense requires.

1 El señor no estudia el francés (but) **el español.**
2 No es comerciante (but) **profesor.**
3 Yo no estudio el español, (but) **mi hermano lo estudia.**
4 No ponemos los libros en la mesa (but) **en la estantería.**
5 Es un muchacho inteligente, (but) **es perezoso** (lazy).

Exercise No. 44—Preguntas

1 ¿Dónde cenan Uds.?
2 ¿Qué tanto por ciento dan Uds. al camarero como propina?
3 ¿Cuánto es la propina?
4 ¿Dónde tiene Ud. su maleta pesada?
5 ¿Cuánto pesa la maleta en kilos? ¿En libras?
6 ¿Qué se usa en España para medir las distancias, kilómetros o millas?
7 ¿Quién sabe cambiar kilómetros en millas?
8 ¿Qué artículos compra la Sra. Adams en una tienda?
9 ¿Cuál es el tema de la próxima conversación?
10 ¿Qué refrán (proverb) usa la Sra. Adams?

CHAPTER 14

¿QUÉ HORA ES?

PRIMERA PARTE

1 La hora punta. Todo el mundo quiere saber — ¿Qué hora es? ¿A qué hora llega el avión? ¿A qué hora sale el tren? ¿A qué hora comienzan los exámenes? ¿A qué hora comienza la película? ¿A qué hora comienza la función? Y un millón de otras preguntas.

2 Sra. Adams, yo voy a hacer el papel de taquillero en la taquilla de la estación de ferrocarril. Ud. va a hacer el papel de viajero que quiere comprar un billete y pide información. Haga el favor de comenzar.

3 Buenos días, señor. Quiero comprar un billete para Barcelona.

4 ¿De primera o de segunda clase?

5 De primera, por favor. ¿Cuánto vale el billete?

6 954 (novecientas cincuenta y cuatro) pesetas por un billete sencillo,[1] o 1.908 (mil novecientas ocho) pesetas por un billete de ida y vuelta.

7 Haga el favor de darme un billete de ida y vuelta. Quiero salir el lunes.

8 Aquí tiene Ud. el billete.

9 Gracias. ¿A qué hora sale el tren y cuándo llega a Barcelona?

10 Sale a mediodía y llega a las ocho menos veinte y cinco de la tarde.[2]

11 Muchas gracias, señor.

12 De nada.

13 Excelente, Sra. Adams. Ud. puede hacerse entender en España.

1 The rush hour. Everybody wants to know: what time is it? At what time does the plane arrive? At what time does the train leave? At what time do the examinations begin? At what time does the film begin? At what time does the performance begin? And a million other questions.

2 Mrs. Adams, I am going to play the role of booking clerk at the window in the railway station. You are going to take the part of a traveller who wants to buy a ticket and is asking for information. Please begin.

3 Good day, sir. I wish to buy a ticket for Barcelona.

4 First or second class?

5 First class, please. How much is the ticket?

6 954 pesetas for a single ticket or 1,908 pesetas for a return ticket.

7 Please give me a return ticket. I want to leave on Monday.

8 Here is the ticket.

9 Thanks. At what time does the train leave and when does it arrive at Barcelona?

10 It leaves at midday and arrives at 7.35 in the evening.[2]

11 Many thanks, sir.

12 Don't mention it.

13 Excellent, Mrs. Adams. You can make yourself understood in Spain.

NOTE: 1. Also **billete de ida**. 2. Official timetables use the 24-hour clock.

1 Ahora yo hago el papel de taquillero de un cine. Ud., Sra. Adams, pide información sobre la función.[1] Hage el favor de comenzar.

2 Por favor, señor, ¿a qué hora comienzan las funciones del cine?

3 Hay dos funciones. La primera comienza a las 7.30 (las siete y media) de la tarde, y la segunda a las 10.30 (las diez y media) de la noche.

4 ¿Hay noticiario?

5 ¿Cómo no? Veinte minutos antes de cada película.

6 ¿Cuánto cuestan las entradas?

7 Cincuenta pesetas cada una. Si Ud. viene temprano va a obtener buenos asientos.

8 Haga el favor de darme dos entradas para la segunda función.

9 Aquí las tiene. Muchas gracias.

10 Admirable, Sra. Adams. Repito — Ud. puede hacerse entender en España.

1 Now I am playing the part of the ticket seller at a cinema. You, Mrs. Adams, ask for information about the show. Please begin.

2 Please, sir, at what time do the performances begin?

3 There are two showings. The first begins at 7.30 in the evening, and the second at 10.30 in the evening.

4 Is there a newsreel?

5 Of course. Twenty minutes before each picture.

6 How much do the tickets cost?

7 Fifty pesetas each. If you come early you will obtain good seats.

8 Please give me two tickets for the second showing.

9 Here they are. Thank you very much.

10 Admirable, Mrs. Adams. I repeat: you can make yourself understood in Spain.

NOTE: 1. Also **sesión**.

Pronunciation Aids

1 Practise:

comienza (ko-ˈmjen-θa)	**millas** (ˈmi-ʎas)
exámenes (ek-ˈsa-me-nes)	**correctamente** (ko-rrek-ta-ˈmen-te)
cualquiera (kwal-ˈkje-ra)	**cumpleaños** (kum-ple-ˈa-njos)

vacaciones (va-ka-'θjo-nes) or   **taquilla** (ta-'ki-ʎa)
(ba-ka-'θjones)

Building Vocabulary

A. **Sinónimos** (Synonyms):

1 **comenzar (ie)**	**empezar (ie)**	to begin
2 **de nada**	**no hay de qué**	don't mention it
3 **el diario**	**el periódico**	newspaper

B. Words dealing with Trains:

1 **¿A qué hora sale el tren para—?**
At what time does the train leave for—?
2 **¿Cuándo llega el tren de—?**
When does the train arrive from—?
3 **El tren sale (llega) a las dos.**
The train leaves (arrives) at 2 o'clock.
4 **un billete de ida, billete sencillo**
a single ticket
5 **un billete de primera (segunda)**
a first (second) class ticket
6 **un billete de pullman**
a pullman ticket
7 **un billete de ida y vuelta**
a round trip ticket
8 **¿Cuánto cuesta (vale) el billete?**
How much is the ticket?

Expresiones Importantes

1 **todo el mundo**	everybody
2 **desde uno hasta ciento**	from 1 to 100
3 **hacer el papel de**	to play the part (role) of
4 **pedir información**	to ask for information
5 **Haga el favor de comenzar**	please begin
6 **Aquí tiene Ud. el billete**	Here is the ticket
7 **Ud. puede hacerse entender**	You can get along (*lit.* you can make yourself understood)
8 **La próxima vez**	next time

Exercise No. 45—Completion of Text

1 **¿A qué hora comienza** (the film)?
2 **¿A qué hora comienza** (the performance)?
3 **¿Tienen Uds.** (other questions)?

4 **El taquillero está en la** (ticket office).
5 **¿Dónde está** (the railway station)?
6 **Ud. es un viajero que** (is asking for information).
7 **Haga el favor de darme** (a return ticket).
8 **¿A qué hora** (does the train leave)?
9 **¿Llega** (at nine in the evening)?
10 (Many thanks.)
11 (Don't mention it.)
12 **Ahora** (I play the role) **de taquillero.**

SEGUNDA PARTE

Grammar Notes

1 Verbs with Stem Changes **e** to **i**—**pedir** to ask for, **repetir** to repeat

I ask for, you ask for, etc.   I repeat, you repeat, etc.

pido	**pedimos**	**repito**	**repetimos**
pides	**pedís**	**repites**	**repetís**
pide	**piden**	**repite**	**repiten**

(a) The stem change **e** to **i** does not occur in the **nosotros-as** (*we*) and the **vosotros-as** (*you, fam.*) forms.

(b) Verbs with stem changes from **e** to **i**, like **pedir** and **repetir**, will be indicated in the vocabulary as follows: **pedir(i), repetir(i).**

2 Time of Day

¿Qué hora es?	What time is it?
Es la una.	It is one o'clock.
Son las dos.	It is two o'clock.
Son las tres.	It is three o'clock.
Son las cuatro.	It is four o'clock
Son las cinco y media.	It is half past five.
Son las seis y cuarto.	It is a quarter past six.
Son las seis y veinte.	It is twenty minutes past six.
Son las siete menos cuarto.	It is a quarter to seven.
Son las siete menos veinte.	It is twenty minutes to seven.

¿A qué hora? A la una en punto.	At what time? At one o'clock sharp.
A las ocho de la mañana.	At eight o'clock in the morning (a.m.)
A las cinco de la tarde.	At five o'clock in the afternoon (p.m.)
A la una de la noche.	At one o'clock at night (a.m.)
A mediodía. A medianoche.	At noon. At midnight.

(a) Use the singular verb **es** in all time expressions involving **la una.**

(1.12) **Es la una y doce.**   (1.30) **Es la una y media.**

(b) Use the plural verb **son** for all other time expressions.

(c) **y** (*and*, *after*) is used for time after the hour (**cuarto, media, minutos**)

Menos (*less*, *to*) is used for time before the hour.

(d) Base time expressions after the half hour on the following hour.

(6.40) **Son las siete menos veinte.** It is twenty minutes to seven.

(e) If no clock time is mentioned, use **por la mañana, por la tarde** and **por la noche** for in the morning, in the afternoon, and at night. With clock time use **de la mañana, de la tarde** and **de la noche.**

Trabajo por la mañana.	I work in the morning.
Trabajo a las ocho de la mañana.	I work at 8 o'clock in the morning.

TERCERA PARTE

Ejercicios (Exercises) No. 46A–46B–46C

46A. Read these sentences giving the time in Spanish.

Ejemplo: El tren de Sevilla llega a las cinco y media de la tarde.

1 **El tren de Sevilla llega a** (5.30 p.m.)
2 **El tren llega a Irún a** (8.15 p.m.)
3 **El tren para Vigo sale a** (9.55 a.m.)
4 **El tren para Guadalajara sale a** (10.50 a.m.)
5 **La primera función comienza a** (8 p.m.)
6 **Le segunda función comienza a** (11 p.m.)
7 **Los domingos la función comienza a** (4.30 p.m.)
8 **El noticiario comienza a** (6.50 p.m.)
9 **Vamos a tomar la cena a** (9.45 p.m.)
10 **Tomamos el almuerzo** (at 2 p.m.)

46B. Fill in the correct form of the verbs in parentheses.

Ejemplo: Yo pido informes.

1 **Yo** (pedir) **información.**
2 **Nosotros** (comenzar) **a comer.**
3 **Ellos** (repetir) **las preguntas.**
4 **¿Quién** (pedir) **información?**
5 **Yo** (comenzar) **a trabajar.**
6 **¿**(Empezar) **Ud. a trabajar ahora?**
7 **¿Qué** (pedir) **tú, niña?**
8 **¿Qué** (pedir) **Uds.?**
9 **El maestro** (repetir) **la respuesta.**
10 **¿Por qué no** (comenzar) **la función?**

46C. Translate into Spanish:

1 I want a return ticket.
2 He is asking for information.
3 When does the train for Bilbao leave?
4 Do you know when the train arrives from Madrid?
5 It arrives at 5.30 in the afternoon.

6 At what time does the first performance begin?
7 It begins at 7.30 in the evening.
8 Do they repeat the performance?
9 Yes, they repeat the performance twice (**dos veces**).
10 Here are the tickets.

Exercise No. 47—Preguntas

1 ¿Qué quiere saber todo el mundo?
2 ¿Quién hace el papel de viajero?
3 ¿Quién hace el papel de taquillero?
4 ¿Qué clase de billete quiere comprar?
5 ¿Cuánto cuesta un billete de ida y vuelta?
6 ¿Quién hace el papel de taquillero de un cine?
7 ¿Quién pide información?
8 ¿Cuántas funciones tiene este cine?
9 ¿Para qué función compra el señor dos entradas?
10 ¿Cuánto paga por las dos entradas?

REVISION 3

CHAPTERS 10–14 PRIMERA PARTE

Repaso de Palabras

NOUNS

1 el agua	16 el duro	31 el pájaro
2 el billete	17 la entrada	32 el pan
3 el bolsillo	18 el equipaje	33 el platillo
4 el camarero	19 la estación	34 el plato
5 la cesta	20 la fecha	35 la propina
6 la cena	21 la flor	36 el pueblo
7 el cine	22 la fruta	37 el tamaño
8 la clase	23 la función	38 la taquilla
9 la comida	24 la hora	39 el taquillero
10 el comprador	25 el jarro	40 el tipo
11 el dibujo	26 la llegada	41 la tienda
12 la cuenta	27 la maleta	42 el viajero
13 el cumpleaños	28 el mercado	43 el vaso
14 la libra esterlina	29 el modo	44 el uso
15 el dinero	30 el número	

1 water	17 ticket (in a cinema or	32 bread
2 ticket	theatre)	33 saucer
3 pocket	18 baggage	34 plate
4 waiter	19 station	35 tip
5 basket	20 date	36 people, town
6 dinner	21 flower	37 size
7 cinema	22 fruit	38 ticketwindow
8 class	23 performance	39 ticket-seller, booking
9 meal	24 hour	clerk
10 buyer	25 jar, pitcher	40 type
11 drawing	26 arrival	41 shop
12 bill	27 suitcase	42 traveller
13 birthday	28 market	43 glass
14 pound sterling	29 way	44 use
15 money	30 number	
16 5-peseta coin	31 bird	

VERBS

1 caer	10 decir (i)	19 pensar (ie)
2 cambiar	11 demandar	20 poder (ue)
3 contar (ue)	12 empezar (ie)	21 poner
4 comprar	13 hacer	22 venir
5 continuar	14 llegar	23 pedir (i)
6 comer	15 mirar	24 querer (ie)
7 comenzar (ie)	16 necesitar	25 saber
8 creer	17 obtener	26 tomar
9 dar	18 pagar	27 traer

28 telefonear
29 repetir (i)
30 recibir

31 saber
32 salir (de)
33 tener

34 valer
35 vender
36 hemos dicho

1 to fall
2 to change
3 to count
4 to buy
5 to continue
6 to eat
7 to begin
8 to believe
9 to give
10 to say
11 to demand
12 to begin

13 to make, do
14 to arrive
15 to look at
16 to need
17 to obtain
18 to pay
19 to think
20 to be able
21 to put
22 to come
23 to ask for
24 to want, wish

25 to know (how)
26 to take
27 to bring
28 to telephone
29 to repeat
30 to receive
31 to know
32 to leave
33 to have
34 to be worth
35 to sell
36 we have said

ADJECTIVES

1 alguno
2 antiguo
3 cada
4 cierto
5 conocido
6 correcto
7 corriente

8 cualquier
9 diario
10 diligente
11 fino
12 igual
13 ligero
14 más

15 mismo
16 necesario
17 nuestro
18 pesado
19 propio
20 sencillo
21 todo

1 some
2 old
3 each
4 certain
5 known
6 correct
7 ordinary

8 any
9 daily
10 diligent
11 fine
12 equal
13 light
14 more

15 same
16 necessary
17 our
18 heavy
19 own
20 simple
21 all

ADVERBS

1 aprisa
2 ahora
3 ahora mismo
4 correctamente
5 entretanto

6 lentamente
7 más
8 solamente
9 tan
10 tan rico como

1 quickly
2 now
3 now, right away
4 correctly
5 meanwhile

6 slowly
7 more
8 only
9 so, as
10 as rich as

PREPOSITIONS

1 antes de
2 desde

3 hasta
4 sobre

5 acerca de

1 before
2 from

3 to, until
4 on, upon

5 about, concerning

IMPORTANT EXPRESSIONS

1 aquí tiene Ud.	15 hoy día
2 creo que sí	16 ir de compras
3 creo que no	17 hacerse entender
4 de cambio	18 nada más
5 de este modo	19 pasar sin
6 de la misma manera	20 pensar en
7 ¿Qué quiere decir-?	21 por cierto
8 ¡qué cosa!	22 por todas partes
9 tener prisa	23 todo el mundo
10 tener que	24 todo lo posible
11 tener razón	25 ¡ya lo creo!
12 en efecto	26 Más vale tarde que nunca
13 es decir	27 El ejercicio hace al maestro
14 haga el favor de darme	

1 here is, are	15 nowadays
2 I think so	16 to go shopping
3 I think not	17 to make oneself understood
4 in change	18 nothing more
5 in this way	19 to get along without
6 in the same way	20 to think of
7 What is the meaning of . . . ?	21 indeed, certainly
8 the idea!	22 everywhere
9 to be in a hurry	23 everybody
10 to have to	24 everything possible
11 to be right	25 yes indeed!
12 in fact	26 Better late than never
13 that is to say	27 Practice makes perfect
14 please give me	

SEGUNDA PARTE

Ejercicio 48 Answer the following questions in the affirmative in complete sentences.

Ejemplo: 1. Sí, pienso en mi amigo.

1 ¿Piensa Ud. en su amigo?
2 ¿Quiere Ud. hacer un viaje a España?
3 ¿Puede Ud. comprar un coche?
4 ¿Pone Ud. la lámpara en el piano?
5 ¿Sale Ud. mañana de la ciudad?
6 ¿Cuenta Ud. siempre el cambio?
7 ¿Dice Ud. las palabras·dos veces?
8 ¿Continúa Ud. la lección?
9 ¿Le[1] da Ud. una propina al camarero?
10 ¿Sabe Ud. contar en español?

NOTE: 1. le *to him*, is not translated here.

Ejercicio 49 Answer the following questions in the negative in complete sentences. Be sure to use the **nosotros** (*we*) form.

Ejemplo: 1. No repetimos las respuestas.

1 ¿Repiten Uds. las respuestas?
2 ¿Hacen Uds. muchas preguntas?
3 ¿Piden Uds. informes?
4 ¿Tienen Uds. prisa?
5 ¿Vienen Uds. temprano a casa?
6 ¿Creen Uds. el cuento (story)?
7 ¿Traen Uds. el equipaje?
8 ¿Toman Uds. la cena?
9 ¿Necesitan Uds. dinero?
10 ¿Tienen Uds. que trabajar?

Ejercicio 50 Select the phrase in the right-hand column which best completes the sentence begun in the left-hand column.

1 Este tipo de cerámica   (a) hace al maestro.
2 Estos dibujos son de flores   (b) es conocido en todas partes.
3 Cada negociante piensa   (c) antes de las nueve.
4 Ud. sabe que el ejercicio   (d) y ésos son de animalitos.
5 Vamos a continuar   (e) para comprar dos billetes.
6 No puedo llegar   (f) cuando hablo español.
7 Voy a la taquilla   (g) primero tiene.
8 Sé a qué hora   (h) en comprar y vender.
9 Él me comprende   (i) este tema interesante.
10 Quien primero viene   (j) comienza la función.

Ejercicio 51 Complete the following sentences by choosing the proper expression from those listed below.

1 (How much does it cost?) **Cada turista** (must know) **esta expresión.**
2 **El turista** (asks for information) **en la estación de ferrocarril.**—¿(At what time) **llega el tren de Burgos? Dice el empleado**—(At 7.30) **de la tarde.**
3 **El turista** (is hungry). **Toma una** (meal) **en un restaurante.** (He pays the bill) **con un billete de cien pesetas. Recibe diez pesetas** (in change). **Le da al camarero** (a tip) **de nueve pesetas** (that is to say), **diez por ciento.**
4 (Thinks) **el turista**—(Everywhere) **son necesarios los números y** (money).

tiene que saber	tiene hambre	es decir
¿a qué hora?	paga la cuenta	el dinero
¿Cuánto cuesta?	una comida	piensa
a las siete y media	en todas partes	una propina
pide informes	de cambio	tiene sed

Ejercicio 52 Translate the demonstrative adjectives in parentheses.

1 (this) **cena**	7 (that-*dist.*) **montaña**
2 (these) **echarpes**	8 (those) **tejidos**
3 (that) **viajero**	9 (these) **casas**
4 (those) **vasos**	10 (those) **fechas**
5 (this) **tipo**	11 (that-*dist.*) **cielo**
6 (that) **estación**	12 (those-*dist.*) **montañas**

Ejercicio 53 From Column II select antonyms for each word in Column I.

I	**II**
1 comprar	(a) recibir
2 venir	(b) tarde
3 dar	(c) aprisa
4 antes de	(d) salir de
5 temprano	(e) vender
6 dividir	(f) ir
7 llegar a	(g) después de
8 más	(h) multiplicar
9 lentamente	(i) comprador
10 vendedor	(j) menos

TERCERA PARTE
Diálogo

Practise the Spanish aloud.

Una turista pide información acerca de la cerámica española

1 Haga el favor de decirme, señor — ¿De qué lugares de España son los mejores ejemplares de cerámica española? Deseo comprar un juego de tazas, platillos y platos.

2 Pues, cada lugar tiene su propio estilo. La cerámica de Talavera y la de Manises es conocida en todas partes.

3 ¿Tengo que ir a aquellos pueblos para obtener los mejores ejemplares?

4 De ninguna manera. Ud. puede comprar cerámica de todos los pueblos aquí mismo en la capital.

5 ¿Cuesta más aquí?

6 Por supuesto cuesta más. Pero hay un surtido excelente.

7 Haga el favor de decirme los nombres de algunas tiendas de cerámica.

8 Hay muchas en El Rastro.

9 ¿Se vende cerámica allí?

10 ¡Ya lo creo! La mejor de España.

11 Muchas gracias, señor.

12 De nada, señorita.

1 Please tell me, sir: from which places in Spain come the best examples of Spanish pottery? I want to buy a set of cups, saucers and plates.

2 Well, each place has its own style. The pottery of Talavera and Manises is well known everywhere.

3 Have I to go to those towns to obtain the best examples?

4 By no means. You can buy pottery from all the towns right here in the capital.

5 Does it cost more here?

6 Of course it costs more. But there is an excellent assortment.

7 Please tell me the names of a few pottery shops.

8 There are many in the Rastro.

9 Do they sell pottery there?

10 I should say so! The best in Spain.

11 Many thanks, sir.

12 Don't mention it, Miss.

Exercise No. 54—La familia de la señora Adams viene a visitar su oficina

Es la primera vez que la familia Adams viene a visitar la oficina de la señora Adams. El señor Adams y sus (their) cuatro hijos entran en un edificio muy grande y suben (go up) al quinto piso en ascensor (lift). Anita, la hija menor, que tiene solamente cinco años, es muy curiosa y hace muchas preguntas a su (her) papá sobre la oficina.

Cuando llegan a la oficina, la madre se levanta y dice, — Me gusta mucho veros (to see you) a todos aquí. ¡Qué agradable (pleasant) sorpresa!

Los niños admiran los objetos que ven en la oficina: la máquina de escribir, el ordenador, el micro-ordenador,[1] los diversos artículos importados (imported) de España, las revistas españolas y los carteles de muchos colores. Todos están muy contentos.

Felipe, el hijo mayor, mira por la alta ventana y ve el cielo azul y el sol brillante. Abajo (below) ve los coches que pasan por la calle. Desde el quinto piso parecen (they seem) bastante pequeños.

Después de (after) la visita toda la familia va a un restaurante que no está lejos de la oficina. Comen con mucho gusto, sobre todo los hijos, porque tienen mucha hambre.

NOTE: 1. **Una computadora**—a big computer; **un ordenador**—a small computer; **un micro-ordenador**—a microcomputer.

Exercise No. 55—Una fábula moderna

A Anita, la menor de los hijos del Sr. Adams, le gustan mucho las fábulas antiguas de Esopo. Le gusta también esta fábula moderna que el Sr. López ha escrito (has written) para ella. Sigue[1] 'La Fábula del Coche y del Burro.'

Un coche pasa por el camino y ve un burro. El pobre burro lleva una grande y pesada (heavy) carga de madera.

El coche se para (stops) y dice al burro — Buenos días. Ud. anda muy despacio. ¿No desea Ud. correr rápidamente como yo?

— ¡Sí, sí, señor! Pero dígame, ¿Cómo es posible?

— No es difícil, dice el coche. — En mi depósito hay mucha gasolina. Tiene Ud. que beber un poco.

— No, gracias, la gasolina no es para mí. Prefiero la hierba fresca.

— Que anticuado[2] es Ud.! Y el coche se ríe del burro burlonamente.[3] El coche se va y corre rápidamente. A unos kilómetros más lejos el burro ve el coche parado.

— Buenos días, Sr. coche, ¿Qué hace Ud. aquí parado?

— No tengo gasolina y no puedo continuar, responde el coche.

— Ah, Sr. coche, dice el burro — coma hierba. Es quizás (perhaps) anticuado, pero más abundante que la gasolina.

Y el burro sigue despacio su camino mientras que (while) el coche burlón se queda en la carretera.

NOTE: 1. The Fable . . . follows. The infinitive of **sigue** is **seguir.**
NOTE: 2. **Anticuado**—old-fashioned.
NOTE: 3. **Reirse burlonamente**—to make fun of, laugh at.

CHAPTER 15

EL CINE

PRIMERA PARTE

1 Sra. Adams, Ud. sabe pedir información sobre las funciones del cine. ¿Es Ud. amiga del cine?

2 Pues sí, me gusta una buena película, pero la mayor parte de los films no me interesan.

3 ¿Le gusta más a Ud. el teatro?

4 Sí. Mi esposo y yo lo preferimos. Vamos a menudo al teatro para ver un buen drama o una producción musical.

5 ¿Y sus hijos? ¿Prefieren el teatro?

6 ¡Claro que no! Les encantan los filmes policíacos y los filmes musicales en colores y las discotecas que a nosotros nos aburren.

7 Ellos conocen[1] a todas las estrellas de la pantalla y de la televisión, ¿verdad?

8 Claro está, las conocen. Conocen también a las estrellas de la televisión y de la radio.

9 Uds. viven en la zona residencial, en las afueras. ¿Hay un cine cerca de su casa?

10 Sí, a cosa de un kilómetro. Podemos ir allí a pie en quince minutos más o menos.

11 ¿Dónde prefieren Uds. sentarse, en las primeras filas o atrás?

12 Nos gusta más sentarnos en las filas catorce o quince. Desde allí es posible ver y oír bien. Desde allí la luz y los movimientos en la pantalla no hacen daño a los ojos.

13 ¿Qué hacen Uds. si la mayor parte de los asientos están ocupados?

14 Entonces pido ayuda a la acomodadora. Nos sentamos en cualquier asiento desocupado, delante, atrás o al lado. Pero no nos gustan aquellos asientos y por eso venimos temprano. Tampoco nos gusta estar de pie en el cine.

15 ¡Estupendo, Sra. Adams! Ud. puede hacerse entender en España.

16 Tengo que darle las gracias a Ud., Sr. López.

1 Mrs. Adams, you know how to ask for information about the performances of the cinema. Are you fond of the cinema?

2 Well yes, I like a good picture but most films do not interest me.

3 You prefer the theatre?

4 Yes. My husband and I prefer it. We often go to the theatre to see a good play or a musical show.

5 And your children? Do they prefer the theatre?

105

6 Of course not! Detective dramas and musical pictures in colour and discotheques which bore us enchant them.

7 They know all the stars of the screen and television don't they?

8 Of course, they know them. They also know the stars of television and radio.

9 You live in the suburbs. Is there a cinema near your house?

10 Yes, about one kilometre. We can go there on foot in fifteen minutes more or less.

11 Where do you prefer to sit, in the first rows or in back?

12 We prefer to sit in rows fourteen or fifteen. From there it is possible to see and hear well. From there the light and the movements on the screen do no harm to the eyes.

13 What do you do if most of the seats are taken?

14 Then I ask the usherette for help. We sit in any unoccupied seat, in front, in back or at the side. But we do not like those seats and therefore we come early. Nor do we like to stand in the cinema.

15 Marvellous, Mrs. Adams! You can get along in Spain! (*Lit.* You can make yourself understood in Spain.)

16 I have to thank you, Mr. López.

NOTE: 1. **conocer** to know (to be acquainted with persons or things). **saber** to know (facts).

Pronunciation and Spelling Aids

1 Practise:

asientos (a-ˈsjen-tos) **película** (pe-ˈli-ku-la)
pantalla (pan-ˈta-ʎa) **estrella** (es-ˈtre-ʎa)
acomodadora (a-ko-mo-ða-ˈðo-ra) **prefiero** (pre-ˈfje-ro)

2 **la función, las funciones; la lección, las lecciones; la estación, las estaciones.** Nouns ending in **ción** drop the accent in the plural.

Building Vocabulary

A. **Sinónimos:**

1 **el noticiario — las actualidades** the newsreel
2 **por eso — por consiguiente** therefore
3 **prefiero — me gusta más** I prefer
4 **el film — la película** film
5 **a menudo — muchas veces** often

B. **Antónimos:**

1 **antes de** before (time) **despúes de** after
2 **delante de** in front of **detrás de** behind
3 **ocupado** occupied **desocupado** unoccupied

C. Words dealing with the Cinema:

1	**el cine**	the cinema
2	**la película, el filme**	the picture
3	**la función**	the performance
4	**el noticiario**	the newsreel
5	**la taquilla**	the ticket office
6	**el papel**	the part, role
7	**la estrella**	the star
8	**la pantalla**	the screen
9	**el asiento**	the seat
10	**la fila**	the row
11	**la acomodadora**	the usher
12	**la entrada**	the ticket (in cinema or theatre)

Expresiones Importantes

1 **tener que: tener,** to have, followed by **que** means to have to, must.

Tengo que repetir	I have to (*must*) repeat
Ud. tiene que aprender	You have to (*must*) learn
¿Tiene él que escribir?	Does he have to (*must he*) write
Ella no tiene que ir	She does not have to go
2 **ir a pie**	to go on foot
3 **estar de pie**	to stand

Grammar Notes

1 Direct Object Pronouns. Summary. Study the following sentences which summarize the direct object pronouns. Note their meanings and position in relation to the verb.

1 ¿Compra Pablo el pan? *Lo* compra.
2 ¿Compra Ana la crema? *La* compra.
3 ¿Ve Ud. al padre? *Le* veo (a él).
4 ¿Ve Ud. a la madre? *La* veo (a ella).
5 ¿Ve Ud. a los padres? *Los* veo (a ellos).
6 ¿Ve Ud. a las madres? *Las* veo (a ellas).
7 ¿Tiene Ud. los billetes? *Los* tengo.
8 ¿Tienen Uds. las cartas? *Las* tenemos.
9 *Le* esperamos *a Ud.,* Sr. Adams.
10 *La* esperamos *a Ud.,* Sra. López.
11 *Los* esperamos *a Uds.,* señores.
12 *Las* esperamos *a Uds.,* señoras.
13 *¿Me* buscas, mamá?
14 *Te* busco, hijito.
15 ¿Quién *nos* busca?

1 Does Paul buy the bread? He buys *it*.
2 Does Anna buy the cream? She buys *it*.
3 Do you see the father? I see *him*.
4 Do you see the mother? I see *her*.
5 Do you see the fathers? I see *them*.
6 Do you see the mothers? I see *them*.
7 Have you the tickets. I have *them*.
8 Have you the letters? We have *them*.
9 We are expecting *you*, Mr. Adams.
10 We are expecting *you*, Mrs. López.
11 We are expecting *you*, gentlemen.
12 We are expecting *you*, ladies.
13 Are you looking for *me*, mother?
14 I am looking for *you*, sonny.
15 Who is looking for *us*?

Chart of Direct Object Pronouns

Singular		Plural	
me	me	**nos**	us
te	you (*fam.*)	**os**	you (*fam.*)
lo (*m*)	it	**los** (*m*)	them, you
le (*m*)	him, you	**las** (*f*)	them, you
la (*f*)	it, her, you		

(a) Object pronouns usually stand directly before the verb.

(b) When the pronoun is the object of an infinitive or of an affirmative command, it follows the verb and is attached to it.

La Sra. Adams va a saludar*le*.   Mrs. Adams goes to greet *him*.
Díga*me*.   Tell *me*.

(c) **a Ud.** and **a Uds.** are usually added after the verb to distinguish the meaning *you* from the other meanings of **le, la, los, las, a él, a ella, a ellos** and **a ellas** may also be added to make the meaning clear.

Ejercicios (Exercises) No. 56A–56B–56C

56A. Read each Spanish question. Then read the answer, using the correct direct object pronoun in place of the dash. Be sure the object pronouns have the same number and gender as the nouns for which they stand.

Ejemplo: Sí, *los* compro.

1 ¿Compra Ud. los billetes?   Sí, —— compro.
2 ¿Comienza Ud. el ejercicio?   Sí, —— comienzo.
3 ¿Quiénes tienen la radio?   Los niños —— tienen.
4 ¿Ven Uds. bien la pantalla?   No, no —— vemos bien.

5 ¿Espera el señor a su amigo? Sí, —— espera.
6 ¿Prefieren Uds. las primeras No, no —— preferimos.
  filas?
7 ¿Conocen los niños a la estrella? Sí —— conocen.
8 ¿Conocen Uds. a estos hombres? Sí, —— conocemos.
9 ¿Conocen Uds. a estas mujeres? Sí, —— conocemos.
10 ¿Quiénes esperan al profesor? Los niños —— esperan.

56B. Read each Spanish sentence. Then put the corresponding English sentence into Spanish. Where do the object pronouns go?

Ejemplo: La criada la lleva.

1 La criada lleva la cuchara. 1 The maid brings it.
2 Los niños comen el (or la) azúcar. 2 The children eat it.
3 Pongo los platillos en la mesa. 3 I put them on the table.
4 Digo las frases al estudiante. 4 I tell them to the student.
5 ¿Por qué no saluda Ud. al 5 Why don't you greet him?
  hombre?
6 ¿Visitas tú a tu hermana? 6 Do you visit her?

56C. Translate into Spanish:

1 I see you, Mrs. Adams.
2 Do you see me?
3 Who sees us?
4 The teacher sees you (pl.), boys.
5 We see the house. We see it.
6 I take the plate. I take it.
7 She writes the verbs. She writes them.
8 We have the chairs. We have them.
9 I expect you, ladies.
10 We expect you, gentlemen.

Exercise No. 57—Preguntas

1 ¿Quién sabe pedir información?
2 ¿Qué prefieren los señores Adams, el teatro o el cine?
3 ¿Qué prefieren los niños?
4 ¿Conocen los niños a las estrellas del cine?
5 ¿Dónde vive la familia Adams?
6 ¿A qué distancia está el cine de la casa de ellos?
7 ¿Qué filas del cine prefieren?
8 ¿Es posible ver y oír desde allí?
9 ¿A quién piden ayuda en el cine?
10 ¿Vienen temprano o tarde?

CHAPTER 16

LAS CALLES Y LOS HOMBRES CÉLEBRES

PRIMERA PARTE

1 Si el turista no sabe nada de la historia de España, los nombres de las calles pueden enseñarle mucho. Como en todas las ciudades del mundo, en las ciudades de España hay calles nombradas en memoria de los hombres célebres del país.

2 Una de las avenidas mas importantes de la ciudad es la Granvía. Hay una Granvía en todas las grandes ciudades. Había antes una Avenida del Generalísimo Franco. Actualmente en España hay una Monarquía constitucional. Juan Carlos I es el rey, casado con Sofía de Grecia. Tienen dos hijas, las Infantas, Cristina y Elena, y un hijo, el Príncipe Felipe.

3 En la ciudad hay otras calles muy interesantes desde el punto de vista histórico. Sus nombres recuerdan a los grandes hombres del pasado. La calle de Prim recuerda al general que combatió en las guerras de Africa en 1859 (mil ochocientos cincuenta y nueve). La calle de José Ortega y Gasset recuerda al ensayista y filósofo que murió en 1955 (mil novecientos cincuenta y cinco); la Plaza de Cánovas del Castillo al político y escritor del siglo pasado; la calle de Núñez de Balboa al conquistador que murió en 1517 (mil quinientos diez y siete); y la Plaza de Cristóbal Colón al célebre navegante que descubrió América.

4 ¿Sra. Adams, le interesan a Ud. estos nombres?

5 Sí, sí. Me interesan mucho. Un día voy a caminar por las calles cuyos nombres recuerdan a los hombres célebres, y voy a recordar las palabras de mi maestro y amigo, el señor López.

6 Ahora es favor que Ud. me hace a mí.[1]

7 No es favor. Es verdad. Pero veo que las fechas también son importantes. ¿Hay en España fechas importantes como el 23 (veinte y tres) de abril en Inglaterra — la fiesta de San Jorge?

8 Sí, hay muchos días de fiesta en España. Y son verdaderas fiestas, porque la gente no trabaja. Algunas de estas fechas son: el 19 (diez y nueve) de marzo, la fiesta de San José; el 25 de julio, la fiesta de Santiago, el santo patrón de España; el 1° (primero) de noviembre, la fiesta de Todos los Santos; y Ud. sabe lo que significa la fecha 25 (veinte y cinco) de diciembre—la Navidad. Hay otros días de fiesta nacionales—y además cada pueblo y aldea celebra la fiesta de su propio santo patrón. San Jorge es el patrón de Cataluña.

9 En Gran Bretaña, dice la señora Adams, hay tan pocos días de fiesta. ¡Qué lástima!

1 If the tourist knows nothing about the history of Spain, the names of the streets can teach him a great deal. As in all the cities in the world, so in the cities of Spain there are streets named in memory of the famous men of their home country.

2 One of the most important avenues of the city is the Granvía (the Great Way). There is a Granvía in all the big cities. There used to be an avenue of Generalissimo Franco. Spain is now a constitutional monarchy. Juan Carlos I is the King, married to Sofia of Greece. They have two daughters, the Infantas (Princesses), Christina and Elena and one son, Prince Philip.

3 In the city there are other very interesting streets from the historical point of view. Their names recall the great men of the past. Prim Street recalls the general who fought in the wars in Africa in 1859. José Ortega y Gasset Street recalls the essayist and philosopher who died in 1955; Cánovas del Castillo Square the politician and writer of the last (*lit.* past) century; Núñez de Balboa Street the conquistador who died in 1517; and Christopher Columbus Square the famous navigator who discovered America.

4 Mrs. Adams, do these names interest you?

5 Yes, yes. They interest me very much. Some day I am going to walk along the streets whose names recall famous men and I will recall the words of my teacher and friend, Mr. López.

6 Now you flatter *me*.

7 It is not flattery. It is the truth. But I see that dates are also important. Are there in Spain important dates like April 23 in England—St. George's Day?

8 Yes, there are many feast days in Spain. And they are true holidays, because the people do not work. Some of these dates are; March 19, St. Joseph's Day; July 25, St. James's Day, the patron saint of Spain; November 1, All Saints' Day; and you know what the date December 25 means—Christmas. There are other national holidays—and in addition each town or village celebrates the feast day of its own patron saint. Saint George is the patron saint of Catalonia.

9 'In Great Britain,' says Mrs. Adams, 'there are so few feast days. What a pity.'

NOTE: 1. **a mí** *to me*, added for emphasis.

Pronunciation Aids

Practise:

historia (is-ˈto-rja)   **significa** (siɣ-ni-ˈfi-ka)
recordar (rre-kor-ˈðar)   **recuerda** (rre-ˈkwer-ða)

Gran Via (ɤran ˈvi-a) or
(ɤram ˈbi-a)

Vocabulary Building

A. Antónimos:

1 **contra** against **por** for   2 **enseñar** to teach **aprender** to learn

B. Palabras Relacionadas:

1 **interesar**	to interest	**interesante**	interesting
2 **la historia**	history	**histórico**	historical
3 **luchar**	to fight	**la lucha**	the fight
4 **caminar**	to walk	**el camino**	the road
5 **recordar**	to recall, remember	**el recuerdo**	the remembrance
6 **resistir**	to resist	**la resistencia**	resistance
7 **comenzar**	to begin	**el comienzo**	beginning

C. Los grandes hombres the great men. The adjective **grande** placed before a noun means great. After a noun it means *big*. Thus:

un hombre grande a big man   **un gran hombre** a great man

Note that **grande** (*not* **grandes**), before a noun, becomes **gran**.

Expresiones Importantes

1 **en memoria de** in memory of 2 **desde ... hasta** from ... to, until

Exercise No. 58—Completion of Text

1 (They know nothing) **de la historia de España.**
2 **Las calles** (can) **enseñarles mucho.**
3 **Hay calles nombradas** (in memory of) **los hombres célebres de la** (fatherland).
4 **Una de las avenidas** (most important) **es la Granvía.**
5 **Esta avenida** (is more commonly called) **la Gran Vía.**
6 **La calle de José Ortega y Gasset recuerda al** (essayist and philosopher).
7 **Son interesaptes** (from the point of view) **histórico.**
8 **Cánovas del Castillo fue un escritor y político** (of the last century).
9 **Cristóbal Colón** (discovered America).
10 (These names) **me interesan mucho.**
11 **Voy a** (walk) **por las calles** (whose) **nombres recuerdan a los hombres célebres.**
12 **Voy a** (recall) **las palabras de mi maestro.**

Grammar Notes

1 The Present Tense of **recordar(ue)** to remember and **oír** to hear.

I remember, you remember, etc.   I hear, you hear, etc.

recuerdo	**recordamos**	**oigo**	**oímos**
recuerdas	**recordáis**	**oyes**	**oís**
recuerda	**recuerdan**	**oye**	**oyen**

2 Ordinal Numbers

primero (a)	first	**sexto (a)**	sixth
segundo (a)	second	**séptimo (a)**	seventh
tercero (a)	third	**octavo (a)**	eighth
cuarto (a)	fourth	**noveno (a)**	ninth
quinto (a)	fifth	**décimo (a)**	tenth

(a) Ordinal numbers are used much less in Spanish than in English. After the tenth they are seldom used.

(b) Like other adjectives they agree with their nouns in number and gender.

la primera fila   la segunda fila   el décimo piso

(c) Before a masculine singular noun **primero** and **tercero** drop the **-o.** When alone, they keep the ending.

el primer año   el primero   el tercer mes   el tercero

3 Dates

1° de mayo de 1968   (el primero de mayo) May 1, 1968
5 de mayo de 1861   (el cinco de mayo) May 5, 1861

(a) **Primero** is used for the first day of the month. After that the cardinal numbers **dos, tres,** etc. are used.

(b) The order for a date is: (day) **de** (month) **de** (year).

(c) The numbers in the year are read like numbers in general.

1968 (mil novecientos sesenta y ocho)
1861 (mil ochocientos sesenta y uno)

4 Pronouns with Prepositions

para mí	for me	**para nosotros -as**	for us
para ti	for you (*fam. sing.*)	**para vosotros -as**	for you (*fam. plur.*)
para Ud.	for you	**para Uds.**	for you
para él	for him	**para ellos**	for them (*masc. pl.*)
para ella	for her	**para ellas**	for them (*fem. pl.*)

(a) Pronouns with prepositions, except **mí** (*me*) and **ti** (*you*), are the same as the subject pronouns.

(b) With the preposition **con, mí** and **ti** become **conmigo** *with me*, and **contigo** *with you*.

(c) The accent mark on **mí** (*me*) distinguishes it from mi (*my*).

Ejercicios (Exercises) No. 59A–59B

59A. Complete the Spanish sentences so that they correspond fully to the English sentences.

Ejemplo: 1. Hablamos de Ud., señor.

1 We are speaking of you, sir.	**1 Hablamos de —— , señor.**
2 They do not work for us (m.).	**2 No trabajan para —— .**
3 He is standing near them (f.).	**3 Está de pie cerca de —— .**
4 They are seated behind me.	**4 Están sentados detrás de —— .**
5 You can go with me.	**5 Ud. puede ir —— .**
6 I want to go with you, Johnny.	**6 Quiero ir —— , Juanito.**
7 We are for them, not against them.	**7 Estamos por —— , no contra —— .**
8 We prefer to go without you, Anna.	**8 Preferimos ir sin —— , Ana.**
9 The ashtray is in front of her.	**9 El cenicero está delante de —— .**
10 We are going to have dinner with him.	**10 Vamos a cenar con —— .**

59B. Translate in two ways:

> **Ejemplo:** Where is your book, Anna? **¿Dónde está su libro (el libro de Ud.), Ana?**

1 Where is her book?	5 Where are your parents, boys?
2 Where is his book?	6 Where is your house, Mrs. A?
3 Where are her books?	7 Where are their chairs?
4 Where are his books?	8 Where is their room?

Exercise No. 60—Preguntas

1 ¿Cuál es la fecha de la fiesta de Santiago?
2 ¿Qué gobierno tiene España?
3 ¿Quién es el Rey de España?
4 ¿Qué santo es el patrón de Cataluña?
5 ¿Cuál es el nombre del general que combatió en las guerras de Africa?
6 ¿Quién fue un filósofo y ensayista célebre?
7 ¿Cuándo murió?
8 ¿Cuál es el nombre de uno de los conquistadores?
9 ¿Interesan estos nombres a la señora Adams?
10 ¿Qué palabras va a recordar?
11 ¿Cuántos días de fiesta hay en España?
12 ¿Hay más días de fiesta que en Gran Bretaña?

CHAPTER 17

CALLES, RÍOS Y MONTAÑAS

PRIMERA PARTE

1 Ya sabe Ud., señora Adams, que hay muchas calles en Madrid cuyos nombres recuerdan a los españoles célebres. También hay calles cuyos nombres recuerdan ciudades y regiones españolas — Toledo, Alcalá, Ibiza y muchas otras.

2 Además se encuentran calles que tienen nombres de los escritores españoles más conocidos — Miguel de Cervantes, que escribió *Don Quijote*, y cuyo nombre conocemos todos; José de Espronceda, el poeta románticon del siglo XIX (diez y nueve); Lope de Vega, que nació en 1562 (mil quinientos sesenta y dos) y murió en 1635 (mil seiscientos treinta y cinco), y que escribió más de 1.500 (mil quinientas) comedias. Los nombres de otras calles celebran a algunos de los pintores más famosos: Goya, Zurbarán y Velázquez, por ejemplo.

3 Realmente, una persona que tiene la costumbre de caminar por las calles de Madrid puede educarse bien y barato.

4 A propósito, señora Adams, ¿Me permite Ud. hacerle algunas preguntas acerca de la geografía?

5 Por supuesto. Y, ¿voy a recibir un premio por las respuestas correctas?

6 No, señora Adams, éste no es un programa de televisión. Vamos a empezar. ¿Cuál es el río más grande del mundo?

7 El Misisipí es el río más grande.

8 Está Ud. equivocada. El Misisipí es mucho más pequeño que el río Amazonas. Éste es el más voluminoso, no solamente de las Américas sino también del mundo entero. Tiene más de 4.600 millas de largo y cruza todo el Brasil. Y, ¿cuál es el pico más alto de América del Sur?

9 No me acuerdo del nombre pero está en los Andes. Es más alto que cualquier pico de las Américas, de Europa o de África. Pero hay picos más altos en el Himalaya en Asia.

10 Se llama Aconcagua, aquel pico altísimo. Bien, una pregunta más. ¿Sabe Ud. los nombres de algunos ríos y picos de España?

11 Creo que sí. Hay los ríos Ebro, Guadalquivir, Tajo y Duero. Tres picos son: Aneto, Mulhacén y Moncayo.

12 Muy bien, señora Adams. Sus conocimientos de geografía son excelentes.

13 ¿Cómo no? Una importadora tiene que conocer la geografía, ¿verdad?

1 You already know, Mrs. Adams, that there are many streets in Madrid whose names recall famous Spaniards. Also there are streets whose names recall Spanish cities and regions—Toledo, Alcalá, Ibiza and many others.

2 In addition there are streets (*lit.* streets meet themselves) which have names of the most well-known Spanish writers—Miguel de Cervantes, who wrote *Don Quixote*, and whose name we all know; José de Espronceda, the Romantic poet of the 19th century; Lope de Vega, who was born in 1562 and died in 1635, and who wrote more than 1,500 plays! The names of other streets celebrate some of the most famous painters: Goya, Zurbarán and Velázquez, for example.

3 Indeed, a person who has the habit of walking through the streets of Madrid can educate himself well and cheaply.

4 By the way, Mrs. Adams, will you permit me to ask you some questions about geography?

5 Of course. And will I receive a prize for the correct answers?

6 No, Mrs. Adams, this is not a television programme. Let us begin. What is the largest river in the world?

7 The Mississippi is the largest river.

8 You are mistaken. The Mississippi is much smaller than the river Amazon. This is the biggest not only in the Americas but also in the whole world. It is more than 4,600 miles long and crosses all Brazil. And what is the highest peak in South America?

9 I do not remember the name but it is in the Andes. It is higher than any mountain in the Americas, Europe or Africa. But indeed, there are higher peaks in the Himalayas of Asia.

10 That very high peak is called Aconcagua. Well then, one more question. Do you know the names of a few rivers and peaks in Spain?

11 I think so. There are the rivers Ebro, Guadalquivir, Tagus and Duero. Three peaks are: Aneto, Mulhacén and Moncayo.

12 Very good, Mrs. Adams. Your knowledge (*note that Spanish says* 'knowledges') of geography is excellent.

13 Of course! An importer has to know geography, hasn't she?

Pronunciation Aids

Practise:

cuyos ('ku-jos)
escritores (es-kri-'to-res)
encuentran (eŋ-'kwen-tran)
geografía (xe-o-ɣra-'fi-a)
cruza ('kru-θa)

celebrar (θe-le-βrar)
costumbre (kos-'tum-bre)
el río Amazonas (el 'ri-o
   a-ma-'θo-nas)
cualquiera (kwal-'kje-ra)

Aconcagua (a-koŋ-'ka-γwa)
nació (na-'θjo)
recuerdan (rre-'kwer-ðan)

Asia ('a-sja)
Velázquez (ve-'laθ-keθ) or
(be-'laθ-keθ)
murió (mu-'rjo)

Building Vocabulary

A. Sinónimos:

1	realmente	verdaderamente	claro está	indeed
2	el sabio	el hombre de ciencia	el científico	the scientist
3	conseguir	obtener	adquirir	to obtain

B. Antónimos:

1	barato	cheap	caro	dear
2	alto	high	bajo	low
3	el más largo	the longest	el más corto	the shortest
4	fácil	easy	difícil	hard

C. Palabras Relacionadas:

1	educar	to educate	educación	education
2	la ciencia	science	el científico	the scientist
3	historia	history	histórico	historical

Expresiones Importantes

1	dar un paseo	to take a walk
2	hacer preguntas	to ask questions
3	cualquier montaña	any mountain

Exercise No. 61—Completion of Text

1 Hay muchas calles (whose) **nombres** (recall) **grandes hombres.**

2 Otras calles recuerdan (Spanish cities).

3 Otras calles tienen nombres de los escritores (most well-known).

4 Además (one can meet with = there meet themselves) **calles que** **tienen nombres de pintor.**

5 (Indeed) **una persona puede** (get a good and inexpensive education) **en las calles de Madrid.**

6 (By the way) Sra. **Adams, quiero hacerle a Ud. algunas preguntas** (about) **la geografía.**

7 **Ud. no va a** (receive) **un premio.**

8 ¿**Es** (larger) **el Misisipí que el Amazonas?**

9 **El Misisipí es** (smaller) **que el Amazonas.**

10 **Este río es** (the largest) **y** (the longest) **del mundo.**

11 **El pico de Aconcagua es** (higher) **que cualquier pico de las Américas.**

12 **Hay picos** (higher) **en el Himalaya.**
13 (Your knowledge) **de geografía son excelentes.**
14 (He has to know) **la geografía.**

SEGUNDA PARTE

Grammar Notes

1 Comparison of Adjectives in Spanish.

> **grande,** large
> **más grande,** larger
> **el (la) más grande,** largest

notable, notable	**notable,** notable
más notable, more notable	**menos notable,** less notable
el (la) más notable, most notable	**el (la) menos notable,** least notable

(a) These adjectives follow and agree with their nouns as usual. In the superlative the definite article or a possessive adjective precedes the noun.

las avenidas más hermosas	the most beautiful avenues
mi profesor más amable	my kindest teacher

(b) After a superlative use **de** not **en** for *in*.

el río más largo del mundo	the longest river in the world

(c) as . . . adj. . . . as, is expressed in Spanish as **tan . . . adj. . . . como.**

Carlos es tan alto como Ana.	Charles is as tall as Anna.
El Tíber no es tan largo como el Rin.	The Tiber is not as long as the Rhine.

(d) In comparison, *than* is usually **que.** Before a number *than* is **de.**

Londres es más grande que Nueva York.	London is larger than New York.
Tenemos más de cien libras.	We have more than £100.

2 Irregular Comparisons

bueno, good	**mejor,** better	**el (la) mejor,** best
malo, bad	**peor,** worse	**el (la) peor,** worst
grande, big	**mayor,** older **más grande,** bigger	**el (la) mayor,** oldest **el (la) más grande,** biggest
pequeño, small	**menor,** younger **más pequeño,** smaller	**el (la) menor,** youngest **el (la) más pequeño,** smallest

(a) The irregular forms of **grande** and **pequeño** refer to age. The regular forms of **grande** and **pequeño** refer to size.

Felipe es mayor que Guillermo.	Philip is older than William.
Felipe es más grande que Guillermo.	Philip is bigger than William.
Es el mayor de la familia.	He is the oldest in the family.
Es el más grande de la familia.	He is the biggest in the family.
Anita es menor que Rosita.	Annie is younger than Rosie.
Anita es más pequeña que Rosita.	Annie is smaller than Rosie.
Es la menor de la familia.	She is the youngest in the family.
Es la más pequeña de la familia.	She is the smallest in the family.

3 The ending -ísimo(a) may be used instead of **muy**.

alto	tall	**altísimo**	very tall
largo	long	**larguísimo**	very long
bueno	good	**bonísimo**	very good
rico	rich	**riquísimo**	very rich
El Aneto es un pico altísimo.		Aneto is a very high peak.	

Exercise No. 62

Complete the Spanish sentences so that they correspond fully to the English sentences.

Ejemplo: Pablo es tan alto como Juan.

1 Paul is as tall as John.
2 My pen is better than John's.
3 Mary is nicer than Elsie.
4 I have the best pen of all.
5 The black ink is not as good as the blue.
6 I want the newest book.
7 My exercises are more difficult than yours.
8 Jane is tall. Marie is taller than Jane.
9 Isabel is the tallest girl of the three.
10 Mr. García has the worst luck.
11 Philip is the oldest child.
12 The capital has the most modern buildings.
13 The pen is bad but the pencil is worse.
14 Why are you not as happy as he?
15 He is the laziest man in the office.
16 Annie is the youngest child.

1 Pablo es —— alto —— Juan.
2 Mi pluma es —— que la de Juan.
3 María es —— simpática —— Elsa.
4 Tengo la —— pluma de todas.
5 La tinta negra no es —— buena —— la tinta azul.
6 Quiero el libro —— nuevo.
7 Mis ejercicios son —— difíciles —— los de Ud.

8 Juana es alta. María es —— grande —— Juana.
9 Isabel es la muchacha —— de las tres.
10 El señor García tiene la ——[1] suerte.
11 Felipe es el hijo ——.
12 La capital tiene los edificios ——.
13 La pluma es mala, pero el lápiz es ——.
14 ¿Por qué no está Ud. —— contento —— él?
15 Él es el hombre más perezoso —— la oficina.
16 Anita es la hija ——.

NOTE: 1. **mejor** and **peor** often precede the noun.

Exercise No. 63—Preguntas

1 ¿Cuál es el río más grande de América del Sur?
2 ¿Cuál es la ciudad más grande del mundo?
3 ¿Cuál es el pico más alto de América del Sur?
4 ¿Qué ciudad es más grande que Nueva York?
5 ¿Es Madrid tan grande como Londres?
6 ¿Es Nueva York tan antigua como Madrid?
7 ¿Qué ciudad es más antigua — Londres o Nueva York?
8 ¿Qué ciudad tiene los edificios más altos del mundo?
9 ¿Cuál es el país más pequeño de Centro América?
10 El Sr. García es un hombre de cuarenta y cinco años de edad. Tiene £100.000 (cien mil libras).
El Sr. Rivera es un hombre de cincuenta años. Tiene £80.000 (ochenta mil libras). El Sr. Torres es un hombre de sesenta años. Tiene £50.000 (cincuenta mil libras).

(a) ¿Quién es el menor de los tres?
(b) ¿Quién es el mayor de los tres?
(c) ¿Es el Sr. Rivera mayor que el Sr. García?
(d) ¿Quién es el más rico?
(e) ¿Quién es el menos rico?
(f) ¿Es el Sr. Torres tan rico como el Sr. García?

CHAPTER 18

EL DÍA DE LA SEÑORA ADAMS

PRIMERA PARTE

1 Sra. Adams, ¿me permite preguntarle cómo pasa Ud. un día típico?

2 ¿Cómo no? Cuando voy a la oficina, me levanto a las seis y media. Ud. ve que soy madrugadora. Me lavo y tomo un baño y me ducho y me visto en treinta minutos más o menos. A eso de las siete me siento a la mesa en el comedor para tomar el desayuno. Mi esposo, que también es madrugador, se levanta temprano y desayunamos juntos. Naturalmente me gusta mucho esta costumbre. Tenemos la oportunidad de hablar de los niños ye de otras cosas de interés.

4 Para el desayuno tomo zumo[1] de naranja, café, panecillos o tostadas y huevos. De vez en cuando tomo te en vez de café.

5 ¿Y después del desayuno?

6 A las siete y media estoy lista para salir a tomar el tren. Ud. sabe que vivo fuera de la ciudad. Voy en coche a la estación. Dejo allí el coche hasta la tarde, cuando vuelvo de la ciudad. El tren sale para la ciudad a las ocho menos cuarto en punto. Raras veces sale tarde. Llega a la ciudad a las nueve menos cuarto en punto. Casi siempre llega a tiempo. Desde la estación de ferrocarril voy a la oficina en metro. Llego a eso de las nueve. En la oficina leo las cartas, dicto las respuestas a la taquígrafa, hablo por teléfono a varios clientes y hago una cantidad de cosas que tiene que hacer una negociante.

7 ¿Y cuándo toma Ud. el almuerzo?

8 Casi siempre a la una. Lo tomo en cosa de 30 minutos.

9 Es muy poco tiempo. En España va a ver Ud. que son muy distintas las costumbres. El negociante español pasa mucho más tiempo en las comidas. Pero en otra ocasión vamos a hablar más de esto. ¿Qué toma Ud. para almorzar?

10 Ordinariamente tomo un bocadillo con café y tal o cual postre — una manzana cocida, una torta, o helado.

11 ¿Qué hace Ud. después del almuerzo?

12 Hago lo mismo que por la mañana. Muchas veces algunos clientes vienen a visitarme por la tarde y de vez en cuando salgo a visitar a otros clientes.

13 ¿A qué hora termina Ud. el trabajo?

14 A las cinco en punto salgo de la oficina y tomo el tren de las cinco

y media. Llego a casa a eso de las siete menos cuarto y me siento a la mesa para tomar la cena.

15 Ud. debe de estar cansada después de semejante día.

16 — ¡Ya lo creo! — responde la señora Adams.

1 Mrs. Adams, may I ask you how you spend a typical day?

2 Certainly. When I go to the office, I get up at six-thirty. You see that I am an early riser. I wash and take a bath or a shower and dress in thirty minutes more or less. At about seven, I sit down at the table in the dining-room to have breakfast. My husband, who is also an early riser, gets up early and we have breakfast together. Naturally I like this custom very much. We have an opportunity to talk about the children and other interesting things.

3 What do you have for breakfast?

4 For breakfast I have orange juice, coffee, rolls or toast, and eggs. Sometimes I have tea instead of coffee.

5 And after breakfast?

6 At seven-thirty I am ready to leave to catch the train. You know that I live outside the city. I go by car to the station. I leave the car there until the afternoon, when I return from the city. The train leaves for the city at a quarter to eight sharp. It seldom leaves late. It arrives at the city at quarter to nine sharp. It almost always arrives on time. From the railway station, I go to my office by underground. I arrive at about nine. In the office I read letters, dictate answers to the shorthand-typist, talk on the telephone to various clients and do a number of things that a businesswoman has to do.

7 And when do you have lunch?

8 Almost always at one. I take it in about 30 minutes.

9 It is very little time. In Spain you will see that customs are very different. The Spanish businessman spends much more time at meals. But another time we will speak more of this. What do you have for lunch?

10 Usually I have a sandwich and coffee and some dessert or other— a baked apple, a cake or ice cream.

11 What do you do after lunch?

12 I do the same as in the morning. Often some clients come to visit me in the afternoon and from time to time I go out to visit other clients.

13 At what time do you stop work?

14 At five o'clock sharp I leave the office and take the five-thirty train. I arrive home at about a quarter to seven and I sit down at table to have dinner.

15 You must be tired after such a day.

16 'Yes, indeed!' answers Mrs. Adams.

NOTE: 1. **Jugo** is also extensively used.

Pronunciation Aids

1 Practise:

preguntar (pre-ɣun-'tar)
madrugador (ma-ðru-ɣa-'ðor)
madrugadora (ma-ðru-ɣa-'ðo-ra)
desayuno (ðe-sa-'ju-no)
desayunarse (ðe-sa-ju-'nar-se)
desayunamos (ðe-sa-ju-'na-mos)
oportunidad (o-por-tu-ni-'ðað)
panecillos (pa-ne-'θi-ʎos)

tostadas (tos-'ta-ðas)
huevos ('we-vos) or ('we-βos)
afuera (a-'fwe-ra)
taquígrafa (ta-'ki-ɣra-fa)
teléfono (te-'le-fo-no)
clientes ('kljen-tes)
bocadillo (bo-ka-'ði-ʎo)

2 tostada a piece of toast

Building Vocabulary

A. Sinónimos:

1 **tomar el desayuno**	**desayunarse**	to have breakfast
2 **naturalmente**	**por supuesto**	of course
3 **platicar**	**charlar**	to chat
4 **algunas veces**	**de vez en cuando**	sometimes

B. Antónimos:

1 **después del desayuno**	after breakfast	**antes del desayuno**	before breakfast
2 **poco tiempo**	little time	**mucho tiempo**	much time

C. Palabras Relacionadas:

1 **comer,** to eat **comedor,** dining-room **la comida,** the meal
2 **el desayuno,** the breakfast **desayunarse,** to have breakfast

D. Zumos (Juices)

1 **zumo de naranja**	orange juice	4 **zumo de uvas**	grape juice
2 **zumo de tomate**	tomato juice	5 **zumo de piña**	pineapple juice
3 **zumo de pomelo**	grapefruit juice	6 **zumo de limón**	lemon juice

Expresiones Importantes

1 **a eso de las siete**	at about seven
2 **a las cinco en punto**	at five o'clock sharp
3 **de costumbre**	generally
4 **ponerse**	to become
5 **Me pongo enfermo**	I become sick
6 **Tomo un baño**	I take a bath
7 **Me ducho**	I take a shower

B. Expressions with **vez**:

1 **una vez**	one time	7 **ninguna vez**	at no time
2 **dos veces**	two times	8 **cuántas veces**	how many
3 **otra vez**	another time		times
4 **algunas veces**	sometimes	9 **cada vez**	each time
5 **muchas veces**	many times	10 **de vez en cuando**	from time to
6 **raras veces**	seldom		time
		11 **en vez de**	instead of

Exercise No. 64—Completion of Text

1 Sra. Adams, ¿me permite Vd. (to ask you at what time) **se levanta Ud.?**
2 **Me levanto** (at 6.30).
3 **Soy** (an early riser). **Mi esposo es** (an early riser).
4 **Siempre se levanta** (early).
5 **A las siete y media** (I am ready to leave).
6 (I read) **las cartas y** (I dictate) **las respuestas.**
7 **Para el almuerzo tomo** (a sandwich with coffee and some dessert or other).
8 (Often) **algunos clientes vienen** (to visit me).
9 **Termino el trabajo** (at five o'clock sharp).
10 (The customs) **son muy distintas en España.**

PARTE SEGUNDA

Grammar Notes

1 Present Tense of Model Reflexive verb. **lavarse** to wash oneself

me lavo	I wash myself
te lavas	you wash yourself (*fam.*)
Ud. **se lava**⎱	you wash yourself
se lava⎰	he washes himself
	she washes herself
	it washes itself
nos lavamos	we wash ourselves
os laváis	you wash yourselves (*fam.*)
Uds. **se lavan**⎱	you wash yourselves
se lavan⎰	they wash themselves

(a) Observe that the reflexive pronoun **se** means *oneself, yourself, himself, herself, itself, yourselves,* and *themselves.*

(b) Like other object pronouns reflexives usually precede the verb. Used with the infinitive, they follow the verb and are attached to it.

lavarse, to wash oneself   **Quiero lavarme,** I want to wash myself.

2 Present Tense of **sentarse(ie)** to sit down (seat oneself), **vestirse(i)** to dress oneself.

I sit down, etc.		I dress myself, etc.	
me siento	**nos sentamos**	**me visto**	**nos vestimos**
te sientas	**os sentáis**	**te vistes**	**os vestís**
Ud. se sienta⎫	**Uds. se sientan⎫**	**Ud. se viste⎫**	**Uds. se visten⎫**
se sienta⎭	**se sientan⎭**	**se viste⎭**	**se visten⎭**

3 Other Reflexive Verbs

Some Spanish reflexive verbs are not translated by a reflexive verb in English.

sentarse, to sit down (to seat oneself)	**Me siento,** I sit down
levantarse, to get up (to raise oneself)	**Me levanto,** I get up
acostarse(ue), to go to bed	**Me acuesto,** I go to bed
llamarse, to be called (to call oneself)	**Me llamo,** My name is ...
encontrarse(ue), to be (to find oneself)	**Me encuentro,** I am (somewhere)
comerse, to eat up	**Me como el pan.** I eat up the bread.
llevarse, to take away	**Se lleva el echarpe.** He takes away the shawl.
irse, to go away	**Me voy de esta ciudad.** I am going away from this city.
acordarse(ue), to remember	**Nos acordamos de él.** We remember him.
ponerse, to become	**Se ponen enfermos.** They become (get) ill.
bañarse	**Me baño**
ducharse	**Me ducho**

Ejercicios (Exercises) No. 65A–65B

65A. Translate the following questions and answers. Then practise the Spanish aloud.

1 ¿A qué hora se acuesta Ud?
 Me acuesto a las once de la noche.
2 ¿A qué hora se levanta Ud?
 Me levanto a las siete de la mañana.
3 ¿Se lava Ud. antes de vestirse?
 Sí, me lavo antes de vestirme.
4 ¿Dónde se encuentra Ud. al mediodía?
 Me encuentro en mi oficina.
5 ¿Cuándo se va Ud. de aquí?
 Mañana me voy de aquí.

6 ¿Se pone Ud. enfermo cuando come muchos dulces?

Sí, me pongo enfermo.

7 ¿En qué fila del cine se sientan Uds?

Nos sentamos en la fila catorce o quince.

8 ¿Se acuerdan Uds. de nuestras conversaciones?

Sí, nos acordamos de ellas.

65B. Make the Spanish sentences correspond to the English by inserting the correct form of the reflexive pronoun.

Ejemplo: 1. La Sra. Adams se sienta en el comedor.

1 Mrs. Adams sits down in the dining-room.

2 She gets up at seven o'clock.

3 She washes and dresses herself.

4 At what time do you go to bed?

5 I go to bed at 10 o'clock.

6 What is his name?

7 Mr. and Mrs. Adams are (find themselves) in the living-room.

8 When do you get up?

9 We get up about seven.

10 I don't remember the name.

1 La Sra. Adams —— sienta en el comedor.

2 —— levanta a las siete.

3 —— lava y —— viste.

4 ¿A qué hora —— acuesta Ud.?

5 —— acuesto a las diez.

6 ¿Cómo —— llama?

7 Los señores Adams —— encuentran en la sala.

8 ¿Cuándo —— levantan Uds.?

9 —— levantamos a eso de las siete.

10 No —— acuerdo del nombre.

NOTE: **señores** can mean Mr. and Mrs.

Exercise No. 66—Preguntas

66. Answer the following in complete sentences.

1 ¿A qué hora se levanta la Sra. Adams?

2 Entonces, ¿qué hace?

3 ¿En cuántos minutos se viste?

4 ¿Qué hace a eso de las siete?

5 ¿Se levanta su esposo temprano?

6 ¿Desayunan ellos juntos?

7 ¿Qué toma ella para el desayuno?

8 ¿Qué toma de vez en cuando en vez de café?

9 ¿A qué hora está lista para salir?

10 ¿Cómo va la Sra. Adams a la estación?
11 ¿A qué hora llega a su oficina?
12 ¿Cuándo toma el almuerzo?
13 ¿Qué toma para el almuerzo?
14 ¿Vienen clientes a visitarla por la tarde?
15 ¿A qué hora termina el trabajo?

REVISION 4

CHAPTERS 15–18 PRIMERA PARTE

Repaso de Palabras

NOUNS

1 el almuerzo	11 la estrella	21 el panecillo
2 el asiento	12 la fiesta	22 la tostada
3 la cara	13 la historia	23 la película
4 el camino	14 el huevo	24 el metro
5 el cliente	15 el zumo	25 el postre
6 el coche	16 la luz	26 el recuerdo
7 el comienzo	17 la manzana	27 el río
8 la costumbre	18 la naranja	28 el sur
9 el bocadillo	19 el norte	29 el turista
10 el desayuno	20 el ojo	30 el teléfono

1 lunch	11 star	21 roll
2 seat	12 holiday	22 piece of toast
3 face	13 history	23 film
4 road	14 egg	24 underground
5 customer	15 juice	25 dessert
6 car	16 light	26 remembrance
7 beginning	17 apple	27 river
8 custom	18 orange	28 south
9 sandwich	19 north	29 tourist
10 breakfast	20 eye	30 telephone

VERBS

1 acordarse	15 irse	29 preferir(ie)
2 buscar	16 hallar	30 reír(i)
3 caminar	17 lavar	31 sonreír(i)
4 celebrar	18 lavarse	32 recordar(ue)
5 comer	19 levantar	33 sentarse(ie)
6 comerse	20 levantarse	34 sentir(ie)
7 cruzar	21 llevar	35 sentirse(ie)
8 deber	22 llevarse	36 significar
9 dejar	23 llamar	37 tratar
10 desayunarse	24 llamarse	38 terminar
11 dormir(ue)	25 poner	39 vestir(i)
12 dormirse	26 ponerse	40 vestirse
13 encontrar(ue)	27 oír	41 volver(ue)
14 encontrarse	28 permitir	42 fue

1 to remember	5 to eat	9 to let, to leave
2 to look for	6 to eat up	10 to breakfast
3 to walk	7 to cross	11 to sleep
4 to celebrate	8 to owe, ought to	12 to fall asleep

13 to meet, to find	23 to call	33 to sit down
14 to be (somewhere)	24 to be named	34 to feel, regret
15 to go away	25 to put	35 to feel (sad, weak, etc.)
16 to find	26 to become	36 to mean
17 to wash	27 to hear	37 to try
18 to wash oneself	28 to permit	38 to end
19 to raise	29 to prefer	39 to dress
20 to get up	30 to laugh	40 to dress oneself
21 to carry, wear	31 to smile	41 to return
22 to take away	32 to recall	42 he (she) was

ADJECTIVES

1 ancho	5 chico	9 ocupado
2 barato	6 desocupado	10 oscuro
3 caro	7 junto	11 raro
4 conocido	8 mayor	12 tal

1 wide	5 small	9 busy, occupied
2 cheap	6 unoccupied	10 dark
3 dear	7 together	11 rare
4 well-known	8 older	12 such

ADVERBS

1 ordinariamente	2 naturalmente	3 temprano

1 ordinarily	2 naturally	3 early

PREPOSITIONS

1 contra	2 lejos de	3 en vez de

1 against	2 far from	3 instead of

IMPORTANT EXPRESSIONS

1 a pie	10 en punto
2 a eso de	11 hacer daño
3 a ver	12 más o menos
4 a tiempo	13 me gusta más
5 acabo de + infin.	14 no solamente
6 claro está	15 sino también
7 estar de pie	16 por consiguiente
8 desde luego	17 Ud. debe de estar cansado
9 de vez en cuando	18 dar un paseo

1 on foot	10 sharp, on the dot
2 at about	11 to hurt
3 let's see	12 more or less
4 on time	13 I prefer
5 I have just	14 not only
6 of course	15 but also
7 to stand	16 consequently
8 of course	17 you must be tired
9 from time to time	18 to take a walk

SEGUNDA PARTE

Ejercicio 67   Select the group of words in Column I which best completes the sentence begun in Column II.

I

1 Los niños Adams conocen
2 Desde la fila catorce
3 En Madrid hay calles
4 El 26 de julio es
5 Una de las avenidas más hermosas de Madrid
6 El río más grande del mundo
7 El Tajo y el Duero
8 Un madrugador se levanta
9 Para comenzar el desayuno la señora
10 Para llegar a la oficina viaja

II

(a) muy temprano.
(b) es la Gran Vía.
(c) es el Amazonas.
(d) la fiesta de Santiago.
(e) se puede ver y oír bien.
(f) en tren, en metro, y a pie.
(g) toma zumo de naranja.
(h) son dos ríos de España.
(i) a las estrellas de la pantalla.
(j) nombradas en memoria de los hombres célebres de España.

Ejercicio 68   Read the Spanish questions and then make your answer in Spanish correspond to the English answer following the question:

1 ¿Invita Ud. a sus amigos a su casa?
    Yes, I invite them from time to time.
2 ¿Prefiere Ud. el cine?
    No, I do not prefer it.
3 ¿Conocen los niños a las estrellas del cine?
    Yes, they know them well.
4 ¿Nos esperan Uds.?
    Yes, we are waiting for you.
5 ¿Dónde pone la criada las tazas?
    She puts them on the table.
6 ¿Me busca Ud.?
    No, I am not looking for you, sir.
7 ¿A qué hora se levanta Ud.?
    I get up at eight o'clock.

8 ¿Se lavan Uds. antes de comer?
  Yes, we wash ourselves before eating.
9 ¿En qué fila se sientan los Adams?
  They sit in row fifteen.
10 ¿Cómo se llama su padre?
   My father's name is ——.

Ejercicio 69 Complete these sentences by writing all English words in Spanish.

1 El Amazonas es el río (the largest in the world).
2 Londres es (bigger than) Manchester.
3 Mi padre es (older than) mi madre.
4 No soy (so tall as) mi hermano.
5 Anita es (the youngest in) la familia.
6 El domingo es (the first day) de la semana.
7 Hoy es (January 30, 1968).
8 ¿Desea Vd. ir (with me) al teatro?
9 Pablo prefiere ir (without me).
10 Cuando (I hear) una palabra española (I remember it).

Ejercicio 70 The following expressions are used in the sentences below. See if you can apply them correctly.

tener que + infinitive	hacer preguntas
darse la mano	dar un paseo
por consiguiente	acostarse
a eso de	de vez en cuando
deber de + infinitive	otra vez

1 Los amigos (shake hands).
2 (We must study) todos los días.
3 (I go to bed) a las once.
4 El profesor (asks many questions).
5 El mio está enfermo. (Consequently) no puede ir a la escuela.
6 Voy al teatro (from time to time).
7 Me gusta (to take a walk) por la noche.
8 (You must be) muy cansado, señor.
9 Dígame su nombre (again), por favor.
10 Me levanto (at about 7.30 a.m.).

TERCERA PARTE

Practise the Spanish aloud: **Diálogo**

En el mercado

Estamos cerca de un puesto donde se venden mantas.
Comprador: ¿Cuánto cuesta ésta blanca y negra?
Vendedor: 200 (doscientas) pesetas.

Comprador: Es demasiado. Le doy a Ud. 125 (ciento veinte y cinco).
Vendedor: No, señor. Esta es muy fina. Por 175 (ciento setenta y cinco).
Comprador: Es mucho. Le doy 140 (ciento cuarenta).
Vendedor: Es barato, señor. Mire Ud. Es muy grande. Es para cama de
matrimonio. Déme 160 (ciento sesenta).
Comprador: Yo soy soltero. No voy a casarme. Le doy 145 (ciento
cuarenta y cinco).
Vendedor: No puedo, señor. Tengo mujer y seis niños. Tenemos que vivir.
155 (ciento cincuenta y cinco). Es el último precio.
Comprador: Muy bien.

**Da al vendedor 155 pesetas y se lleva la manta negra y blanca. Es
costumbre regatear¹ y los dos se quedan² muy contentos.**

We are near a stand where blankets are sold.
Buyer: How much does this black and white one cost?
Seller: 200 pesetas.
Buyer: It's too much. I'll give you l25.
Seller: Well, no sir. It's very fine. For 175 pesetas it's yours.
Buyer: It's too much. I'll give you 140.
Seller: It is cheap sir. Look. It's very big. It's for a marriage bed. Give
me 160.
Buyer: I am a bachelor. I'm not going to get married. I'll give you 145.
Seller: I cannot do it, sir. I have a wife and six children. We have to live.
155. It's the final price (offer).
Buyer: Very well.

He gives the seller 155 pesetas and takes away the black and white
blanket. It is customary to bargain and both are (remain) pleased.

Note: 1. **Regatear** (to bargain) is very little used nowadays and is
mostly restricted to gypsy traders.
Note: 2. **Quedarse** (to remain) may be used instead of **estar** (to be).

LECTURA

Exercise No. 71—Una visita a Soho

Es sábado. La señora Adams se levanta a las ocho, y mira por la
ventana. El cielo es de color azul. Hay un sol brillante. Dice a su
esposo, — Hoy vamos a visitar Soho. Es un distrito internacional. Allí
se venden periódicos y revistas españolas, y hay tiendas españolas. Está
cerca de los cines, de manera que (so that) por la tarde podemos ver
una buena película.

— Está bien, dice su esposo.

A las nueve suben (get into) al coche y después de cuarenta y cinco
minutos de viaje llegan a Soho. Bajan (they get out) del coche y comienzan a pasearse (to walk) por las calles. Al poco tiempo (in a little while)
ven a un grupo de muchachas que están de pie (are standing) cerca de
una tienda, y que hablan muy rápidamente en español.

La señora Adams saluda a las muchachas y empieza a charlar con ellas. Sigue la conversación:

— Buenos días, ¿son Uds. españolas?

— Sí, señora. Yo soy estudiante. Estoy en Londres para aprender el inglés.

— Yo también soy española. Trabajo en una casa particular (a private house). Ayudo a la señora y cuido (look after) a sus niños.

— Yo, señora, soy inglesa, pero sé hablar bien el español. Tengo muchas amigas españolas y ellas son mis profesoras. En casa tengo libros en español y estudio mucho. A propósito, ¿es Ud. española?

— No, yo soy inglesa también, y como Ud. estudio el español. Me gusta mucho la lengua. Parece (it seems) que en Londres hay muchas personas que estudian el español. Hoy quiero comprar unas botellas de vino español. Dígame, ¿conoce Ud. una buena tienda?

— Sí, señora. En la esquina hay una tienda excelente. Allí se vende (*lit.* there sells itself) un vino de Málaga muy bueno.

— Muchas gracias, dice a la muchacha, hasta la vista.

— Hasta luego, señora.

Los señores Adams van a la tienda.

— ¡Qué muchacha tan simpática! dice la señora Adams a su esposo. Y entonces (then) traduce (she translates) la frase, porque éste no comprende el español: 'What a nice girl!'

— ¡Ya lo creo! responde sonriendo (smiling) el señor Adams, que después de todo (after all) sabe decir unas pocas palabras en español.

CHAPTER 19

¡QUÉ TIEMPO TAN LLUVIOSO!

PRIMERA PARTE

1 Está lloviendo mucho. La criada abre la puerta de la casa de los señores Adams. Entra el señor López.

2 La criada dice — Buenas noches, señor López. ¡Qué tiempo tan lluvioso! Pase Ud., pase Ud. Está Ud. bastante mojado. Por favor, déme el impermeable y el sombrero. Ponga el paraguas en el paragüero.

3 El señor López responde — Gracias. Ahora estoy bien. Llueve a cántaros, pero no hace frío. Estoy seguro de que no voy a coger un resfriado. ¿Está en casa la señora Adams?

4 Sí. Le espera a Ud. en la sala. Aquí está ella misma.

5 Buenas tardes, señor López. Mucho gusto en verle, pero Ud. no debería salir de su casa con este tiempo. Venga conmigo al comedor y tome una taza de té con ron para calentarse un poquito.

6 Gracias, señora Adams. Tengo un poco de frío. Me gusta mucho tomar una taza de té con Ud., y mientras bebemos el té con ron vamos a charlar sobre el tiempo. Es un tópico de conversación común y en este momento está muy a propósito.

7 Pasan al comedor charlando en voz animada. Se sientan a la mesa y la criada les trae una bandeja con dos tazas y platillos, una tetera con té caliente, un azucarero y unas cucharitas. Los pone en la mesa junto con una botella de ron que toma del aparador. Luego sale del comedor.

8 — Permítame servirle a Ud., señor López, — dice la señora Adams. Echa té y una porción generosa de ron en las tazas.

9 Mientras toman el té con ron siguen charlando en voz animada.

10 Afuera sigue lloviendo.

1 It is raining hard. The maid opens the door of the house of Mr. and Mrs. Adams. Mr. López enters.

2 The maid says, 'Good evening, Mr. López. What rainy weather! Come in, come in. You are quite wet. Give me, please, your raincoat and hat. Put your umbrella in the umbrella stand.'

3 Mr. López answers, 'Thank you. Now I feel all right. It is pouring with rain (*lit.* it is raining buckets), but it is not cold. I am sure that I will not catch cold. Is Mrs. Adams at home?'

4 Yes. She is waiting for you in the living-room. Here she is herself.

5 Good evening, Mr. López. I am very glad to see you, but you

should not go out of your house in weather like this. Come with me to the dining-room and drink a cup of tea with rum to warm yourself a bit.

6 Thank you, Mrs. Adams. I am a little cold. I am very glad to have a cup of tea with you and while we drink the tea with rum, we will chat about the weather. It is a common topic of conversation and just now is very appropriate.

7 They go into the dining-room chatting in animated voices. They sit down and the maid brings them a tray with two cups and saucers, a tea pot with hot tea, a sugar-bowl and some teaspoons. She puts them on the table together with a bottle of rum which she takes from the sideboard. Then she leaves the dining-room.

8 'Allow me to serve you, Mr. López,' says Mrs. Adams. She pours tea and a generous portion of rum into the cups.

9 While they are drinking the tea with rum they continue chatting in lively voices.

10 Outside it continues raining.

Pronunciation and Spelling Aids

1 In the combinations **gua, guo** (ɣwa, ɣwo), the **u** is pronounced: (pa-ˈra-ɣwas).

2 In the combination **gue, gui**, the **u** is silent. It is there to show that the **g** is hard (not like g in **gente**). **si-guen, se-guir** (ˈsi-ɣen, se-ˈɣir).

3 In the combinations **güe, güi** (ɣwe, ɣwi), the ¨ (diaerisis) over the **u** shows that the **u** is pronounced: **paragüero** (pa-ra-ˈɣwe-ro).

Building Vocabulary

A. 1 **él mismo**   he himself   3 **ellos mismos**   they themselves (*m*)
   2 **ella misma** she herself   4 **ellas mismas**   they themselves (*f*)

B. **tomar** may mean to take, to eat, to drink, to catch (in *catch cold*)

Expresiones Importantes

A. Expressions of Weather

In Spanish we say: What weather does it *make* (**hace**)? It *makes* (**hace**) heat, cold, etc., *not* What is the weather? It is hot, cold etc.

In Spanish we say *I have* (**tengo**) warmth, cold, etc.; not *I am* warm, cold. etc.

1 **¿Qué tiempo hace?**
   What's the weather?
2 **Hace buen (mal) tiempo.**
   The weather is (bad) nice.

3 **Hace calor, hace frío, hace fresco.**
   It is warm (hot), it is cold, it is cool.
4 **Hace mucho calor. Hace mucho frío.**
   It is very hot. It is very cold.
5 **Hace viento. Hace sol (hay sol).**
   It is windy. It is sunny.
6 **Hay polvo (lodo).**
   It is dusty (muddy).
7 **Llueve (está lloviendo).**
   It is raining.
8 **Nieva (está nevando).**
   It is snowing.
9 **Tengo calor, frío.**
   I am warm (hot), cold.
10 **Tengo mucho calor, mucho frío.**
   I am very warm (hot), very cold.

Exercise No. 72—Completion of Text

1 **La criada dice —¡** (What rainy weather)!
2 (Come in, come in). **Ud. está bastante** (wet).
3 (Give me) **el impermeable y el sombrero.**
4 (Put) **el paraguas en el paragüero.**
5 **Llueve** ('buckets').
6 (Come with me) **al comedor.**
7 (Drink) **una taza de té con ron.**
8 (Permit me) **servirle a Ud.**
9 (While they are drinking) **el té siguen charlando.**
10 **Afuera** (it continues raining).

SEGUNDA PARTE

Grammar Notes

1 The Imperative or Command Forms of the Verb.

Infinitive	1st Person Singular		Imperative Singular	
hablar	**hablo**	I speak	**hable Ud.**	speak
pensar (ie)	**pienso**	I think	**piense Ud.**	think
contar (ue)	**cuento**	I count	**cuente Ud.**	count
comer	**como**	I eat	**coma Ud.**	eat
poner	**pongo**	I put	**ponga Ud.**	put
abrir	**abro**	I open	**abra Ud.**	open
venir	**vengo**	I come	**venga Ud.**	come
repetir (i)	**repito**	I repeat	**repita Ud.**	repeat

Infinitive	1st Person Singular		Imperative Singular	
oír	**oigo**	I hear	**oiga Ud.**	hear
traer	**traigo**	I bring	**traiga Ud.**	bring

Imperative Plural

hablen Uds.	speak
piensen Uds.	think
cuenten Uds.	count
coman Uds.	eat
pongan Uds.	put
abran Uds.	open
vengan Uds.	come
repitan Uds.	repeat
oigan Uds.	hear
traigan Uds.	bring

(a) To form the imperative take these steps:

1 Remove the **-o** from the first person singular.

2 For the imperative singular add **-e** to the stem of **-ar** verbs, and **-a** to the stem of **-er** and **-ir** verbs.

3 For the imperative plural add **-en** to the stem of **-ar** verbs, and **-an** to the stem of **-er** and **-ir** verbs.

Thus the endings of the imperative are the reverse of the endings of the present tense, where **-ar** verbs have **-a** and **-an,** and **-er** and **-ir** verbs have **-e** and **-en.**

4 Use **Ud.** and **Uds.** after the verb. They may, however, be omitted like *you* in English.

2 Irregular Imperatives

Infinitive	Imperative Singular		Imperative Plural	
dar	**dé Ud.**	give	**den Uds.**	give
estar	**esté Ud.**	be	**estén Uds.**	be
ser	**sea Ud.**	be	**sean Uds.**	be
ir	**vaya Ud.**	go	**vayan Uds.**	go

3 The Imperative with Object Pronouns

(a) Object pronouns follow and are attached to the affirmative imperative form.

An accent mark must be added to hold the verb stress where it was before the pronoun was added.

Abra Ud. la puerta.	Open the door.
Ábrala Ud.	Open *it.*
Dejen Uds. los platos.	Leave the plates.
Déjenlos Uds.	Leave *them.*
Óigame.	Hear *me.*
Dígame.	Tell *me.*

(b) In the negative imperative, object pronouns precede the verb.

No abra Ud. la puerta.	Do not open the door.
No *la* abra.	Do not open *it*.
No tomen Uds. los platos.	Do not take the plates.
No *los* tomen.	Do not take *them*.

Ejercicios (Exercises) No. 73A–73B

73A. Rewrite each sentence, changing the direct object noun into an object pronoun. First, revise 'Grammar Notes 3'.

Ejemplo: Póngala Ud. en la mesa.

1 Ponga Ud. *la tetera* en la mesa.
2 No abra Ud. *la puerta.*
3 Repita Ud. *las preguntas.*
4 No deje Ud. *el paraguas* en el vestíbulo.
5 Traiga Ud. *los platos* al comedor.
6 No tomen Uds. *el pan.*
7 Saluden Uds. *a sus amigos.*
8 Compren Uds. *los billetes.*
9 Inviten Uds. *al profesor.*
10 Hagan Uds. *el ejercicio.*

73B. Write the first person singular, present; and the imperative, singular and plural, of the following verbs. Give the meaning of each form.

Ejemplo: entrar, entro I enter   entre Vd. entren Vds. enter.

1 escribir	4 ver	7 repetir	9 dar
2 leer	5 preguntar	8 ir	10 ser
3 tener	6 recibir		

Exercise No. 74—Preguntas

1 ¿Hace buen o mal tiempo?
2 ¿Quién abre la puerta?
3 ¿Dónde pone el Sr. López el paraguas?
4 ¿Dónde espera al Sr. López la Sra. Adams?
5 ¿A dónde pasan la señora Adams y el señor López?
6 ¿Qué toman en el comedor?
7 ¿Qué pone la criada en la mesa?
8 ¿Qué hace ella luego?
9 ¿Quién sirve al Sr. López?
10 ¿Qué echa la Sra. Adams en las tazas?

CHAPTER 20

EL CLIMA DE ESPAÑA

PRIMERA PARTE

1 Todavía están sentados la Sra. Adams y el Sr. López en el comedor. Todavía están charlando y tomando el té. Todavía está lloviendo afuera. Ya no tiene frío el Sr. López.

2 La señora Adams dice — El clima de Gran Bretaña y el de España son muy distintos, ¿verdad? Aquí en Gran Bretaña tenemos cuatro estaciones y cada estación es diferente.

3 Es cierto. En verano hace calor; a veces hace mucho calor. En invierno hace frío; muchas veces hace mucho frío y de vez en cuando nieva. En primavera comienza a hacer buen tiempo pero a menudo llueve, como esta noche. Normalmente hace tiempo agradable y hay sol. En el otoño hace fresco y hace viento. ¿Qué estación prefiere Ud.?

4 Prefiero la primavera, cuando toda la naturaleza se pone verde; pero me gusta también el otoño con sus colores vivos. Bien, basta del clima de Gran Bretaña. Dígame algo del clima de España.

5 Bueno. Oiga Ud. bien.

6 Acabamos de hablar del clima en Gran Bretaña. Ahora vamos a hablar del clima de la Península Ibérica. Ud. va a viajar en avión. Va a ver abajo el gran panorama de sierras con sus altos picos y grandes altiplanicies. España le va a parecer una tierra de montañas y altas llanuras. Es la verdad. Al atravesar la Península en coche se sube a una altura de 2.200 pies[1] sobre el nivel del mar en Madrid. La ciudad está situada en la Meseta Central, cuya altura media es de unos 1.800 pies. España es un país de altas tierras. Excepto las dos mesetas, la Meseta Norte y la Meseta Sur, los valles del Ebro y del Guadalquivir, la mayor parte de la Península es muy montañosa. En el norte, en los Pirineos, la cima más elevada es la del Aneto, con una altura de 11.168 (once mil ciento sesenta y ocho) pies. La cima más elevada de la Cordillera Bètica es la del Mulhacén, 11.420 (once mil cuatrocientos veinte) pies.

7 La señora Adams dice — ¡De veras! España sí que es una tierra de montañas. Y este hecho determina en gran parte el clima de España, ¿verdad?

8 — Tiene Ud. razón. La mayor parte de la Península es una zona seca, donde hay mucho sol y pocas lluvias. Solamente en la provincia de Galicia, que se halla en el noroeste de la Península, y en toda la costa Cantábrica, hay mucha lluvia. Con su clima lluvioso y sus campos verdes

139

se parece mucho a Gran Bretaña. En la Meseta Central y en las altas montañas hace mucho frío en invierno, y los picos de Aneto y Mulhacén están coronados de nieve todo el año.

9 Hay de hecho dos zonas en España — la zona seca y la zona húmeda. Hay muchos contrastes en el clima de la Península. En el norte y en el noroeste es lluvioso, en el Levante es muy templado todo el año, en la Meseta Central y en las montañas hace gran frío en invierno, y en las tierras calientes de Andalucía en el sur, el calor es muy pesado en verano. Pero ya es tarde. Vamos a continuar con este tema la próxima vez.

1 Mrs. Adams and Mr. López are still seated in the dining-room. They are still chatting and drinking tea. It is still raining outside. Mr. López is no longer cold.

2 Mrs. Adams says, 'The climate of Great Britain and that of Spain are very different, are they not? Here in Great Britain we have four seasons and each season is different.'

3 That's true. In summer it is hot; sometimes it is very hot. In winter it is cold; often it is very cold and from time to time it snows. In spring it begins to be good weather but often it rains like tonight. Usually the weather is pleasant and the sun shines. In autumn it is cool and windy. Which season do you prefer?

4 I prefer the spring when all nature turns green; but I also like autumn with its bright colours. Well, enough of the climate of Great Britain. Tell me something about the climate of Spain.

5 Good. Listen carefully.

6 We have just talked about the climate of Great Britain. Now we are going to talk about the climate of the Iberian Peninsula. You are going to travel by plane. You will see below the great panorama of mountain ranges and large plateaux. Spain will seem to you a land of mountains and high plains. It is a fact. In crossing the Peninsula by car one climbs to an altitude of 2,200 feet[1] above sea level at Madrid. The city is situated on the Central Plateau, whose average altitude is some 1,800 feet. Spain is a country of high lands. Except for the two plateaux Northern and Southern, and the valleys of the Ebro and the Guadalquivir, the greater part of the Peninsula is very mountainous. In the north, in the Pyrenees, the highest peak is that of Aneto, with a height of 11,168 feet. The highest peak of the Andalusian Ranges is that of Mulhacén, 11,420 feet.

7 Mrs. Adams says: 'Really! Spain is indeed a land of mountains. And this fact largely (*lit.* in large part) determines the climate of Spain, doesn't it?'

8 You are right. The greater part of the Peninsula is a dry zone, where there is much sun and few rains. Only in the province of Galicia, which is (*lit.* finds itself) in the north-west of the Peninsula, and on the Cantabrian coast, is there a lot of rain. With its rainy climate and green

fields it is very much like Great Britain. In the Central Plateau and in the high mountains it is very cold in winter, and the peaks of Aneto and Mulhacén are crowned with snow all year.

9 There are in fact two zones in Spain—the dry zone and the wet zone. There are many contrasts in the climate of the Peninsula. In the north and north-west it is rainy, in the east it is very temperate all the year, in the Central Plateau and the mountains it is very cold in winter, and in the warm lands of Andalusia in the south the heat is very heavy in summer. But it's already late. Let us continue this topic next time.

NOTE: 1. 2,200 feet = 730 metres.

Pronunciation Aids

Practise:

naturaleza (na-tu-ra-'le-θa) **llanura** (ʎa-'nu-ra)
altiplanicie (al-te-pla-'ni-θje) **Mulhacén** (mul-a-'θen)
Andalucía (an-da-lu-'θi-a) **Galicia** (ɣa-'li-θja)
cordillera (kor-ði-'ʎe-ra)

Building Vocabulary

1 **Las cuatro estaciones** (the four seasons)
la primavera, spring; **el verano**, summer; **el otoño**, autumn; **el invierno**, winter

Expresiones Importantes

1 **no importa,** it doesn't matter
2 **en efecto,** in fact
3 **ponerse,** to become
   La naturaleza se pone verde, Nature becomes green;
   to put on
   Me pongo el abrigo, I put my overcoat on
4 **todavía,** still
5 **ya no,** no longer **Ya no tiene frío,** He is no longer cold.

Exercise No. 75—Completion of Text

1 (It is raining) **afuera.**
2 **Todavía los señores** (are chatting and drinking) **té con ron.**
3 **En el verano** (it is hot); **en el invierno** (it is cold).
4 **¿Qué estación** (do you prefer)?
5 (Tell me) **algo del clima de España. Bueno.** (Listen well.)
6 (We have just spoken) **del clima de Gran Bretaña.**
7 (In crossing) **España** (one climbs) **hasta una altura de mil ochocientos**
   (1,800) **pies o sea unos 640 metros.**

8 **Desde la Meseta Central** (rise) **grandes montañas.**
9 **El pico Mulhacén es la cima** (highest in Spain).
10 **El pico Aneto está en** (the Pyrenees).

SEGUNDA PARTE

Grammar Notes

1 The Present Tense of **seguir (i)** to follow, **servir (i)** to serve.

I follow, continue, etc.		I serve, etc.	
sigo	**seguimos**	**sirvo**	**servimos**
sigues	**seguís**	**sirves**	**servís**
sigue	**siguen**	**sirve**	**sirven**

Imperative		Imperative	
siga Ud.	**sigan Uds.**	**sirva Ud.**	**sirvan Uds.**

(a) Verbs ending in **-guir**, like **seguir**, drop the silent **u** before the ending **-o** and **-a**.

(b) **seguir (i)** and **servir (i)** belong in the same stem-changing group as **pedir (i)**, **repetir (i)**.

2 The Present Progressive Tense of **hablar, aprender, vivir.**

Singular

> **estoy hablando (aprendiendo, viviendo)**
> I am speaking (learning, living)
> **estás hablando (aprendiendo, viviendo)**
> you are speaking (learning, living)
> Ud. **está hablando (aprendiendo, viviendo)**
> you are speaking (learning, living)
> **está hablando (aprendiendo, viviendo)**
> he, she, it is speaking (learning, living)

Plural

> **estamos hablando (aprendiendo, viviendo)**
> we are speaking (learning, living)
> **estáis hablando (aprendiendo, viviendo)**
> you are speaking (learning, living)
> Uds. **están hablando (aprendiendo, viviendo)**
> you are speaking (learning, living)
> **están hablando (aprendiendo, viviendo)**
> they are speaking (learning, living)

(a) The present progressive tense in Spanish is formed by the present tense of **estar** and the present participle of a verb.

(b) To form the present participle: remove the infinitive ending **-ar, -er,** or **-ir.** Add **-ando** to the remaining stem of **-ar** verbs; add **-iendo** to the stem of **-er** verbs and **-ir** verbs. The endings **-ando** and **-iendo** are equivalent to the English ending *-ing.*

hablando speaking   **aprendiendo** learning   **viviendo** living

(c) The simple present tense in Spanish may be translated into the English progressive form. However, to stress continuing action use the progressive tense:

No están saliendo ahora.   They are not leaving now.

3 Present Participle of Some common Verbs

desear	to want	**deseando**	wanting
estudiar	to study	**estudiando**	studying
pensar (ie)	to think	**pensando**	thinking
contar (ue)	to count	**contando**	counting
hacer	to make, do	**haciendo**	making, doing
poner	to put	**poniendo**	putting
querer (ie)	to wish	**queriendo**	wishing
abrir	to open	**abriendo**	opening
leer	to read	**leyendo**	reading
creer	to believe	**creyendo**	believing
traer	to bring	**trayendo**	bringing
caer	to fall	**cayendo**	falling
ir	to go	**yendo**	going
repetir (i)	to repeat	**repitiendo**	repeating
pedir (i)	to ask for	**pidiendo**	asking for
ser	to be	**siendo**	being

(a) The Spanish does not permit an unaccented **i** between two vowels. Therefore, **-iendo** becomes **-yendo** in the following verbs.

**leer, leyendo   creer, creyendo   oír, oyendo   caer, cayendo
traer, trayendo**

(b) No Spanish word may begin with **ie.** Therefore: **yendo** going.

4 Position of Object Pronouns with Present Participles

Object pronouns follow the present participle and are attached to it, as in the case of the infinitive. An accent mark must be added to hold the stress on the first syllable of **-ando** and **-iendo:**

Está escribiendo la carta.	He is writing the letter.
Está escribiéndola.	He is writing it.
Estamos esperando al maestro.	We are expecting the teacher.
Estamos esperándole.	We are expecting him.
Estoy sentándome.	I am seating myself.

Ejercicios (Exercises) No. 76A–76B–76C

76A. Rewrite each sentence, changing the direct object noun into an object pronoun.

Ejemplo: Estamos estudiándo*las*.

1 Estamos estudiando *las lecciones*.
2 Carlos está escribiendo *la carta*.
3 ¿Estás leyendo *el cuento*, niño?
4 La criada está poniendo *la mesa*.
5 Los señores están tomando *el té*.
6 Juan y yo estamos contando *el dinero*.
7 ¿Están comprando Uds. *los billetes*?
8 No estoy leyendo *las revistas*.
9 ¿Quién está escribiendo *las cartas*?
10 Están vendiendo *los echarpes*.

76B. Rewrite each sentence replacing the English direct object pronouns by the correct Spanish pronouns.

Ejemplo: No estamos esperándola a Ud., señora.

1 No estamos esperando (you), señora.
2 No estamos esperando (you), señor.
3 No están mirando (you), señores.
4 No están mirando (you), señoras.
5 ¿Quién está buscando (me)?
6 Yo estoy buscando (you), hijita.
7 El señor López está enseñando (us) a hablar español.

76C. Translate, using the present progressive tense. Omit all subject pronouns except **Ud.** and **Uds.**

1 We are studying
2 He is putting
3 We are opening
4 Are you (**Ud.**) reading?
5 She is bringing
6 Who is waiting?
7 Are you (**Ud.**) taking?
8 You (**tú**) are speaking
9 I am not writing
10 Is Mary working?
11 He is looking for
12 They are teaching

Exercise No. 77—Preguntas

1 ¿De qué están hablando los señores?
2 ¿Qué tiempo hace normalmente en primavera?
3 ¿Se pone verde la naturaleza en invierno?
4 ¿Qué ve abajo un viajero que viaja por avión en España?
5 ¿Dónde está situado Madrid?
6 ¿Qué altura tiene Madrid?

7 ¿Cuál es la cima más alta de la Península?
8 ¿Qué determina en gran parte el clima de España?
9 ¿Cuántas zonas hay en la Península?
10 ¿En qué parte de España hace mucho calor?

CHAPTER 21

EL CLIMA DE ESPAÑA (CONTINUACIÓN)

PRIMERA PARTE

1 Esta tarde seguimos charlando del clima de España y de las estaciones.

2 En Gran Bretaña hay cuatro estaciones. En España también hay cuatro estaciones. España es una tierra de fuertes contrastes: en la zona templada del Levante parece que hace buen tiempo todo el año, mientras que en la Meseta Central los fríos del invierno son intensos, y el calor del verano es sofocante en el sur.

3 Voy a llegar a Madrid el treinta y uno de mayo, es decir casi al comienzo del verano.

4 Está bien. La primavera es una estación muy agradable allí.

5 ¿Hace sol?

6 ¡Ya lo creo! Los meteorólogos dicen que Madrid goza de muchos más días sin nubes que casi cualquier otra ciudad de Europa.

7 ¿Y es posible verse sorprendido por la lluvia?

8 En Madrid, no. Pero si Ud. quiere visitar Galicia, vale la pena llevar consigo un impermeable o un paraguas.

9 ¿Nunca hace frío en Madrid?

10 Por la noche puede hacer fresco, y un abrigo ligero o un jersey son de utilidad. Pero tenga cuidado del sol. Cuando el sol es muy fuerte en junio y en julio, es peligroso caminar o quedarse al sol sin sombrero.

11 Muchas gracias por estos consejos.[1] Voy a acordarme de ellos. Y al hacer la maleta no voy a olvidar el impermeable, un jersey y un abrigo ligero.

12 La próxima vez vamos a hablar de los alimentos y bebidas. ¿Le gusta este tema?

13 ¡Ya lo creo! responde la señora Adams.

1 This evening we continue chatting about the climate of Spain and the seasons.

2 In Great Britain there are four seasons. In Spain also there are four seasons. Spain is a land of strong contrasts: in the temperate zone in the east it seems to be spring all year, while in the Central Plateau the cold (*lit.* colds) of winter is intense, and the heat of the summer is suffocating in the south.

146

3 I shall arrive in Madrid on May 31, that is to say almost at the beginning of the summer.

4 That's good. Spring is a very pleasant season there.

5 Is there any sun?

6 I should say so! The meteorologists say that Madrid enjoys more cloudless (*lit.* without clouds) days than almost any other city of Europe.

7 And is it possible to be (*lit.* to see oneself) surprised by the rain?

8 In Madrid, no. But if you wish to visit Galicia, it is worth the trouble to take with you a raincoat or an umbrella.

9 Is it never cold in Madrid?

10 At night it can be cool, and a light coat or a sweater are useful. But be careful of the sun. When the sun is very strong in June and July, it is dangerous to walk or remain in the sun without a hat.

11 Many thanks for this advice. I shall remember it. And on packing my bag I shan't forget my raincoat, a sweater and a light coat.

12 Next time we are going to talk about food and drink. Does this topic please you?

13 I should say so! replies Mrs. Adams.

NOTE: 1. Spanish says: *advices.*

Pronunciation Aids

Practise:

lluvias (ˈʎu-vjas) or (ˈʎu-βjas) **llover** (ʎo-ˈver) or (ʎo-ˈβer)
sorprendido (sor-pren-ˈdi-ðo) **veces** (ˈve-θes) or (ˈbe-θes)
estaciones (es-ta-ˈθjo-nes) **bebidas** (be-ˈβi-ðas)
cuidado (kwi-ˈða-ðo) **ligero** (li-ˈxe-ro)

Building Vocabulary

A. Antónimos:

1 **algo**	something	**nada**	nothing
2 **antes de mi llegada**	before my arrival	**después de mi llegada**	after my arrival
3 **comenzar**	to begin	**terminar**	to end
4 **siempre**	always	**nunca**	never
5 **alguien**	somebody	**nadie**	nobody

Expresiones Importantes

1 **no importa,** it doesn't matter
2 **por lo tanto, por eso,** therefore
3 **esta noche,** tonight

4 **tenga cuidado (con),** be careful (of)
5 **al hacer mi maleta,** on packing my valise
6 **Refrán** (Proverb): **Más vale algo que nada.** *Lit.* Something is worth more than nothing. *English proverb.* Half a loaf is better than none.

Exercise No. 78—Completion of Text

1 **Esta noche** (we continue speaking) **del clima.**
2 **España es una tierra** (of strong contrasts).
3 **Madrid** (enjoys) **mucho más** (days without clouds) **que las otras ciudades.**
4 **¿Es posible** (to be surprised by the rain)?
5 (It's worth the trouble) **llevar un impermeable.**
6 (Never) **hace frío** (except) **en las montañas.**
7 (Be careful of) **el sol.**
8 **Es peligroso** (to remain) **en el sol** (without) **sombrero.**
9 **Voy a** (remember) **de estos consejos.**
10 (On packing) **mi maleta no voy** (to forget) **el impermeable.**

SEGUNDA PARTE

Grammar Notes

1 Negative Words

   (a) Common negative words are:

nadie	nobody	**nunca (jamás)**	never
ninguno	no, none, not any	**ni . . . ni**	neither . . . nor
nada	nothing	**tampoco**	neither, not . . . either

   (b) If these negative words follow the verb, **no** must precede the verb. If the negative words precede the verb or stand alone, **no** is not required.

Nadie viene hoy. **No** viene **nadie** hoy. *Nobody* is coming today.
Ningún cliente viene. *No* viene **ningún** cliente. *No* customer is coming.
Nunca (jamás) hace frío. **No** hace **nunca** (jamás) frío. It is *never* cold.
Nada tengo. **No** tengo **nada.** I have *nothing*.
No tiene **ni** amigos **ni** dinero. He has *neither* friends *nor* money.
¿Qué quiere Vd.? **Nada.** What do you want? *Nothing.*
Pablo no desea ir. **Tampoco yo. (Ni yo tampoco.)** Paul doesn't want to go. *Neither* do I.

NOTE: **ninguno** becomes **ningún** before a noun.

2 Infinitives after Prepositions

   After prepositions the Spanish uses an infinitive where the English uses a present participle.

al cruzar España	on crossing Spain
sin trabajar	without working
después de comer	after eating
antes de comer	before eating

3 **Consigo,** with oneself (himself, herself, yourself, yourselves, themselves)

| **Lo trae consigo.** | He brings it with him (self). |
| **Uds. lo traen consigo.** | You bring it with you (yourselves). |

Exercise No. 79

Complete the following, replacing the English words by **nadie, ningún (o, a, os, as) nunca, nada, ni . . . ni, tampoco,** as needed.

1 **Muchos turistas no saben** (nothing) **de la historia de España.**
2 (Nothing) **es más fácil.**
3 (Never) **hace frío en la capital.**
4 **No es posible pasar sin números.** (Nor) **es posible comprar sin dinero.**
5 (Nobody) **puede vivir sin comer.**
6 **No hay** (nobody) **en la taquilla.**
7 **Más vale tarde que** (never).
8 **No anda** (never) **en el sol sin sombrero.**
9 **El hombre no está bien.** (Neither) **está contento.**
10 **No tenemos** (neither) **tiempo** (nor) **dinero.**
11 (No) **hombre puede vivir sin comer.**
12 **No vemos a** (no) **niño en la calle.**
13 **¿Tiene Ud. dinero? No tengo** (any).
14 **No hay** (any) **faja en esta cesta.**
15 **Más vale algo que** (nothing).

Exercise No. 80—Preguntas

1 **¿Dónde parece que hace primavera todo el año?**
2 **¿Hace calor en invierno en la Meseta Central?**
3 **¿Quién dice que Madrid goza de muchos días sin nubes?**
4 **¿En qué parte de la Península llueve mucho?**
5 **¿Hace frío en la capital?**
6 **¿Por qué es de utilidad un abrigo ligero?**
7 **¿Por qué es peligroso caminar en el sol sin sombrero?**
8 **¿Qué no va a olvidar la Sra. Adams al hacer su maleta?**
9 **¿De qué van a hablar la próxima vez?**
10 **¿Le gusta a la señora Adams este tema?**

CHAPTER 22

LA COMIDA ESPAÑOLA

PRIMERA PARTE

1 Señora Adams, ¿le gusta la cocina española?

2 Sí, mucho, contesta la señora Adams. Conozco un buen restaurante español aquí en Londres. A mi esposo y a mí nos gusta mucho cenar en aquel restaurante.

3 Y, ¿cuáles platos les gustan más?

4 Nos gusta la paella valenciana.

5 ¿Sabe Ud. de qué hacen la paella?

6 Creo que sí. Se hace con arroz y con trozos de pollo, chorizo, pimiento, cangrejos, almejas y muchas otras cosas, me parece.

7 Muy bien. Pero Ud. olvida el ingrediente más importante — el aceite. El aceite es la base misma de la cocina española. También es la causa de muchos malestares turísticos. ¿Le gusta el aceite?

8 Sí, pero es un poco difícil acostumbrarse a su sabor. Me gusta comer una paella, pero después me siento, a veces, un poco débil. ¿Qué puedo hacer para acostumbrarme a los alimentos españoles? ¿Qué me aconseja Ud.?

9 Tenga cuidado con los platos típicos de las regiones de España — bacalao a la vizcaína, pollo a la chilindrón, cochinillo a la Segoviana, gambas al ajillo. Son muy sabrosos, pero al principio es mejor tomar platos conocidos — jamón, una chuleta, un bistec, etcétera.

10 Pero, continúa el señor López, hay platos típicos más ligeros — por ejemplo, el gazpacho, que es una sopa fría hecha de legumbres. Algunos dicen que el gazpacho es una ensalada líquida. Hay muchos alimentos típicos de España. Y no olvide Ud. la célebre tortilla.

11 Pero la tortilla es un alimento de México, ¿verdad?, pregunta la señora Adams.

12 Es verdad. La tortilla es el pan de México, y la hacen del maíz. Pero la tortilla española es otra cosa. La hacen de huevos, patatas, cebollas, y aceite de oliva.

13 ¡La conozco muy bien! En inglés la llamamos 'Spanish omelette', ¿verdad?

14 Exacto. Es un plato muy nutritivo. Y se puede comer frío también. ¿Y le gustan los vinos españoles?

15 ¡Por supuesto! Ud. olvida que a nosotros los británicos nos gusta el Jerez, y que aquí se pueden comprar excelentes vinos tintos y blancos.

16 ¿Y hay muchas clases de postres?

17 A los españoles les gusta comer un dulce, un flan o una de las muchas frutas que se venden en el mercado.

18 Debo saber leer el menú en un restaurante, ¿verdad?

19 Sí, y también debe Ud. probar los alimentos de España. Pero todo con moderación. El estómago británico no se acostumbra rápidamente a los alimentos picantes de España, y Ud. no quiere tener dolor de estómago. No lo olvide — Comemos para vivir; no vivimos para comer.

20 No voy a olvidarlo. Y no voy a olvidar ninguno de sus buenos consejos.

21 Y no olvide tampoco que a los españoles les gusta comer más tarde que a los británicos. La hora de la comida es a las dos o dos y media de la tarde, y la de la cena a eso de las diez de la noche.

22 ¡Veo que voy a tener que acostumbrarme también a la hora española!, dice la señora Adams.

1 Mrs. Adams, do you like Spanish cooking?

2 'Yes, very much,' replies Mrs. Adams. 'I know a good Spanish restaurant here in London. My husband and I like dining in that restaurant a lot.'

3 And which dishes do you like most?

4 We like the Valencian *paella*.

5 Do you know what they make the *paella* from?

6 I think so. It is made with rice and with pieces of chicken, sausage, pepper, crayfish, clams and many other things, it seems to me.

7 Very good. But you are forgetting the most important ingredient— the olive oil. Olive oil is the very basis of Spanish cooking Also it is the cause of many tourist indispositions. Do you like olive oil?

8 Yes, but it is a little difficult to get used to its taste. I like eating a *paella*, but afterwards I sometimes feel a little weak. What can I do to get used to Spanish foods? What do you advise me?

9 Take care with the typical dishes of the regions of Spain—cod in the Biscayan fashion, chicken *a la chilindrón* (*fried in oil and garlic with a rich sauce of, amongst other things, onion, tomatoes and peppers*), sucking pig in the Segovian fashion, prawns fried with garlic. They are very tasty, but at the beginning it is better to have familiar dishes— ham, a chop, steak, etc.

10 'But,' continues Mr. López, 'there are lighter typical dishes—for example, *gazpacho*, which is a cold soup made from vegetables. Some say that *gazpacho* is a liquid salad. There are many foods typical of Spain. And don't forget the famous *tortilla*.'

11 'But the *tortilla* is a Mexican food, isn't it?' asks Mrs. Adams.

12 That's true. The *tortilla* is the bread of Mexico, and they make it from maize, but the Spanish *tortilla* is a different thing. They make it from eggs, potatoes, onions, and olive oil.

13 I know it very well. In English we call it a Spanish omelette, don't we?

14 That's right. It is a very nutritive dish. And it can also be eaten cold. And do you like Spanish wines?

15 Of course! You are forgetting that we British like sherry, and that here excellent red and white wines can be bought.

16 And are there many kinds of desserts?

17 Spaniards like to eat a sweet, custard or one of the many fruits that are sold in the market.

18 I should know how to read the menu in a restaurant, shouldn't I?

19 Yes, and you should also try the Spanish foods. But everything in moderation. The British stomach does not accustom itself quickly to the sharp foods of Spain, and you don't want stomach-ache. Don't forget. We eat to live; we do not live to eat.

20 I will not forget. And I will not forget any of your good advice.

21 And don't forget either that the Spaniards like to eat later than the British. Lunchtime is two or two-thirty, and that of dinner at about ten at night.

22 'I see that I am going to have to get used to Spanish time as well!' says Mrs. Adams.

Pronunciation Aids

Practise:

acostumbrado (a-kos-tum-'bra-ðo)   Jerez (xe-'reθ)
aceite (a-'θej-te)   aconseja (a-kon-'se-xa)
vizcaína (viθ-ka-'i-na) or   huevos ('we-vos) or ('we-βos)
  (biθ-ka-'i-na)   tortilla (tor-'ti-ʎa)
ajillo (a-'xi-ʎo)

Building Vocabulary

A. **Frutas** Fruits

el plátano [1]	banana	**la naranja**	orange
la cereza	cherry	**la pera**	pear
la fresa	strawberry	**la piña**	pineapple
el melocotón	peach	**el pomelo**	grapefruit
la lima	lime	**la uva**	grape
el limón	lemon		

B. **Carne** Meat   **Pescados** Fish

el bacalao	cod	**el pato**	duck
el bistec	steak	**el pavo**	turkey
la chuleta	chop	**el pescado**	fish
el cochinillo	sucking pig	**el pollo**	chicken
el cordero	lamb	**el puerco**	pork

el chorizo	blood sausage	**el rosbif**	steak
el hígado	liver	**la salchicha**	sausage
el jamón	ham	**la ternera**	veal
la langosta	lobster	**el tocino**	bacon

C. **Legumbres y Verduras** Vegetables and Greens

el ajo	garlic	**los guisantes**	peas
el arroz	rice	**las habas**	broad beans
la cebolla	onion	**las judías**	green beans
la col	cabbage	**la lechuga**	lettuce
la coliflor	cauliflower	**la patata**	potato
los espárragos	asparagus	**la seta**	mushroom
los garbanzos	chick peas	**la zanahoria**	carrot

NOTE: 1. **Banana** in Hispano America.

Expresiones Importantes

1	**dolor de cabeza**	headache	3 **dolor de estómago**	stomach-ache
2	**dolor de muelas**	toothache	4 **eso es**	that's right

Exercise No. 81—Completion of Text

1 (It is made) **con arroz y con** (pieces of chicken).
2 **El aceite es la base de la** (Spanish cooking).
3 **Es la causa** (of many tourist indispositions).
4 **¿Qué puedo hacer** (to accustom myself) **a los alimentos españoles?**
5 (Take care) **con los platos típicos.**
6 **Al principio es mejor tomar** (familiar dishes).
7 **El gazpacho es una** (liquid salad).
8 (They make it with eggs) **patatas y cebollas.**
9 (I know it) **muy bien.**
10 **Es un plato** (very nutritive).
11 **También** (it can be eaten cold).
12 **Ud.** (should) **probar los alimentos.**
13 (We eat) **para vivir.** (We do not live) **para comer.**
14 **No voy** (to forget) **sus consejos.**

SEGUNDA PARTE

Grammar Notes

1 The Present Tense of **sentir (ie)** to feel, to regret, **conocer** to know

I feel, etc.		I know, etc.	
siento	**sentimos**	**conozco**	**conocemos**
sientes	**sentís**	**conoces**	**conocéis**
siente	**sienten**	**conoce**	**conocen**

(a) **parecer** to seem, and **traducir** to translate, are irregular in the first person singular, like **conocer**. Thus: **parezco, pareces,** etc.; **traduzco, traduces,** etc.

2 Special Uses of the Reflexive Verb

(a) The reflexive verb is often used instead of the passive.

Se venden frutas.	Fruits are sold (fruits sell themselves).
Se abre la puerta.	The door is opened (the door opens itself).
Aquí se habla español.	Here Spanish is spoken.
Se ve mucha gente en el parque.	Many people are seen in the park.

(b) The reflexive verb is used in certain impersonal constructions where the English has an indefinite subject such as one, people, they or you.

se dice	one says	people say they say it is said
¿cómo se dice?	how does one say?	how do you say?
se puede	one may	can
se sube	one goes up	

(c) The reflexive verb is at times used with a different meaning than the simple verb:

comer	to eat	**ir**	to go
comerse	to eat up	**irse**	to go away
parecer	to seem	**encontrar**	to meet
parecerse	to resemble	**encontrarse**	to be (somewhere); to meet someone

3 conocer, saber

(a) **saber** means to know facts and things (never persons) by means of the mind, **saber** also means to *know how*.

Sabemos dónde vive Juan.	We know where John lives.
Sabemos cuántos años tiene.	We know how old he is.
Sabemos los números en español.	We know the numbers in Spanish.
Sé cantar esta canción.	I know how to sing this song.

(b) **conocer** means to know in the sense of to be acquainted with a person or thing; to recognize; to know by sight, hearing or any of the senses.

Conozco a Juan.	I know (am acquainted with) John.
Conozco esta casa.	I know (recognize by sight) this house.
Conocemos este restaurante. Es muy bueno.	We know this restaurant. It is very good.
Conozco esta canción.	I know (recognize on hearing) this song.

Ejercicios (Exercises) No. 82A–82B

82A. Replace the English words by the correct Spanish reflexive verbs.

1 ¿(May one) **entrar en el parque?**
2 ¿(How does one say) **en inglés — Permítame?**
3 **Aquí** (are sold) **flores.**
4 **Muchos coches** (are seen) **en los caminos.**
5 (People say) **que el presidente viene hoy.**
6 **Aquí** (Spanish is spoken).
7 (They eat up) **todos los alimentos.**
8 ¿(Do you know) **a aquellos profesores?**
9 (I do not know them).
10 ¿(Do you know how) **contar hasta ciento?**
11 **Mañana** (I go away).
12 (We know how) **cantar estas canciones.**
13 **La tortilla** (resembles) **a nuestra 'omelette'.**
14 **Tengo** (a stomach-ache).

82B. Match up the Spanish words in Group II with the English words in Group I.

Group I	Group II
1 the peas	(a) el postre
2 the steak	(b) las habas
3 the pear	(c) el arroz
4 the corn	(d) la carne
5 the dessert	(e) el jamón
6 the rice	(f) la pera
7 the beans	(g) el pan
8 the ham	(h) la salchicha
9 the meat	(i) los guisantes
10 the chicken	(j) las chuletas
11 the bread	(k) el maíz
12 the sausage	(l) la naranja
13 the chops	(m) el bistec
14 the foods	(n) el pollo
15 the orange	(o) la manzana
16 the apple	(p) los alimentos

Exercise No. 83—Preguntas

1 ¿Dónde comen los señores Adams la paella?
2 ¿Cuál es la base de la cocina española?
3 ¿Qué causa el aceite?
4 ¿Qué plato se llama una ensalada líquida?
5 ¿Cuál es el pan de México?

6 ¿De qué hacen la tortilla española?
7 ¿Se puede comer la tortilla solamente caliente?
8 ¿Qué clase de postres comen los españoles?
9 ¿Por qué es mejor probar los alimentos típicos de España con moderación?
10 ¿A qué hora cenan los españoles?

REVISION 5

CHAPTERS 19–22 PRIMERA PARTE

Repaso de Palabras

NOUNS

1 el abrigo	14 la estación	27 la nieve
2 el aceite	15 el flan	28 el otoño
3 la altura	16 la gente	29 el paraguas
4 el arroz	17 el hecho	30 la pera
5 el bacalao	18 el impermeable	31 el pie
6 la botella	19 el invierno	32 el pollo
7 la bebida	20 el jamón	33 el pico
8 la carne	21 el menú	34 la primavera
9 el clima	22 la lluvia	35 la tortilla
10 el cochinillo	23 el maíz	36 la sierra
11 el consejo	24 el mar	37 el sombrero
12 las chuletas	25 el melón	38 el verano
13 el estado	26 la naturaleza	

1 overcoat	14 season	26 nature
2 olive oil	15 crème caramel,	27 snow
3 height	custard	28 autumn
4 rice	16 people	29 umbrella
5 cod	17 fact	30 pear
6 bottle	18 raincoat	31 foot
7 drink	19 winter	32 chicken
8 meat	20 ham	33 peak
9 climate	21 menu	34 spring
10 sucking pig	22 rain	35 omelette
11 advice	23 corn	36 mountain range
12 chops	24 sea	37 hat
13 state	25 melon	38 summer

VERBS

1 acostumbrarse	8 olvidar	14 quedar
2 aconsejar	9 parecer	15 seguir (i)
3 bajar	10 parecerse	16 servir (i)
4 conocer	11 ponerse	17 sentirse (ie)
5 charlar	12 preocuparse	18 subir
6 descansar	13 probar (ue)	19 traer
7 llover (ue)		

1 to accustom oneself	7 to rain	14 to remain
2 to advise	8 to forget	15 to follow, continue
3 to go down; get out	9 to seem	16 to serve
(of a car)	10 to resemble	17 to feel (weak, ill, etc.)
4 to know	11 to become	18 to go up; get into
5 to chat	12 to worry	(a car)
6 to rest	13 to try	19 to bring, carry

157

ADJECTIVES

1 agradable	7 frío	13 mismo
2 caliente	8 fuerte	14 peligroso
3 común	9 húmedo	15 picante
4 débil	10 ligero	16 sabroso
5 diferente	11 lluvioso	17 seguro
6 distinto	12 mojado	18 seco

1 pleasant	7 cold	13 same
2 hot	8 strong	14 dangerous
3 common	9 damp	15 sharp, spicy
4 weak	10 light	16 tasty
5 different	11 rainy	17 certain
6 different	12 wet	18 dry

ADVERBS

1 afuera	3 entonces	5 todavía
2 abajo	4 solamente	6 todavía no

1 outside	3 then	5 still
2 below	4 only	6 not yet

PREPOSITIONS

1 junto con	2 antes de	3 cerca de

1 together with	2 before	3 near

PRONOUNS

1 algo	2 alguien	3 consigo

1 something	2 somebody	3 with himself, herself, themselves

NEGATIVES

1 nada	4 nunca	7 jamás
2 nadie	5 ni . . . ni	8 todavía no
3 ninguno	6 tampoco	

1 nothing	4 never	7 never
2 nobody	5 neither . . . nor	8 not yet
3 no, none, not any	6 neither, not . . . either	

IMPORTANT EXPRESSIONS

1 a menudo	8 dolor de muelas
2 acabar de	9 hacer la maleta
3 con su permiso	10 no importa
4 de veras	11 por lo tanto
5 en coche	12 tener cuidado
6 es cierto	13 vale la pena
7 dolor de cabeza	14 eso es

1 often
2 to have just
3 with your permission
4 indeed
5 by car
6 it is true
7 headache

8 toothache
9 to pack the suitcase
10 it does not matter
11 therefore
12 to be careful
13 it is worth the trouble
14 that's right

SEGUNDA PARTE

Ejercicio 84. From Group 2 select the opposite for each word in Group 1.

1 antes de comer
2 frío
3 siempre
4 alguien
5 comenzar
6 recordar

7 fuerte
8 trabajar
9 lluvioso
10 despacio
11 algo
12 ahora

(a) caliente
(b) después de comer
(c) nada
(d) de prisa
(e) seco
(f) entonces

(g) nunca
(h) olvidar
(i) débil
(j) terminar
(k) nadie
(l) descansar

Ejercicio 85 Complete the following sentences in Spanish.

1 **Cuando hace frío** (I am cold).
2 **Cuando hace calor** (I am warm).
3 **En verano** (the weather is nice).
4 **En primavera** (it rains a great deal).
5 **En otoño** (it is cool).
6 **En invierno** (it is cold).
7 **Cuando llueve** (I wear a raincoat).
8 **Cuando nieva** (I wear an overcoat).
9 **Cuando hace calor** (it is dusty).
10 **Me gustan** (all the seasons).

Ejercicio 86 Select the group words in the right-hand column which best complete the sentences begun in the left-hand column.

1 Prefiero la primavera
2 No me gusta el invierno
3 Voy a decir algo sobre
4 Es verdad que España
5 Se venden frutas
6 Lleve Ud. un paraguas consigo
7 A los españoles les gusta
8 No voy a olvidar
9 Sabemos
10 Conocemos bien

(a) el clima de España.
(b) es una tierra de contrastes.
(c) en todos los mercados.
(d) porque hace buen tiempo.
(e) comer platos con aceite.
(f) porque hace mucho frío.
(g) contar en español.
(h) porque está lloviendo.
(i) a los alumnos de esta clase.
(j) ningunos de sus consejos.

Ejercicio 87 Read each command. Then translate the sentence that follows it. Watch out for the position of the object pronoun!

Ejemplo: **Cuenta Ud. el dinero.** I count it. **Lo cuento.**

1 **Abra Ud. la puerta.** I open it.
2 **Cuente Ud. los picos.** I count them.

3 **Coma Ud. la carne.** I eat it.
4 **Ponga Ud. la mesa.** I set it.
5 **Repita Ud. las preguntas.** I repeat them.
6 **Dejen Uds. los platos.** We leave them.
7 **Tomen Uds. las tazas.** We take them.
8 **Aprendan Uds. las lecciones.** We learn them.
9 **Escriban Uds. el ejercicio.** We write it.
10 **Lean Uds. el periódico.** We read it.

Ejercicio 88 Substitute the present participle for the infinitive in parentheses to make the present progressive tense.

Ejemplo: 1. Está lloviendo a cántaros.

1 Está (llover) a cántaros.
2 Estamos (echar) el café.
3 Están (pedir) informes.
4 Estoy (leer) las cartas.
5 ¿Está (pensar) Ud. en su padre?
6 ¿Quién está (traer) la tetera?
7 ¿Quiénes están (oír) al maestro?
8 ¿No están (contar) el dinero?
9 ¿La criada está (poner) la mesa?
10 ¿Qué está (hacer) Carlos?

TERCERA PARTE
Diálogo

Practise the Spanish aloud:

En el restaurante

—¿Qué hay en el menú[1] del día? — pregunta la Sra. Adams al camarero.
¿Quiere Ud. tomar algunos platos españoles, Sra. Adams?
Pues, todavía no. Acabo de llegar a España y es mejor, al principio, comer platos conocidos.
¿Me permite Ud. recomendar el filete mignon a la parrilla?
Debe de estar muy bueno, pero prefiero probar las chuletas.
Chuletas de ternera, entonces. Y puede escoger Ud. dos legumbres.
Patatas y zanahorias. Como postre, déme flan, por favor. Es un postre español que me gusta mucho.
¿Y de beber?
Café con leche, por favor.
Muy bien, Sra. Adams.
Y hágame el favor de traer la cuenta.
Aquí la tiene, Sra. Adams.
Muchas gracias.
A Ud., señora.

NOTE: 1. or **minuta.**

'What is there on the set menu?' Mrs. Adams asks the waiter.
Do you want to eat some Spanish dishes, Mrs. Adams?

Well, not yet. I have just arrived in Spain and it is better, at first, to eat customary dishes.

Will you permit me to recommend the grilled filet mignon?

It must be very good but I prefer to try the chops.

Veal chops, then. And you may choose two vegetables.

Potatoes and carrots. As dessert, give me crème caramel, please. It is a Spanish dessert that I like very much.

And to drink?

Coffee with milk, please.

Very well, Mrs. Adams.

And please bring me the bill.

Here it is, Mrs. Adams.

Many thanks.

Thank you, madam.

LECTURA

Exercise No. 89—A Felipe no le gusta estudiar la aritmética

Un día, al volver (upon returning) de la escuela, dice Felipe a su madre, — No me gusta estudiar la aritmética. Es tan difícil. ¿Para qué necesitamos tantos (so many) ejercicios y problemas hoy día? ¿No es verdad que tenemos máquinas calculadoras (adding machines)?

La señora Adams mira a su hijo y dice, — No tienes razón, hijito. No es posible pasar sin números. Por ejemplo, siempre es necesario cambiar dinero, hacer compras, calcular distancias y ... y ...

La madre deja de (stops) hablar al ver (on seeing) que Felipe no presta atención a lo que (what) ella dice.

— A propósito, continúa la madre con una sonrisa (smile), — el fútbol tampoco (either) te interesa, hijo mío?

— Ya lo creo, mamá.

— Pues, si el Chelsea ha ganado (have won) treinta partidos (games) y ha perdido (have lost) diez, ¿sabes qué tanto por ciento de los partidos ha ganado?

Al oír (On hearing) esto Felipe abre la boca y exclama, — Tienes razón, mamá. Los números, la aritmética y las matemáticas son muy importantes incluso para manejar bien una calculadora. Creo que voy a estudiar mucho más.

CHAPTER 23

EL PUEBLO[1] DE ESPAÑA

PRIMERA PARTE

1 Voy a hacerle algunas preguntas acerca del pueblo[1] de España, dice la señora Adams. ¿Está Ud. listo? ¿Quiere Ud. otro puro? Aquí tiene las cerillas y el cenicero.

2 Gracias, señora Adams. Estoy muy bien. Continúe, por favor.

3 Ante todo, ¿quiénes son los españoles?

4 No sabemos mucho de los orígenes del pueblo. Los primeros habitantes de la Península fueron los íberos. A través de los siglos el país sufrió muchas invasiones, por ejemplo, las de los celtas, los romanos, los visigodos y los árabes.

5 ¿Cuántos habitantes hay ahora en España?

6 Hoy día hay en España más o menos 34 (treinta y cuatro) millones de habitantes. Se dice que los españoles son el pueblo más monárquico del mundo, y que por eso hay en España 34 millones de reyes. El sentido de la independencia, del honor y del orgullo es muy típico del pueblo.

7 ¿Dónde vive la mayor parte de los habitantes, en la ciudad o en el campo?

8 Hay ciudades grandes muy modernas y grandes industrias. Casi dos millones y medio de personas viven en Madrid, una ciudad muy hermosa. Pero todavía hay gente que vive en el campo y trabaja en la agricultura.

9 ¿Cuáles son los productos más importantes?

10 España produce y exporta una variedad de productos — trigo, arroz; naranjas, limones y aceite pero actualmente la industria del automóvil exporta mucho más.

11 Además de ser agricultores y industriales, los españoles son artistas y artesanos, ¿verdad?

12 Son muy trabajadores, pero saben también vivir. Y conocen a fondo como hacer cosas artísticas.

13 ¿De qué artes[2] se ocupan?

14 Mucha gente se ocupa de las artes populares — la cerámica, el tejido; hace cestas, artículos de cuero, de cobre, de hojalata, de oro, de plata y de laca.

15 A propósito, acabo de recibir un envío de algunos artículos de España. ¿Quiere Ud. venir a mi oficina el jueves a las tres de la tarde para verlos? Entonces volveremos a hablar de las artes populares.

162

16 Con mucho gusto, Sra. Adams. Tenemos cita para el jueves a las tres, ¿verdad?

17 Hasta el jueves, entonces.

18 Hasta luego. Que Ud. lo pase bien.

1 'I am going to ask you some questions about the people of Spain,' says Mrs. Adams. 'Are you ready? Do you want another cigar? Here are the matches and the ashtray.'

2 Thank you, Mrs. Adams. I am very comfortable. Continue, please.

3 First of all, who are the Spaniards?

4 We do not know much of the origins of the people. The first inhabitants of the Peninsula were the Iberians. Throughout the centuries the country suffered many invasions, for example, those of the Celts, the Romans, the Visigoths and the Arabs.

5 How many inhabitants are there now in Spain?

6 Today Spain has more or less 34 million inhabitants. It is said (*lit.* it says itself) that the Spanish are the most monarchic people in the world and because of this there are in Spain 34 million kings. The feeling of independence, honour and pride is very typical of the people.

7 Where do the majority of the inhabitants live, in the city or in the country?

8 There are big, very modern cities and big industries. Almost two and a half million persons live in Madrid, a very beautiful city. But there are still people who live in the country and work in agriculture.

9 What are the most important products?

10 Spain produces and exports a variety of products—wheat, rice, oranges, lemons and oil but at present the car industry exports a lot more.

11 Besides being agriculturalists and industrialists, Spaniards are artists and artisans, are they not?

12 They are very hardworking but they also know how to live. And they know thoroughly how to make artistic things.

13 What arts are they engaged in?

14 Many people are engaged in the popular arts—ceramics, weaving; they make baskets, leather goods, things of copper, tin, gold, silver and lacquer.

15 By the way, I have just received a shipment of some articles from Spain. Do you want to come to my office on Thursday at three in the afternoon to look at them? Then we will talk again about the popular arts.

16 With pleasure, Mrs. Adams. We have an appointment for Thursday at three, haven't we?

17 Until Thursday, then.

18 Good-bye. Good luck to you.

NOTE: 1. **Pueblo** can mean town, people or population.

NOTE: 2. **Las artes,** arts and crafts; **El Arte,** Art on a high plane; **Las Bellas Artes,** fine arts; **artesanía,** craftsmanship.

Pronunciation Aids

1 Practise:

continúe (kon-ti-ˈnu-e)   **cerámica** (θe-ˈra-mi-ka)
industrias (in-ˈdus-trjas)   **tejido** (te-ˈxi-ðo)
variedad (va-rje-ðað) or   **envío** (en-ˈvi-o) or (em-ˈbi-o)
  (ba-rje-ðað)   **hojalata** (o-xa-ˈla-ta)
embellecer (em-be-ʎe-ˈθer)   **cuero** (ˈkwe-ro)
trabajadores (tra-βa-xa-ˈðo-res)   **cobre** (ˈko-βre)
artísticos (ar-ˈtis-ti-kos)

2 **y** and **e** mean *and*. **e** is used instead of **y** when the next word begins with the letter **i,** to avoid repetition of the **i** (ee) sound: agricultura **e** industria.

o and **u** mean *or*. **u** is used instead of **o** when the next word begins with **o** to avoid repetition of the **o** sound: septiembre **u** octubre.

Building Vocabulary

A. **Materias Primas** (Raw Materials)

el algodón	cotton	**el oro**	gold
el cobre	copper	**la paja**	straw
el cuero	leather	**el petróleo**	petroleum
el hierro	iron	**la plata**	silver
la lana	wool	**el plomo**	lead
la madera	wood	**la seda**	silk

B. **Sinónimos:**

el idioma	**la lengua**	language
acabar	**terminar**	to finish
el cigarro	**el puro**	cigar
la cerilla	**el fósforo**	match
encantado	**con mucho gusto**	with great pleasure

Expresiones Importantes

a causa de	because of	**a fondo**	fully, completely, thoroughly
ante todo	first of all	**ocuparse de**	to be engaged in (to busy oneself with)
que Ud. lo pase bien	good luck to you (may you get along well)		

Exercise No. 90—Completion of Text

1 **Voy a** (ask you) **algunas preguntas.**
2 **Son** (about the people) **de España.**
3 (Here are) **las cerillas.** (Continue), **por favor.**
4 ¿(Who) **son los españoles?**
5 ¿**Cuántos habitantes viven** (nowadays) **en España?**
6 **En España hay** (34 million kings).
7 **España produce y exporta** (a variety of products).
8 **El aceite es** (an important product).
9 **Son** (artists and artisans).
10 ¿**De qué artes** (are they engaged)?
11 (They are engaged) **de las artes populares.**
12 **Hacen** (baskets and leather articles).
13 (I have just received) **un envío de España.**
14 (We will talk again) **de las artes populares.**
15 (Good luck to you).

SEGUNDA PARTE

Grammar Notes

1 Present Tense of **volver (ue)** to return, go back; **volver a hablar** to speak again

I return, etc.		I speak again, etc.	
vuelvo	**volvemos**	**vuelvo a hablar**	**volvemos a hablar**
vuelves	**volvéis**	**vuelves a hablar**	**volvéis a hablar**
vuelve	**vuelven**	**vuelve a hablar**	**vuelven a hablar**

(a) **Vuelvo a casa.** I return home. **Volvemos al cine.** We return to the cinema.

(b) **Volver a,** plus an infinitive, means to do something again.

Vuelvo a escribir la carta I am writing the letter again.
Hoy volvemos a hablar de las artes. Today we shall speak again of the arts.

Another way of expressing the same idea:

Escribo la carta otra vez. **Hoy hablamos de las artes otra vez.**

2 **acabar** to finish, **acabar de recibir** to have just received

(a) **Acabo el trabajo.** I finish the work.

¿**Acaban Uds. la lección?** Are you finishing the lesson?

(b) **acabar de** plus an infinitive, means to have just done something.

Acabo de recibir un envío. I have just received a shipment.
Acaba de enseñar la lección. He has just taught the lesson.

Ejercicios (Exercises) No. 91A–91B

91A. Repeat aloud the Spanish sentences many times.

1 **¿Acaba Ud. de comer?** Have you just eaten?
2 **Sí, acabo de comer.** Yes, I have just eaten.
3 **¿Acaba de dormir el niño?** Has the child just slept?
4 **No, no acaba de dormir.** No, he has not just slept.
5 **¿Acaban de tomar la cena?** Have they just eaten supper?
6 **Sí, acaban de tomarla.** Yes, they have just eaten it.
7 **¿Cuándo vuelve Ud. a casa?** When do you return home?
8 **Vuelvo a casa a las siete.** I return home at seven.
9 **Vuelven a leer el libro.** They are reading the book again.
10 **Carlos vuelve a venir acá.** Charles is coming here again.

NOTE: **acá** here, and **allá** there, are used instead of **aquí** and **allí** with verbs of motion.

91B. Translate:

1 When do they return home?
2 They return home at ten o'clock in the evening.
3 The students are writing the exercises again.
4 I am reading the guide book (**la guía de viajero**) again.
5 We have just received a shipment of merchandise (**mercancía**).
6 I have just spoken about the climate.
7 She has just returned from the jewellery shop (**joyería**).
8 They have just bought silver earrings (**pendientes** (or **orejeras**) **de plata**).
9 Have you just come from the cinema?
10 We are finishing the work (**el trabajo**).

Exercise No. 92—Preguntas

1 **¿Quién va a hacer algunas preguntas?**
2 **¿Cuál es la primera pregunta?**
3 **¿Cómo se llaman los primeros habitantes de la Península?**
4 **¿Cuántos habitantes tiene España?**
5 **¿Qué sentido es típico del pueblo?**
6 **¿Cuáles son los productos de España?**
7 **¿Cuál es el producto más importante de España?**
8 **¿De qué artes se ocupan muchas personas?**
9 **¿De qué materiales hacen cosas artísticas?**
10 **¿Quién acaba de recibir un envío de mercancía de España?**

CHAPTER 24

LAS ARTES POPULARES

PRIMERA PARTE

1 En la oficina de la Sra. Adams. Acaba de recibir unas cajas de mercancía de España y ha invitado al Sr. López a verlas con ella.

2 Vamos a ver los artículos de España, Sr. López. Acabo de recibirlos.

3 Con mucho gusto. Y entretanto podemos hablar de las artes populares.

4 Sabemos, Sr. López, que algunos de los artículos más artísticos que hacen los artesanos españoles son los de uso diario. Así es que el vestido es también un arte popular?

5 En los bailes folklóricos se llevan vestidos tradicionales. El traje tradicional de los vascos es muy sencillo pero hermoso: los hombres llevan una camisa blanca, pantalones blancos y una faja roja. ¡Qué contraste con los colores brillantes del traje tradicional de los gitanos en Andalucía! ¿Le mandan faldas de colores?

6 Desgraciadamente, no. Pero acabo de recibir esos echarpes tejidos de lana, de algodón y de seda. ¿Son muy bonitos, verdad? ¡Qué graciosos son los dibujos!

7 Son muy hermosos, pero me gustan más aquellos objetos de cerámica.

8 A mí también me gustan, señor López. Mire Ud. esos jarros y vasos. Mire los dibujos — éstos de pájaros y ésos de animalitos que adornan los jarros. Aquellas botellas son muy bonitas y prácticas — están envueltas en cuero, que sirve para proteger el vidrio.

9 De veras, toda esta cerámica es hermosísima[1] y estoy seguro de que se vende bien. Viene de Talavera, ¿verdad?

10 En efecto. Y esos objetos de cerámica son de Manises. Tengo también muñecas hechas de cerámica que representan señoras y toreros. Espero también recibir muy pronto un envío de objetos de arte hechos de hojalata y de cobre. Y van a mandarme cestas de varios tamaños y estilos, dice la señora Adams.

11 Hemos hablado de las fiestas, pero ¿qué sabe Ud. de las fiestas?

12 Sé muy poco de las fiestas.

13 Entonces tenemos que hablar de las fiestas la próxima vez. ¿Le parece bien el martes a las ocho?

14 Me parece bien.

167

15 Hasta el martes, Sra. Adams.

16 Que Ud. lo pase bien, Sr. López.

1 In the office of Mrs. Adams. She has just received some boxes of merchandise from Spain and has invited Mr. López to look at them with her.

2 Let us look at the things from Spain, Mr. López. I have just received them.

3 With pleasure. And meanwhile we can talk about the popular arts.

4 We know, Mr. López, that some of the most artistic things that the Spanish craftsmen make are those articles of daily use. So it is that the clothing is also a popular art, is it not?

5 The folk dancers traditional dress. The traditional costume of the Basques is very simple but beautiful. The men wear a white shirt, white trousers and a red sash. What a contrast with the brilliant colours of the traditional costume of the gipsies in Andalusia! Do they send you coloured skirts?

6 Unfortunately, no. But I have just received those shawls, woven in wool, cotton and silk. They are very pretty, aren't they? Aren't the designs lovely!

7 They are very beautiful, but I prefer those ceramic objects.

8 I like them too, Mr. López. Look at those jugs and vases. Look at the designs—these of birds and those of little animals which decorate the jugs. Those bottles are very pretty and practical—they are covered in leather, which serves to protect the glass.

9 Indeed, all this ceramic ware is very beautiful, and I am sure it sells well. It comes from Talavera, doesn't it?

10 It does. And those ceramic objects are from Manises. I also have some dolls made of pottery which represent Spanish ladies and bull-fighters. I also hope I shall soon receive a shipment of art objects made from tin plate and copper. And they are going to send me baskets of various sizes and styles, says Mrs. Adams.

11 We have spoken of fiestas, but what do you know about the fiestas?

12 I know very little about fiestas.

13 Then, we must talk about fiestas the next time. Is Tuesday at eight all right with you?

14 It is all right with me.

15 Until Tuesday, Mrs. Adams.

16 Good luck to you, Mr. López.

NOTE: 1. The ending **-ísimo, -a** is equivalent to *very*: **malo** bad, **malísimo, -a** very bad.

Pronunciation Aids

Practise:

sencillos (sen-'θi-ʎos)
brillantes (bri-'ʎan-tes)
gitano (xi-'ta-no)
desgraciadamente
 (ðes-ɣra-θja-ða-'men-te)

botella (bo-'te-ʎa)
vestido (ves-'ti-ðo) or (bes-'ti-ðo)
cestas ('θes-tas)
hojalata (o-xa-'la-ta)

Building Vocabulary

A. **la mano,** the hand. Nouns ending in -o are masculine. **La mano** is an exception.

B. **La Ropa**   Clothing, Wearing Apparel

el abrigo	coat	**el impermeable**	raincoat
la blusa	blouse	**las medias**	stockings
los calcetines	socks	**los pantalones**	trousers
la camisa	shirt	**el pañuelo**	handkerchief
la corbata	tie	**el sombrero**	hat
el echarpe	shawl	**el traje**	suit, costume
la faja	sash	**el vestido**	dress
la falda	skirt	**los zapatos**	shoes
los guantes	gloves	**los leotardos**	tights
los vaqueros	jeans		

Expresiones Importantes

1	**entretanto**	meanwhile
2	**de seguro**	certainly
3	**¿Le parece (a Ud.) bien?**	Is it all right with you?
4	**Me parece bien.**	It's all right with me.
5	**Se visten con blusas**	They dress in blouses.

Exercise No. 93—Completion of Text

1 **Vamos** (to look at) **los artículos de España.**

2 (In the meanwhile) **vamos a hablar de** (the folk arts).

3 **Estos artículos son** (of daily use).

4 **Llevan blusas** (with simple embroidery).

5 **Las mujeres se visten de** (long skirts).

6 **Los hombres llevan** (a white shirt).

7 **El traje de los vascos** (is simple but beautiful).

8 **¡Qué contraste con** (the brilliant colours) **del traje tradicional** (of the gipsies).

9 (I like) **los dibujos de pájaros.**

10 **La faja está tejida** (of wool or cotton).
11 **El cuero** (serves to protect) **el vidrio.**
12 (Of course) **van a mandarme** (baskets of various sizes).
13 (We must talk) **de las fiestas.**
14 Is Tuesday all right with you?
15 It's all right with me.

SEGUNDA PARTE

Grammar Notes

1 Demonstrative Pronouns

(a)

este dibujo **y ése**	*this* sketch and *that* (*one*)
esta casa **y aquélla**	*this* house and *that* (*one*)
estos libros **y ésos**	*these* books and *those*
esa tienda **y ésta**	*that* shop and *this* (*one*)
esos trajes **y éstos**	*those* costumes and *these*.
aquel coche **y éste**	*that* car and *this one*

When the noun is omitted after a demonstrative adjective, the adjective becomes a demonstrative pronoun. The demonstrative pronoun takes an accent mark and agrees in number and gender with the omitted noun.

(b) **esto, eso, aquello.** These are neuter forms of the demonstrative pronoun. They are used to point out a thing not yet mentioned, and to refer to a whole sentence or idea. They do not have an accent mark.

¿Qué es *esto*? What's *this*? (pointing to it)
Es perezoso. *Eso* es verdad. He is lazy. *That* is true.

2 The Former, the Latter

éste means the latter; **aquél** and **ése,** the former. They agree in number and gender with the nouns to which they refer. The accent mark is usually omitted over capitals.

El Sr. Adams y su esposa están en casa.	Mr. Adams and his wife are at home.
***Esta* lee una revista.**	*The latter* is reading a magazine.
***Aquél* escribe una carta.**	*The former* is writing a letter.

Ejercicios (Exercises) No. 94A–94B–94C

94A. Write each sentence putting the verbs into Spanish. Remember: **vestir (i)** to dress, **vestir de** to dress in, **vestirse** to dress oneself, **llevar** to wear.

1 (I dress) **al niño.**
2 I dress myself.

7 (I wear) **mi vestido nuevo.**
8 **¿Quiénes** (wear) **echarpes?**

3 (They dress in) **faldas bordadas.**
4 (We dress) **a los niños.**
5 **Las niñas** (dress themselves).
6 **¿Qué** (do you — **Ud.** — wear)
  los domingos?

9 **Las señoritas** (wear) **guantes.**
10 (We are wearing) **zapatos**
  nuevos.

94B. Complete these sentences using the correct demonstrative adjectives and pronouns.

Ejemplo: Este dibujo es antiguo, ése es moderno.

1 (This) **dibujo es antiguo,** (that one) **es moderno.**
2 (These) **echarpes tienen dibujos de animalitos,** (those) **tienen dibujos de pájaros.**
3 (Those) **faldas son de lana,** (these) **son de algodón.**
4 (This) **blusa tiene bordados sencillos,** (that one) **es moderna.**
5 (That—*distant*) **casa es antigua,** (this one) **es moderna.**
6 **El Sr. López y la Sra. Adams son amigos.** (The latter) **es negociante,** (the former) **es profesor.**
7 **Ana y María son alumnas.** (The latter) **aprende el español,** (the former) **aprende el francés.**
8 **¿Qué es** (this)? **¿Qué es** (that)?
9 **El hombre es rico.** (That) **es verdad.**
10 **Felipe trabaja diligentemente. Todos saben** (that).

94C. Repeat the Spanish sentences aloud many times.

1 **¿Qué está comprando Ud.?**
2 **Estoy comprando un sombrero.**
3 **¿Qué está comprando su hermana?**
4 **Está comprando una faja.**

1 What are you buying?
2 I am buying a hat.
3 What is your sister buying?
4 She is buying a sash.

1 **¿Tiene Ud. un echarpe?**
2 **No tengo echarpe.**
3 **¿Tiene Ud. un pañuelo?**
4 **No tengo pañuelo.**

1 Have you a shawl?
2 I have no shawl.
3 Have you a handkerchief?
4 I have no handkerchief.

1 **¿Lleva Ud. guantes en invierno?**
2 **Sí, llevo guantes en invierno.**
3 **¿Lleva Ud. abrigo?**
4 **Llevo abrigo cuando hace frío.**

1 Do you wear gloves in winter?
2 Yes, I wear gloves in winter.
3 Do you wear an overcoat?
4 I wear an overcoat when it is cold.

Exercise No. 95—Preguntas

1 **¿Quién acaba de recibir una caja de mercancía de España?**
2 **¿Qué da a los campesinos un aspecto pintoresco?**
3 **¿Quién viste la faja roja?**

4 ¿De qué están tejidos los echarpes?

5 ¿Qué clase de dibujos adorna los jarros?

6 ¿En qué están envueltas las botellas?

7 ¿Para qué sirve el cuero?

8 ¿De dónde viene la cerámica que vende la señora Adams?

9 ¿De qué sabe muy poco la Sra. Adams?

10 ¿Qué dice la Sra. Adams al Sr. López cuando éste sale de su casa?

CHAPTER 25

LOS DÍAS DE FIESTA

PRIMERA PARTE

1 — ¿Cuáles son los días de fiesta en España?, pregunta la señora Adams al señor López.

2 Hay fiestas en varios días en un pueblo u otro. Estas fiestas están dedicadas al santo ¯patrón del lugar. Todas se celebran con procesiones, ferias, juegos, cohetes y otros fuegos artificiales.

3 Por supuesto, los españoles celebran la Navidad[1].

4 Sí. En la Navidad celebran el nacimiento de Jesucristo, visitan las iglesias y se cantan villancicos. Pero, como en Gran Bretaña, la fiesta de Navidad es también una fiesta mundana.

5 ¿Ud. quiere decir que comen mucho?

6 Sí. A los españoles les gusta escoger y comer el pavo tradicional y turrón[2]. En la Nochebuena, es decir la víspera de Navidad, algunos van a misa del gallo.

7 Y en las casas particulares, ¿hay también árboles de Navidad?

8 Sí, pero además cada familia tiene su nacimiento, con figuritas de barro que representa la escena de Belén.

9 Y ¿qué dicen los españoles cuando se encuentran en la fiesta de Navidad?

10 Se desean 'Felices Pascuas'. A própósito, diciembre es el mes del gran sorteo de la lotería. Al que escoge un buen billete, el mejor regalo de todos es un premio, quizás el premio gordo. En general no es costumbre dar regalos de Navidad, pero los niños reciben regalos doce días después, en el Día de Reyes. El cinco de enero los Tres Reyes desfilan por las calles, y por la noche dejan regalos para los niños buenos.

11 Y el primero de mayo, ¿se celebra el Primero de Mayo?

12 Sí. Como en muchos otros países del mundo, nadie trabaja en la Fiesta del Trabajo. La gente va de jira a los parques o al campo.

13 ¿Hay fiestas en la Semana Santa?

14 ¡Claro está! Las fiestas de la Semana Santa en Sevilla son las más importantes de España, y gozan de fama internacional. Más de cincuenta cofradías desfilan por las calles. Y el esplendor de las procesiones es magnífico.

15 ¡Que lástima que no puedo verlas! dice la señora Adams.

16 Pero Ud. sí debe asistir al Encierro de Pamplona el siete de julio, dice el señor López con una sonrisa. En aquel día de fiesta los toros corren libres por las calles. Dicen es deporte. Sin embargo, hay españoles que están en contra los Toros.

17 — Ah, es algo así como los ingleses que quieren prohibir la caza del zorro ¿verdad? responde la señora Adams.

NOTE: 1. Can also be in plural **Navidades,** but meaning remains unchanged. 2. A sweet (sort of nougat) eaten at Christmas time; it is the 'Christmas Pudding' of Spain. 3. Midnight mass.

1 'What are the fiesta days in Spain?' Mrs. Adams asks Mr. López.

2 There are fiestas on various days in one town or another. These fiestas are dedicated to the patron saint of the place. All are celebrated with processions, fairs, games, rockets and other fireworks.

3 Of course, the Spaniards celebrate Christmas.

4 Yes. At Christmas they celebrate the birth of Jesus Christ, they visit the churches, and Christmas carols are sung. But, as in Great Britain, the feast of Christmas is also a worldly feast.

5 You mean they eat a lot?

6 Yes. The Spaniards like to choose and eat the traditional turkey and 'turrón'. On Holy Night, that is to say Christmas Eve, some people go to midnight mass.

7 And in private houses, are there also Christmas trees?

8 Yes, but also each family has its crib, with little clay figures, which represents the scene in Bethlehem.

9 And what do the Spanish people say when they meet one another at Christmas time?

10 They wish one another Merry Christmas. By the way, December is the month of the big draw in the lottery. To the one who chooses a good ticket, the best present of all is a prize, perhaps the first (*lit.* the fat) prize. In general it is not the custom to give Christmas presents, but the children receive presents twelve days after, at Epiphany (*lit.* the Day of the Kings, i.e. the Wise Men). On January 5, the Three Kings parade through the streets and at night leave presents for good children.

11 And on May 1 do they celebrate May Day?

12 Yes, but it is a religious holiday. As in many other countries of the world, nobody works on May Day. People go for picnics in the parks or in the country.

13 Are there fiestas in Holy Week?

14 Yes indeed! The fiestas of Holy Week in Seville are the most important in Spain, and are internationally famous. Over 50 'brotherhoods' process through the streets. And the splendour of the processions is magnificent.

15 'What a pity I can't see them!' says Mrs. Adams.

16 'But you should indeed be present at the "Encierro" at Pamplona on July 7,' says Mr. López with a smile. 'On that fiesta day the bulls run free through the streets. They say it is a sport. However, there are Spaniards who are against bullfighting.'

17 'Ah, it is something like the English who wish to ban fox-hunting, isn't it?' replies Mrs. Adams.

Pronunciation Aids

Practise:

Navidad (na-vi-'ðað) or (na-βi-'ðað)
villancicos (vi-ʎan-'θi-kos) or (bi-ʎan-'θi-kos)
Nochebuena (no-tʃe-'βwe-na)
Felices Pascuas (fe-'li-θes 'pas-kwas)

cofradía (ko-fra-'ði-a)
diciembre (ði-'θjem-bre)
árbol ('ar-βol)
nacimiento (na-θi-'mjen-to)
quizás (ki-'θas)
Encierro (en-'θje-rro)

Building Vocabulary

A. Palabras relacionadas

1 **jugar**	to play	4 **regalar**	to give a present
juego	game	**regalo**	present
2 **correr**	to run	5 **trabajar**	to work, labour
corrida	bullfight	**trabajo**	work, labour
	(*lit.* running)	6 **prohibir**	to ban, prohibit
3 **nacer**	to be born		
nacimiento	birth		

B. Partes de la Cara   Parts of the Face

la boca	mouth	**los oídos**	ears (internal)
los dientes	teeth	**las orejas**	ears (external)
los labios	lips	**los ojos**	eyes
la nariz	nose	**las mejillas**	cheeks

Expresiones Importantes

1 **Felices Pascuas**	Merry Christmas
2 **el premio gordo**	the first prize
3 **ir de jira**	to go for a picnic
4 **¡qué lástima!**	what a pity!
5 **estar en contra**	to be against, to oppose
6 **Ud. debe asisitir a**	you should be present at

Exercise No. 96—Completion of Text

1 **Hay fiestas** (in some town or other).
2 **Todas** (are celebrated) **con procesiones y juegos.**
3 (Of course) **celebran la Navidad.**
4 Christmas carols are sung.
5 **La fiesta de Navidad es** (also a worldly feast).
6 (You mean) **que comen mucho.**
7 **En las calles** (are roasted) **castañas.**
8 **Diciembre es el mes** (of the big draw) **de la lotería.**
9 **Los niños reciben regalos** (twelve days after).
10 **Nadie trabaja** (on May Day).
11 **La gente** (goes for picnics).
12 ¡(What a pity) **que no puedo verlas!**

13 It is a magnificent sport!
14 **No quiero** (to see bullfighting).

SEGUNDA PARTE

Grammar Notes

1 Present Tense of

coger to catch, pick up,

    I catch, etc.

escoger to choose,

    I choose, etc.

cojo	cogemos	escojo	escogemos
coges	cogéis	escoges	escogéis
coge	cogen	escoge	escogen

      Imperative   Imperative

coja Ud.   cojan Uds.   **escoja Ud.   escojan Uds.**

NOTE: Before the endings **-o** and **-a, g** becomes **j,** so as to keep the same sound as is found in the infinitive (**-ger**).

2 Shortened Adjectives

The following adjectives drop the ending **-o** when used before a masculine noun:

(uno)	**un hombre**	one man
(alguno)	**algún pueblo**	some town
(ninguno)	**ningún padre**	no father
(bueno)	**un buen hombre**	a good man
(malo)	**un mal hombre**	a bad man
(primero)	**el primer día**	the first day
(tercero)	**el tercer año**	the third year

NOTE: **algún** and **ningún** have an accent mark to hold the stress on the syllable **-gún.**

3 Present Participle of Stem-Changing Verbs. **pedir (i),** and verbs like it, which have the stem change **e** to **i** in the present tense, have the same change in the present participle.

Infinitive	Present Tense	Present Participle
pedir	**(yo) pido**	**pidiendo**
repetir	**(yo) repito**	**repitiendo**
servir	**(yo) sirvo**	**sirviendo**
despedirse	**(yo) me despido**	**despidiéndome**

Ejercicios (Exercises) No. 97A–97B

97A. Complete these sentences in Spanish.

1 **Enero es el** (first) **mes del año.**
2 **Marzo es el** (third) **mes del año.**
3 **Vamos a pasar un** (good) **rato.**
4 **Tenemos un** (good) **maestro.**
5 **El científico Einstein es un** (great) **hombre. No es un hombre** (big, tall).
6 **Tenemos asientos en la** (third) **fila.**
7 **Hace** (bad) **tiempo en invierno.**
8 **El** (first) **de enero.**
9 **Ellos tienen** (good) **asientos.**
10 (Some) **día Ud. irá a España.**

97B. Write each sentence putting all the verbs into Spanish.

1 (They sing) **villancicos.**
2 (We celebrate) **la Navidad.**
3 (They visit) **las iglesias.**
4 (They choose) **el pavo tradicional.**
5 (I am preparing) **la comida.**
6 ¿(Do you use) **un bolígrafo?**
7 **La cesta** (contains) **panecillos.**
8 **Un niño** (tries to) **correr.**
9 **Todos** (pick up) **los libros.**
10 **Los Reyes Magos** (bring) **los regalos.**

Exercise No. 98—Preguntas

1 **¿Cómo se titula** (entitled) **esta lectura** (reading selection)?
2 **¿Cómo se celebran las fiestas de los santos patrones?**
3 **¿Cuál es un elemento casi esencial de estas fiestas?**
4 **¿Qué celebra la fiesta de Navidad?**
5 **¿Qué se come?**
6 **¿A dónde van algunos españoles en la Nochebuena?**
7 **¿Qué representa un 'nacimiento'?**

8 ¿Cuándo se hace el gran sorteo de la lotería?
9 ¿Cuándo reciben los niños regalos?
10 ¿Qué fiesta se celebra el primero de mayo?
11 ¿Qué fiestas de la Semana Santa son las más importantes de España?
12 ¿Qué se puede ver el siete de julio en Pamplona?

Regiones o Comunidades Autonomas
Regions of Spain

The constitution of 1978 recognises and guarantees the right of autonomy
(self government) to all the regions of Spain.

CHAPTER 26

¿QUÉ LUGARES QUIERE VD. VISITAR, SRA. ADAMS?

PRIMERA PARTE

1 Pronto Ud. va a salir para España, Sra. Adams. ¿Ha decidido qué lugares quiere visitar?

2 No pienso en otra cosa y estoy leyendo mucho en las varias guías del viajero.

3 Viajaré en avión a la capital. Tomando el centro de la ciudad como punto de partida, visitaré lugares de interés en la capital, en los alrededores y en otras partes del país.

4 En la capital, veré el Parque del Retiro con sus árboles y avenidas hermosas, y el Jardín Botánico. Y pasaré al menos un día en el Museo del Prado, que está muy cerca. Visitaré los museos de Arte Contemporáneo, de Artes Decorativas, del Pueblo Español y del Teatro. Voy a ver el Palacio Real, las muchas iglesias, y muchos lugares más de interés. También tengo ganas de ir a ver los mercados y el Rastro, donde podré comprar artículos de interés folklórico.

5 En los alrededores visitaré el Valle de los Caídos. Se dice que es muy imponente, con su cruz gigante. Y mientras estoy en la capital visitaré los alrededores y algunos de los pueblos cercanos.

6 No deje Ud. de visitar también Alcalá de Henares, donde nació Cervantes. Ud. visitará La Complutense Universidad, que fue muy célebre, sobre todo en los siglos XV y XVI.

7 Iré al Escorial, el monasterio construído por orden de Felipe II. Está situado en la sierra de Guadarrama, ye se dice que es un lugar muy popular en verano porque allí hace fresco y en invierno por el esquí.

8 Es verdad. Y Ud. hallará muchas cosas de interés en Segovia, una ciudad típica de Castilla. Verá el acueducto romano, que funciona todavía, y el Alcázar, la fortaleza de la ciudad. Hay muchos pueblos bonitos no lejos de Madrid. Estoy seguro de que Ud. irá también a Talavera, y Manises, pueblos célebres por su cerámica.

9 Sin falta. E iré a todos los pueblos conocidos por sus artes populares y sus plateros y . . .

10 Sus proyectos son muy ambiciosos. Veo que siempre es Ud. la negociante, señora Adams.

11 No es eso. Mi viaje es un viaje de negocios y quiero aprovecharme de ello, pero también me interesa el pueblo de España que vive fuera de los

179

grandes centros. Quizás veré también los monumentos árabes de Andalucía, y conoceré a los gitanos que viven en las cuevas.
  12 Tengo ganas de acompañarla, señora Adams, pero no es posible.
  13 ¡Qué lástima, señor López!

  1 Soon you are going to leave for Spain, Mrs. Adams. Have you
decided what places you want to visit?
  2 I think of nothing else and I am reading a great deal in the various
guide books.
  3 I shall travel by plane to the capital. Taking the centre of the city
as a point of departure, I shall visit places of interest in the capital, in
the surrounding area and in other parts of the country.
  4 In the capital, I shall see the Retiro Park with its trees and beautiful avenues, and the Botanical Garden. And I will spend at least one
day in the Prado Museum, which is very near. I shall visit the museums of
Contemporary Art, of Decorative Arts, of the Spanish People and of the
Theatre. I shall go to see the Royal Palace, many of the churches, and
many more places of interest. I also have a desire to go to see the
markets and the flea-market, where I shall be able to buy articles of
folklore interest.
  5 In the surrounding area I shall visit the Valley of the Fallen. It is
said that it is very impressive with its gigantic cross. And while I am in
the capital I shall visit the suburbs and some of the nearby towns.
  6 Don't fail to visit Alcalá de Henares too, where Cervantes was
born. You will visit the Complutense University, which was very famous,
above all in the 15th and 16th centuries.
  7 I shall go to the Escorial, the monastery built by order of Philip II. It is
situated in the Guadarrama mountains, and it is said that it is a very popular
place in summer because it is very cool there and in winter for ski-ing.
  8 It's true. And you will find much of interest in Segovia, a typical
city of Castile. You will see the Roman aqueduct, which still works, and
the Alcázar, the fortress of the city. There are many pretty towns not
far from Madrid. I am sure you will also go to Talavera and Manises,
towns famous for their pottery.
  9 Without fail. And I shall go to all the other towns known for
their folk arts and their silversmiths and . . .
  10 Your projects are very ambitious. I see that you are always the
businesswoman, Mrs. Adams.
  11 It is not that. My trip is a business trip and I want to profit from
it, but also I am interested in the Spanish people who live outside the
big centres. Perhaps I shall also see the Arabic monuments of Andalusia,
and get to know the gipsies who live in the caves.
  12 I would like to go with you, Mrs. Adams, but it is not possible.
  13 What a pity, Mr. López!

Pronunciation Aids

Practise:

alrededores (al-re-ðe-ˈðo-res)   **Caídos** (ka-ˈi-ðos)
Henares (e-ˈna-res)   **acueducto** (a-kwe-ˈðuk-to)
Alcázar (al-ˈka-θar)   **Andalucía** (an-da-lu-ˈθi-a)

Building Vocabulary

A. Sinónimos:

1 **contestar**	**responder**	to answer
2 **desear**	**querer**	to wish, want
3 **estoy seguro**	**estoy cierto**	I am sure
4 **el lugar**	**el sitio**	place

B. Expressions of Future

1 **mañana**	tomorrow
2 **pasado mañana**	day after tomorrow
3 **la próxima vez (semana)**	next time (week)
4 **el próximo año**	next year
5 **el año que viene**	next year
6 **mañana por la mañana**	tomorrow morning

Expresiones Importantes

1 **estoy seguro**	I am sure
2 **No deje Ud. de (ver, etc.)**	do not fail to (see, etc.)
3 **pensar en**	to think of
4 **tengo ganas**	I have a desire (a mind to)

Exercise No. 99—Completion of Text

1 (I am reading) **en las varias guías.**
2 (I shall travel) **en avión.**
3 (I shall visit) **lugares de interés.**
4 (I shall see) **el Palacio Real.**
5 (I shall spend) **un día en el parque del Retiro.**
6 (I am sure) **de que irá Ud. a los mercados.**
7 **Iré** (to the flea market).
8 (In the surrounding area) **visitaré el Valle de los Caídos.**
9 **Se dice** (that it is very impressive).
10 (While I am in the capital) **visitaré los alrededores.**
11 (Do not fail to) **visitar Alcalá de Henares.**
12 (You will find) **muchas cosas de interés en Segovia.**
13 Without fail.

14 **Me interesa el pueblo que vive** (outside the big centres).
15 (I have a desire) **de acompañarla, señora Adams.**

SEGUNDA PARTE

Grammar Notes

1 The Future Tense. Model Verb, **hablar.**

hablar-é	I shall speak
hablar-ás	you will speak
hablar-á	$\begin{cases}\text{you, he}\\ \text{she, it}\end{cases}$ will speak
hablar-emos	we shall speak
hablar-éis	you will speak
hablar-án	$\begin{cases}\text{you (pl.),}\\ \text{they}\end{cases}$ will speak

(a) The future endings of *all* verbs are:

singular **-é -ás -á**   plural **-emos -éis -án**

(b) To form the regular future add these endings to the *whole infinitive* as a base.

hablaré	**hablarás**	etc.	**viviré**	**vivirás**	etc.
estaré	**estarás**	etc.	**seré**	**serás**	etc.
aprenderé	**aprenderás**	etc.	**abriré**	**abrirás**	etc.

2 The Irregular Future

In a few common verbs there is a change in the infinitive base when the future endings are added. Thus:

saber to know		**tener** to have		**salir** to leave	
I shall know, etc.		I shall have, etc.		I shall leave, etc.	
sabré	**sabremos**	**tendré**	**tendremos**	**saldré**	**saldremos**
sabrás	**sabréis**	**tendrás**	**tendréis**	**saldrás**	**saldréis**
sabrá	**sabrán**	**tendrá**	**tendrán**	**saldrá**	**saldrán**

querer to wish		**venir** to come		**valer** to be worth	
I shall wish, etc.		I shall come, etc.		I shall be worth	
querré	**querremos**	**vendré**	**vendremos**	**valdré**	**valdremos**
querrás	**querréis**	**vendrás**	**vendréis**	**valdrás**	**valdréis**
querrá	**querrán**	**vendrá**	**vendrán**	**valdrá**	**valdrán**

poder to be able		**decir** to say		**hacer** to do, make	
I shall be able, etc.		I shall say, etc.		I shall do, make, etc.	
podré	**podremos**	**diré**	**diremos**	**haré**	**haremos**
podrás	**podréis**	**dirás**	**diréis**	**harás**	**haréis**
podrá	**podrán**	**dirá**	**dirán**	**hará**	**harán**

Ejercicios (Exercises) No. 100A–100B–100C

100A. Translate:

1 Visitaremos Salamanca.
2 Pasaré una semana allí.
3 Me gustará ver la Universidad.
4 ¿Quién viajará a España?
5 Ellos no trabajarán mucho.
6 ¿Estudiarán Uds. la lección?
7 ¿Tomará Ud. café?
8 Felipe no escribirá la carta.

9 No tendré frío.
10 El no vendrá acá.
11 Saldremos a las ocho.
12 Haré este papel.
13 Querrán comer.
14 Ella lo pondrá en la mesa.
15 No podré ir allá.

100B. Answer these questions in complete sentences (in the future), with the help of the words in parentheses.

Ejemplo: ¿A dónde irá Ud. esta noche? (al cine) Esta noche iré al cine.

1 ¿Qué comprará Ud.? (una corbata)
2 ¿Cuánto costará? (cien pesetas)
3 ¿A dónde irá Ud. en el verano? (al campo)
4 ¿Quién irá con Ud.? (mi hermano)
5 ¿A qué hora volverá Ud. del cine? (a las nueve de la tarde)
6 ¿A quién verá Ud. en la estación? (a mi amigo Guillerno)
7 ¿A qué hora saldrá Ud. de su casa? (a las ocho de la mañana)
8 ¿A qué hora tomarán Uds. la cena? (a las siete)
9 ¿A quiénes visitarán Uds. en la ciudad? (a nuestros amigos)
10 ¿Qué estudiarán Uds. esta tarde? (nuestras lecciones de español)

100C. Translate:

1 I shall learn
2 He will write
3 They will go
4 We shall eat
5 She will speak
6 Will you work?
7 Will John see?
8 Who will visit?
9 I shall not travel
10 Will they study?
11 I shall make
12 He will come
13 You (Ud.) will put
14 They will not want
15 Will you (Ud.) go out?
16 I shall have
17 They will be here
18 Will you (Uds.) go?

Exercise No. 101—Preguntas

1 ¿Cómo se titula esta lectura?
2 ¿Quién va a salir pronto para España?
3 ¿Qué clase de libros está leyendo ella?
4 ¿Cómo viajará?
5 ¿Qué lugar tomará como punto de partida?
6 ¿Cómo se llama el parque que está cerca del Museo del Prado?
7 ¿Cuánto tiempo pasará la Sra. Adams en el Museo del Prado?
8 ¿Qué espera comprar en el Rastro?
9 ¿Quién nació en Alcalá de Henares?

10 ¿Quién hizo construir (had built) **el monasterio del Escorial?**

11 ¿Cómo se llama la fortaleza de Segovia?

12 ¿Cuáles son los nombres de dos pueblos célebres por su cerámica?

13 ¿Qué monumentos verá quizás la Sra. Adams en Andalucía?

14 ¿Quién tiene ganas de acompañar a la Sra. Adams?

REVISION 6

CHAPTERS 23–26 PRIMERA PARTE

Palabras

NOUNS

1 el artista	14 el cuero	27 el oro
2 el arbol	15 la falda	28 el pavo
3 el arte	16 la guía	29 la plata
4 el algodón	17 el idioma	30 los pantalones
5 el baile	18 el juego	31 el pañuelo
6 la blusa	19 el juguete	32 el platero
7 la boca	20 el jardín	33 el regalo
8 la castaña	21 la lana	34 la ropa
9 la camisa	22 la madera	35 el sastre
10 la canción	23 la mano	36 el tejido
11 los calcetines	24 las medias	37 el traje
12 la cara	25 la nariz	38 el vestido
13 la corbata	26 el ojo	39 el zapato

1 artist	14 leather	27 gold
2 tree	15 skirt	28 turkey
3 art	16 guide	29 silver
4 cotton	17 language	30 trousers
5 dance	18 game	31 handkerchief
6 blouse	19 toy	32 silversmith
7 mouth	20 garden	33 present
8 chestnut	21 wool	34 clothing
9 shirt	22 wood	35 tailor
10 song	23 hand	36 cloth
11 socks	24 stockings	37 suit
12 face	25 nose	38 dress
13 necktie	26 eye	39 shoe

VERBS

1 bailar	8 durar	15 ocuparse de
2 cantar	9 emplear	16 representar
3 celebrar	10 escoger	17 romper
4 coger	11 llevar	18 vestir
5 contener	12 mandar	19 vestirse
6 cubrir	13 mirar	20 volver
7 decidir	14 observar	

1 to dance	8 to last	15 to be busy with
2 to sing	9 to employ	16 to represent
3 to celebrate	10 to choose	17 to break
4 to pick up, to catch	11 to bring, wear	18 to dress
5 to contain	12 to send	19 to dress oneself
6 to cover	13 to look at	20 to return
7 to decide	14 to observe	

185

ADJECTIVES

1 cubierto	5 hecho	9 pintoresco
2 cercano	6 imponente	10 precioso
3 chico	7 lleno	11 popular
4 envuelto	8 magnífico	12 tejido

1 covered	5 made	9 picturesque
2 near	6 impressive	10 precious
3 pretty, little	7 full	11 folk, popular
4 covered (surrounded by)	8 magnificent	12 woven

ADVERBS

1 de antemano	2 entretanto	3 todavía

1 beforehand	2 in the meantime	3 still

PREPOSITIONS

1 acerca de	2 a causa de	3 fuera de

1 concerning	2 because of	3 outside of

IMPORTANT EXPRESSIONS

1 acabar de + infin.	7 ir de jira
2 al fin	8 vestir de
3 al principio	9 volver a + infin.
4 llegar a + infin.	10 a la derecha
5 ¿le parece bien?	11 a la izquierda
6 me parece bien	

1 to have just	7 to go for a picnic
2 finally	8 to dress in
3 at first	9 to do again
4 to succeed in	10 to the right
5 is it all right with you?	11 to the left
6 it is all right with me	

SEGUNDA PARTE

Ejercicio 102. From Group II select the synonym for each word or expression in Group I.

Group I		Group II	
1 contestar	7 me acuerdo	(a) terminar	(g) vestir de
2 desear	8 vuelvo a	(b) lengua	(h) el año que
3 acabar	escribir	(c) responder	viene
4 llevar	9 por eso	(d) lugar	(i) recuerdo
5 sitio	10 idioma	(e) querer	(j) escribo otra
6 el año próximo	11 por supuesto	(f) por lo tanto	vez
	12 me gusta más		(k) prefiero
			(l) claro está

Ejercicio 103 Complete the following sentences by translating the given words.

Remember: 1. **ponerse** = to put on. 2. Use the definite article **(el, la, los, las)** instead of the possessive adjective **(mi, tu, su,** etc.) with clothing, when the meaning is clear.

NOTE: Another meaning of **ponerse** is to become. **Los árboles se ponen verdes.** The trees become green.

Ejemplo: Me pongo la camisa (*not* **mi camisa**). I put on my shirt.

1 **Me pongo** (my trousers).	6 **Nos ponemos** (our shoes).
2 **Te pones** (your hat).	7 **Uds. se ponen** (your gloves).
3 **El se pone** (his suit).	8 **Ellos se ponen** (their shirts).
4 **Ud. se pone** (your tie).	9 **Ellas se ponen** (their dresses).
5 **Ella se pone** (her sash).	10 **Póngase** (your overcoat).

Ejercicio 104 Select the group of words in the right-hand column which best completes the sentence in the left-hand column.

Remember: **se lleva** = is worn, one wears   **se llevan** = are worn, one wears

1 **Se lleva abrigo**	(a) **cuando se juega al tenis.**
2 **Se lleva impermeable**	(b) **para proteger la cabeza.**
3 **Se lleva sombrero**	(c) **cuando hace frío.**
4 **Se llevan zapatos**	(d) **para proteger las manos.**
5 **Se llevan guantes**	(e) **cuando llueve.**
6 **Se lleva traje de deporte**	(f) **para proteger los pies.**

Ejercicio 105 Complete these sentences, putting all the English words into Spanish.

1 (The baker) **vende pan en la** (bakery).
2 (The silversmith) **hace artículos de plata en la** (the silversmith's shop).
3 (The shoemaker) **vende zapatos en la** (shoe shop).
4 **El** (tailor) **hace trajes en la** (tailor's shop).
5 **Quien vende es** (a seller).
6 **Quien compra es** (a buyer).
7 **Comemos y hablamos con la** (mouth).
8 **Oímos con los** (ears).
9 **Vemos con los** (eyes).
10 **Otras partes de la** (face) **son** (the nose) **y** (the lips).

TERCERA PARTE

Diálogo 1

Practise the Spanish aloud:

En el autobús

1 Perdóneme, señor, ¿dónde me apeo para la Central de Correos

(para la Plaza de Colón)? (para la Puerta de Toledo)? (para la embajada de Gran Bretaña)? (para la estación de ferrocarril)? (para el mercado)? etc.

2 Ud. baja en la esquina de la calle de Alcalá con el Paseo del Prado (etc.).

3 ¿A cuántas manzanas de aquí?

4 Más o menos diez (cinco, etc.) manzanas, señor.

5 ¿En cuántos minutos llegaremos?

6 En unos minutos.

7 Muchas gracias, señor.

In the Bus

1 Excuse me, sir, where do I get off for the General Post Office? (for Columbus Square)? (for the Toledo Gate)? (for the embassy of Great Britain)? (for the railway station)? (for the market)? etc.

2 You get off at the corner of Alcalá Street and the Prado Avenue (etc.).

3 How many blocks from here?

4 More or less ten (five, etc.) blocks, sir.

5 In how many minutes will we get there?

6 In a few minutes.

7 Thank you very much, sir.

Diálogo 2

Practise the Spanish aloud:

Sobre el correo

1 Sra. Adams, por supuesto tiene Ud. mucha correspondencia. ¿Hay un buzón en su edificio?

2 Naturalmente. Tenemos un buzón en donde echamos nuestras cartas. Pero enviamos a la Central de Correos los paquetes postales.

3 ¿Quién los lleva allá?

4 Nuestro chico de oficina. Él nos compra también los muchos sellos que necesitamos — sellos de correo aéreo, etc.

5 ¿Dónde está la oficina principal de correos?

6 No está lejos de aquí.

About the Mail

1 Mrs. Adams, of course you have much correspondence. Is there a letter-box in your building?

2 Of course. We have a letter-box where we post our letters. But we send parcel post packages to the main post office.

3 Who takes them there?

4 Our office boy. He also buys us the many stamps that we need—air mail stamps, etc.

5 Where is the main post office?
6 It is not far from here.

Exercise No. 106—El cumpleaños de la señora Adams

Es el veintidós de marzo, día del cumpleaños (birthday) de la señora Adams. Hoy cumple (she is) treinta y cinco años de edad. Para celebrar este día, la familia Adams va a cenar (dine) a un restaurante español de Londres.

Cuando entran en el restaurante ven una hermosa canasta (basket) llena de (full of) rosas rojas en el centro de la mesa reservada para los Adams. Naturalmente la señora Adams está muy sorprendida y da mil gracias y besos (kisses) a su querido esposo.

Después de una sabrosa comida, Anita, la hija menor, dice en voz baja (in a low voice) a sus hermanos, — ¡Ya! (Ready) Y cada uno de los cuatro hijos saca (take out) de debajo de la mesa una bonita caja. Son regalos para su madre.

Anita le da un pañuelo de seda; Rosita, una blusa de algodón; Guillermo, un par de guantes y Felipe, un echarpe de lana.

La semana próxima papá Adams calcula la cuenta de aquel día, que es como sigue:

Cena—Treinta y seis libras y setenta peniques	£36.70
Propina—Tres libras y ochenta peniques	3.80
Flores—Doce libras y veinticinco peniques	12.25
Regalos—Treinta y seis libras y quince peniques	36.15
Total—Ochenta y ocho libras y noventa peniques	£88.90

CHAPTER 27

LA SRA. ADAMS ESCRIBE UNA CARTA A SU AGENTE

PRIMERA PARTE

1 La Sra. Adams y el Sr. López están sentados en la sala de la primera. Es la penúltima cita antes de la salida de la Sra. Adams para España. La Sra. Adams tiene en la mano una copia de su carta a su agente, el Sr. Carrillo, y la respuesta de éste, que acaba de llegar.

2 Sr. López, voy a leerle mi carta al Sr. Carrillo.

3 Me gustará mucho oírla.

4 La Sra. Adams lee la siguiente carta:

Londres, 4 de mayo de 1978

Sr. Rufino Carrillo
Calle de la Princesa, 40
Madrid, España

Muy señor mío:

Tengo el gusto de informarle que voy a hacer un viaje a España. Saldré de Londres por avión el 31 de mayo y llegaré al aeropuerto de Madrid. Tengo la intención de permanecer en la capital dos meses. Será un viaje de recreo y también de negocios. Tomando la capital como punto de partida, haré viajes a lugares de interés en España. Espero también ir por avión a Tenerife, y tal vez a las otras Islas Canarias.

Siempre le he apreciado mucho a causa de sus excelentes servicios por nuestra casa y ahora espero aprovechar la oportunidad de conocerle a Ud. personalmente. Tenga la bondad de informarme sobre la fecha más conveniente para una cita. Sé que está Ud. muy ocupado y que viaja mucho. Por eso le escribo de antemano, esperando tener el gusto de verle a Ud.

Estará sorprendido Ud. de saber que desde hace cinco meses tomo lecciones de conversación española. Ud. sabe que yo sabía leer el español bastante bien, pero no sabía ni escribirlo ni hablarlo. Esta carta, espero, le mostrará a Ud. que he adelantado un poco en escribir. Espero poder conversar con Ud. en su hermoso idioma. Creo que no tendrá Ud. mucha dificultad en entenderme. Mi profesor es el Sr. Eugenio López, compatriota de Ud.

En espera de sus gratas noticias, quedo de Ud. atto. y s.s.,

Juana Adams

5 Estupendo, Sra. Adams. No hay ninguna falta en toda la carta.

6 Y ahora ¿me hará Ud. el favor de leerme la respuesta que ha recibido del Sr. Carrillo?

7 Con mucho gusto, señor López.

   Continúa en el Capítulo 28

1 Mrs. Adams and Mr. López are seated in the living-room of the former. It is the penultimate appointment before the departure of Mrs. Adams for Spain. Mrs. Adams has in her hand a copy of her letter to her agent, Mr. Carrillo, and the latter's answer, which has just arrived.

2 Mr. López, I am going to read you my letter to Mr. Carrillo.

3 I would like very much to hear it.

4 Mrs. Adams reads the following letter:

London, May 4, 1978

Mr. Rufino Carrillo
40 Princess St.
Madrid, Spain

Dear Sir,

I am pleased to tell you that I am going to make a trip to Spain. I shall leave London by plane on May 31 and will arrive at the airport of Madrid. I intend to remain in the capital two months. It will be a pleasure trip and also a business trip. Taking the capital as a point of departure, I shall take trips to places of interest in Spain. I hope also to go by plane to Tenerife and perhaps to the other Canary Isles.

I have always appreciated you very much because of your excellent services to our firm and now I hope to take advantage of the opportunity to meet you personally. With this in mind I beg you to let me know the most convenient date for an appointment. I know that you are very busy and that you travel a great deal. For that reason I am writing you beforehand hoping to have the pleasure of seeing you.

You will be surprised to learn that for five months I have been taking lessons in Spanish conversation. You know that I could read Spanish fairly well but I could neither write it nor speak it. This letter, I hope, will show you that I have made a little progress in writing. I hope to be able to talk with you in your beautiful language. I think you won't have much difficulty in understanding me. My teacher is Mr. Eugene López, a fellow-countryman of yours.

I look forward to hearing from you.

Yours faithfully,
Jane Adams

5 Wonderful, Mrs. Adams. There is not a single error in the whole letter.

6 And now, will you kindly read me the answer you have received from Mr. Carrillo?

7 With great pleasure, Mr. López.

Continued (*lit.* it continues) in Chapter 28

Pronunciation Aids

1 Practise:

aeropuerto (a-e-ro-ˈpwer-to)
apreciado (a-pre-ˈθja-ðo)
aprovechar (a-pro-ve-ˈʧar) or
  (a-pro-βe-ˈʧar)
personalmente (per-so-ˈnal-ˈmen-te)
conveniente (kon-ve-ˈnjen-te) or
  (kom-be-ˈnjen-te)
sorprendido (sor-pren-ˈdi-ðo)
entenderme (en-ten-ˈder-me)
compatriota (kom-pa-ˈtrjo-ta)
comercial (ko-mer-ˈθjal)

bondadosa (bon-da-ˈðo-sa)
siguiente (si-ˈɣjen-te)
servicios (ser-ˈvi-θjos) or
  (ser-ˈβi-θjos)
oportunidad (o-por-tu-ni-ˈðað)
antemano (an-te-ˈma-no)
adelantado (a-ðe-lan-ˈta-ðo)
correspondencia
  (ko-rres-pon-ˈden-θja)
encabezamiento
  (en-ka-βe-θa-ˈmen-to)
conclusiones (koŋ-klu-ˈsjo-nes)

Building Vocabulary

A. Sinónimos:

1 bello	hermoso	beautiful
2 comprender	entender (ie)	to understand
3 el idioma	la lengua	language
4 mostrar (ue)	enseñar	to show
5 por eso	por lo tanto	therefore

6 Tenga la bondad de ... ⎫
  Hágame el favor de ... ⎭ please
(*Lit.* Have the kindness to; do me the favour of)

B. Palabras Relacionadas

1 la mano	the hand	5 a la izquierda	to the left
2 la mano derecha	the right hand	6 de antemano	beforehand
3 la mano izquierda	the left hand	7 hecho a mano	handmade
4 a la derecha	to the right		

Expresiones Importantes

A. Salutation: Business Letters

1 Muy señor mío	Dear Sir	3 Muy señora mía	Dear Madam
2 Muy señores míos	Gentlemen		

B. Conclusion: Business Letters

En espera de sus gratas noticias, quedo de Ud.   Awaiting your reply,
                                                                    I remain

atentamente le saluda	yours faithfully, yours very truly
atto. (atento)	attentive[1]
afmo. (afectísimo)	most affectionate[2]
s.s. (su servidor)	your servant[3]

NOTES: 1-3 are literal translations, all meaning 'Yours faithfully'.

Exercise No. 107—Completion of Text

1 **Voy** (to read to you) **mi carta.**
2 (I will be very glad) **oírla.**
3 **Tengo el gusto** (to inform you) **que saldré el 31 de mayo.**
4 **Siempre** (I have appreciated you).
5 (Kindly) **informarme sobre la fecha** (most convenient).
6 **Sé que Ud. está** (very busy).
7 (Therefore) **le escribo** (in advance).
8 **Espero tener el gusto** (of seeing you).
9 **Esta carta** (will show you) **que he adelantado.**
10 **Ud. no tendrá dificultad** (in understanding me).
11 (There is not any) **falta en la carta.**
12 **Tengo que** (give my sincere thanks to you).
13 You are very kind.
14 ¿(Will you kindly) **leerme la respuesta?**

SEGUNDA PARTE

Grammar Notes

1 The Indirect Object

As in English the indirect object is the *to* (sometimes *for*) object. It indicates the person or persons *to* whom, sometimes *for* whom, the action is performed.

Escribo una carta a mi agente.	I write a letter to my agent.

2 The Indirect Object Pronouns

Observe the indirect object pronouns in the following sentences.

Carlos *me* da el vaso.	Charles gives *me* the glass.
Juan *te* escribe una carta.	John writes *you* (*fam.*) a letter.
Pablo *le* da (a Ud.) el dinero.	Paul gives *you* the money.
Ana *le* lleva (a él) la silla.	Anna brings *him* the chair.
Yo *le* leo (a ella) el cuento.	I read *her* the story.
El profesor *nos* da la lección.	The teacher gives *us* the lesson.
La criada *les* da (*a Uds.*) los platos.	The servant gives *you* the plates.

| **Nosotros *les* vendemos (*a ellos*) el coche.** | We sell *them* (*m.*) the car. |
| **Los niños *les* traen (*a ellas*) las flores.** | The children bring *them* (*f.*) the flowers. |

(a) The Indirect Object Pronouns are:

me (to) me	**le ... a Ud.** (to) you	**les ... a Uds.** (to) you
te (to) you (*fam.*)	**le ... a él** (to) him	**les ... a ellos** (to) them (*m.*)
nos (to) us	**le ... a ella** (to) her	**les ... a ellas** (to) them (*f.*)
os (to) you (*fam. pl.*)		

(b) The indirect object pronouns, **me, te, nos, os** are like the direct object pronouns.

(c) The indirect object pronoun **le** can mean *to you, to him* or *to her*. The indirect object pronoun **les** can mean *to you* (*pl.*), *to them* (*m.*), *to them* (*f.*).

If necessary to make the meaning clear, add: **a Ud., a él, a ella, a Uds., a ellos, a ellas,** immediately after the verb.

(d) Like the direct object, the indirect object precedes the verb, except when used with the infinitive, the present participle, or the affirmative imperative.

3 Familiar Verbs which may take Indirect Objects

dar	to give	**traer**	to bring
enseñar	to show, teach	**entregar**	to deliver
mostrar (ue)	to show	**leer**	to read
enviar	to send	**escribir**	to write
mandar	to send	**decir (i)**	to say
llevar	to carry		

4 Indirect Objects with **gustar, parecer, importar.**

(a) **gustar,** to be pleasing to

Me gusta el cuento. I like the story. (*Lit.* To me is pleasing the story.)
¿Les gustan a Uds. los cuentos? Do you like the stories?

(b) **parecer** to seem

Me parece bien. It seems (is) all right to me.
Le parece bien a ella. It seems (is) all right to her.

(c) **importar** to be important to (another meaning of **importar**)

No nos importa. It is not important to us. It does not concern us.
No les importa a ellos. It is not important to them. It does not concern them.

Ejercicios (Exercises) No. 108A–108B

108A. Translate:

1 ¿Le dará Ud. a él las naranjas?
2 Tráigame Ud. los zapatos.
3 Tenga la bondad de leernos la carta.
4 Le escribiré una carta a ella cuanto antes.
5 ¿Me enseñará Ud. las palabras nuevas?
6 No podemos mandarles a Uds. el dinero.

7 ¿Quién nos leerá el cuento?
8 Dígame — ¿qué hace María en la cocina?
9 No me gustará la corrida de toros.
10 ¿Le parece bien esa fecha?
11 No me parece bien.
12 No me importan estas cosas.

108B. Complete the Spanish sentences, filling in the correct indirect object pronouns, so that the Spanish sentences correspond exactly to the English.

Remember: **le** = to you (*sing.*), to him, to her; **les** = to you (*plur.*), to them (*m.* and *f.*).

Ejemplo: I am writing *you* a letter. **Le escribo una carta.**

1 Will you give *him* the money?
2 They bring *us* the clothing.
3 Will you teach *her* the lesson?
4 I like your hats.

5 They like your garden.
6 Tell *me* the truth.
7 It's of no concern *to them.*
8 The booking clerk will give *you* the tickets.
9 I like sweets.
10 Their parents are buying *them* the toys.
11 I shall speak *to you (fam.)* on the telephone, Henry.
12 I am bringing *you* the umbrella, sir.
13 Bring us the coffee, please.

14 It seems good to me.
15 They seem good to us.

1 ¿—— dará Ud. el dinero?
2 —— traen la ropa.
3 ¿—— enseñará Ud. la lección?
4 —— gustan los sombreros de Uds.
5 —— gusta a ellos su jardín.
6 Díga —— la verdad.
7 No —— importa a ellos.
8 El taquillero —— dará a Uds. las entradas.
9 —— gustan los dulces.
10 Sus padres están comprándo —— los juguetes.
11 —— hablaré por teléfono, Enrique.
12 Estoy trayendo —— a Ud. el paraguas, señor.
13 Tráiga —— Ud. el café, por favor.
14 —— parece bien.
15 —— parecen bien.

Exercise No. 109—Preguntas

1 ¿Dónde están sentados la Sra. Adams y el Sr. López?
2 ¿Qué tiene en la mano la señora Adams?
3 ¿Qué va a leerle al Sr. López?
4 ¿A quién le gustará mucho oírla?
5 ¿Cuál es la fecha de la carta?
6 ¿A quién escribe la carta la Sra. Adams?
7 ¿Qué saludo usa la Sra. Adams?
8 ¿Quién irá de viaje a España?
9 ¿Cuándo saldrá la Sra. Adams de Londres?
10 ¿Cuándo llegará al aeropuerto de Madrid?
11 ¿Cuánto tiempo permanecerá en la capital?
12 ¿A dónde hará viajes?
13 ¿A dónde irá tal vez en avión?
14 ¿De quién ha apreciado los servicios la Sra. Adams?
15 ¿A quién quiere conocer personalmente?

CHAPTER 28

LA SEÑORA ADAMS RECIBE UNA CARTA

PRIMERA PARTE

La Sra. Adams tiene en la mano la respuesta que acaba de recibir de su agente, el Sr. Carrillo. Está leyéndola.

1 Muy señora mía:

2 Estoy muy agradecido por su carta del 4 de mayo en la que Ud. tiene la bondad de informarme de su visita a España.

3 Tengo el gusto de informarle que estaré en la capital durante los meses de junio y julio y quiero aprovechar la oportunidad de ponerme enteramente a sus órdenes.

4 Tendré gran placer en saludarle en el aeropuerto el 31 de mayo. Espero poder facilitar su estancia en esta capital tanto en las diversiones como en los negocios.

5 Con mucho gusto hablaré con Ud. en español y estoy seguro de que Ud. lo habla perfectamente. Por cierto, lo escribe Ud. sumamente bien. Quiero felicitarles a Ud. y a su profesor, el Sr. López.

6 Esperando la pronta oportunidad de conocerla a Ud., le saluda muy atentamente, s.s.

Rufino Carrillo

7 Es una carta muy amable, dice el señor López. Hasta ahora Ud. ha conocido y ha apreciado al señor Carrillo solamente como un buen representante. Sin duda alguna, Ud. verá que es también muy simpático, como tantos. Pero Ud. verá por sí misma.

8 Estoy segura de que estaré muy contenta entre la gente de España. Y lo mejor es que podré hablar con ellos en su propio idioma.

9 Claro está. Bueno, Sra. Adams, el martes que viene es nuestra última cita antes de su salida para España. Nos veremos en su oficina, ¿verdad?

10 Sí. ¿Y me dará Ud. unos últimos consejos?

11 Con mucho gusto, Sra. Adams.

Mrs. Adams has in her hand the reply which she has just received from her agent, Mr. Carrillo. She is reading it.

1 Dear Madam,

2 I am much obliged to you for your letter of May 4 in which you have the kindness to tell me of your visit to Spain.

3 I am very pleased to tell you that I shall be in the capital during the months of June and July and I want to take advantage of the opportunity of putting myself entirely at your service.

4 I shall be delighted to greet you at the airport on May 31. I hope to be able to facilitate your stay in this capital in matters of recreation as well as in matters of business.

5 With much pleasure, I will talk with you in Spanish and I am sure that you speak it perfectly. Indeed you write it extremely well. I want to congratulate you and your teacher, Mr. López.

6 Looking forward to meeting you soon, I remain.

Yours faithfully,
Rufino Carrillo

7 It is a very kind letter, says Mr. López. Until now you have known and appreciated Mr. Carrillo only as a good representative. Without any doubt, you will find that he is also very nice like so many Spaniards. But you will see for yourself.

8 I am sure that I shall be very happy among the people of Spain. And the best is that I shall be able to speak to them in their own language.

9 Very true. Well, Mrs. Adams, next Tuesday is our last appointment before your departure for Spain. We shall meet in your office, shan't we?

10 Yes, and will you give me some final advice?

11 With great pleasure, Mrs. Adams.

Pronunciation Aids

1 Practise:

agradecido (a-ɣra-ðe-ˈθi-ðo)
aprovechar (a-pro-ve-ˈtʃar)
enteramente (en-te-ra-ˈmen-te)
estancia (es-ˈtan-θja)
diversiones (ði-ver-ˈsjo-nes) or
  (ði-βer-ˈsjo-nes)
perfectamente (per-ˈfek-ta-ˈmen-te)

sumamente (su-ma-ˈmen-te)
felicitarles (fe-li-θi-ˈtar-les)
apreciado (a-pre-ˈθja-ðo)
represento (rre-pre-ˈsen-to)
perdóneme (per-ˈðo-ne-me)
orgulloso (or-ɣu-ˈʎo-so)

Building Vocabulary

Sinónimos:

1 **informar — avisar,** to inform
2 **enteramente — completamente,** entirely
3 **tendré gran placer en — me gustará mucho,** I shall be pleased to
4 **dispénseme — perdóneme,** pardon me

Expresiones Importantes

A. 1 **aprovechar la oportunidad de,** to take advantage of the opportunity to
2 **esperando la pronta oportunidad de conocerle,** looking forward to meeting you soon
3 **a sus órdenes,** at your service
4 **estoy muy agradecido,** I am much obliged
5 **lo mejor es,** the best is; **lo peor es,** the worst is
6 **quiero felicitarle a Ud.,** I want to congratulate you
7 **sin duda alguna,** without any doubt
8 **Ud. tiene a bien informarme,** you have the kindness to inform me

B. Salutations: Letters to Friends

Querido Pablo; Querida Elena	Dear Paul; dear Ellen, etc.[1]
Querido amigo; Querida amiga	
Estimado amigo; Estimada amiga	

C. Conclusions: Letters to Friends

Su sincero amigo Su sincera amiga	Your sincere friend
Sinceramente Afectuosamente	Sincerely Affectionately
Le saluda cordialmente su amigo (a)	Cordial greetings from your friend[2]
Reciba un abrazo de su amigo (a)	Receive an embrace from your friend[3]

NOTE: 1. **Querido (a)** is not used freely like the English Dear —, which is the form of address even for business letters.

NOTES: 2 and 3. These are literal translations. The English equivalent is 'Kindest regards' or 'Best wishes'.

Exercise No. 110—Completion of Text

A. Complete these sentences by putting all English words into Spanish.

1 **La Sra. Adams tiene** (a letter in her hand).
2 (I am much obliged) **por su carta del 4 de mayo.**
3 **Ud. tiene la bondad** (to inform me) **de su visita a España.**
4 (I shall take great pleasure) **en esperarle en el aeropuerto.**
5 (I shall speak) **con Ud. en español.**
6 (I am sure that) **Ud. lo habla perfectamente.**
7 **Quiero** (to congratulate you) **a Ud. y a su profesor.**
8 (Without any doubt) **Ud. verá que el Sr. Carrillo es** (very congenial).
9 (Pardon me). **Estoy muy** (proud) **de mi pueblo.**
10 **Ud. verá** (for yourself) **que los españoles son** (very friendly).
11 (I am sure) **de que** (I will be able) **hablar con ellos en su propio idioma.**
12 (The best is) **que puedo hablar español.**

13 (The worst is) **que Ud. no puede ir conmigo.**
14 (Each other) **veremos en su oficina.**
15 **Le daré a Ud.** (some final advice).

SEGUNDA PARTE

Grammar Notes

1 Use of **hacer** in Time Expressions.

(a) ¿Cuánto tiempo hace que estudia Ud. el español?
(How much time does it make that you are studying Spanish?)

1 How long have you been studying Spanish?

(b) Hace cinco meses que estudio el español.
(It makes five months that I am studying Spanish.)

2 I have been studying Spanish five months.

(c) Estudio el español hace cinco meses.
(I am studying Spanish it makes five months.)

3 I have been studying Spanish for (since) five months.

To express an action which began in the past and is still going on, the Spanish uses **hace** (it) makes, plus an expression of time, plus **que**, plus the present tense of the verb (ex. b).

If the **hace** expression comes after the verb, **que** is omitted (ex. c).

2 Use of the Definite Article in place of the Possessive Adjective.

1 **El señor tiene una carta en la mano.**

The gentleman has a letter in his hand.

2 **Ana se pone el sombrero en la cabeza.**

Anna puts her hat on her head.

The definite article is used instead of the possessive adjective with parts of the body and clothing when there is no doubt who is meant.

3 Reflexive Pronouns with a Reciprocal Meaning.

Nos veremos.	We shall see each other.
No se conocen (el uno al otro).	They do not know each other.
Juana y Ana se admiran (la una a la otra).	Jane and Anna admire each other.

(a) When the reflexive pronoun is used with a reciprocal meaning, **el uno al otro (la una a la otra)**, *one another*, may be added for clarity.

Ejercicios (Exercises) No. 111A–111B–111C

111A. Complete these sentences by putting the English words into Spanish.

Ejemplo: 1. ¿Cuánto tiempo hace que estudia Ud. el español?

1 ¿(How long) **hace que estudia Ud. el español?**
2 (For six months) **que estudio el español.**
3 (For ten years) **que el Sr. López es profesor.**
4 (For 45 minutes) **que esperamos.**
5 (For three days) **que mi madre está enferma.**
6 **Hace seis meses que** (I have known him).
7 **Hace cinco semanas que** (they have lived in this house).
8 **Hace tres horas que** (the children have been in the cinema).
9 **Hace diez años que** (he has been in this country).
10 **Hace cinco días que** (I have been here).

111B. Change the following affirmative commands into negative commands.

Remember: 1. In affirmative commands object pronouns follow the verb. 2. In negative commands they precede it.

Ejemplo: Déme el libro. No me dé el libro.

1 **Pónganlos Uds. en la mesa.**
2 **Escríbales Ud. las cartas.**
3 **Tráiganlos a la casa.**
4 **Dígame las respuestas.**
5 **Mándele los artículos.**
6 **Tráigame la carne y el pescado.**
7 **Déme un billete de ida y vuelta.**
8 **Cómpreme una bolsa de cuero.**
9 **Léanles todos los cuentos.**
10 **Véndale el coche.**

NOTE: The singular imperative of **dar, dé Ud.**, takes an accent mark to distinguish it from **de** (of).

111C. Answer the following questions in the future with both **sí** and **no**. Use an object pronoun in each answer.

Remember: If the question has **Ud.** as subject, the answer has **(yo)** as subject: if the question has **Uds.**, the answer has **(nosotros)**.

Ejemplos: ¿Comerá Ud. la carne? Sí, la comeré. No, no la comeré.
　　　　　¿Comerán Uds. la carne? Sí, la comeremos. No, no la comeremos.

1 **¿Visitará Ud. el museo?**
2 **¿Escribirá Ud. la carta?**
3 **¿Comprará Ud. el coche?**
4 **¿Traerá Ud. los cestos?**
5 **¿Tomará Ud. el té?**
6 **¿Pedirán Uds. los billetes?**
7 **¿Venderán Uds. la casa?**
8 **¿Querrán Uds. las frutas?**
9 **¿Seguirán Uds. a sus amigos?**
10 **¿Repetirán Uds. las preguntas?**

Exercise No. 112—Preguntas

1 ¿Qué acaba de recibir la Sra. Adams?
2 ¿Cuándo estará en la capital el Sr. Carrillo?
3 ¿Dónde esperará a la Sra. Adams?
4 ¿En qué lengua conversará con ella?
5 ¿De qué está seguro él?
6 ¿A quiénes quiere felicitar el Sr. Carrillo?
7 ¿Qué verá la Sra. Adams por sí misma?
8 ¿Cuándo será la última cita de la Sra. Adams y el Sr. López?
9 ¿Dónde se verán?

CHAPTER 29

LOS CONSEJOS DEL SEÑOR LÓPEZ

PRIMERA PARTE

1 Hace calor en la oficina de la señora Adams. No hace viento. Por la ventana abierta se oyen los ruidos de la calle.

2 — Me alegro de salir de la ciudad, — dice la señora Adams al señor López.

3 — Tengo ganas de ir a España también, — contesta el señor López.

4 ¿No puede Ud. ir allá este año?

5 Desgraciadamente, no es posible.

6 Por lo menos, ¿me hace Ud. el favor de darme unos últimos consejos? ¿Es muy distinta la vida en España de la vida en Gran Bretaña?

7 Sí, señora Adams, hay muchas costumbres diferentes. En general, la vida en España es más formal. Son muy importantes las formalidades. Y eso de la cortesía tenía antes una significación profunda. Quería decir que cada hombre era digno de respeto. Las cosas han cambiado.

8 — Es verdad, — responde la señora Adams.

9 He notado que entre los negociantes también hay más formalidades en España que en Gran Bretaña. Les gusta charlar un rato acerca de otras cosas antes de emprender un negocio. Quieren llegar a conocerse bien.

10 Estaré muy contenta allí.

11 Se dice que en general la vida es más tranquila allí. Espero que sí. Estoy cansada de ir siempre con prisas.

12 A propósito, Sra. Adams, ¿ha leído Ud. los libros sobre España que le he recomendado? Hoy en día hay mucho bullicio y ruido.

13 Sí, los he leído todos. Me han sido muy útiles e interesantes.

14 Bueno. He dicho muchas veces que Ud. se entenderá muy bien en España. En cuanto a mí, pasaré el verano en Londres. He gozado de nuestras conversaciones y voy a echarla de menos.

15 Pensaré en Ud. a menudo y le escribiré de vez en cuando.

16 Me gustará mucho recibir sus cartas desde España. Pues bien, tenemos que despedirnos. Hágame el favor de saludar de mi parte al señor Adams y a sus hijos.

17 Gracias y mucha suerte, Sr. López.

18 Buen viaje, Sra. Adams.

Se dan la mano.

1 It is hot in Mrs. Adams's office. There is no wind. Through the open window the noises of the street can be heard.

2 'I shall be glad to get away from the city,' says Mrs. Adams to Mr. López.

3 'I wish I were going to Spain, too,' says Mr. López.

4 Can't you go there this year?

5 Unfortunately, it is not possible.

6 At least, will you please give me some final advice? Is life in Spain very different from life in Great Britain?

7 Yes, Mrs. Adams, there are many different customs. In general, life in Spain is more formal. The formalities are very important. And the matter of courtesy used to have a profound significance—it meant that every man was worthy of respect. Things have changed.

8 'That is true,' answers Mrs. Adams.

9 I have noticed that among businessmen too there is more formality in Spain than in Great Britain. They like to chat a little about other things before taking up business. They want to get to know one another.

10 I shall be very happy there.

11 They say that in general life is more tranquil there. I hope so. I am tired of being in a hurry.

12 By the way, Mrs. Adams, have you read the books on Spain which I have recommended to you? Today there is a lot of noise.

13 Yes, I have read them all. They have been very useful and interesting to me.

14 Good. I have said many times that you will get along in Spain. As for me, I shall spend the summer in London. I have enjoyed our conversations and I am going to miss you.

15 I shall think of you often and I shall write you from time to time.

16 I shall be glad to receive your letters from Spain. Well then, we have to take leave of each other. Kindly give my regards to Mr. Adams and to your children.

17 Thank you and good luck, Mr. López.

18 Happy voyage, Mrs. Adams.

They shake hands.

Pronunciation Aids

1 Practise:

viento ('vjen-to) or ('bjen-to)
ruidos ('rrwi-ðos)
acompañarla (a-kom-pa-'njar-la)
desgraciadamente
    (ðes-ɣra-'θja-ða-'men-te)
cortesías (kor-te-'si-as)

acostumbrarse (a-kos-tum-'brar-se)
apresurarse (a-pre-su-'rar-se)
despedirnos (ðes-pe-'ðir-nos)
leído (le-'i-ðo)
caído (ka-'i-ðo)
creído (kre-'i-ðo)

significado (siγ-ni-fi-'ka-ðo) **oído** (o-'i-ðo)
formalidad (for-ma-li-'ðað)

2 The combinations (diphthongs) **ai, oi, ei** become separate vowels, **a-í, o-í,** and **e-í,** when the **í** has an accent mark.

Building Vocabulary

A. Sinónimos:

1 **alegrarse (de)**	**estar contento (de)**	to be happy (to)
2 **a menudo**	**muchas veces**	often
3 **ir con prisas**	**tener prisa**	to be in a hurry
4 **hay que**	**es necesario**	it is necessary, one must

Expresiones Importantes

1 **en cuanto a mi**	as for me
2 **espero que sí**	I hope so
3 **espero que no**	I hope not
4 **He gozado de nuestras conversaciones**	I have enjoyed our conversations.
5 **Voy a echarle de menos**	I am going to miss you.

Exercise No. 113—Completion of Text

1 (I shall be glad) **salir de la ciudad.**
2 (I wish I were) **de ir a España también.**
3 (At least) **haga el favor de** (to give me) **algunos consejos.**
4 (The matter of courtesy) **tenía una significación profunda.**
5 (It meant) **que cada hombre** (was worthy) **de respeto.**
6 (They like) **charlar un rato** (about) **otras cosas.**
7 **Quieren llegar a** (to know each other).
8 (As I have told you), **es mejor no apresurarse.**
9 (People say) **que en general la vida es más tranquila.** (I hope so.)
10 **Estoy cansada** (of being in a hurry).
11 ¿(Have you read) **los libros sobre España?**
12 (As for me) **me quedaré aquí en Londres.**
13 (I have enjoyed) **de nuestras conversaciones.**
14 **Tenemos que** (take leave of each other).
15 They shake hands.

SEGUNDA PARTE

Grammar Notes

1 The Present Perfect Tense—Model Verbs: **hablar, aprender, vivir.** This is one of the tenses used to indicate past time.

Singular

he hablado (aprendido, vivido)
   I have spoken (learned, lived)
has hablado (aprendido, vivido)
   you have spoken (learned, lived)
Ud. **ha hablado (aprendido, vivido)**
   you have spoken (learned, lived)
ha hablado (aprendido, vivido)
   he, she, it has spoken (learned, lived)

Plural

hemos hablado (aprendido, vivido)
   we have spoken (learned, lived)
habéis hablado (aprendido, vivido)
   you have spoken (learned, lived)
Uds. **han hablado (aprendido, vivido)**
   you have spoken (learned, lived)
han hablado (aprendido, vivido)
   they have spoken (learned, lived)

(a) As in English, the present perfect tense in Spanish is formed by the present tense of the auxiliary (helping) verb, **haber** (*to have*) plus the past participle of the verb.

(b) The endings of the auxiliary verb **haber** are: singular **-e, -as, -a;** plural **-emos, -éis, -an.** You have learned that these are also the endings in the future tense (see Chapter 26). In the future, however, all the endings except **-emos** have an accent mark.

(c) To form the regular past participle of an **-ar** verb, drop the **-ar** and add **-ado.** To form the past participle of an **-er** or **-ir** verb drop the **-er** or **-ir** and add **-ido.**

(d) The subject may never, as in English, come between the auxiliary verb and the past participle. Object pronouns precede the auxiliary verb.

¿**Ha escrito Carlos la carta?**   Has Charles written the letter?
Sí, la ha escrito.   Yes, he has written it.

2 The Past Participles of some familiar Verbs

he comprado	I have bought	**he querido**	I have wished
he enseñado	I have taught	**he vendido**	I have sold
he tomado	I have taken	**he comido**	I have eaten

he trabajado	I have worked	he bebido	I have drunk
he andado	I have walked	he tenido	I have had
he deseado	I have wanted	he ido	I have gone
he pasado	I have passed	he sido	I have been
he estado	I have been	he venido	I have come

3 Past Participles with an Accent Mark

When the stem of the verb ends in a vowel, the **i** of **-ido** has an accent mark.

he leído	(le-í-do)	I have read
he caído	(ca-í-do)	I have fallen
he oído	(o-í-do)	I have heard
he traído	(tra-í-do)	I have brought
he creído	(cre-í-do)	I have believed

4 Irregular Past Participles

Most past participles are regular. The most common irregulars are:

abrir	he *abierto*	I have opened
cubrir	he *cubierto*	I have covered
decir	he *dicho*	I have said
escribir	he *escrito*	I have written
hacer	he *hecho*	I have done
poner	he *puesto*	I have put
ver	he *visto*	I have seen
volver	he *vuelto*	I have returned
morir	ha *muerto*	he has died
romper	he *roto*	I have broken

NOTE: the proverb **(refrán): Dicho y hecho.** No sooner said than done. *Lit.* Said and done.

5 **haber** and **tener**

haber, to have, as you have seen, is used as an auxiliary verb to form the present perfect tense.

tener, to have, means to *possess*. It is never used as an auxiliary verb.

He vendido la casa.	I have sold the house.
He tenido una casa.	I have had (possessed) a house.
Tengo una casa.	I have (possess) a house.

Ejercicios (Exercises) No. 114A–114B–114C

114A. Translate:

1 Hemos tenido un buen viaje.
2 Los lápices han caído al suelo.
3 No han dicho nada.
4 ¿Qué ha hecho Pablo con el dinero?
5 Nadie ha abierto las puertas.

6 No hemos leído esos periódicos.   9 Nunca he creído ese cuento.
7 ¿Han estado Uds. en el cine?   10 ¿Qué han dicho ellos?
8 ¿Ha estado enferma la niña?

114B. Translate:

1 I have noted
2 He has said
3 They have not read
4 (ser) They have been
5 (estar) We have been
6 I have not worked
7 Have you taught (Ud.)?
8 Who has not written?
9 What have you done (Vds.)?
10 You (tú) have opened.
11 What has John said?
12 She has taken
13 I have not believed
14 We have heard
15 Have you (Uds.) heard?

114C. Change the following sentences 1. to the future, 2. to the present perfect. Do not change the subject.

      Ejemplo: Compro un sombrero. Compraré un sombrero. He
                comprado un sombrero.

1 El Sr. García vende su casa.
2 Trabajo en la ciudad.
3 Escribimos una carta.
4 Leen las revistas.
5 ¿Toma Ud. la cena a las ocho?
6 Tú no aprendes la lección.
7 ¿Busca el niño a su madre?
8 ¿Compran Uds. zapatos nuevos?
9 Salgo de la ciudad.
10 Entran en la casa.

Exercise No. 115—Preguntas

1 ¿Dónde se encuentran los señores Adams y López?
2 ¿Qué tiempo hace?
3 ¿Qué se oye por la ventana?
4 ¿Quién se alegra de irse de la ciudad?
5 ¿Quién tiene ganas de ir a España también?
6 ¿Qué responde el Sr. López a la pregunta — No puede ir Ud. allá este año?
7 ¿Es la vida en España más formal que la vida en Gran Bretaña?
8 ¿Qué quiere decir la importancia de la cortesía en España?
9 ¿Qué ha notado el Sr. López entre los negociantes?
10 ¿Quién está cansada de ir con prisas?
11 ¿Quién ha leído libros sobre España?
12 ¿Quién ha recomendado estos libros?
13 En cuanto al Sr. López, ¿dónde pasará el verano?
14 ¿En quién pensará a menudo la Sra. Adams?
15 ¿Le escribirá cartas al Sr. López de vez en cuando?

CHAPTER 30

LA SEÑORA ADAMS SALE PARA ESPAÑA

PRIMERA PARTE

1 Hace cinco meses que la señora Adams estudia el español. Ha pasado muchas horas en conversación con su profesor, el señor López. También ha aprendido la gramática necesaria y ha leído mucho sobre España. Verdaderamente ha trabajado mucho. Ahora habla español bastante bien y espera hacerse entender muy bien en España.

2 La señora Adams ha obtenido los billetes para el vuelo y su pasaporte. Por supuesto la señora Adams ha escrito una carta a su agente en España haciéndole saber la hora de llegada del avión a la capital. Este ha prometido recibirla en el aeropuerto.

3 Al fin llega el 31 de mayo, día de la salida. El avión de la señora Adams sale del Aeropuerto de Londres a las diez y media de la mañana. Ella tiene que estar en el aeropuerto una media hora antes para mostrar su billete y hacer pesar su equipaje. La familia no va a acompañarla a España porque los hijos tienen que terminar el año escolar y su esposo tiene que quedarse en casa porque tiene negocios importantes en Londres. Además, viajar con cuatro niños desde cinco hasta diez años de edad no es solamente difícil sino también bastante caro.

4 Por supuesto toda la familia está muy animada. Los niños no han dormido mucho y a las cinco de la mañana todos están despiertos.

5 A las ocho de la mañana la familia entera está lista para salir para el aeropuerto. La señora Adams ha hecho dos maletas y las pone en el coche. Entonces suben todos al coche que se pone en marcha y llega al aeropuerto a eso de las diez menos cuarto. La señora Adams hace revisar su billete y hace pesar su equipaje. Tiene que pagar tres libras de exceso porque el peso total excede las 44 libras permitidas gratis.

6 Luego la señora Adams se despide de su esposo y de sus hijos que le dan 'el buen viaje'. Sube al avión saludando a su esposo y a sus hijos que están mirándola con mucha emoción. A las diez y media en punto despega el avión.

7 La señora Adams está en camino.

1 Mrs. Adams has been studying Spanish for five months. She has spent many hours in conversation with her teacher, Mr. López. Also she has learned the necessary grammar and has read a great deal about

Spain. She really has worked very hard. Now she speaks Spanish quite well and she expects to get along very well in Spain.

2 Mrs. Adams has obtained the tickets for the flight, and her passport. Of course Mrs. Adams has written a letter to her agent in Spain letting him know the time of arrival of the plane at the capital. The latter has promised to meet her at the airport.

3 At last May 31st, the day of departure, arrives. Mrs. Adams's plane leaves London Airport at ten-thirty in the morning. She must be at the airport half an hour before to show her ticket and have her baggage weighed. Her family is not going with her to Spain because her children have to finish the school year and her husband has to remain at home because he has important business in London. Besides, travelling with four children from five to ten years of age is not only difficult but quite expensive.

4 Of course the whole family is very excited. The children have not slept very much and at five in the morning all are awake.

5 At eight in the morning the whole family is ready to leave for the airport. Mrs. Adams has packed two suitcases and puts them in the car Then all get into the car which starts off and arrives at the airport at about 9.45. Mrs. Adams has her ticket checked and has her baggage weighed. She has to pay £3 extra because the total weight exceeds the 44 pounds allowed free.

6 Then Mrs. Adams takes leave of her husband and children, who wish her 'a happy voyage'. She goes up into the plane waving to her husband and children who are watching her with great excitement. At 10.30 o'clock sharp the plane takes off.

7 Mrs. Adams is on her way.

Pronunciation Aids

1 Practise:

verdaderamente	**dormido** (ðor-'mi-ðo)
(ver-ða-ðe-ra-'men-te) or	**despierto** (ðes-'pjer-to)
(ber-ða-ðe-ra-'mente)	**revisar** (rre-vi-'sar)
pasado (pa-'sa-ðo)	**despedirse** (ðes-pe-'ðir-se)
aprendido (a-pren-'di-ðo)	**se despide** (se ðes-'pi-ðe)
hecho ('e-tʃo)	**equipaje** (e-ki-'pa-xe)
conseguido (kon-se-'ɣi-ðo)	**aeropuerto** (a-e-ro-'pwer-to)
prometido (pro-me-'ti-ðo)	

Building Vocabulary

A. **Antónimos:**

1	**empezar (ie)**	to begin
	acabar, terminar	to finish

2	**abrir**	to open
	cerrar (ie)	to close
3	**abierto**	open
	cerrado	closed
4	**acostarse (ue)**	to go to bed
	levantarse	to get up
5	**dormir (ue)**	to sleep
	estar despierto	to be awake
6	**dormirse**	to go to sleep
	despertarse	to wake up
7	**despedirse (de)**	to take leave (of)
	saludar (a)	to greet
8	**llegar (a)**	to arrive (at)
	salir (de)	to leave (from)
9	**la llegada**	the arrival
	la salida	the departure
10	**suben al coche**	they get into the car
	bajan del coche	they get out of the car

Expresiones Importantes

1	**cuidar a los niños**	to take care of the children
2	**haciéndole saber**	letting him know
3	**hacer una maleta**	to pack a suitcase
4	**no solamente ... sino también**	not only ... but also
5	**quedar en casa**	to remain at home

Exercise No. 116—Completion of Text

1 (For five months) **que la Sra. Adams estudia el español.**

2 **La Sra. Adams** (has obtained) **los billetes.**

3 (Of course) **la Sra. Adams ha escrito a su agente.**

4 (Finally) **llega el 31 de mayo.**

5 **La familia no va** (to accompany her).

6 **Viajar con cuatro niños** (is not only) **difícil** (but also) **bastante caro.**

7 **La familia** (is ready) **para salir.**

8 **La Sra. Adams** (has packed two suitcases).

9 **Todos** (get into the car).

10 (It starts off) **y llega al aeropuerto** (about) **las diez.**

11 **El peso total** (of her baggage) **excede las 44** (pounds).

12 **Por eso** (she has to) **pagar £3 (tres libras) de exceso.**

13 **La negociante** (takes leave of) **su esposo y de sus hijos.**

14 (At 11 o'clock sharp) **despega el avión.**

15 Mrs. Adams is on her way.

SEGUNDA PARTE

Grammar Notes

1 Present Tense of **dormir (ue)** to sleep, **despedirse (i)** to take leave.

I sleep, etc.		I take leave, etc.	
duermo	**dormimos**	**me despido**	**nos despedimos**
duermes	**dormís**	**te despides**	**os despedís**
duerme	**duermen**	**se despide**	**se despiden**

Imperative		Imperative	
duerma Ud.	**duerman Uds.**	**despídase Ud.**	**despídanse Uds.**

2 Present Perfect of **dormir (ue)** and **despedirse (i)**.

I have slept, etc.		I have taken leave, etc.	
he dormido	**hemos dormido**	**me he despedido**	**nos hemos despedido**
has dormido	**habéis dormido**	**te has despedido**	**os habéis despedido**
ha dormido	**han dormido**	**se ha despedido**	**se han despedido**

In the present perfect tense of a reflexive verb, the reflexive pronoun must precede the auxiliary verb.

No me he lavado. I have not washed myself.

¿Se ha lavado Ud.? Have you washed yourself?

3 Past Participles used as Adjectives.

Study the following expressions, noting in each a past participle used as an adjective.

1 **el libro abierto**   the open book
2 **El libro está abierto**   The book is open
3 **La ventana cerrada**   the closed window
4 **La ventana está cerrada.**   The window is closed.

(a) Past participles may be used as adjectives. Like other adjectives they agree in number and gender with the nouns they modify.

(b) Past participles as predicate adjectives, are generally used with **estar**.

Ejercicios (Exercises) No. 117A–117B–117C

117A. Translate:

    1 **Estamos comenzando la lección.**
    2 **Hemos comenzado el ejercicio.**
    3 **No me acuerdo de él.**
    4 **Me he acordado de ella.**
    5 **¿Están sentándose?**
    6 **¿Se han sentado?**

7 ¿Están repitiendo Uds. las palabras?
8 ¿Han repetido Uds. las palabras?
9 La criada está poniendo la mesa.
10 La criada no ha puesto la mesa.
11 La mesa está puesta.
12 Ella está sirviendo el café.
13 Ella ha servido el té.
14 ¿Qué frutas prefiere Ud.?
15 ¿Qué frutas ha preferido Ud.?
16 Los niños están acostándose.
17 Ya se han acostado.
18 ¿Están pidiendo Uds. información?
19 ¿Han pedido Uds. información?
20 El trabajo no está acabado.

117B. Complete by putting the English words into Spanish.

1 La ventana está (open).
2 La puerta está (closed).
3 Los niños están (awake).
4 La mesa está (set).
5 La casa está (sold).

6 Los muchachos están (dressed).
7 Los señores están (seated).
8 Las cartas están (written).
9 El año escolar está (finished).
10 El traje está (made) a mano.

117C. Translate:

1 I sleep.
2 He is sleeping (prog. tense).
3 They sleep.
4 Do you (Ud.) sleep?
5 I take leave.
6 They take leave.
7 We do not take leave.
8 I have slept.

9 Have you (Ud.) slept?
10 We have not slept.
11 I have taken leave.
12 They have not taken leave.
13 Have you (Uds.) taken leave?
14 Sleep (Ud.).
15 Do not sleep (Uds.).

Exercise No. 118—Preguntas

1 ¿Cuánto tiempo hace que la Sra. Adams estudia el español?
2 ¿Con quién ha pasado muchas horas en conversación?
3 ¿Qué ha aprendido?
4 ¿Cómo ha trabajado?
5 ¿Cómo habla español ahora?
6 ¿Qué ha obtenido la Sra. Adams?
7 ¿A quién ha escrito la Sra. Adams?
8 ¿Qué le ha prometido su agente?
9 ¿A qué hora están despiertos todos los niños?
10 ¿A qué hora sale el avión del aeropuerto?

11 ¿Qué tiene que mostrar cada pasajero?
12 ¿Va a acompañar a la Sra. Adams su familia?
13 ¿Qué tienen que terminar sus niños?
14 ¿Para qué tiene que quedarse en casa el señor Adams?

REVISION 7

CHAPTERS 27–30 PRIMERA PARTE
Repaso de Palabras

NOUNS

1 el aeropuerto	9 la entrada	17 el punto
2 el aire	10 la luna	18 un rato
3 los alrededores	11 el modismo	19 el ruido
4 el cariño	12 las noticias	20 el servicio
5 la cortesía	13 el negocio	21 los servicios
6 la corrida de toros	14 la partida	22 el sitio
7 la cultura	15 el pasaporte	23 la visita
8 la dirección	16 el placer	24 la vista

1 airport	9 entrance, ticket	17 point
2 air	10 moon	18 a while, time
3 suburbs	11 idiom	19 noise
4 affection	12 news	20 service
5 courtesy	13 business	21 toilet
6 bullfight	14 departure	22 place
7 culture	15 passport	23 visit
8 address	16 pleasure	24 view

VERBS

1 acompañar	8 cuidar	15 felicitar
2 alegrarse	9 despedirse de	16 gozar de
3 aprovechar	10 extender(ie)	17 irse
4 apreciar	11 envidiar	18 mostrar(ue)
5 ayudar	12 informar	19 pesar
6 cansarse	13 faltar	20 prometer
7 confesar(ie)	14 facturar	21 usar

1 to accompany	8 to take care of	15 to congratulate
2 to be glad	9 to take leave of	16 to enjoy
3 to take advantage of	10 to extend	17 to go away
4 to appreciate	11 to envy	18 to show
5 to help	12 to inform	19 to weigh
6 to get tired	13 to be lacking	20 to promise
7 to confess	14 to check (baggage)	21 to use

ADJECTIVES

1 abierto	6 cierto	11 ocupado
2 amable	7 conveniente	12 orgulloso
3 bello	8 despierto	13 siguiente
4 bondadoso	9 digno	14 sorprendido
5 caro	10 entero	15 último

1 open	6 certain	11 busy
2 friendly	7 convenient	12 proud
3 beautiful	8 awake	13 following
4 kind	9 worthy	14 surprised
5 dear	10 entire	15 final

ADVERBS

1 atentamente	3 enteramente	5 perfectamente
2 desgraciadamente	4 entretanto	6 sumamente

1 attentively	3 entirely	5 perfectly
2 unfortunately	4 meanwhile	6 completely

IMPORTANT EXPRESSIONS

1 a menudo	12 hace algún tiempo
2 bastante bien	13 hay que
3 de antemano	14 hecho a mano
4 de seguro	15 por lo menos
5 dispénseme	16 qué lástima
6 echar de menos	17 ponerse en marcha
7 en cuanto a mí	18 sin duda alguna
8 espero que sí	19 tener la intención
9 espero que no	20 la mano izquierda
10 ir con prisas	21 la mano derecha
11 estar en camino	

1 often	12 some time ago
2 quite well	13 it is necessary
3 beforehand	14 hand-made
4 surely	15 at least
5 pardon me	16 what a pity
6 to miss	17 to set out
7 as for me	18 without any doubt
8 I hope so	19 to intend
9 I hope not	20 the left hand
10 to be in a hurry	21 the right hand
11 to be on the way	

SEGUNDA PARTE

Ejercicio 119   From Group II select the antonyms for each word in Group I.

Group I		Group II	
1 me acuesto	6 abro	(a) comienzo	(f) me levanto
2 me despido	7 aprendo	(b) cierro	(g) enseño
3 duermo	8 mando	(c) saludo	(h) recibo
4 acabo	9 subo a	(d) vendo	(i) bajo de
5 compro	10 llego a	(e) estoy despierto	(j) salgo de

Ejercicio 120   Complete the following sentences by selecting expressions from those listed (**a** to **j**).

Be sure to use the correct forms of the verbs.

1 (Pardon me), **señor, tengo que despedirme.**	(a) **tener la intención de**
2 (It is necessary) **obtener un pasaporte.**	(b) **a menudo**
3 **Estudiamos el español** (for some time).	(c) **dispénseme**
4 (They intend to) **salir para España mañana.**	(d) **estar de prisa**
5 (Often) **he pensado en Ud.**	(e) **por lo menos**
6 **No puedo hablar más porque** (I am in a hurry).	(f) **hay que**
7 **María** (will remain at home) **porque está enferma.**	(g) **quedarse en casa**
8 ¿(At least) **me dará Ud. algunos consejos?**	(h) **bastante bien**
9 (As for me) **pasaré todo el verano en la ciudad.**	(i) **hace algún tiempo**
10 **Me haré entender en España porque hablo español** (quite well).	(j) **en cuanto a mí.**

Ejercicio 121   Select the group of words in the right-hand column which best completes each sentence begun in the left-hand column.

1 **Ahora espero aprovechar la oportunidad**	(a) **lea Ud. algo de sus costumbres.**
2 **La Sra. Adams no es solamente una buena negociante**	(b) **pero tiene que quedarse en Londres.**
3 **Ha aprendido a hablar español**	(c) **porque tengo prisa.**
4 **La carta que he recibido**	(d) **de conocerle personalmente.**
5 **Si Ud. quiere viajar en España**	(e) **sino también una mujer de cultura.**
6 **Después de despedirse de su familia**	(f) **de mi agente es muy amistosa** (friendly).
7 **El Sr. López tiene ganas de ir a España**	(g) **porque quiere visitar a su agente.**
8 **Pensaré a menudo en Ud.**	(h) **entra la Sra. Adams en el avión.**
9 **Ya no puedo quedar aquí**	(i) **que estudio el español.**
10 **Hace cinco meses**	(j) **porque voy a echarle de menos.**

Ejercicio 122   Complete the Spanish sentences so that they correspond to the English sentences. Be careful to use the correct indirect object pronouns.

Ejemplo: Me gusta la carta.

1 I like the letter.	1 —— **gusta la carta.**
2 They like to travel.	2 —— **gusta viajar.**
3 We like the aeroplanes.	3 —— **gustan los aviones.**
4 Do you like the paintings, Madam?	4 ¿—— **gustan las pinturas, señora?**
5 He does not like tomatoes.	5 **No** —— **gustan los tomates.**
6 She does not like this style.	6 **No** —— **gusta esta moda.**

7 Do you like to dance, gentlemen?	7 ¿—— gusta bailar, caballeros?
8 Don't you like to play, Anita?	8 ¿No —— gusta jugar, Anita?
9 It seems all right to us.	9 —— parece bien.
10 It doesn't concern me.	10 No —— importa.

Ejercicio 123 In the following sentences fill in the past participle of the verbs in parentheses.

1 Los pájaros han (cantar) todo el día.
2 ¿Por qué no han (volver) Uds. a casa?
3 ¿Ha (llegar) el tren todavía?
4 ¿Han (put) Uds. los objetos de arte en la mesa?
5 El señor ha (hacer) un viaje de recreo.
6 Los empleados han (abrir) las cajas.
7 Hemos (recibir) una caja de mercancía.
8 Le he (decir) a Ud. la verdad.
9 ¿Han (leer) Uds. muchos libros sobre España?
10 ¿Se han (despedir) todos los viajeros?

Ejercicio 124 Complete the following sentences with a past participle.

Remember: In these sentences the past participle is used as an adjective and therefore must agree with the noun it modifies.

Ejemplo: **1. Las señoritas están sentadas en la sala.**

1 Las señoritas están (sentar) en la sala.	6 Estas cartas están (written) en español.
2 La tierra está (cubrir) de nieve (snow).	7 La mesa está (poner).
3 El viento viene por la puerta (abrir).	8 No hemos visto el ejercicio (escribir).
4 Todos los cuartos están (cerrar).	9 El trabajo está (acabar).
5 Los echarpes están (hacer) a mano.	10 Tiene un libro (abrir) en la mano.

Ejercicio 125. Translate the English sentences. Be careful to use the correct direct object pronouns.

Ejemplo: **1. ¿Ha comprado Ud. la cesta? La he comprado.**

1 ¿Ha comprado Ud. la cesta?	1 I have bought it.
2 ¿Ha abierto Ud. la ventana?	2 I have opened it.
3 ¿Ha oído Ud. el ruido?	3 I have heard it.
4 ¿Ha obtenido Ud. el pasaporte?	4 I have obtained it.
5 ¿Ha ayudado Ud. a sus amigos?	5 I have helped them.
6 ¿Han visto Uds. los echarpes?	6 We have seen them.
7 ¿Han vendido Uds. los billetes?	7 We have sold them.
8 ¿Han completado Uds. el ejercicio?	8 We have completed it.

9	¿Han escrito Uds. las cartas?	9	We have written them.
10	¿Han leído Uds. la revista?	10	We have read it.

Diálogo

En el aeropuerto de Barajas (Madrid)

Practise the Spanish aloud:

— Buenos días, Sr. Carrillo. ¿Espera Ud. a alguien en el próximo avión?

— Sí, estoy esperando a la Sra. Adams de Londres, jefe de la casa que represento en España.

— ¿La conoce Ud. personalmente?

— La conozco solamente por correspondencia. Pero tengo su fotografía y debo reconocerla. Es una mujer de treinta y cinco años de edad.

— ¿Cuándo llega el avión de Londres?

— Debe de llegar a la una menos veinte.

— ¿Llega con retraso?

— No, llega a tiempo. ¡Ah! Ya llega. Está acercándose. Está bajando. Ya está aterrizando.

Dispénseme, señor, voy a saludar a la Sra. Adams.

— Bienvenida a España, Sra. Adams. ¿Ha tenido Ud. un buen viaje?

— ¡Estupendo! Me alegro mucho de estar en España. A menudo he soñado con este momento.

— Bueno. Estoy seguro de que estará Ud. muy contenta aquí.

Good day, Mr. Carrillo. Are you waiting for someone on the next plane?

Yes, I am waiting for Mrs. Adams from London, head of the firm which I represent in Spain.

Do you know her personally?

I know her only by correspondence. But I have her photograph and I should recognize her. She is a woman of 35.

When does the plane arrive from London?

It should arrive at 12.40.

Is it late?

No, it is on time. Ah! It is arriving now. It is approaching. It is coming down. It is landing now.

Excuse me, sir, I am going to greet Mrs. Adams.

Welcome to Spain, Mrs. Adams. Have you had a good trip?

Superb! I am very happy to be in Spain. I have often dreamed of this moment.

Good. I am sure that you will be very happy here.

LECTURA

Exercise No. 126—Un programa extraordinario en el cine

Esta tarde el señor Adams y su esposa van al cine. Al señor Adams no le gusta la mayor parte de las películas de Hollywood, sobre todo aquéllas en que los vaqueros[1] americanos se disparan tiros (fire shots) los unos a los otros. Tampoco le interesan la películas de detectives.

Pero esta tarde se exhibe (is being shown) un programa extraordinario en un cine que está a cosa de un kilómetro de su casa. La película se llama 'Un viaje por España'. Es una película sobre el país que nuestra amiga la Sra. Adams va a visitar dentro de unos meses y que trata de (deals with) su historia, su geografía, sus ríos, montañas, ciudades, etc.; es decir, una película que debe interesar mucho a los turistas.

Los Adams entran en el cine a las ocho y media. Casi todos los asientos están ocupados y por eso tienen que sentarse en la tercera fila. Esto no le gusta a la señora Adams porque los movimientos en la pantalla le hacen daño a los ojos. Afortunadamente pueden cambiar de asientos después de quince minutos y se mudan (move) a la fila trece.

A los Adams les gusta mucho esta película y también aprenden mucho acerca de las costumbres de España.

Al salir (On leaving) del cine, la señora Adams dice a su esposo, ¿Sabes, Carlos? Creo que me haré entender muy bien en España. He entendido (I have understood) casi todas las palabras de los actores y las actrices de esta película.

NOTE: 1. **Vaqueros** is also the word for jeans.

CHAPTER 31

LA SEÑORA ADAMS LLEGA A ESPAÑA

PRIMERA PARTE

FOREWORD

Mrs. Adams is now in Spain and writes ten letters to Mr. López, about some of the places she visits and about some of her experiences and impressions.

There are many references in her letters to things she has discussed with her teacher so that much of the vocabulary of Chapters 3 to 30 is repeated in the letters.

It is therefore very desirable that you re-read all the texts and dialogues of the previous chapters *before* proceeding with Chapter 31. You will be able to do this easily and rapidly, with little or no reference to the English translation. Thus you will in a pleasant manner revise the vocabulary and important expressions.

Chapters 2 to 25 are in the present tense which is by far the most important and most used tense in the affairs of daily life. In Chapters 26 to 30 the future and present perfect tenses were introduced. In Chapter 31 Mrs. Adams begins to relate her experiences, that is to say, what *happened* to her. She will begin to use the preterite tense which is the chief tense for relating what *happened* in definite past time.

Thus in Chapter 31 you will accompany Mrs. Adams not only into Spain, but also into the realm of the preterite tense, which you will find useful.

You should continue your pronunciation practice by reading aloud as often as possible dialogues and parts of conversational texts from previous chapters.

El ejercicio hace al maestro.

Primera Carta de España

Madrid, 4 de junio de 1978

Estimado amigo:

1 Después que llegó el avión al aeropuerto de Barajas, Madrid y los aduaneros me revisaron el equipaje en la aduana, fui a la sala de espera.

2 De repente un apuesto señor se acercó a mí y dijo — Dispénseme, ¿Es Ud. la señora Adams?

3 — Soy yo,[1] — contesté. — Y Ud. es el señor Carrillo, ¿verdad?
Mucho gusto en conocerle.

4 — El gusto es mío, — respondió el señor Carrillo.

5 Ud. recordará, Sr. López, que el Sr. Carrillo es el agente de nuestra
casa en Madrid y que prometió recibirme en el aeropuerto.

6 Cuando salimos juntos a la calle el señor Carrillo llamó un taxi.
Dijo al conductor — Al Hotel Emperador, por favor.

7 Salimos del aeropuerto. Marchando a una velocidad espantosa por
una gran avenida, pensé — El Sr. López está muy equivocado en cuanto
a la tranquila vida española.

8 Por la ventanilla del taxi vi correr por todas partes, a la misma
velocidad espantosa, autobuses, coches y quién sabe qué más.

9 Traté de decir al conductor — ¡Por favor, más despacio! Pero
olvidé por entero el español.

10 — Yo no tengo prisa — grité al fin al conductor.

11 — Ni yo tampoco, señora — me contestó, doblando la calle a toda
velocidad.

12 Bueno, al fin llegamos sanos y salvos al hotel. El coche paró y
bajamos. El Sr. Carrillo y yo entramos en el hotel. Le dije al conserje
— Buenas tardes. ¿Tiene Ud. una habitación con baño?

13 Tenemos una habitación en el segundo piso. Da a la plaza. Es el
número 25.

14 ¿Cuánto cuesta?

15 Mil quinientas pesetas al día, señora.

16 Muy bien. Voy a quedarme aquí varias semanas. Hágame el favor
de mandar a un muchacho para buscar las maletas.

17 Ahora mismo, señora. Habla Ud. el español muy bien. ¿Hace
mucho tiempo que Ud. está aquí en España.

18 — Acabo de llegar, — contesté yo, un tanto orgullosa.

19 — ¿Está Ud. aquí de turista? — preguntó el dependiente.

20 Estoy aquí en viaje de recreo y de negocios.

21 El Sr. Carrillo y yo charlamos un rato más y después nos despedimos. El señor Carrillo prometió llamarme por teléfono para concertar
una cita.

22 Subí en el ascensor a la habitación número 25. Es muy cómoda. No
me falta nada. Vuelvo a decirle, señor López, que voy a estar muy contenta en España.

Le saluda cordialmente su amiga
Juana Adams

Madrid, June 4, 1978

Dear Mr. López,

1 After the aeroplane arrived at the airport of Madrid and the
customs officers examined my luggage in the customs house, I went to
the waiting-room.

2 Suddenly a handsome gentleman approached me and asked, 'Excuse me, are you Mrs. Adams?'

3 'It is I,' I answered. 'And you are Mr. Carrillo, are you not? I am very pleased to meet you.'

4 'The pleasure is mine,' answered Mr. Carrillo.

5 You will remember, Mr. López, that Mr. Carrillo is the agent of our firm in Madrid and that he promised to meet me at the airport.

6 When we went outside together Mr. Carrillo called a taxi. He said to the driver, 'To the Hotel Emperador, please.'

7 We left the airport. Travelling with frightful speed along the great avenue, I thought 'Mr. López is very mistaken as regards the quiet life of Spain!'

8 Through the window of the taxi I saw on all sides, dashing at the same frightening speed, buses, cars and who knows what else?

9 I tried to say to the driver, 'Please, more slowly.' But I forgot my Spanish completely.

10 'I am not in a hurry,' at last I shouted to the driver.

11 'Neither am I, madam,' he answered me, turning a corner at full speed.

12 Well, at last we arrived safe and sound at the hotel. The car stopped and we got out. Mr. Carrillo and I entered the hotel. I said to the clerk, 'Good day. Have you a room with bath?'

13 We have a room on the second floor. It opens onto the plaza. It is number 25.

14 How much is it?

15 One thousand five hundred pesetas a day, madam.

16 Very well. I am going to remain here several weeks. Please send a boy to get my bags.

17 Right away, madam. You speak Spanish very well. You have been in Spain a long time?

18 'I have just arrived,' I answered, somewhat proud.

19 'You are here as a tourist?' asked the clerk.

20 I am here on a pleasure and business trip.

21 Mr. Carrillo and I chatted a while longer and then we said good-bye. Mr. Carrillo promised to telephone me to make an appointment.

22 I went up in the lift to room number 25. It is very comfortable. I lack nothing. I tell you again, Mr. López, that I am going to be very happy in Spain.

Yours sincerely,
Jane Adams

NOTE: 1. **Soy yo** = *it is I*, means literally *I am I. It is you* = **eres tú, es Ud.**; *it is we* = **somos nosotros;** *it is they* = **son ellos, son ellas,** *etc.*

Pronunciation Aids

1 Practise:

conductor (kon-duk-'tor)   velocidad (ve-lo-θi-'ðað) or
espantosa (es-pan-'to-sa)   (be-lo-θi-'ðað)
corriendo (ko-'rrjen-do)   orgullosa (or-ɣu-'ʎo-sa)

2 Be sure to stress these verbs on the last syllable.

salió (sa-'ʎjo)   bajé (ba-'xe)
contestó (kon-tes-'to)   pregunté (pre-ɣun-'te)
respondió (rres-pon-'djo)   contesté (kon-tes-'te)
se acercó (se a-θer-'ko)   olvidé (ol-vi-'ðe) or (ol-βi-'ðe)
prometió (pro-me-'tjo)   grité (ɣri-'te)
entré (en-'tre)

Building Vocabulary

1	ayer	yesterday	4	el año (mes) pasado	last year (month)
2	anteayer	day before yesterday	5	la semana pasada	last week
3	anoche	last night	6	el verano pasado	last summer

Expresiones Importantes

A. 1 **acercarse a,** to approach   **Se acercó a mí.** He approached me
   2 **doblando la calle**   making a turn
   3 **de repente**   suddenly
   4 **tratar de**   to try to
   5 **pienso visitar**   I intend to visit
   6 **por entero**   completely
   7 **revisar el equipaje**   to examine the luggage
   8 **sano y salvo**   safe and sound (*Lit.* sound and safe)
   9 **se dan la mano**   they shake hands (*Lit.* give the hand to each other)

B **Presentaciones** (Introductions)

1 Sr. Carrillo: Quiero presentarle a Ud. a un amigo mío.
2 Sr. Sánchez: Pedro Sánchez, a su disposición. Tengo mucho gusto en conocerle a Ud.
3 Sr. Martínez: Pablo Martínez, servidor de Ud. El gusto es mío. (Se dan la mano.)

1 Mr. Carrillo: I want to present to you a friend of mine.
2 Mr. Sánchez: Peter Sánchez, at your service. I'm very glad to meet you.

3 Mr. Martínez: Paul Martínez, your servant. The pleasure is mine. (They shake hands.)

Notice that the introducer lets the persons introduced say their own names.

Exercise No. 127—Completion of Text

1 **Me revisaron el equipaje** (in the customs).
2 **Fui a** (the waiting-room).
3 (Suddenly) **un señor se acercó a mí.**
4 (Excuse me), **¿es Ud. la Sra. Adams?**
5 **Yo contesté,** — (I am pleased to meet you).
6 — (The pleasure is mine), — **respondió el Sr. Carrillo.**
7 **Pensé** — (Mr. López is very mistaken).
8 (Who knows what else?)
9 — (I am not in a hurry!) — **grité al conductor.**
10 — (Neither am I), **señora** — **me contestó.**
11 **Tenemos una habitación que** (faces the square).
12 **¿Cuánto cuesta?** (150 a day).

SEGUNDA PARTE

Grammar Notes

1 The Preterite Tense. Model Verbs—**hablar, aprender, vivir**

The preterite tense is used in Spanish to tell of things that happened at a definite time in the past.

hablar, to speak I spoke (did speak), etc.	**aprender,** to learn I learned (did learn), etc.	**vivir,** to live I lived (did live), etc.
Singular	Singular	Singular
habl-é	**aprend-í**	**viv-í**
habl-aste	aprend-iste	viv-iste
habl-ó	aprend-ió	viv-ió
Plural	Plural	Plural
habl-amos	**aprend-imos**	**viv-imos**
habl-asteis	aprend-isteis	viv-isteis
habl-aron	aprend-ieron	viv-ieron

(a) To form the regular preterite tense of **-ar** verbs
    1. Drop **-ar** from the infinitive
    2. Add to the remaining stem the endings:
       Singular: **-é, -aste, -ó**   Plural **-amos, -asteis, -aron**

(b) To form the regular preterite tense of **-er** and **-ir** verbs
1. Drop **-er** or **-ir** from the infinitive.
2. Add to the remaining stem the endings:
   Singular: **-í, -iste, -ió**   Plural **-imos, -isteis, -ieron**

The preterite endings of **-er** and **-ir** verbs are exactly the same.

(c) **-ar** and **-ir** verbs have **-amos** and **-imos** respectively in the **nosotros** (we) form of both the present and preterite.

The sense of the sentence will tell you which is meant.

Hoy hablamos	Today we speak.
Ayer hablamos	Yesterday we spoke.
Hoy vivimos.	Today we live.
Ayer vivimos.	Yesterday we lived.

(d) **dije** *I said* and **dijo** *he said* are irregular preterites. You will learn more about these and other irregular preterites later.

2 Preterite of **leer, creer, caer, oír**

I read (did read), etc.	I believed, etc.	I fell, etc.	I heard, etc.
leí	creí	caí	oí
leíste	creíste	caíste	oíste
leyó	creyó	cayó	oyó
leímos	creímos	caímos	oímos
leísteis	creísteis	caísteis	oísteis
leyeron	creyeron	cayeron	oyeron

Note carefully the forms:

leyó, leyeron   creyó, creyeron   cayó, cayeron   oyó, oyeron

Ejercicios (Exercises) No. 128A–128B–128C–128D

128A. Conjugate the following verbs in the preterite tense:

1 entrar   2 comer   3 salir   4 ver   5 sentarse.

128B. Translate:

1 ¿Quién olvidó los billetes?
2 Ayer recibimos las cartas.
3 El hombre compró un vestido nuevo.
4 Anoche no oímos el timbre.
5 ¿Llegó a tiempo el tren?
6 Buscaron el equipaje.
7 El niño cayó delante de la casa.
8 Salieron del aeropuerto en un taxi.
9 ¿Dónde esperó la Sra. Adams a su amigo?
10 ¿Cuánto costó el impermeable?

128C. Answer in the negative in complete Spanish sentences. Use the preterite.

Remember: A question with **Ud.** requires an answer in the singular **(yo)**. A question with **Uds.** requires an answer in the plural **(nosotros)**

Ejemplo: ¿Trabajó Ud. anoche? Did you work last night?
        (Yo) No trabajé anoche. I did not work last night.

1 **¿Compró Ud. ayer un sombrero nuevo?**
2 **¿Volvieron Uds. tarde del teatro anoche?**
3 **¿Escribió Ud. unas cartas esta mañana?**
4 **¿Llegaron Uds. a las ocho en punto?**
5 **¿Salió Ud. a las nueve de la noche?**
6 **¿Pasó Ud. el verano pasado en el campo?**
7 **¿Oyeron Uds. el timbre?**
8 **¿Vendió Ud. su casa?**
9 **¿Dejaron Uds. el dinero en casa?**
10 **¿Trabajaron Uds. toda la noche?**

128D. Translate into Spanish, using the verbs indicated in the preterite tense.

1 **(salir)** I left
2 **(llegar)** we arrived
3 **(examinar)** they examined
4 **(oír)** he heard
5 **(responder)** you **(Ud.)** answered
6 **(preguntar)** I did not ask
7 **(llamar)** she called
8 **(desear)** you **(Uds.)** wanted
9 **(salir)** we got out
10 **(parar)** it stopped
11 **(olvidar)** I did not forget
12 **(gritar)** he shouted
13 **(creer)** they believed
14 **(vender)** we sold
15 **(volver)** did you **(Uds.)** return?
16 **(leer)** did he read?

Exercise No. 129—Preguntas

1 **¿Quiénes revisaron el equipaje?**
2 **¿Quién se acercó a la Sra. Adams en la sala de espera?**
3 **¿Qué dijo el señor?**
4 **¿Qué contestó la Sra. Adams?**
5 **¿Cómo pasó el taxi por una gran avenida?**
6 **¿Qué deseó decir la Sra. Adams al conductor?**
7 **¿Qué olvidó?**
8 **¿Qué vió la Sra. Adams por la ventanilla?**
9 **¿Qué gritó al conductor?**
10 **¿Qué le contestó el conductor?**
11 **¿Cómo llegaron al fin al hotel?**
12 **¿Qué dijo la Sra. Adams al conserje?**

CHAPTER 32

UNA VISITA A LA FAMILIA CARRILLO

PRIMERA PARTE

Segunda Carta de España

Estimado amigo:

1 El lunes pasado el Sr. Carrillo me llamó por teléfono. Quiso invitarme a tomar la merienda en su casa al día siguiente. Así es que tuve la oportunidad de visitar a una familia española.

2 A las cinco de la tarde llegué a una casa grande de piedra roja en los alrededores de Madrid. Me acerqué a la enorme puerta de pesado roble.

3 Toqué el timbre e inmediatamente oí pasos rápidos en el vestíbulo. Una criada me abrió la puerta y me invitó a entrar en la casa.

4 El Sr. Carrillo vino a saludarme. — Está Ud. en su casa, — me dijo, según la costumbre española.

5 Le di las gracias y dije. — Su casa tiene un aspecto verdaderamente romántico. Me parece una casa de cuento de hadas.

6 — Hay muchas casas semejantes en España, — me respondió. — Esta casa fue construída en el siglo diez y siete.

7 Miré las gruesas paredes, los balcones y las altas ventanas con sus rejas de hierro. Me encantó el patio lleno de árboles y flores. Gran parte del suelo estaba[1] cubierto de azulejos. Admiré la fuente de piedra en el centro del patio.

8 Entramos en una sala grande, uno de los muchos cuartos que dan al patio. El Sr. Carrillo me presentó a su esposa y a sus dos hijos, jóvenes muy serios e inteligentes.

9 Los muchachos me dijeron que asisten al Instituto Nacional para Bachillerato. El mayor quiere hacerse médico. El menor quiere ser abogado.

10 Al poco tiempo tuvieron que volver a su cuarto para estudiar.

11 La señora Carrillo me sirvió una taza de chocolate y algunas pastas muy sabrosas. Entretanto el señor Carrillo y yo hablamos de la vida en España, de las costumbres y del arte.

12 Me dijo que vale la pena ver un mercado típico para buscar ejemplares del arte popular. Me dijo que el viernes es el mejor día para visitar los mercados.

13 Le respondí que tenía[1] la intención de ir a un mercado dentro de unos pocos días.

14 Sintió no poder acompañarme.

15 Después de una hora y media muy interesante y divertida nos despedimos y volví a casa, es decir, a mi hotel.

Su sincera amiga
Juana Adams

Dear Mr. López,

1 Last Monday Mr. Carillo called me on the telephone. He wanted to invite me to tea at his house the following day. So I had the opportunity of visiting a Spanish family.

2 At five o'clock in the afternoon I arrived at a big house of red stone in the suburbs of Madrid. I approached the enormous door of heavy oak.

3 I rang the bell and immediately I heard rapid steps in the hall. A servant opened the door and asked me to enter the house.

4 Mr. Carrillo came to greet me. 'My house is yours,' he said to me, according to the Spanish custom.

5 I thanked him and said: 'Your house has a truly romantic appearance. It seems to me a house out of a fairy story.'

6 'There are many similar houses in Spain,' he answered me. 'This house was built in the 17th century.'

7 I looked at the thick walls, the balconies and tall windows with their iron gratings. The courtyard full of trees and flowers enchanted me. Most of the ground was covered with tile. I admired the stone fountain in the centre of the courtyard.

8 We entered a big living-room, one of the many rooms that open onto the courtyard. Mr. Carrillo introduced me to his wife and to his two sons, very serious and intelligent young men.

9 The boys told me that they go to a grammar school (*lit.* National Institute for Baccalaureat). The elder wants to become a doctor. The younger wants to be a lawyer.

10 Within a short time they had to go back to their rooms to study.

11 Mrs. Carrillo served me a cup of chocolate and some very delicious cakes. Meanwhile Mr. Carrillo and I chatted about life in Spain, about its customs and art.

12 He told me that it is worth the trouble to go to see a typical market and to look for samples of folk art. He told me that Friday is the best day to visit the markets.

13 I answered that I intended to go to a market within a few days.

14 He regretted not being able to accompany me.

15 After a very interesting and pleasant hour and a half we took leave of one another and I returned home, that is to say, to my hotel.

Yours sincerely,
Jane Adams

NOTE: 1. Imperfect tense. You will learn this tense later.

Pronunciation Aids

1 Practise:

llegué (ʎe-ˈɣe)

acerqué (a-θer-ˈke)

sirvió (sir-ˈvjo) or (sir-ˈβjo)

sintió (sin-ˈtjo)

repitió (rre-pi-ˈtjo)

romántico (rro-ˈman-ti-ko)

hierro (ˈje-rro)

semejante (se-me-ˈxan-te)

inmediatamente

(in-me-ði-a-ta-ˈmen-te)

enseñanza (en-se-ˈnjan-θa)

2 **el joven, los jóvenes.** The plural must add an accent mark to hold the stress on the syllable **jo-.**

Building Vocabulary

A.

1 **casa de piedra**	stone house	4 **falda de algodón**	cotton skirt
2 **reja de hierro**	iron grating	5 **guantes de lana**	woollen gloves
3 **silla de madera**	wooden chair	6 **vestido de seda**	silk dress

NOTE: In Spanish, what things are made of is indicated by **de** plus the material, not by using the material as an adjective. Thus **casa de piedra** (house of stone).

B. **la merienda,** a light afternoon meal, tea. The Spaniards eat **la cena,** supper, rather late in the evening, about 10 o'clock or later.

Expresiones Importantes

1 **al día siguiente** — on the following day

2 **es decir** — that is to say

3 **hacerse** — to become (*lit.* to make oneself)

   Se hace médico (abogado, ingeniero).

   He becomes a doctor (lawyer, engineer).

4 **llamar por teléfono** — to telephone

   Llamé por teléfono. — I telephoned.

5 **Tener la intención de** — to intend to

   Tengo la intención de salir. — I intend to leave.

Exercise No. 130—Completion of Text

1 El Sr. Carrillo (telephoned me).

2 Quiso invitarme (to have tea) **en su casa.**

3 (The following day) **llegué a su casa.**

4 (I approached) **a la puerta.**

5 Una criada (invited me to enter) **en la casa.**

6 **El Sr. Carrillo** (came to greet me).

7 — (You are in your house) — **me dijo.**

8 **Me saludó** (according to the Spanish custom).

9 (It looks to me like) **una casa de cuento de hadas.**

10 **Hay** (many similar houses) **en España.**

11 (I admired) **la fuente de piedra.**

12 (He presented me) **a la señora Carrillo.**

13 **El hijo mayor quiere** (to become a doctor).

14 (He was sorry) **no poder acompañarme.**

15 (We took leave) **y volví** (home).

SEGUNDA PARTE

Grammar Notes

1 The Irregular Preterite with **-i** Stems.

hacer, to do (make) I did (made), etc.	**querer,** to wish I wished, etc.	**venir,** to come I came, etc.	**decir,** to say I said, etc.
hic-e	**quis-e**	**vin-e**	**dij-e**
hic-iste	**quis-iste**	**vin-iste**	**dij-iste**
hiz-o	**quis-o**	**vin-o**	**dij-o**
hic-imos	**quis-imos**	**vin-imos**	**dij-imos**
hic-isteis	**quis-isteis**	**vin-isteis**	**dij-isteis**
hic-ieron	**quis-ieron**	**vin-ieron**	**dij-eron**

(a) Irregular verbs of this group have an **-i** in the preterite stem.

(b) The ending of the **(yo)** form is unaccented **-e** instead of **-i;** the ending of the **(Ud., él, ella)** form is unaccented **-o** instead of **-ió.**

(c) In the form **hizo, z** replaces **c.**

(d) You know that the **(yo)** form of the present tense of these verbs ends in unaccented **-o.**

> **hago,** I do   **quiero,** I wish   **vengo,** I come   **digo,** I say

The change of stem prevents the present forms from being confused with the preterite forms:

> **hizo,** you, he,
she did   **quiso,** you, he,
she wished   **vino,** you, he,
she came   **dijo,** you, he,
she said

2 An Irregular Preterite with **-u** stem.

In the second letter from Spain at the beginning of this chapter we met the Preterite of the verb **tener** *to have* in the form **tuve** *I had.* The full Preterite is as follows: **tuve, tuviste, tuvo, tuvimos, tuvisteis, tuvieron.** You will meet more verbs with **-u** Stems in the Preterite in the next chapter.

3 The Preterite of Stem-Changing Verbs like **pedir (i)**.

pedir (i), to ask for I asked for, etc.	servir (i), to serve I served, etc.	repetir (i), to repeat I repeated, etc.	vestir (i), to dress I dressed, etc.
pedí	serví	repetí	vestí
pediste	serviste	repetiste	vestiste
pidió	sirvió	repitió	vistió
pedimos	servimos	repetimos	vestimos
pedisteis	servisteis	repetisteis	vestisteis
pidieron	sirvieron	repitieron	vistieron

(a) The preterite of verbs like **pedir (i)** is formed almost exactly like the regular preterite of **-ir** verbs. The only differences are in the stem of the (**Ud., él, ella**) form (**pidió**) and in the (**Uds., ellos, ellas**) form (**pidieron**) where **-i** replaces **-e** in the stem.

(b) Note the same difference in the preterite of **sentir** to regret.

sentí   sentiste   *sintió*   sentimos   sentisteis   *sintieron*

Ejercicios (Exercises) No. 131A–131B–131C

131A. Translate:

1 La criada nos sirvió la merienda.
2 ¿Por qué no quiso Ud. invitarme?
3 Anoche volvimos tarde del teatro.
4 Quise llamarle a Ud. por teléfono.
5 ¿Qué hizo Ud. después de la comida?
6 Dijeron — No tenemos prisa.
7 Repetí todas las respuestas.
8 Mi amigo no vino a tiempo. Lo sentí.
9 Pidieron informes en la oficina de información.
10 Quisieron comprar billetes de ida y vuelta.

131B. Answer in complete sentences the following questions using the suggested words in the answer.

Ejemplo: ¿Qué quiso Ud. comprar? (guantes de lana)
Quise comprar guantes de lana.

1 ¿Qué dijo Ud. al señor? (pase Ud.)
2 ¿Quién hizo un viaje al Perú? (mi hermano)
3 ¿Cuándo vino Ud. a casa? (a las siete)
4 ¿De qué vistieron las mujeres? (de falda de algodón)
5 ¿Qué quiso hacerse el mayor? (médico)
6 ¿Qué sirvió la criada? (una taza de chocolate)
7 ¿Qué pidió el viajero? (información)

8 ¿Qué quisieron Uds. ver? (la nueva película)
9 ¿Cuándo hicieron Uds. un viaje a España? (el año pasado)
10 ¿Qué dijeron Uds. cuando salieron de la casa? (hasta la vista)

131C. Translate. Use the correct forms of **querer (ie)**, **decir (i)**, **hacer**, **servir (i)**, **repetir (i)**, **sentir (ie)**

1 I wished	9 they said
2 I did not say	10 they made
3 he made	11 What did he say?
4 they came	12 What did you (Uds.) say?
5 she served	13 we did not wish
6 they wished	14 I did not come
7 I repeated	15 they regretted
8 we made	

Exercise No. 132—Preguntas

1 ¿Quién llamó a la Sra. Adams por teléfono?
2 ¿A qué hora llegó a la casa del señor Carrillo?
3 ¿Quién le abrió a la Sra. Adams la puerta?
4 ¿Quién vino a saludar a la Sra. Adams?
5 ¿Qué encantó a la Sra. Adams?
6 ¿Qué admiró ella?
7 ¿Quiénes son serios e inteligentes?
8 ¿A qué clase de escuela asisten los jóvenes?
9 ¿Qué quiere hacerse el mayor?
10 ¿A dónde tuvieron que volver los jóvenes?
11 ¿De qué hablaron entretanto los señores?
12 ¿Vale la pena ir a un mercado?
13 ¿Quién quiso ir allá?
14 ¿Después de una hora, quiénes se despidieron?
15 ¿A dónde volvió la Sra. Adams?

CHAPTER 33

UN PASEO POR MADRID

PRIMERA PARTE

Tercera Carta de España

Estimado amigo:

1 ¡Qué hermosa es la Gran Vía! Los edificios son tan imponentes — algunos del estilo tradicional español, algunos de estilo moderno, otros una combinación de los dos estilos. Esta avenida es el centro comercial de Madrid. En ambos lados de la avenida hay tiendas y almacenes elegantes y tengo ganas de gastar todo mi dinero allí.

2 Estaba[1] en la Plaza de España cuando empecé mi paseo. Allí se halla el monumento a Cervantes. Naturalmente, tuve que pensar en nuestra conversación sobre las calles de Madrid. Recordé que en ellas se puede encontrar a los grandes españoles del pasado. Se puede caminar no solamente a través de la historia sino también a través de la literatura y del arte.

3 Ayer pude ver todo esto por mí misma. Era[1] domingo y vi a muchas personas en las calles.

4 Caminé despacio por la Gran Vía hasta la esquina en donde se junta con la Calle de Alcalá. Unos minutos más y estuve en la Plaza de la Cibeles. Entonces caminé a la derecha, por el Paseo del Prado hasta el museo mismo.

5 Miré mi reloj. ¡La una! Los domingos el museo cierra a las dos. Solamente una hora para ver las obras del Greco, de Velázquez, de Goya . . . Es imposible, pensé. Volveré más tarde. Miré el exterior del museo y admiré la arquitectura magnífica del siglo 18, y la estatua de Velázquez, que está delante del museo.

6 Me senté un rato en la Plaza de Cánovas de Castillo, donde hay una fuente muy agradable. Entonces decidí comer en un restaurante cercano.

7 Después de una comida copiosa fui al Jardín Botánico. Pasé un buen rato mirando las flores y los árboles. Su variedad es muy imponente — dicen que hay más de treinta mil especies diferentes.

8 Es muy interesante caminar por Madrid. Cuando vi todos aquellos monumentos y museos comprendí el orgullo de los españoles en el pasado de la nación.

9 Después, me senté, muy cansada, en el parque del Retiro y — tengo que confesarlo — me dormí.

Le saluda cordialmente su amiga
Juana Adams

Dear Mr. López,

1 How beautiful the Gran Vía is! The buildings are so impressive—some in the traditional Spanish style, some in modern style, others a combination of the two styles. This avenue is the commercial centre of Madrid. On both sides of the avenue there are elegant shops and stores, and I am tempted to spend all my money there.

2 I was in the Plaza de España when I began my stroll. That is where the monument to Cervantes stands. Naturally, I recalled our conversation about the streets of Madrid. I remembered that in them one can meet the great Spaniards of the past. One can walk not only through history, but also through literature and art.

3 Yesterday I could see all this for myself. It was Sunday and I saw many people in the streets.

4 I walked slowly along the Gran Vía up to the corner where it joins with the Alcalá Street. Some minutes more and I was in Cybele Square. Then I walked to the right, along the Paseo del Prado to the museum itself.

5 I looked at my watch. One o'clock! On Sundays the museum closes at two. One hour only to see the works of El Greco, Velázquez, Goya... It's impossible, I thought. I shall come back later. I looked at the outside of the museum and admired the magnificent architecture of the 18th century and the statue of Velázquez which is in front of the museum.

6 I sat down a while in Cánovas de Castillo Square, where there is a very pleasant fountain. Then I decided to eat in a nearby restaurant.

7 After a copious lunch I went to the Botanical Garden. I spent a good while looking at the flowers and trees. Their variety is very impressive—they say there are more than 30,000 different species.

8 It is very interesting to walk through Madrid. When I saw all those monuments and museums I understood the pride of the Spaniards in the nation's past.

9 Afterwards, I sat down, very tired, in the Retiro Park and—I must confess it—I fell asleep.

Yours sincerely,
Jane Adams

NOTE: 1. **estaba** and **era** are in the imperfect tense. This will be studied in a later chapter.

Pronunciation Aids

Practise:

imponente (im-po-'nen-te)
pude ('pu-ðe)
esquina (es-'ki-na)

despacio (ðes-'pa-θjo)
Velázquez (ve-'laθ-keθ) or
    (be-'laθ-keθ)

especie (es-'pe-θje)   **orgullo** (or-'ɣu-ʎo)
empecé (em-pe-'θe)

Building Vocabulary

A. Related words:

1 **pasar,** to pass
  el paso, the step, passage
  el pasillo, vestibule
2 **pasear** or **pasearse,** to stroll   **el paseante,** the stroller
  el paseo, the walk, promenade   **dar un paseo,** to take a walk
3 **parecer,** to seem, to appear
  parecerse a, to resemble
  me parece bien. It seems all right to me.
  Jorge se parece a su padre. George resembles his father.

Exercise No. 133—Completion of Text

1 ¡(How beautiful) **es la Gran Vía!**
2 **Es** (the commercial centre) **de Madrid.**
3 **Tengo ganas de** (spend all my money).
4 (I recalled) **en nuestra conversación.**
5 **Se puede caminar** (through history).
6 (Yesterday) **era domingo.**
7 **El museo** (shuts) **a las dos.**
8 **La estatua de Velázquez** (is in front of the museum).
9 **Me senté** (for a while) **en la plaza.**
10 **Tengo que confesarlo,** (I went to sleep).

SEGUNDA PARTE

Grammar Notes

1 Irregular Preterites with **-u** Stems

In the last chapter you learned the irregular preterite of some familiar verbs. Here are more familiar verbs with an irregular preterite.

| **poder,** to be able | **poner,** to put | **tener,** to have |
I was able, etc.	I put (did put) etc.	I had, etc.
pud–e	pus–e	tuv–e
pud–iste	pus–iste	tuv–iste
pud–o	pus–o	tuv–o
pud–imos	pus–imos	tuv–imos
pud–isteis	pus–isteis	tuv–isteis
pud–ieron	pus–ieron	tuv–ieron

estar, to be	saber, to know
I was, etc.	I knew, etc.
estuv-e	**sup-e**
estuv-iste	**sup-iste**
estuv-o	**sup-o**
estuv-imos	**sup-imos**
estuv-isteis	**sup-isteis**
estuv-ieron	**sup-ieron**

(a) Irregular verbs of this group have a **-u** in the preterite stem.

(b) The endings are the same as the irregular preterites (of **hacer,** etc.) you have already learned.

(c) **saber** to know, in the preterite usually means *learned, found out.*
Supe el nombre del médico. I learned the name of the doctor.

2 More Irregular Preterites

dar, to give	ser, to be	ir, to go
I gave, etc.	I was, etc.	I went, etc.
di	**fui**	**fui**
diste	**fuiste**	**fuiste**
dio	**fue**	**fue**
dimos	**fuimos**	**fuimos**
disteis	**fuisteis**	**fuisteis**
dieron	**fueron**	**fueron**

Since **di, dio,** etc. are monosyllables the accent is unnecessary, and is not written.

The verbs **ser** and **ir** have exactly the same forms in the preterite tense. The sense of the sentence will always tell you which verb is meant. Thus:

| **Isabel fue reina de España.** | Isabel was queen of Spain. |
| **Cristóbal Colón fue a la reina.** | Christopher Columbus went to the queen. |

Ejercicios (Exercises) No. 134A-134B-134C

134A. Translate:

1 En Navidad di regalos a todos los niños.
2 No tuve oportunidad de conocerle a Ud. personalmente.
3 No pudimos pagar toda la cuenta.
4 Esta casa fue construída en el siglo diez y seis.
5 El domingo dimos un paseo por el Parque del Retiro.
6 Pude conversar con él en su bello idioma.
7 Él no tuvo dificultad en entenderme.
8 Ella no quiso descansar mucho.

9 La familia de la Sra. Adams no pudo acompañarla.
10 Me puse el sombrero nuevo en la cabeza.

134B. Change these sentences from the present to the preterite. Be sure to keep the same person.

Ejemplo: Pongo la mesa. Puse la mesa.

1 Tengo que estudiar la lección.
2 La Sra. Adams está en el comedor.
3 Los árboles se ponen verdes.
4 Ella da las gracias al Sr. Carrillo.
5 Soy un estudiante atento.
6 Vamos al mercado.
7 Vienen del cine a las once.
8 No digo nada.
9 Uds. no hacen nada.
10 ¿Quieren Uds. comprarlo?

134C. Translate, using the preterite of the given verbs.

1 (tener), I had
2 (poder), you (Ud.) were able
3 (ir), they went
4 (decir), she said
5 (poner), he put
6 (querer), we wished
7 (dar), they gave
8 (ser), I was
9 (estar), you (Uds.) were
10 (encontrarse), we met

Exercise No. 135—Preguntas

1 ¿Cómo se titula esta lectura?
2 ¿De qué estilo son los edificios?
3 ¿Qué hay a ambos lados de la avenida?
4 ¿Dónde se halla el monumento a Cervantes?
5 ¿En qué día fue a pasearse la Sra. Adams?
6 ¿Con qué calle se junta la Gran Vía?
7 ¿A qué hora cierra el museo del Prado los domingos?
8 ¿De qué siglo es su arquitectura?
9 ¿De quién es la estatua delante del museo?
10 ¿Qué comprendió la Sra. Adams cuando vio los monumentos?
11 ¿Dónde se sentó después?
12 ¿Es interesante caminar por Madrid?

CHAPTER 34

EN EL MERCADO

PRIMERA PARTE

Cuarta Carta de España

Querido amigo:

1 La semana pasada fui a un mercado en un pueblecito que está situado a cosa de unas millas de Madrid.

2 Mientras que nuestro coche de línea[1] pasaba por las aldeas vi mujeres hombres que trabajaban en los campos.

3 Era viernes y el mercado estaba lleno de gente. Probablemente la mayor parte de ellos venía del campo, pero había también mucha gente de la ciudad.

4 Uno se puede perder fácilmente en este mercado tan grande. Pero yo no tuve dificultad, porque sabía pedir información en español.

5 Mientras caminaba por una calle de puestos donde se vendían ropa, zapatos y sombreros, vi a un muchacho de siete u ocho años, de aspecto muy serio, cuidando un puesto.

6 Parecía mucho un viejecito con su sombrero de ala ancha y sus pantalones muy grandes. Como los demás vendedores, arreglaba su mercancía con sumo cuidado. También vi que regateaba en serio.

7 En el mercado se vendía toda clase de productos — frutas, flores, cerámica, cestas, ropa, echarpes. Había cosas corrientes y artículos de lujo.

8 Por todas partes veía el sentido estético de muchos de los vendedores. Especialmente entre los puestos de comidas encontré color y arte.

9 Por ejemplo, una mujer estaba sentada en la acera. Delante de ella había unas pocas cebollas y pimientos. Con sumo cuidado los arreglaba en pequeños montones.

10 Junto a ella vi un puesto de frutas con algunas hojas verdes cerca de las naranjas y los limones.

11 Cerca de esos puestos escuché la conversación de las mujeres y pude aprender algo sobre la vida del campo.

12 Supe que los campesinos vienen al mercado no solamente para vender y comprar sino también para divertirse, para charlar y para visitar a sus amigos.

239

13 La gente gritaba, charlaba, compraba, vendía, reía, todos con animación y humor.

14 De veras pasé un día muy interesante y muy divertido en el mercado.

15 Y mientras iba a casa, es decir, a la capital, recordaba nuestras conversaciones en que hablábamos de los mercados de España y de tantas otras cosas.

Cordialmente
Juana Adams

Dear Mr. López,

1 Last week I went to a market in a small town which is about forty miles from Madrid.

2 While our coach passed through the villages, I saw women and men who were working in the fields.

3 It was Friday and the market was full of people. Probably the majority of them came from the country but there were also many people from the town.

4 One can easily lose one's way in this very big market. But I did not have difficulty because I knew how to ask for information in Spanish.

5 While I was walking through a street of stalls where clothing, shoes and hats were being sold, I saw a boy of seven or eight years, looking very serious, minding a stall.

6 He was just like a little old man with his broad-brimmed hat and his very large trousers. Like the rest of the sellers he was arranging his merchandise with extreme care. Also I saw he was bargaining seriously.

7 All kinds of merchandise were being sold in the market—fruit, flowers, pottery, baskets, clothing, shawls. There were ordinary things and luxury articles.

8 Everywhere I was aware (*lit.* I could see) of the aesthetic feeling of many of the sellers. Especially among the food stalls I found colour and art.

9 For example, a woman was sitting on the pavement. Before her there were a few onions and peppers. With extreme care, she was arranging them in little piles.

10 Near her I saw a fruit stall with some green leaves near the oranges and lemons.

11 Near those stalls I listened to the chatting of the women and I could learn something about life in the country.

12 I learned that the country people come to the market not only to sell and to buy but also to enjoy themselves, to chat, and to visit their friends.

13 The people were shouting, chatting, buying, selling, laughing, all with liveliness and humour.

14 Indeed I spent a very interesting and very enjoyable day in the market.

15 And while I was going home, that is to say to the capital, I kept remembering our conversations in which we used to speak of the markets of Spain and of so many other things.

Cordially
Jane Adams

NOTE: 1. **un coche de línea** is a motor-coach which serves different towns and villages.

Pronunciation Aids

1 Practise:

estética (es-'te-ti-ka)
estaba (es-'ta-βa)
caminaba (ka-mi-'na-βa)
arreglaba (a-rre-'ɣla-βa)
regateaba (rre-ɣa-te-'a-βa)
gritaba (ɣri-'ta-βa)

hablábamos (a-'βla-βamos)
comprábamos (kom-'pra-βa-mos)
éramos ('e-ra-mos)
íbamos ('i-βa-mos)
reía (rre-'i-a)
había (a-'βi-a)

Building Vocabulary

A. Palabras Relacionadas

1 **el ánimo,** animation
animado, animated, lively
2 **campo,** country, field
campesino, farmer, peasant, countryman
3 **difícil,** difficult
la dificultad, difficulty
4 **divertirse,** to enjoy oneself
divertido, enjoyable
5 **naranja,** orange
anaranjado, orange-coloured
6 **platicar,** to chat
la plática, chatting, conversation

B. **La gente,** people, requires a singular verb in Spanish.

La gente del campo estaba allí. The country people were there.

Exercise No. 136—Completion of Text

1 (Last week) **fui al mercado.**
2 (I saw) **mujeres** (who) **lavaban ropa.**
3 **El mercado estaba** (full of people).
4 **Venían** (from the country).
5 **Se puede facilmente** (lose one's way).
6 **Yo caminaba** (through a street of stalls).
7 (I saw) **a un muchacho** (of seven or eight years).
8 (Like the other sellers) **arreglaba su mercancía.**
9 **Se vendían en el mercado** (flowers, baskets and clothing).
10 (Among the stands) **encontré color y arte.**

11 **Los campesinos vienen** (to enjoy themselves).
12 **Yo escuché** (the chatting of the women).
13 **Aprendí un poco** (about country life).
14 (I remembered) **nuestras conversaciones.**
15 **Pasé** (a very pleasant day).

SEGUNDA PARTE

Grammar Notes

1 The Imperfect Tense

You have learned two tenses which indicate past time, the present perfect and the preterite. Of the two the preterite is more commonly used.

You will now learn a third tense that refers also to past time—the imperfect. We may call the imperfect the 'was, were or used to' tense because it indicates actions that *were* happening or *used to* happen in past time. Thus:

(a) *We were working,* when he entered.
(b) *He used to do* his lessons in the evening.

In sentence (a), *were working* is in the imperfect; *he entered*, which interrupts the working at a definite moment, is in the preterite.

2 The Imperfect of Model Verbs—**hablar, aprender, vivir.**

Singular	Singular	Singular
I was speaking, etc.	I was learning, etc.	I was living, etc.
habl-aba	**aprend-ía**	**viv-ía**
habl-abas	**aprend-ías**	**viv-ías**
habl-aba	**aprend-ía**	**viv-ía**
Plural	Plural	Plural
habl-ábamos	**aprend-íamos**	**viv-íamos**
habl-abais	**aprend-íais**	**viv-íais**
habl-aban	**aprend-ían**	**viv-ían**

(a) To form the imperfect tense of all -**ar** verbs, *without* exception:

1 Drop -**ar** from the infinitive
2 Add the endings **aba, -abas, -aba; -ábamos, -abais, -aban,** to the remaining stem.

(b) To form the imperfect of all -**er** and -**ir** verbs with the exception of **ver, ser** and **ir**:

1 Drop -**er** or -**ir** from the infinitive.
2 Add the endings -**ía, -ías, -ía; -íamos, -íais, -ían,** to the remaining stem.

(c) The stress is on the first syllable (**a**) in all the **-aba** endings. To prevent it from shifting in the **-ábamos** ending the first **-a** must have an accent mark.

The stress in the **-ía** endings is always on the **i**.

(d) The endings of the **yo** and the (**Ud. él ella**) forms of the verb are alike in the imperfect. The subject pronoun is used when the meaning is not clear.

3 The Imperfect of **ver, ser, ir.**

I was seeing, etc.		I was, etc.		I was going, etc.	
veía	veíamos	era	éramos	iba	íbamos
veías	veíais	eras	erais	ibas	ibais
veía	veían	era	eran	iba	iban

(a) The endings of **veía** are regular. But the endings are added to **ve**-not to **v-**.

(b) In all forms of **era** and **iba** the stress must be on the first syllable.

To prevent it from shifting, an accent mark is added to the first syllable of **éramos** and **íbamos.**

Ejercicios (Exercises) No. 137A–137B–137C

137A. Translate:

1 Llovía a cántaros cuando nos despedimos de los jóvenes.
2 Yo pensaba en Ud. cuando me paseaba en coche por las calles de Madrid.
3 Los turistas y los vendedores regateaban y todos parecían divertirse mucho.
4 Me acercaba a la puerta cuando encontré a los hijos del Sr. Carrillo.
5 Mientras hablábamos sobre las artes populares, la señora Carrillo leía un periódico.
6 Hacía mucho calor cuando volvimos a Sevilla.
7 Cuando el coche se ponía en marcha se acercó un agente de policía (policeman).
8 Los aviones llegaban y salían a todas horas.
9 Estábamos cansados pero no queríamos descansar.
10 Ya eran las cuatro y media de la tarde y teníamos prisa.

137B. Each of these sentences indicates an action that was going on (*imperfect*) and another action which interrupted it at a definite time (*preterite*). Translate the verbs in parentheses, using the correct tense.

1 Mientras (I was eating), **me llamó por teléfono.**
2 Cuando (we were studying), **entraron en nuestro cuarto.**
3 Cuando (he was) **enfermo, le visitamos.**

4 **Mientras** (you were taking leave), **empezó a llover.**
5 **Cuando** (they were taking a walk), **se perdieron.**
6 **Los vendedores** (were shouting) **cuando llegamos al mercado.**
7 **Cayó en la acera cuando** (he was getting out) **del coche.**
8 **No nos oyeron cuando** (we were speaking).
9 **Los encontramos cuando** (they were going) **al mercado.**
10 **Cuando** (we were passing) **por una avenida grande, grité** — no tengo
prisa.

137C. Translate the following verbs in the correct tense, preterite or imperfect, as necessary.

1 **(caminar)** I was walking
2 **(ir)** I was going
3 **(decir)** he said
4 **(jugar)** they were playing
5 **(cantar)** they sang
6 **(ver)** we were seeing
7 **(correr)** they were running
8 **(perder)** you **(Ud.)** lost

9 **(vivir)** they lived
10 **(leer)** she read
11 **(empezar)** it began
12 **(llamar)** they were calling
13 **(entrar)** you **(Uds.)** did not enter
14 **(estar)** were you **(Ud.)**?
(imperfect)
15 **(ser)** we were (imperfect)
16 **(oír)** they heard

Exercise No. 138—Preguntas

1 ¿Por dónde pasaba el coche de línea?
2 ¿Qué lavaban las mujeres?
3 ¿Dónde trabajaban los hombres?
4 ¿Qué día de la semana era?
5 ¿De dónde venía la mayor parte de la gente?
6 ¿Había[1] también gente de la ciudad?
7 ¿Por qué no tenía dificultad la Sra. Adams?
8 ¿A quién vio mientras caminaba?
9 ¿Qué parecía el muchacho?
10 ¿Qué clase de sombrero llevaba?
11 ¿Qué arreglaba el muchacho?
12 ¿Qué veía por todas partes la Sra. Adams?
13 ¿Quién estaba sentada en la acera?
14 ¿Qué había delante de ella?
15 ¿Cuándo recordaba la Sra. Adams sus conversaciones con el Sr.
López?

NOTE: 1. The imperfect of **hay** (there is or there are) is **había** (there
was or there were). The preterite is **hubo** (there was or there were).

CHAPTER 35

SOBRE EL DESCANSO

PRIMERA PARTE

Quinta Carta de España

Querido amigo:
Ud. recordará, amigo mío, sus últimos consejos antes de mi salida para España. Me dijo Ud. — No tenga prisa. Descanse una o dos horas por la tarde. De veras no he olvidado sus consejos acerca del descanso, pero tengo que confesar — no descanso largo rato. Hay tanto que ver, tanto que oír, tanto que descubrir, tanto que hacer.

Ayer, por ejemplo, descansaba al mediodía en un café en la esquina de la Carretera de San Jerónimo con la Calle del Prado. Había brisa, y era muy agradable.

Pero no pude descansar largo rato. Al otro lado de la Calle del Prado veía las muchas tiendas donde se venden objetos de arte, libros, artículos de cuero, de paja, de tela, de plata y de cristal. Muchas veces he visitado aquellas tiendas, pero no pude resistir la tentación de volver a visitarlas.

También tuve que visitar otra vez el Museo de Artes Decorativas. Nunca me canso de mirar las artes populares ni de hacer preguntas a los dependientes en la tienda del Museo y al director.

Saliendo del Museo, que está cerca del Parque del Retiro, volví a visitar el Museo Nacional de Arte Contemporáneo, que está a unas tres manzanas del parque. Me gusta mucho mirar los cuadros de los grandes artistas modernos de España y de los otros países.

Bien, Sr. López, Ud. ve que voy aprendiendo más cada día, sobre todo porque soy muy habladora. Y sus consejos me han sido muy útiles, excepto (tengo que confesarlo otra vez) los que me dió Ud. sobre el descanso.

Cordialmente,
Juana Adams

Dear Mr. López:
You will remember, my friend, your final advice before my departure for Spain. You told me 'Don't be in a hurry. Rest one or two hours in the afternoon.' Indeed I have not forgotten your advice concerning resting, but I must confess—I don't rest very much. There is so much to see, so much to hear, so much to discover, so much to do.

Yesterday, for example, I was resting at noon in a café at the corner of Prado Street and St. Jerome's Road. There was a breeze, and it was very pleasant.

But I was not able to rest very long. On the other side of Prado Street I saw the many shops where they sell art objects, books, things made of leather, straw, cloth, silver and glass. I have often visited those shops but I was not able to resist the temptation to visit them again.

I also had to visit once again the Museum of Decorative Arts. I never tire of observing the folk arts, nor of asking questions of the sales people in the shop of the Museum and of the director.

Leaving the Museum, which is near the Retiro Park, I again visited the National Museum of Contemporary Art which is some three blocks from the park. I very much enjoy looking at the pictures of the great modern artists of Spain and of other countries.

Well, Mr. López, you see I am learning more every day, especially because I am very talkative. And your advice has been very useful to me, except (I must confess again) that which you gave me about resting.

Cordially,
Jane Adams

Exercise No. 139—Completion of Text

1 (Before my departure) **para España, me dijo** — (Don't be in a hurry).
2 (I have not forgotten) **sus consejos.**
3 (I do not rest) **largo rato.**
4 **Hay** (so much to discover).
5 (Yesterday) **descansaba yo** (at noon).
6 **Objetos de arte** (are sold) **en la calle.**
7 (I was not able) **resistir la tentación.**
8 (I never tire of) **mirar las artes populares.**
9 (I visited again) **el Museo Nacional de Arte Contemporáneo.**
10 (I like very much) **los cuadros de los grandes** (painters).

SEGUNDA PARTE

Grammar Notes

1 The Possessive Pronouns

In Spanish as in English there are possessive adjectives and possessive pronouns. The possessive adjectives **mi, tu, su,** etc. are important and useful words and you have learned and used them a great deal. The possessive pronouns are not of great practical importance because there are good and easy ways of avoiding them. However, you should be sufficiently familiar with these pronouns to understand them when you hear or see them used. Study the following examples:

Possessive Adjectives	Possessive Pronouns
(a)	(a)
Mi (*my*) **libro es rojo.**	**El mío** (*mine*) es rojo.
Mi (*my*) **pluma es roja.**	**La mía** (*mine*) es roja.
Mis (*my*) **libros son rojos.**	**Los míos** (*mine*) son rojos.
Mis (*my*) **plumas son rojas.**	**Las mías** (*mine*) son rojas.
(b)	(b)
Es **mi** (*my*) libro.	El libro es **mío** (*mine*)
Es **mi** (*my*) pluma.	La pluma es **mía** (*mine*).
Son **mis** (*my*) libros.	Los libros son **míos** (*mine*).
Son **mis** (*my*) plumas.	Las plumas son **mías** (*mine*).

(a) The possessive pronoun agrees in number and gender with the noun for which it stands. Each form is preceded by **el, la, los** or **las.** (Group a.)

(b) When the possessive pronoun comes after the verb **ser** the definite article is omitted. (Group b.)

(c) The complete table of possessive pronouns:

Singular		Plural		
el mío	**la mía**	**los míos**	**las mías**	mine
el tuyo	**la tuya**	**los tuyos**	**las tuyas**	yours (*fam.*)
el suyo	**la suya**	**los suyos**	**las suyas**	yours, his hers, theirs
el nuestro	**la nuestra**	**los nuestros**	**las nuestras**	ours
el vuestro	**la vuestra**	**los vuestros**	**las vuestras**	yours (*fam.*)

(d) Memorize the following common expressions in which the long form of the possessive follows the noun:

amigo mío, my friend (*m.*)	**un amigo mío,** a friend of mine
amiga mía, my friend (*f.*)	**unos amigos míos,** some friends of mine
amigos míos, my friends	**unos amigos nuestros,** some friends of ours
amigas mías, my friends (*f.*)	**unos amigos suyos,** some friends of yours

2 The Definite Article as a Pronoun

(a) **el libro de Pedro y el libro de Ana.**   Peter's book and Anna's book.

la pluma de Pedro y la pluma de Ana.   Peter's pen and Anna's pen.

los libros de Pedro y los libros de Ana.   Peter's books and Anna's books.

las plumas de Pedro y las plumas de Ana.	Peter's pens and Anna's pens.
(b) **el libro de Pedro y** *el* **de Ana.**	Peter's book and *that* of Anna.
la pluma de Pedro y *la* **de Ana.**	Peter's pen and *that* of Anna.
los libros de Pedro y *los* **de Ana.**	Peter's books and *those* of Anna.
las plumas de Pedro y *las* **de Ana.**	Peter's pens and *those* of Anna.

In group (a), the noun is repeated in each sentence. This, as you see, is monotonous. In group (b), the noun is not repeated and the article that remains is translated *that* (in the singular) and *those* (in the plural).

TERCERA PARTE

Ejercicios (Exercises) No. 140A–140B

140A. Read each sentence on the left and complete the corresponding sentence on the right with the correct possessive pronoun.

Ejemplo: ¿De quién es esta revista? Es (mine) mía.

1 **¿De quién es este traje?**	1 **Es** (mine).
2 **¿De quiénes son estos carteles?**	2 **Son** (yours).
3 **Juan y yo tenemos corbatas.**	3 **Esta es** (mine), **ésa es** (his).
4 **Ana y yo hemos comprado alfombras.**	4 **Estas son** (mine), **ésas son** (hers).
5 **Ud. y yo hemos recibido cartas.**	5 **Estas son** (mine), **y ésas son** (yours).
6 **Pablo y yo compramos billetes ayer.**	6 **Tengo los** (mine), **pero él perdió los** (his).
7 **Las revistas han llegado.**	7 **Yo he leído las** (mine); **él ha leído las** (his).
8 **Fui al cine con mi madre.**	8 **Ella fue con la** (hers).
9 **Fuimos al cine con nuestros amigos.**	9 **Ellos fueron con los** (theirs).
10 **Ellos llevaron sus juguetes.**	10 **Nosotros llevamos los** (ours).

140B. Change these sentences from the present to the imperfect and preterite. Translate each sentence.

Ejemplo: Respondo a su pregunta.	I answer his question.
Respondía a su pregunta.	I was answering his question.
Respondí a su pregunta.	I answered his question.

1 **Salgo del cuarto.**	5 **El conductor me responde.**
2 **Entramos en el museo.**	6 **Ellos no aprenden el francés.**
3 **Vemos las tiendas.**	7 **Estoy en casa.**
4 **Uds. no olvidan mis consejos.**	8 **Los jóvenes van a la corrida.**

Exercise No. 141—Preguntas

1 ¿Qué no ha olvidado la Sra. Adams?
2 ¿Por qué no descansa largo rato?
3 ¿Dónde descansaba al mediodía?
4 ¿Qué veía al otro lado de la calle?
5 ¿Ha visitado la Sra. Adams aquellas tiendas muchas veces o pocas veces?
6 ¿Qué tentación no podía resistir?
7 ¿Se cansa ella de mirar las artes populares?
8 ¿Qué museo volvió a visitar la Sra. Adams?
9 ¿A cuántas manzanas del parque está el Museo Nacional de Arte Contemporáneo?
10 ¿Le gusta mucho a la Sra. Adams mirar las pinturas de los grandes pintores?

REVISION 8

CHAPTERS 31–35 PRIMERA PARTE
Repaso de Palabras
NOUNS

1 el abogado	10 el cristal	18 el joven
2 la aldea	11 el cuadro	19 el médico
3 el ascensor	12 el dependiente	20 el orgullo
4 la brisa	13 el descanso	21 el pintor
5 el campesino	14 la dificultad	22 la sala de espera
6 la cebolla	15 la enseñanza	23 la seda
7 el coche de línea	16 la estatua	24 la tela
8 el corazón	17 la fuente	25 el viejecito
9 el conductor		

1 lawyer	10 glass	18 youth
2 village	11 picture	19 doctor
3 lift	12 employee	20 pride
4 breeze	13 rest	21 painter
5 farmer	14 difficulty	22 waiting-room
6 onion	15 education	23 silk
7 coach	16 statue	24 cloth
8 heart	17 fountain	25 little old man
9 driver		

VERBS

1 acercarse a	7 descubrir	13 hallar
2 arreglar	8 descansar	14 perder
3 asistir a	9 divertirse	15 pintar
4 cansarse	10 encantar	16 regatear
5 aconsejar	11 expresar	17 señalar
6 correr	12 gritar	18 sonar

1 to approach	7 to discover	13 to find
2 to arrange	8 to rest	14 to lose
3 to attend	9 to enjoy oneself	15 to paint
4 to get tired	10 to charm	16 to bargain
5 to advise	11 to express	17 to point out
6 to run	12 to shout	18 to sound

ADJECTIVES

1 afortunado	8 emocionante	14 sabroso
2 alegre	9 enorme	15 salvo
3 cansado	10 apuesto	16 sano
4 cuadrado	11 grueso	17 semejante
5 demasiado	12 impaciente	18 sumo
6 deseoso	13 junto	19 vacío
7 divertido		

1 lucky
2 happy
3 tired
4 square
5 too much
6 eager
7 enjoyable

8 exciting
9 enormous
10 handsome
11 thick
12 impatient
13 together

14 tasty
15 safe
16 sound (healthy)
17 similar
18 greatest
19 empty

ADVERBS

1 ayer

1 yesterday

2 anteayer

2 day before yesterday

3 anoche

3 last night

4 enfrente

4 in front

PREPOSITIONS

1 dentro de

1 inside of

2 excepto

2 except

3 junto a

3 close to

4 según

4 according to

CONJUNCTIONS

1 mientras(que)

1 while

2 antes de que

2 before

3 puesto que

3 since

IMPORTANT EXPRESSIONS

1 al día siguiente
2 de repente
3 dar un paseo
4 es decir
5 largo rato
6 llamar por teléfono

7 pensar (+ infin.)
8 por entero
9 sano y salvo
10 darse la mano
11 voy aprendiendo

1 on the following day
2 suddenly
3 to take a walk
4 that is to say
5 a long time
6 to telephone

7 to intend to
8 entirely
9 safe and sound
10 to shake hands
11 I am learning

Note: **voy aprendiendo = estoy aprendiendo. Ir** is often used like **estar** to form the present progressive.

SEGUNDA PARTE

Ejercicio 142   For each Spanish word give the related Spanish word suggested by the English word in parentheses.

Ejemplo: 1. comer (the meal) — la comida

1 **comer** (the meal)
2 **difícil** (the difficulty)
3 **hablar** (talkative)
4 **divertirse** (enjoyable)
5 **el viaje** (to travel)
6 **segundo** (secondary)
7 **la ventana** (the little window)

8 **caminar** (the road)
9 **pintar** (the painting)
10 **preguntar** (the question)
11 **responder** (the answer)
12 **llegar** (the arrival)
13 **fácil** (easily)
14 **el campo** (the farmer)

Ejercicio 143 Translate each verb form and give the infinitive of the verb.

Ejemplo: **dijeron,** they said, **decir**

1 pudo	6 Ud. dijo	11 Uds. hicieron
2 quise	7 tuvimos	12 vine
3 pusieron	8 di	13 hizo
4 vi	9 fue	14 tuviste
5 leyeron	10 pidió	15 supe

Ejercicio 144 Select the group of words in Column II which best completes each sentence begun in Column I.

I

1 Mientras nuestro coche de línea pasaba por las aldeas,
2 Las mujeres lavaban ropa y
3 Por todas partes había puestos
4 Le gustaba mucho un muchacho
5 Cuando le encontró,
6 Escuchando la conversación de las mujeres,
7 ¿Recuerda Ud. las conversaciones
8 Yo estaba sentado al mediodía en el parque
9 Debajo de los árboles, en el parque
10 Mientras la Sra. Adams se divertía en España.

II

(a) el Sr. López sufría el calor de Londres.
(b) donde se vendían cosas corrientes.
(c) había una brisa fresca.
(d) en que hablábamos de los mercados de España?
(e) los hombres trabajaban en los campos.
(f) charlando con un estudiante.
(g) que cuidaba un puesto.
(h) el muchacho arreglaba su mercancía.
(i) la Sra. Adams podía comprender todo lo que (all that) **decían.**
(j) chocó (it collided) **con otro.**

Ejercicio 145 Complete each sentence by selecting that tense which makes good sense. Translate each sentence.

Ejemplo: 1. **Ayer recibí un paquete.**   Yesterday I received a package.

1 Ayer —— un paquete. (recibí, recibiré, recibo)
2 Mañana —— en casa. (quedé, quedaré, quedo)
3 Anoche no —— al cine. (vamos, iremos, fuimos)
4 Ahora —— las maletas. (hicieron, hacen, harán)
5 El maestro habla y los alumnos ——. (escuchan, escucharán, escucharon)

6 ¿—— Uds. de la ciudad pasado mañana? (salen, saldrán, salieron)
7 ¿Le ——Ud. anteayer? (vio, ve, verá)
8 El año que viene —— en Europa. (viaja, viajé, viajaré)
9 ¿Qué está diciendo él? No —— oirle. (pudimos, podemos, podremos)
10 Yo —— la semana pasada. (llegué, llego, llegaré)

TERCERA PARTE

Diálogo

En la gasolinera

Practise the Spanish aloud:

La Sra. Adams necesita gasolina y ha entrado en una gasolinera.
En seguida se acerca al coche un joven para servirla.
— Buenas tardes, — le saluda el joven.
— Muy buenas, — le contesta la Sra. Adams. — ¿Me hace el favor de llenarme el depósito de gasolina?
— ¿Regular o super?
— Super. ¿Y quiere Ud. comprobar el aceite, el agua y el aire?
— Con mucho gusto, señora, — le contesta el empleado.
El joven llena el depósito, revisa el aceite, el agua y la presión de aire en los neumáticos. Luego vuelve a la Sra. Adams.
— Todo está bien, — le dice a nuestra turista.
— Muchas gracias, ¿y cuánto le debo?
Dos mil pesetas.
La Sra. Adams le da un billete de cinco mil pesetas. El joven se[1] lo cambia, entregándole tres mil pesetas. La Sra. Adams cuenta el cambio y ve que todo está en orden.
— Está bien, — le dice al empleado. — Muchas gracias y muy buenas tardes.
— Muy buenas y feliz viaje, — le contesta el joven.

Mrs. Adams needs petrol and has gone into a petrol station.
Immediately a young man approaches the car to serve her.
'Good afternoon,' the young man greets her.
'Good afternoon to you,' Mrs. Adams answers. 'Will you please fill the tank with petrol?'
'Regular or super?'
'Super. And do you want to check the oil, the water and the air?'
'With pleasure, madam,' the employee replies.
The young man fills the tank, checks the oil, the water and the air pressure in the tyres. Then he returns to Mrs. Adams.
'Everything is all right,' he says to our tourist.
'Many thanks, and how much do I owe you?'
'2,000 pesetas.'
Mrs. Adams gives him a five-thousand-peseta note. The young man

changes it for her, returning to her 3,000 pesetas. Mrs. Adams counts the change and sees that everything is in order.

'All right,' she says to the employee. 'Many thanks and very good afternoon.'

'Very good afternoon and happy voyage,' the young man answers her.

NOTE: 1. The indirect objects **le** (*to* or *for him, her, you*) and **les** (*to* or *for them, you*) become **se** before any other object pronoun that begins with the letter **l**. Complete treatment of *two object pronouns* will be found in Capítulo 39.

LECTURA 1
Exercise No. 146—Una visita a La Granja

En cierta ocasión la Sra. Adams llevó a los hijos del Sr. Carrillo a una excursión al pueblo de La Granja, que está situado a unos 3.500 pies sobre el nivel del mar, en la Sierra de Guadarrama.

El pueblo no está muy lejos de la capital y nuestra amiga llegó sin dificultad. Al llegar (On arriving) al pueblo, tuvo una idea muy luminosa. Propuso (She proposed) una merienda al aire libre, cerca del Palacio Real. Los muchachos aceptaron el proyecto con entusiasmo.

La Sra. Adams entró en una tienda de comestibles, compró dos latas (tins) de sardinas con salsa de tomate. Luego compró unas tortas y unos pasteles en una pastelería. Por último, compró unas naranjas y varios tomates en una verdulería.

Quedó (There remained) el problema de los refrescos. Entonces uno de los muchachos tuvo una idea luminosa. — ¿Por qué no comprar unas botellas de gaseosa? Siempre hay muchos vendedores de refrescos fríos.

— Estupenda idea, — comentó la Sra. Adams.

Luego empezaron a explorar La Granja. El rey Felipe V escogió este sitio tranquilo y hermoso para su residencia de verano. Hizo construir un palacio. Se dice que el palacio con sus jardines se parece a Versalles en miniatura. Hay fuentes y un lago artificial. A la Sra. Adams le interesó también la antigua fábrica de vidrio. Después de su paseo, hallaron un lugar muy tranquilo. La Sra. Adams abrió las latas de sardinas y preparó unos bocadillos que comieron con los tomates. Para beber tuvieron la gaseosa que habían comprado y por fin tuvieron de postre las sabrosas naranjas. Era una merienda estupenda y los muchachos quedaron (were—*lit.* remained) encantados. No olvidarán esta experiencia en muchos años.

LECTURA 2
Exercise No. 147—En el Rastro

En todas las grandes ciudades del mundo hay un 'mercado de pulgas'. En Madrid se llama el Rastro. ¿Quiere Ud. comprar una sartén o un traje de luces usado de un torero? Aquí, en este mercado pintoresco, hallará Ud. todo. El Rastro se compone de dos partes — en una parte se venden antigüedades, en la otra artículos de segunda mano. Un domingo por la mañana la Sra. Adams fue al Rastro y pasó allí unas horas muy agradables y divertidas. Miró todas las mercancías. La encantaron sobre todo unos dibujos del siglo 18, y unos artículos de cerámica del siglo pasado. Por supuesto, compró todo lo que podía. Vio también unas sillas antiguas, pero le faltaba el dinero. Además, pensó, eran demasiado grandes y pesadas. En su próxima visita las comprará sin falta.

CHAPTER 36

LA PLAZA

PRIMERA PARTE

FOREWORD

In Chapters 36–41 there is no parallel translation of the texts. However, the new words and expressions that appear are given in the vocabularies which follow each text. There is also the Spanish–English vocabulary in the Appendix to which you can refer for words you may have forgotten.

You should therefore have no difficulty in reading and understanding the texts. As a means of testing your understanding a series of English questions to be answered in English are given under the heading 'Test of Reading Comprehension', instead of the usual Spanish Preguntas. You can check your answers in the Answers Section of the Appendix.

LA PLAZA

Sexta Carta de España

Querido amigo:

En nuestras conversaciones hemos hablado de muchas cosas, pero no me acuerdo de ninguna conversación sobre las plazas españolas. Tengo ganas de escribirle a Ud. mis impresiones sobre ellas.

He notado que cada pueblo en España tiene su 'corazón'. Es la plaza. Todo el mundo va a la plaza para el descanso, para los negocios, para el recreo, para todo.

Así pensaba yo mientras estaba sentada en una de las pequeñas plazas de Madrid.

Cada plaza es distinta. Algunas son redondas, otras son cuadradas. Grandes arboles crecen en algunas. En otras no se ven más que algunas pocas hojas secas de quién sabe qué pobre arbolito.

Muchas veces hay arcadas a un lado o a dos lados de la plaza. En los portales se encuentran (*are found*) toda clase de tiendas — papelerías, farmacias, mercerías, joyerías, librerías. Casi siempre hay un café. Allí se reúnen los hombres (*the men get together*) por la tarde, para charlar o para leer el periódico mientras toman un chato, es decir un pequeño vaso de vino tinto o blanco, y comen pinchos — trocitos de pescado frito o de chorizo, gambas o queso.

Antes de la cena, se reúnen en los cafés las tertulias. La tertulia es un grupo de amigos que se reúne regularmente para discutir todos los asuntos.

El hotel del pueblo puede estar en la plaza principal. También se ve allí una iglesia antigua.

El aspecto de la plaza cambia a cada hora. Por la mañana temprano se ven (*one sees*) solamente algunos viajeros cansados que van al mercado. Más tarde vienen los niños que son demasiado pequeños para ir a la escuela. Las madres se sientan en los bancos para charlar.

Durante las horas de la siesta hay pocas personas en la plaza. Algunos descansan en los bancos, otras duermen. Hace calor. A eso de las cuatro comienza otra vez la vida de la plaza.

El domingo por la tarde se reúne todo el mundo en la plaza para 'el paseo'. Los muchachos caminan en una dirección (*in one direction*), las muchachas en la otra (*in the other*).

Finalmente llega la noche. La plaza se pone tranquila. Se ven solamente algunos viajeros que vienen del mercado. La plaza duerme.

Reciba un cordial saludo de su amiga,
Juana Adams

Vocabulario

la arcada	arcade	**el trocito**	little piece
el aspecto	appearance	**la tertulia**	regular gathering of
el asunto	subject, topic		friends
el contrario	opposite	**discutir**	to discuss
el corazón	heart	**el paseo**	promenade
la farmacia	chemist's	**el rumbo**	direction
la hoja	leaf	**crecer**	to grow
la joyería	jewellery shop	**reunirse**	to get together
la iglesia	church	**cansado**	tired
la librería	book shop	**cuadrado**	square-shaped
la mercería	haberdashery	**cuidado**	kept, cared for
la papelería	stationery shop	**redondo**	round
la plaza	square	**seco**	dry
el chato	small glass of wine	**mientras tanto**	in the meantime
el pincho	tidbit		

Exercise No. 148—Test of Reading Comprehension

Answer these questions in English. They will test your comprehension of the text.

1 What has every town?
2 Why does everybody go to the plaza?
3 What grows in some plazas?

4 What does one see in others?
5 Name six kinds of shops which are found in the arcades.
6 For what purpose do the men get together in the café in the evenings?
7 What do they drink?
8 What do they eat?
9 What does one see in the main plaza?
10 What do some people do in the plaza during the siesta hour?
11 At what time does the life of the plaza begin again?
12 What happens on Sunday afternoons?
13 How do the boys and girls promenade?
14 Whom does one see in the plaza at night?

Exercise No. 149—Completion of Text

1 (The heart of each town) **es la plaza.**
2 **Así pensaba yo** (while I was seated) **en la plaza.**
3 (One sees nothing more) **que unas pocas hojas secas.**
4 **Hay arcadas** (where one finds) **toda clase de tiendas.**
5 **Los hombres** (get together) **en el café** (in the evening).
6 **Toman chatos** (of red or white wine).
7 **Comen** (tidbits), **trocitos de** (fried fish or sausage).
8 **También se ve allí** (an old church).
9 (One sees) **algunos viajeros** (tired).
10 (Later) **vienen los niños** (who) **son** (too small) **para ir a la escuela.**

SEGUNDA PARTE

Grammar Notes

1 The Present and Preterite of **dormir (ue)** to sleep.

Present		Preterite	
I sleep, etc.		I slept, etc.	
duermo	**dormimos**	**dormí**	**dormimos**
duermes	**dormís**	**dormiste**	**dormisteis**
duerme	**duermen**	**durmió**	**durmieron**

Present Participle: **durmiendo**

2 Relative Pronouns

(a) **que,** who, whom, which, that

que is the most commonly used relative. Like the English *that* it can refer to persons or things, except with prepositions, when it may refer only to things.

El sombrero que compré me sienta mal.   The hat which I bought fits me badly.

¿Dónde está el muchacho que perdió su libro?	Where is the boy who lost his book?
¿Dónde está la cesta de que Ud. habló?	Where is the basket of which you spoke?

(b) **quien, quienes** (plural), who, whom

quien and **quienes** refer only to persons. When they are used as a direct object the personal **a** is required.

Los hombres de quienes hablé son abogados.	The men of whom I spoke are lawyers.
El niño a quien buscábamos está en casa.	The child whom we were looking for is at home.

(c) **lo que** what (that which), **todo lo que,** all that

Sé lo que dijo.	I know what he said.
Le diré a Ud. todo lo que he aprendido.	I will tell you all that I have learned.

(d) **cuyo (o, os, as)** whose, must immediately precede the noun it modifies, and must agree with it in number and gender.

Buscan las calles *cuyos* nombres son fechas.	They are looking for the streets whose names are dates.
¿Dónde está el hombre *cuya* casa hemos comprado?	Where is the man whose house we have bought?

(e) **donde, en donde, a donde, de donde** may often take the place of a relative pronoun.

La casa *en donde* vive es antigua.	The house in which (where) he lives is old.
No conozco la escuela *a donde* van los niños.	I do not know the school to which (where) the children go.

(f) **el cual (la cual, los cuales, las cuales),** that, which, who, whom

These longer forms of the relative pronouns are used to make clear to which of two possible antecedents the relative clause refers.

Visité a la esposa del Sr. Carrillo, la cual toca bien el piano.	I visited the wife of Mr. Carrillo, who plays the piano well.

TERCERA PARTE
Ejercicios (Exercises) No. 150A–150B

150A. Use the correct verb forms with these subjects:

1 (**Yo**) sleep
2 (**Yo**) am not sleeping
3 (**Quién**) sleeps?
4 (**Nosotros**) sleep
5 Do you sleep (**Ud.**)?
6 Sleep (**Ud.**) (*Imperative*)
7 Do not sleep (**Uds.**)
8 (**El niño**) sleeps

9 **(La niña)** is not sleeping   11 **(Ellos)** sleep

10 **(Quiénes)** sleep?   12 **(Nadie)** is sleeping

150B. Complete these sentences by using the correct relative pronoun.

Ejemplo: Déme el lápiz que compré.

1 **Déme el lápiz** (which) **compré.**

2 **¿Dónde está el alumno** (whose) **libro tengo?**

3 **Los muchachos** (who) **eran diligentes aprendieron mucho.**

4 **Aquí está la pintura** (of which) **hablábamos.**

5 **Las palabras** (which) **aprendemos son difíciles.**

6 (What, that which) **le dije a Ud. es verdad.**

7 **Me dio** (all that) **quise.**

8 **La casa** (which) **compró es de piedra.**

9 **Allí están las señoritas** (of whom) **hablábamos.**

10 **La Sra. Adams,** (who) **estaba sentada detrás de su escritorio, se levantó.**

NOTE: Use **que** for *who* (sentence 3). If the relative clause can be omitted without changing the sense or clarity of the sentence use **quien** (sentence 10).

CHAPTER 37

UN PASEO AL VALLE DE LOS CAÍDOS

PRIMERA PARTE

Séptima Carta de España

Querido amigo:

Ayer llamé por teléfono a los hijos del Sr. Carrillo y les pregunté — ¿Quieren Uds. pasear en coche conmigo? Aceptaron con alegría.

Quería (*I wanted*) volver a tiempo para ir a un concierto por la noche. Así es que muy temprano nos encontramos (*we met*) los tres delante de mi hotel. Saqué (*I took out*) el coche del garaje donde lo había alquilado (*I had rented*) para el día. Charlando y riendo con animación nos pusimos en marcha (*we set out*).

Pasamos por los alrededores de la ciudad. Vimos de vez en cuando unas casas pequeñas. Más allá (*further on*) vimos las montañas a lo lejos.

Yo conducía el coche y de repente oí un sonido que inmediatamente conocí. — ¿Qué pasa? — preguntaron los jóvenes.

Paré (*I stopped*) el coche y bajamos. — Tenemos un pinchazo, — contesté yo.

Yo quería cambiar el neumático y los jóvenes estaban muy deseosos de ayudarme. Los dos, muy contentos, comenzaron a buscar el gato. ¡Ay! No había ningún gato (*there was no jack*) en la maleta. ¿Qué hacer?

De vez en cuando pasaba un coche a toda velocidad. A pesar de nuestras señales nadie paró. Era casi mediodía y había mucho sol. Nos sentamos bajo un pequeño árbol al lado del camino, para esperar.

Pronto Carlos vio en el horizonte un gran camión. Se acercó (*It approached*) rápidamente y paró delante de nuestro árbol. El conductor bajó.

— ¿Tienen Uds. un pinchazo? — dijo sonriendo. ¿Me permiten Uds. ayudarles?

— ¡Ya lo creo! — le respondí. Tenemos un pinchazo y nos hace falta un gato.

El conductor nos prestó su gato y nos ayudó a cambiar la rueda. Afortunadamente teníamos un neumático de repuesto (*a spare tyre*)[1].

Le di mil gracias al hombre y le ofrecí cien pesetas, pero no quiso aceptarlas. Entonces nos dimos la mano y nos despedimos.

Seguimos nuestro camino hasta que llegamos al Valle de los Caídos, en Cuelgamuros, que está entre el Escorial y Guadarrama. Hay una basílica subterránea y una necrópolis construídas en homenaje a las víctimas de la Guerra Civil. Encima se alza (*rises*) una magnífica cruz gigante, que tiene 135 m de altura. Los jóvenes subieron corriendo al pie de la cruz. Yo subí muy despacio, pero sin embargo llegué a la cima algo jadeante (*somewhat out of breath*). Desde allí, como Ud. sabe, hay una vista maravillosa del valle entero.

Después de tomar la comida que me habían preparado (*they had prepared*) en el hotel, subimos otra vez al coche y regresamos, cansados pero muy contentos.

Le saluda cordialmente su amiga
Juana Adams

NOTE: 1. Or **rueda de recambio.**

Vocabulario

el camión	lorry	**riendo**	laughing
el gato	car-jack, cat	**sonreír**	to smile
la maleta	boot (of car); suitcase	**ancho**	wide
		deseoso	eager
el neumático	tyre	**jadeante**	out of breath
(de repuesto)[1]	(spare)	**subterráneo**	underground
el paseo	walk, stroll, ride	**el valle**	valley
el pinchazo	puncture, flat tyre	**los Caídos**	the fallen
		la víctima	the victim (always feminine, even when the 'victim' is a man)
la señal	signal		
el sonido	sound		
la tierra	land		
correr	to run	**el homenaje**	homage
ofrecer	to offer	**entero**	entire
conducir	to drive	**a pesar de**	in spite of
regresar	to return	**algo**	somewhat, something
reír	to laugh	**!ay!**	oh!

NOTE: 1. or **de recambio.**

Expresiones Importantes

a lo lejos	in the distance	**hacer falta**	to be missing
a tiempo	on time	**nos hace falta un gato**	we need a jack
a toda velocidad	at full speed		
dar mil gracias	to thank a thousand times	**pasear en coche**	to go on a car ride
		ponerse en marcha	to set out
nada más que	nothing but, only	**sin embargo**	nevertheless
de vez en cuando	from time to time		

Exercise No. 151—Test of Reading Comprehension

Answer these questions in English:

1 Where did Mrs. Adams want to go?
2 Whom did she invite to go with her?
3 Where did they meet at an early hour?
4 How had Mrs. Adams obtained a car?
5 What did they see on the road from time to time?
6 What did they see in the distance?
7 What happened when Mrs. Adams was driving?
8 Why weren't they able to change the tyre?
9 What time of day was it?
10 How did they finally manage to put on the spare tyre?
11 How did Mrs. Adams try to show her appreciation of the lorry driver's help?
12 How did Mrs. Adams climb to the foot of the giant cross, and how did she feel on reaching the top?
13 How did the boys go up?
14 What can one see from the foot of the cross?
15 How did they feel when they returned?

Exercise No. 152—Completion of Text

1 ¿Irá Ud. (with me by car) **al Valle de los Caídos?**
2 (The young men accepted) **la invitación** (with joy).
3 (We met) **delante de mi hotel.**
4 (I took the car) **del garaje.**
5 (I had rented it) **para el día.**
6 (Chatting and laughing) **subimos en el coche.**
7 (From time to time) **vimos unas pequeñas casas.**
8 (We saw nothing but) **las montañas.**
9 (Suddenly) **oí un sonido.**
10 ¿(What happened?) — **preguntaron.**
11 **Yo quería** (to change the tyre) **pero** (there was no jack).
12 (In spite of) **nuestras señales nadie** (stopped).
13 **Dijimos al conductor** — (We need a jack).
14 **Nos prestó un gato** (and helped us change the tyre).
15 **Entonces** (we shook hands) **y** (took leave of one another).

SEGUNDA PARTE

Grammar Notes

1 The Past Perfect Tense. Model Verbs, **hablar, aprender, vivir.**

Singular

había hablado (aprendido, vivido)	I had spoken (learned, lived)
habías hablado (aprendido, vivido)	you had spoken (learned, lived)
Ud. **él** **había hablado** **ella** **(aprendido, vivido)**	**you** **he, it** had spoken **she, it** (learned, lived)

Plural

habíamos hablado (aprendido, vivido)	we had spoken (learned, lived)
habíais hablado (aprendido, vivido)	you had spoken (learned, lived)
Uds. **ellos** **habían hablado** **ellas** **(aprendido, vivido)**	**you** **they** had spoken (learned, lived)

(a) As in English, the past perfect tense in Spanish is formed by the auxiliary verb **había** (*had*), plus the past participle of the verb. **Había** is the imperfect of **haber,** *to have.*

2 Verbs with Spelling Changes.

Note the Spelling Changes in these verbs.

sacar, to take out

present		preterite	
saco	**sacamos**	*saqué*	**sacamos**
sacas	**sacáis**	**sacaste**	**sacasteis**
saca	**sacan**	**sacó**	**sacaron**

imperative

saque Ud.   *saquen Uds.*

llegar, to arrive

present		preterite	
llego	**llegamos**	*llegué*	**llegamos**
llegas	**llegáis**	**llegaste**	**llegasteis**
llega	**llegan**	**llegó**	**llegaron**

imperative

llegue Ud.   *lleguen Uds.*

(a) In verbs whose infinitives end in **-car** or **-gar, c** must become **qu** and **g** must become **gu** before the endings **e** and **en,** in order to keep the pronunciation of **c** and **g,** as found in the infinitive.

(b) Other verbs ending in **-car** or **-gar** are: **buscar** to look for; **acercarse (a)** to approach; **pagar** to pay.

TERCERA PARTE

Ejercicios (Exercises) No. 153A–153B

153A. In the following sentences fill in the correct auxiliary verb in the past perfect tense. Translate the sentence.

Ejemplo: **(Nosotros) habíamos aprendido español en España.**

We had learned Spanish in Spain.

1 (Nosotros) —— **visto la película.**
2 ¿—— **leído Ud. muchos libros?**
3 ¿Quién —— **abierto la ventana?**
4 **Los hijos no** —— **dormido durante la noche.**
5 **Yo no** —— **creído el cuento.**
6 (Nosotros) —— **volado sobre las montañas.**
7 **Ellos** —— **ido al teatro.**
8 ¿—— **tenido Ud. un buen viaje?**
9 **Uds. no** —— **dicho nada.**
10 ¿—— **comido (tú) los dulces, Juanito?**

153B. Complete in Spanish:

1 (He had bought) **los billetes.**
2 (I had seen) **la película.**
3 (We had eaten) **la comida.**
4 ¿(Had they received) **la carta?**
5 ¿(Had you set) **la mesa?**
6 (You **[Uds.]** had not heard) **el cuento.**
7 (You **[tú]** had not slept) **bien.**
8 **El hombre** (had seated himself) **en el banco.**
9 (They had had) **un pinchazo.**
10 (We had said) **nada.**
11 ¿**Qué** (had happened)?
12 (They had not found) **el gato.**
13 ¿**Por qué** (had they not changed) **el neumático?**
14 **El conductor** (had approached) **a nosotros.**

CHAPTER 38

LA SEÑORA ADAMS COMPRA UN BILLETE DE LOTERÍA

PRIMERA PARTE

Octava Carta de España

Querido amigo:

Yo no soy jugadora, Sr. López. Es decir, hasta la semana pasada nunca había sido (*I had never been*) jugadora.

¿Qué pasó? Oiga bien. Le contaré a Ud. todo.

Como Ud. sabe mejor que yo, hay en todas las esquinas del centro de la capital un vendedor, y muchas veces dos vendedores, de billetes de lotería. Cuando llegué a España noté inmediatamente que todo el mundo compraba billetes de lotería. ¿Quién no quiere hacerse rico (*to get rich*)? Yo pensaba en la posibilidad de ganar uno de los muchos premios menores o, tal vez el premio gordo. El año que viene haría (*I would take*) viajes por toda España. Llevaría (*I would take*) conmigo a toda la familia. Los niños aprenderían (*would learn*) a hablar español. Podría (*I would be able*) volver a visitar a mis amigos en España. Pasaría (*I would spend*) mucho tiempo en las ciudades y pueblos de España que todavía no conozco.

Caminaría (*I would walk*) por todos los mercados para hablar con la gente del campo y para aprender más de la vida y de las costumbres de España. Compraría (*I would buy*) objetos de arte, pero no para venderlos, sino para mi casa.

Así soñaba yo.

El miércoles de la semana pasada paseaba por la Gran Vía. Vi en la esquina, como siempre, a una señora que vendía billetes de lotería. Como siempre, me dijo la señora — Compre Ud. este billete afortunado.

— Pero, señora, — le respondí, — todos estos billetes son afortunados, ¿verdad?

— No, señora, — me dijo. — Le he guardado a Ud. (*I have kept for you*) éste. Mire Ud. Tiene tres ceros.

Yo no sabía que quería decir 'tres ceros'. Pero una voz por dentro (*within*) me dijo — ¡Compra!

Y me hice jugadora.

Al día siguiente yo leía en el periódico los números que ganaron. Naturalmente no esperaba nada. De repente vi un número con tres ceros, el número 26.000. ¡Yo había ganado un premio de doscientas mil (200.000) pesetas!

266

Busqué (*I looked for*) mi billete. Y mientras buscaba, hacía (*I was making*) viajes con toda la familia. ...

Al fin encontré el billete en un bolsillo. Muy impaciente lo miré. Había tres ceros. Había un dos. Pero — ¡qué lástima! Había también un '5'. Yo tenía el número veinticinco mil (25.000).

¿Pero qué importa? Desde aquel momento, fui jugadora.

Le saluda cordialmente su amiga.

Juana Adams

Vocabulario

el billete de lotería	lottery ticket	**ganar**	to win
el bolsillo	pocket	**guardar**	to keep
la esquina	corner	**hacerse**	to become
el cero	zero	**pasar**	to happen, to pass
el jugador	player, gambler	**pasear**	to stroll
el premio	prize	**soñar (ue)**	to dream
el premio gordo	first (grand) prize	**afortunado**	lucky
		gordo	fat
la voz	voice	**impaciente**	impatiently
buscar	to look for	**siguiente**	following
busqué	I looked for		

me hice jugador, -a   I became a gambler

Note the difference between **sonar (*ue*)** to sound, ring; and **soñar (ue)** to dream. **Tengo sueño:** I am sleepy.

Exercise No. 154—Test of Reading Comprehension

Answer these questions in English.

1 What kind of woman had Mrs. Adams never been?
2 What had she noted when she came to Spain?
3 What possibility was she thinking of?
4 After winning the first prize, to what country would she take trips?
5 Whom would she visit again?
6 What would she buy for her house?
7 From whom did Mrs. Adams buy a ticket with three zeros?
8 What was she reading in the newspaper next day?
9 What did she suddenly see?
10 What did she think when she saw the number with three zeros?
11 What was she dreaming of doing while she looked for her ticket?
12 What number did Mrs. Adams have?
13 What number won the prize?
14 What expression does Mrs. Adams use to show that she doesn't take the matter seriously?
15 Translate: **Desde aquel momento, fui jugadora.**

Exercise No. 155—Completion of Text

1 **Cuando** (I arrived) **a España** (everybody) **compraba billetes de lotería.**

2 **Había vendedores** (on all corners).

3 **Tal vez ganaré** (the first prize).

4 **Podría** (to visit again) **a mis amigos.**

5 **Llevaría conmigo** (the whole family).

6 **Así** (I was dreaming).

7 **Compré el billete** (with three zeros).

8 **No sabía** (what the three zeros meant).

9 (The numbers which won) **estaban en el periódico.**

10 (I looked for) **mi billete.**

11 (At last) **lo encontré** (in a pocket).

12 **Sí** (there were) **tres ceros, pero** (there was not) **un seis.**

SEGUNDA PARTE

Grammar Notes

1 The Present Conditional. Model Verbs—**hablar, aprender, vivir.**

The conditional may be called the *would* form of the verb. Its use in Spanish is much the same as in English.

hablar-ía	I would speak		**hablar-íamos**	we would speak	
hablar-ías	you would speak		**hablar-íais**	you would speak	
Ud. ⎫	you ⎫		**Uds.** ⎫	you ⎫	
él ⎬ **hablar-ía**	he, it ⎬ would speak		**ellos** ⎬ **hablar-ían**	you ⎬ would speak	
ella ⎭	she, it ⎭		**ellas** ⎭	they ⎭	

(a) The conditional endings of all verbs are:

singular: **-ía, -ías, -ía**   plural: **-íamos, íais, -ían**

(b) To form the regular conditional add these endings to the *whole* infinitive just as you do with the endings of the future. Thus: **hablar-ía, aprender-ía, vivir-ía, ser-ía, estar-ía.**

(c) The endings of the conditional are the same as those of **-er** and **-ir** verbs in the imperfect. But remember:

The endings of the conditional are added on to the *whole infinitive*. The endings of the imperfect are added to the *stem of the verb* after the infinitive ending has been removed.

imperfect		conditional	
aprendía	I was learning	**aprendería**	I would learn
vivía	I was living	**viviría**	I would live

2 The Irregular Conditional

Those verbs that have a change in the infinitive base for the future have the same changes in the conditional.

Infinitive	Future	Conditional
	I shall, etc.	I would, etc.
saber	(yo) sabré	(yo) sabría
poder	podré	podría
querer	querré	querría
decir	diré	diría
hacer	haré	haría
haber	habré	habría
venir	(yo) vendré	(yo) vendría
tener	tendré	tendría
salir	saldré	saldría
poner	pondré	pondría
valer	valdré	valdría

Ejercicios (Exercises) No. 156A–156B

156A. Change the following sentences from the future to the present conditional. Translate each sentence in the conditional.

> **Ejemplo:** Future: **Haremos viajes.** We shall take trips.
> Conditional: **Haríamos viajes.** We would take trips.

1 Iremos a la Puerta del Sol.
2 Juan venderá sus billetes de sombra.
3 No ganarán el premio.
4 Ud. encontrará a sus amigos.
5 Leeré muchas guías de viajero.
6 ¿Llevará Ud. a su familia a España?
7 ¿Les gustarán a Uds. los mercados?
8 Saldré de mi casa a las siete.
9 No podremos hacer los ejercicios.
10 No dirán nada.

156B. Translate:

1 I would learn
2 he would write
3 they would go
4 we would eat
5 she would speak
6 would you (**Ud.**) work?
7 would John see?
8 who would visit?
9 I would not travel
10 would they study?
11 I would make
12 he would come
13 they would not want
14 would you (**Ud.**) go out?
15 you (**Uds.**) would put

CHAPTER 39

LA SEÑORA ADAMS APRENDE MÁS COSAS DE ESPAÑA, CONSERVACIÓN, DEPORTES Y JUEGOS

PRIMERA PARTE

Novena Carta de España

Querido amigo:

Era sábado. Yo había visitado al Sr. Carrillo en su oficina y estábamos para salir (*we were about to leave*). Vi un anuncio de una corrida de Toros en el periódico que estaba sobre la mesa y pregunté al Sr. Carrillo: ¿Son los españoles muy aficionados a los Toros?—El Sr. Carrillo sonrió y me dio una respuesta inesperada.—Aparte de Andalucía en el sur, lo que entusiasma a los españoles no son los Toros sino el Fútbol. Hay tantos hinchas (*fans*) como en Inglaterra. El Fútbol es en realidad la verdadera Fiesta Nacional. Los Toros subsisten por el apoyo tradicional de una minoría, y se fomentan con fines turísticos.

Ya sé,—continuó mi amigo,—que los españoles tienen mala reputación respecto al trato de los animales. Pero no se la merecen completamente. Hay un puñado de gentes totalmente consagradas al cuidado, protección y supervivencia del mundo animal y de la Naturaleza virgen. Por Decreto de 27 de octubre de 1969, España creó el Parque Nacional de Doñana de 32.000 hectáreas.

Doñana está situada en las marismas del río Guadalquivir. Es un paraíso en donde se encuentran muchas especies de aves acuáticas y también otros animales como el lince español. El organismo internacional cuya sigla es WWF (World Wildlife Fund en inglés, o sea Fondo mundial para los animales salvajes) ayudó a salvar Doñana que estuvo en peligro de desaparecer.

España cuenta por el momento con varios Parques Nacionales.* El Parque Nacional de Covadonga o de Peña Santa fue el primero que se creó en España en 1918. Tiene una fauna abundante y variada: gato montés, jabalíes, zorros, lobos y algunos osos.

En el mismo año se declaró también Parque Nacional el Valle de Ordesa en el Pirineo Aragonés. El Parque Nacional del Teide, Tenerife (Canarias) se creó en 1954 así como el de la Caldera de Teburiente, también en Canarias. En 1955 se crearon los de Aïgues Tortes y el Lago de San Maurico en el Pirineo, Tablas de Daimiel en La Mancha y más recientemente dos más en Canarias.[1]

NOTE: 1. 1981 Timanfaya en la isla de Lanzarote y Garajonai en la isla de Gomera.
*The official body for conservation is ICONA (Instituto de Conservacion de la Naturaleza). Can be equated to the British Nature Conservancy Council. There are also private bodies, e.g. ADELPHA (Asociacion de Defensa Ecologic del Patrimonio Ecológico Histórico-Artístico.

Hay mucho que hacer todavía en este aspecto, especialmente en cuanto a la educación. Pero, con el desarrollo tan rápido de la industria y la polución que resulta, el español actual (*present-day*) está empezando a volverse de espaldas a la ciudad e interesarse por la naturaleza virgen. Es un buen comienzo y hemos puesto ya nuestro granito de arena en la Conservación y respeto al medio ambiente. Nuestro gran pensador José Ortega y Gasset dijo—El hombre se cree estar en el centro del Universo y sólo le pertenece un rinconcito—. El español actual empieza a darse cuenta de que esto tiene sentido.

Pero no se acabó aquí el Sr. Carrillo. Continuó—También se practican deportes de invierno, especialmente el esquí (*skiing*), en los Centros deportivos del Guadarrama a unos pocos kilómetros de Madrid y en los Pirineos. España tuvo hace años, una medalla de oro en los Juegos Olímpicos de invierno.

Actividades más sosegadas como el ajedrez (*chess*) también se practican en toda España. En muchísimos pueblos del Nordeste, en Cataluña, es el juego corriente de los lugareños en los cafés.

Quedé muy impresionada por la plática del Sr. Carrillo, que me ofreció un nuevo aspecto de España que ignoraba (*which I was unaware of*) como lo ignoran la mayor parte de los turistas.

Ud. verá que sigo aprendiendo muchas cosas nuevas de España.

Cordialmente,
Juana Adams.

Vocabulario

el aficionado	amateur, fan	**el desarrollo**	development
el aficionado al	football fan	**la polución**	pollution
fútbol or		**virgen**	virgin,
hincha			unspoiled
el apoyo	support	**el granito de**	grain of sand
el trato	treatment	**arena**	
el puñado	handful	**el medio**	environment
el decreto	decree	**ambiente**	
la hectárea	hectare	**la supervivencia**	survival
la marisma	marsh	**los toros**	bulls, bullfight
el paraíso	paradise	**pertenecer**	to belong to
el lince	lynx	**consagrar**	to devote
el organismo	organisation	**fomentar**	to promote
la sigla	abbreviation	**la plática**	short talk
	(in initials)		(Mexican—
salvaje	wild		**la charla** is
el gato montés	wild cat		used in Spain)
el jabalí	wild boar	**sosegado-a**	peaceful
el zorro	fox	**el lugareño**	countryman
el lobo	wolf		
el oso	bear		

Expresiones Importantes

contar con	to number	**estar para** + inf.	to be about to
en cuanto a	with regard to	**en peligro de**	in danger of
volverse de espaldas	to turn one's back on	**tener sentido**	to make sense
darse cuenta de	to realise		

Exercise No. 157—Test of Reading Comprehension

Answer these questions in English.

1 What did Mrs. Adams see in the paper?
2 What did Sr. Carrillo say about Bullfighting and Football in Spain?
3 Do Spaniards like and respect wild life?
4 What are the side effects of the sudden industrial development of Spain?
5 Do people of the Spanish cities enjoy going into the country?
6 What did José Ortega y Gasset say about man?
7 When was the National Park of Doñana created?
8 What is Doñana?
9 What is World Wild Life in Spanish?
10 Where is Covadonga?
11 What animals can you find in the National Parks?
12 What sports do Spaniards practise in Winter?
13 Where are the main ski resorts in Spain?
14 Is chess a popular game in Spain?

Exercise No. 158—Completion of Text

1 (We were about to leave).
2 **El Sr. Carrillo sonrió y me dio** (an unexpected reply).
3 **Los Toros subsisten por** (the traditional support) **de una minoría.**
4 **Doñana estuvo** (in danger of) **desaparecer.**
5 **Este Parque** (was the first) **que se creó en España.**
6 (There is much to do) **especialmente en cuanto a la educación.**
7 **El hombre** (believes himself to be) **en el centro del Universo.**
8 **Lo que dijo José Ortega y Gasset** (makes sense).
9 **Pero el Sr. Carrillo** (did not end here).
10 **Actividades como el ajedrez** (are also practised).
11 (I was very impressed) **por la plática del Sr. Carrillo.**
12 (It gave me) **un nuevo aspecto de España** (which I was unaware of).

SEGUNDA PARTE

Grammar Notes

1 Two Object Pronouns

Note in the following Spanish and English sentences the position of the indirect object (a person or persons) and the direct object (a thing or things).

1 Carlos *me lo* da.	1 Charles gives *it* (m.) *to me*.
2 Ana *me los* trae.	2 Anna brings *them* (m.) *to me*.
3 Juan *nos la* manda.	3 John sends *it* (f.) *to us*.
4 María no *nos las* presta.	4 Mary does not lend *them* (f.) *to us*.
5 *Te lo* damos, hijito.	5 We give it *to you*, sonny.

(a) In Spanish, when there are two pronoun objects, the indirect object precedes the direct object.

(b) In English, the opposite is true.

2 Two Object Pronouns (continued)

Study the following examples and note what happens to the indirect object pronouns le (*to you, to him, to her*) and les (*to you*, pl., *to them*).

1 *Se lo* digo a Ud.	1 I tell *it to you*.
2 *Se la* traigo a él.	2 I bring *it* (f.) *to him*.
3 *Se las* prestamos a ella.	3 We lend *them to her*.
4 *Se lo mando* a ellos.	4 I send *it* (m.) *to them*.
5 *Se los* doy a Uds.	5 I give *them* (m.) *to you* (pl.)

(a) Le (*to you, to him, to her*) and les (*to you*, pl., *to them*) may not be used before another object pronoun that begins with the letter l. In such cases le and les must become se.

(b) Thus se may mean *to you* (sing. and plural), *to him, to her, to them* (masc. and fem.).

a Vd., a él, a ella, etc., after the verb, make the meaning clear.

3 Two Object Pronouns after the Verb

Like single object pronouns, two object pronouns follow the verb with the affirmative imperative, with the infinitive and with the present participle. Study the two object pronouns in the following examples.

1 Díga*melo*.	1 Tell *it to me*.
2 Díga*selo* a él.	2 Tell *it to him*.
3 Dé*sela* a ella.	3 Give *it* (f.) *to her*.
4 Dé*noslos*.	4 Give *them to us*.
5 Mánde*selos a ellos*.	5 Send *them to them*.

(a) When two object pronouns follow the verb they are attached to it and to each other.

(b) An accent mark is added to the stressed syllable of the verb to keep the stress from shifting.

Ejercicios (Exercises) No. 159A–159B–159C–159D

159A. Practise the Spanish questions and answers aloud many times. They will give you a 'feeling' for the two object pronouns construction.

1 ¿Le ha escrito la Sra. Adams la carta a su agente?
Sí, se la ha escrito.

1 Has Mrs. Adams written the letter to her agent?
Yes, she has written it to him.

2 ¿Le ha dado Ud. el regalo a su madre?
Sí, se lo he dado.

2 Have you given the gift to your mother?
Yes, I have given it to her.

3 ¿Me prestará Ud. su pluma?
Sí, se la prestaré.

3 Will you lend me your pen?
Yes, I will lend it to you.

4 ¿Nos mandarán Uds. las flores?
Sí, se las mandaremos.

4 Will you send us the flowers?
Yes, we will send them to you.

5 ¿Les prestaron el dinero a Uds.?
Sí, nos lo prestaron.

5 Did they lend you the money?
Yes, they lent it to us.

6 ¿Les contó Ud. los cuentos a los niños?
Sí, se los conté.

6 Did you tell the stories to the children?
Yes, I told them to them.

159B. Before doing this exercise review Grammar Notes 1.

I. Translate into English:

1 Los niños me los traen.
2 Los alumnos nos las mandan.
3 Ellos no nos los venden.
4 Te lo doy, hijito.

II. Translate into Spanish:

1 Charles gives it (*m.*) to me.
2 Anna lends them (*m.*) to us.
3 The teacher says it (*m.*) to us.
4 We give it (*f.*) to you, child.

159C. Before doing this exercise review Grammar Notes 2.

I. Translate into English:

1 Se lo decimos a Ud.
2 Se lo traemos a Uds.
3 Se los damos a él.
4 Se las mandamos a ellos.

II. Translate into Spanish:

1 John tells it (*m.*) to you (*sing.*).
2 Mary writes it (*f.*) to him.
3 The teacher gives them (*m.*) to you (*pl.*).
4 We send them (*f.*) to her.

159D. Before doing this exercise review Grammar Notes 3.

I. Translate into English:

1 Dígamelo.
2 Dénoslo.
3 Préstemelos.
4 Mándeselos a él.

II. Translate into Spanish:

1 Lend them (*m.*) to me.
2 Send it (*m.*) to us.
3 Tell it (*f.*) to him.
4 Give them (*m.*) to her.

CHAPTER 40

LA SEÑORA ADAMS SALE DE ESPAÑA

PRIMERA PARTE

Décima Carta de España

Muy amigo mío:

Cuando me fui (*I went away*) de Londres, como Ud. ya sabe, había aprendido algo acerca de España. Había leído varios libros muy interesantes sobre su (*its*) historia y sus costumbres. Ya sabía hablar español bastante bien.

Aquí en España he visitado muchos lugares. En nuestras conversaciones, que recuerdo bien, hemos hablado de algunos de ellos. En mis cartas podía describirle un poco de lo mucho que he visto y he aprendido. Lo demás (*the rest*) espero decírselo personalmente.

Como Ud. puede imaginar, me gustan mucho los lugares de interés histórico, el paisaje, el arte y las artes populares. Pero más me interesa el pueblo de España con su cariño y su generosa hospitalidad. Me gustan su humor y su filosofía frente a las dificultades.

Me gusta mucho la vida de España. De veras es más tranquila que la de Londres, a pesar de (*in spite of*) mis primeras impresiones en el taxi que me llevó con velocidad espantosa desde el aeropuerto hasta mi hotel.

Ud. sabe que vine a España en viaje de recreo y también de negocios. Afortunadamente terminé pronto los negocios y pude dedicarme enteramente al recreo.

No pude ir a Tenerife, ni a las otras Islas Canarias. ¡Qué lástima! Pero preferí llegar a conocer (*to get to know*) mejor la Península. Hay tanto que ver, tanto que hacer, tanto que aprender. Me encantó todo.

Tendré mucho que decirle de las personas muy simpáticas que he conocido, los lugares que he visitado y todo lo que he aprendido de las costumbres, de la vida, del idioma y de las artes de España.

Claro está que pronto volveré de nuevo a España. Quiero volver el año que viene. Pero entonces llevaré conmigo a la familia entera. Estoy segura de que (*I am sure that*) no tendré ninguna dificultad. No he ganado el premio gordo en la lotería; pero de todos modos, volveré.

Esta es la última carta que le escribo antes de salir para México el primero de agosto. Tendré mucho gusto en escribirle y darle mis impresiones de ese país, y compararlo con España.

Entretanto cordialmente,

Juana Adams

Vocabulario

el cariño	affection	**dedicar**	to dedicate
el paisaje	landscape	**encantar**	to charm
la filosofía	philosophy	**enteramente**	entirely
la hospitalidad	hospitality	**frente a**	in the face of

Expresiones Importantes

de todos modos	anyway
llegar a conocer	to get to know
cuanto antes	as soon as possible

Exercise No. 160—Test of Reading Comprehension

Answer these questions in English.

1 Before leaving for Spain how had Mrs. Adams obtained some knowledge of the country?
2 How much was she able to describe in her letters?
3 What interests Mrs. Adams most in Spain?
4 Mention four qualities of the people that she likes.
5 How does Mrs. Adams compare life in London with that in Spain?
6 When did she get a different impression?
7 Why didn't she go to Tenerife or the other Canary Islands?
8 Whom will she take with her on her next trip to Spain?
9 What is she sure of?
10 When is she leaving for Mexico?
11 What will she be glad to do when she arrives in Mexico?
12 Which are the two countries she is going to compare?

SEGUNDA PARTE

Grammar Notes

1 **saber** and **poder**

(a) **saber** plus an infinitive means *to know how to do* something.

Sabe escribir en español.   He can (knows how to) write Spanish.

(b) **poder** plus an infinitive means to have the physical ability or the opportunity to do something.

Hoy no puede escribir, porque está enfermo.	Today he cannot (is not able to) write, because he is ill.

2 Untranslated **que**

(a) You have learned that **tener que** means *to have to*. Thus:

Tengo que estudiar la lección.	I must (have to) study the lesson.

(b) **que** appears in a number of other expressions where it is not translated:

Tendré mucho que decirle.	I will have much to tell you.
Tengo una carta que escribir.	I have a letter to write.
Hay tanto que ver.	There is so much to see.

TERCERA PARTE

Ejercicios (Exercises) No. 161A–161B–161C

161A. Translate the following sentences accurately. Be sure the tense is correct.

Ejemplo:	**Me fui de Londres.**	I left London.
	Me iré de Londres.	I shall leave London.

1 **Leeré varios libros.**
2 **Había leído varios libros.**
3 **He leído varios libros.**
4 **Hemos visitado España.**
5 **Habíamos visitado España.**
6 **Visitaremos España.**
7 **Puedo describirlo.**
8 **Podía describirlo.**
9 **Podré describirlo.**
10 **Me gusta su carta.**
11 **Me gustó su carta.**
12 **Me gustará su carta.**
13 **Terminan los negocios.**
14 **Terminaron los negocios.**
15 **Han terminado los negocios.**
16 **Tienen mucho que decirme.**
17 **Tendrán mucho que decirme.**
18 **Tuvieron mucho que decirme.**
19 **Volveremos a casa.**
20 **Volvimos a casa.**

161B. Complete with the correct form of **saber, conocer** or **poder** as needed:

1 **¿Quién** (knows) **todas las respuestas?**
2 (We know) **a ese hombre, pero** (we do not know) **dónde vive.**
3 (I cannot) **hacer el viaje con Ud.**
4 **La Sra. Adams quiere** (to know) **mejor a su agente.**
5 **Ahora** (they know each other) **mejor.**
6 (I know how) **jugar al fútbol.**
7 **Si Ud.** (know) **el sistema monetario, Ud.** (can) **regatear en el mercado.**
8 **Ud.** (know) **aquellas calles mejor que yo.**

9 **Mucho gusto en** (know you).
10 (They are not able) **cambiar el neumático.**

161C.

1 Have you learned much about Spain?
2 Yes, I have been **(estado)** there, and I have read many books.
3 Can you speak Spanish?
4 Yes, I speak it quite well.
5 Do you remember the places of which **(de que)** we have spoken?
6 I remember them well.
7 Are you able to describe them in Spanish?
8 Yes, I can describe them.
9 What did you like most in Spain?
10 I liked the people most.
11 Is the life of Spain quieter than that of London?
12 Indeed it is more quieter
13 Is there much to see in Spain?
14 There is much to see, much to hear, much to do, much to learn.
15 My trip is finished.

REVISION 9

CHAPTERS 36–40 PRIMERA PARTE

NOUNS

1 la alegría	10 la gasolina	19 el refresco
2 el aficionado	11 la gasolinera	20 la risa
3 el banco	12 la joya	21 la señal
4 la biblioteca	13 la librería	22 el sonido
5 el bolsillo	14 la lotería	23 la sombra
6 la carretera	15 la posibilidad	24 el sueño
7 los dulces	16 el premio gordo	25 la tela
8 la esquina	17 el paisaje	26 el tabaco
9 el garaje	18 el recreo	27 el valle

1 joy	10 petrol	19 refreshment
2 amateur, fan	11 petrol station	20 laugh
3 bench, bank	12 jewel	21 signal
4 library	13 bookshop	22 sound
5 pocket	14 lottery	23 shade
6 road, highway	15 possibility	24 sleep, dream
7 sweets	16 first prize	25 cloth
8 corner	17 landscape	26 tobacco
9 garage	18 recreation	27 valley

VERBS

1 alquilar	7 ganar	13 regresar
2 anunciar	8 matar	14 reunirse
3 conducir	9 nombrar	15 sacar
4 crecer	10 ofrecer	16 señalar
5 dormir(ue)	11 parar	17 soñar(ue)
6 dormirse	12 prestar	

1 to rent, hire	7 to win	13 to return (go back)
2 to announce	8 to kill	14 to meet together
3 to drive	9 to name	15 to take out
4 to grow	10 to offer	16 to point to
5 to sleep	11 to stop	17 to dream
6 to fall asleep	12 to lend	

PREPOSITIONS

1 durante	2 a pesar de	3 hacia
1 during	2 in spite of	3 towards

IMPORTANT EXPRESSIONS

1 a lo lejos	4 estar para + infin.
2 de todos modos	5 en seguida
3 estar de acuerdo con	6 faltaba una hora

279

7 no me falta nada
8 más allá
9 no (verb) más que

10 ¡qué importa!
11 sin embargo
12 tener sueño

1 in the distance
2 anyway
3 to be in agreement with
4 to be about to
5 immediately
6 it was one hour before

7 I lack nothing
8 further on
9 (verb) nothing but, only
10 what does it matter?
11 nevertheless
12 to be sleepy

SEGUNDA PARTE

Ejercicio 162 Translate the following sentences accurately. All the tenses you have learned and the imperative are here illustrated.

1 ¿Quién pedirá información en la estación de ferrocarril?
2 Pablo ya había tomado el almuerzo cuando le vi.
3 ¿Querrían Uds. hacer un viaje a todos los países de Europa?
4 Conozco a ese hombre, pero no sé dónde vive.
5 Escribíamos nuestras cartas cuando el profesor entró en la sala.
6 Tomen Uds. estos papeles y pónganlos en mi escritorio.
7 Hemos comprado los diarios y los hemos leído.
8 No podía describirles todo lo que había visto.
9 Vine a España y me recibieron con cariño.
10 Guillermo hablaba toda la tarde mientras yo no decía nada.
11 No me gustó la corrida y por eso no asistiré a otra.
12 Los padres trabajaban mientras que los niños dormían.
13 Estábamos en el mercado cuando comenzó a llover.
14 Eran las ocho y media de la mañana y todavía dormían los niños.
15 No vendrán aquí porque no tendrán tiempo.
16 Niños, ¿no jugaréis en el patio?
17 Mi tío viajó por todos los países de América del Sur.
18 A la Sra. Adams le gustaban los alimentos picantes, pero recordaba los consejos de su maestro y no los comía.
19 Yo quería los juguetes, pero Carlos no me los daba.
20 Si encuentro platos con dibujos de animalitos, se los mandaré a Ud.
21 Él pidió cambio de un billete de mil pesetas y el cajero (cashier) se lo dio.
22 Ud. tiene el sombrero de María. Devuélvaselo.

Ejercicio 163 Complete these sentences in Spanish.

1 La Sra. Adams (is a businesswoman of London).
2 Hizo (a trip to Spain in order to visit) a su agente.
3 Quería (to know him better).
4 Antes de salir para España (she learned to speak Spanish).
5 También (she had read many books) sobre España.
6 Desde España escribió cartas (to her friend and teacher, Mr. López).

7 **Le gustaron mucho a ella** (the places of historic interest).

8 **A pesar de sus primeras impresiones** (Mrs. Adams found the life in Spain more tranquil than that of London).

9 **Pensó** (of the taxi which took her to her hotel).

10 **No le gustó** (the fearful speed of that taxi).

11 **Afortunadamente** (she finished her business matters quickly).

12 **Sin embargo** (she was not able to visit Tenerife).

13 **Había** (so much to see, so much to hear, so much to do, so much to learn).

14 **Pero la Sra. Adams** (will return to Spain).

15 **Llevará consigo** (the whole family).

16 **Ésta es** (Mrs. Adams's last letter) **desde España.**

17 (No doubt) **escribirá una carta al Sr. López** (and give her impressions of Mexico).

LECTURA

Exercise No. 164—Toledo

La ciudad de Toledo está situada a 70 km al sur de Madrid, en el margen[1] (*bank*) derecho del rio Tajo. Tiene 516 m de altura sobre el nivel del mar, y tiene unos 41.000 habitantes. Es una diudad muy antigua y una de las más célebres de España. No es solamente una ciudad, sino también un monumento nacional, de manera que su arquitectura y carácter quedan y quedarán intactos.

En la Edad Media (*Middle Ages*) vivieron en la ciudad cristianos (*Christians*), árabes y judíos (*Jews*). Convivieron en paz (*peace*) y todos contribuyeron (*contributed*) a hacer de Toledo un centro de cultura y de gran variedad de artes.[2]

El turista no puede dejar de visitar la catedral. Su construcción se inició en 1226 y se terminó aproximadamente (*approximately*) en 1492, el año del descubrimiento (*discovery*) de América. Vale la pena también ver el Alcázar.

Aproximadamente en 1575 llegó a Toledo un inmigrante (*immigrant*) cuyo nombre es conocido en el mundo entero. Vino de Creta (*Crete*) y se llamaba Dominico[3] Theotocopuli, pero le conocemos mejor bajo el nombre de 'El Greco' (*The Greek*). Vivió en Toledo hasta su muerte (*death*), en 1625. Podemos ver sus pinturas en los grandes museos del mundo y en la ciudad misma de Toledo. En efecto, dicen que Toledo es un gran museo dedicado al Greco.

Quérido lector (*reader*), no deje Ud. de visitar esta hermosísima ciudad.

NOTE: 1. '**Margen**' belongs to the so-called 'ambiguous' gender, but in this particular case referring to the banks of a river it is **masculine**. 2. Toledo was well-known in the Middle Ages for its 'Escuela de Traductores', or School of Translators, who translated classical texts from Greek and Latin. 3. Also **Domingo**.

CHAPTER 41

LA SEÑORA ADAMS LLEGA A MÉXICO

PRIMERA PARTE

Primera Carta de México

Estimado amigo:

Hace una semana que llegué a la ciudad de México. El Licenciado Sr. González de la Vega, Director de una importante compañía exportadora de artículos de artesanía, me esperaba en el aeropuerto, y me llevó al hotel. Ya desde el aire, antes de aterrizar, pude ver la magnífica ciudad muy antigua y moderna a la vez, que fue en tiempo antiguo la capital azteca de Tenotchtitlán. No muy lejos se encuentran los dos impresionantes volcanes de Popocatepetl y Ixtactihuatl. !Que son difíciles de pronunciar esos nombres indios! Y luego en la ciudad hay grandes avenidas modernas como el Paseo de la Reforma.[1]

He visitado, entre muchas otras cosas, el Museo Antropológico en donde se puede seguir la historia del México precolombino. Esta capital ofrece grandes contrastes desde lo precolombino a lo muy moderno pasando por lo colonial y otras influencias históricas como la francesa.

La ciudad moderna fue construída sobre las ruinas de la antigua Tenotchtitlán en 1521 y en ella se fundó la primera Universidad de América, ahora la Universidad Nacional Autónoma de renombre cultural. Restos de la antigua gloria colonial se pueden ver en la gran plaza de El Zócalo. Allí se encuentra la catedral, edificada en donde antes se hallaba el palacio del último Emperador azteca, Moctezuma. También el Ayuntamiento (*Town Hall*). Partiendo de la Plaza hay una serie de calles estrechas que son como el corazón de la ciudad, en gran contraste con las grandes avenidas. He visitado también la ciudad de Monterrey, ciudad de aire hispánico, que tiene un célebre Instituto Tecnológico.

Los mexicanos son muy corteses y hospitalarios pero mucho más reservados y pausados que los españoles. Las mujeres son más sumisas y muy bonitas. He notado que los mexicanos se interesan muchísimo por todo lo cultural. Desde la Revolución a principios de siglo, México es un país políticamente estable—por eso ha podido desarrollarse mucho mas rápidamente que otros países de la América Hispana.

Su gobierno es presidencial y su república federal. México es el paraíso de los arqueólogos con sus Pirámides escalonadas y restos de las antiguas civilizaciones Toltecas, Aztecas y Mayas.

La semana que viene el Sr. González piensa llevarme a Yucatán al Sur de México a visitar los restos de la antigua civilización Maya. Hay todavía mucha población india en México que conservan sus tradiciones y lenguas especialmente en esas tierras Mayas.

Luego, de regreso, podré visitar los Centros de la industria petrolera ya que el hijo del Sr. González es ingeniero químico y trabaja para la PEMEX.[2] Es imposible en una sola carta contarle todo lo de México. Es un país muy antiguo y muy moderno y sobre todo de gran porvenir. Salgo para Londres dentro de 15 días y espero encontrarle allí para contarle con más detalle todas mis impresiones de ese hermoso país.

Cordialmente,
Juana Adams.

NOTE: 1. This has nothing to do with the Reformation. It is a period of Mexican history in the mid-nineteenth century.

NOTE: 2. **Pemex: Petróleos Mexicanos.**

Vocabulario

el licenciado	courtesy title given to university graduate	**el renombre**	renown, fame
artesanía	craft	**escalonado**	stepped
impresionante	impressive	**estable**	stable
el volcán	volcano	**la población**	population
precolombino	pre-Columbian	**el ingeniero**	engineer
las ruinas	ruins	**químico**	chemical
los restos	traces, remains	**aterrizar**	to land
Emperador	Emperor	**edificar**	to build
hospitalario	hospitable	**fundar**	to found
cortés	polite	**exportar**	to export
pausado	slow, deliberate	**desarrollarse**	to develop
sumiso	submissive, humble	**el porvenir**	future

Expresiones Importantes

Desde el aire	from the air
a la vez	at the same time, simultaneously
de regreso	on one's (my) return
salir para	to leave for

Exercise No. 165—Test of Reading Comprehension

Answer these questions in English.

1 Where did Mrs. Adams go after leaving Spain?
2 Who was at the airport waiting for her?

3 What did she visit in Mexico City?
4 Which was the first University to be founded in the New World?
5 Where is Mexico City Cathedral?
6 What are Mexicans like?
7 What is one of their main interests?
8 Is Mexico a stable country?
9 What sort of government have they got?
10 What regions of Mexico of archaeological interest did Mrs. Adams visit?
11 Is industry important in Mexico?

Exercise No. 166—Completion of Text

1 (A week ago) **llegué a la Ciudad de México.**
2 **El Sr. González** (was waiting for me) **en el aeropuerto.**
3 **Desde el aire** (before landing) **pude ver la ciudad.**
4 **Es una ciudad antigua y moderna** (at the same time).
5 (I have visited) **el Museo Antropológico.**
6 **La ciudad moderna** (was built) **en las ruinas de Tenotchtitlán.**
7 **Partiendo de la Plaza hay** (a series of narrow streets).
8 **Los mexicanos son muy** (hospitable and polite).
9 **Se interesan mucho** (about everything cultural).
10 **El Sr. González** (intends to take me) **a Yucatán.**
11 (On my return) **visitaré los centros de la industria petrolera.**
12 **Es imposible en una sola carta contarle** (all about Mexico).

SEGUNDA PARTE

Grammar Notes

1 **Para** and **por**

Para and **por** are important prepositions which are frequently confused by the student of Spanish, since both can translate the English "for". Their uses can be summarised as follows:

Para
(a) destination

El tren salió para Madrid.	The train left for Madrid.
Este regalo es para mi madre.	This present is for my mother.

(b) purpose, in order to

Comemos para vivir.	We eat in order to live.

(c) suitability, aptitude for

Papel para escribir.	Writing paper.
Madera para sillas.	Wood for chairs.

(d) in certain expressions, e.g. **estar para salir, hablar para sí**

El tren está para salir.	The train is about to leave.
Está hablando para sí.	He is talking to himself.

Por

(a) reason or motive

Por esta razón.	For this reason.
Por miedo.	Through fear.

(b) indicates the agent by whom something is done

Hamlet fue escrito por Shakespeare.	Hamlet was written by Shakespeare.

(c) way or manner

Prefiero viajar por avión.	I prefer to fly.
Pasamos por las calles.	We pass through the streets.

(d) on behalf of, instead of, as, in favour of

Estamos todos por él.	We are all for him.
Morir por la patria.	To die for one's country.

(e) in exchange for

Cambié mis libras por pesetas.	I changed my pounds for pesetas.

(f) equivalent to English "per" in rates and measures

Diez por ciento.	Ten per cent.
Gana dos libras por hora.	He earns two pounds an hour.

(g) referring to future time

Voy a Francia por dos meses.	I am going to France for two months.

2 Study carefully the following examples contrasting the meanings of **para** and **por.**

¿Por qué robó el dinero?	Why did he steal the money?
Lo robó por necesidad.	(Reason)
Lo robó para su hermana.	(Destination)
¿Por qué necesitan tanto dinero?	Why do they need so much money?
¿Para qué necesitan tanto dinero?	What do they need so much money for?
Trabajo por ser pobre.	(Reason)
Trabajo para ser rico.	(Purpose)

3 Idioms with **por**

¡por Dios!	for heaven's sake!
por ahora	for the time being
por el momento	for (at) the moment
por si acaso	just in case
por supuesto	of course
por eso	for that reason, that's why
por todas partes	everywhere
tres veces por semana	three times a week
por primera vez	for the first time
por ejemplo	for example
por fin	finally

4 Compound prepositions
  Study the following:

además de	as well as
a través de	across, through
alrededor de	around, about
antes de	before
cerca de	near
debajo de	under
delante de	in front of
dentro de	inside
después de	after
detrás de	behind
encima de	on top of
enfrente de	opposite, in front of
fuera de	outside
lejos de	far from
más allá de	beyond

Note. 1. Do not confuse **antes de** (before in time) with **delante de** (before in place).

Desayunó antes de salir.	He breakfasted before going out.
El árbol está delante de la casa.	The tree is in front of the house.

2. **alrededor de** means "about" for place, and **sobre** = about, concerning

Hay una muralla alrededor de la ciudad.	There is a wall about the city.
Escribió un libro sobre España.	He wrote a book about (on) Spain.

TERCERA PARTE

Ejercicios (Exercises) Nos. 167A–167B

167A. Translate the following sentences into Spanish using **para** or **por**.
1 I leave tomorrow for Mexico.
2 He wanted to travel through France.
3 Don Quixote was written by Cervantes.
4 I gave the waiter a tip of ten per cent.
5 She bought a skirt for her mother.
6 I travel by train twice a week.
7 The aeroplane was about to land.
8 All the students are in favour of the teacher.
9 I will give you 500 pesetas for this shawl.
10 The girl is reading to herself.
11 I cannot help you at the moment.
12 This book was written by a father for his children.

167B. Translate the following sentences into Spanish.
1 The child was in front of me.
2 It is an interesting book on the travels of a Frenchman.
3 The university is found outside the city.
4 Your shoes are on the table.
5 Near the square is an ancient cathedral.
6 Is it far from the centre?
7 Before having lunch I want to buy a suitcase.
8 My parents live beyond the main square.
9 As well as the cathedral we visited the university.
10 Around the palace are beautiful gardens.

VOCABULARY—ENGLISH–SPANISH

A

able, to be, poder(ue)
about, de, acerca de; **about 2 o'clock, a** eso de las dos
accept, to, aceptar
accompany, to, acompañar
ache, el dolor; **headache,** dolor de cabeza; **toothache,** dolor de muelas
according to, según
accustom, to, acostumbrar
in addition to, además de
address, la dirección
admire, to, admirar
advice, el consejo
advise, to, aconsejar
aeroplane, el avión
affection, el cariño
after, después de (*prep.*); después que (*conj.*)
afternoon, la tarde; **in the afternoon,** por la tarde; **p.m.,** de la tarde
again, otra vez; **to do again,** volver a + *infin.*
against, contra
agent, el agente
ago: two years ago, hace dos años
agreeable, agradable
aid, la ayuda
aid, to, ayudar
air, el aire; **in the open air,** al aire libre
airmail: by airmail, por correo aéreo
airport, el aeropuerto
almost, casi
alone, solo
along, por
already, ya
also, también
although, aunque
always, siempre
amusement, la diversión
and, y, e (*before* i *or* hi)
announce, anunciar
another, otro, -a
answer, la respuesta
answer, to, contestar, responder
any, cualquier
anyone, alguién, alguno, -a

apple, la manzana
approach, to, acercarse a
arm, el brazo
around, alrededor de
arrange, to, arreglar
arrival, la llegada
arrive, to, llegar
art, el arte (*f*) and (*m*)
article, el artículo
artist, el (la) artista
as . . . as, tan . . . como
ask, to, preguntar; **to ask for,** pedir(i); **to ask questions,** hacer preguntas
assortment, el surtido
at, a, en
attend, to, asistir a
attention, la atención
aunt, la tía
avenue, la avenida
awake, to be, estar despierto, -a
awaken, to (arouse), despertar(ie)

B

bacon, el tocino
bad, malo, -a
badly, mal
baggage, el equipaje
ballpoint pen, el bolígrafo
baker, el panadero
bargain, to, regatear
basket, la cesta, la canasta
bath, el baño; **bathroom,** el cuarto de baño
bathe, to, bañar, bañarse
be, to, ser, estar; **to be in a hurry,** tener prisa, ir con prisas; **to be on the way,** estar en camino; **to be about to,** estar para
beans, las habas, las judías
beautiful, bello, -a; hermoso, -a
because, porque
become, to, ponerse, hacerse; **He becomes ill.** Se pone enfermo; **He is becoming rich.** Se hace rico.
bed, la cama
bedroom, el dormitorio
before, (*time*) antes de; (*place*) delante de

begin, to, comenzar(ie), empezar(ie)

beginning, el principio; at the beginning, al principio

behind, detrás de

believe, to, creer

belt, el cinturón

bench, el banco

better, mejor

between, entre

big, grande

bill, la cuenta

bird, el pájaro

birth, el nacimiento

birthday, el cumpleaños

black, negro, -a

blanket, la manta

block, la manzana

blouse, la blusa

blue, azul

boat, el barco

body, el cuerpo

boiled, cocido, -a

book, el libro

booking clerk, el taquillero

bookshelf, la estantería

bookshop, la librería

boot (of car), la maleta

born, to be, nacer; he was born, nació

bottle, la botella

box, la caja

boy, el muchacho

bread, el pan

break, to, romper

breakfast, el desayuno

breakfast, to have, desayunar, desayunarse; tomar el desayuno

bring, to, traer, llevar

British, británico, -a

brother, el hermano

building, el edificio

bundle, el bulto

bus, el autobús

business, el negocio

businessman, woman, el, la comerciante, negociante

busy, ocupado, -a

but, pero; but on the contrary, sino

buy, to, comprar

buyer, el comprador

C

cake, la pasta

calculator, la calculadora

call, to, llamar

can (be able to), poder(ue)

car, el coche; by car, en coche

caramel cream, el flan

care: Be careful! ¡Cuidado!

carpet, la alfombra

carry, to, llevar; to carry away, llevarse

catch, to, coger; to catch cold, coger, atrapar un resfriado, catarro

celebrate, to, celebrar

century, el siglo

certain, cierto, -a

certainly, por cierto

chair, la silla

change, el cambio; in change, de cambio

change, to, cambiar; to change clothes, cambiar de ropa

chat, to, charlar

cheap, barato, -a

check, to (baggage), facturar

cheese, el queso

chicken, el pollo

child, el niño, la niña

choose, to, escoger

chop, la chuleta

Christmas carol, el villancico

church, la iglesia

cigar, el puro, cigarro

cinema, el cine

city, la ciudad

class, la clase

clean, limpio, -a

clean, to, limpiar

clear, claro, -a

clerk, el dependiente

climate, el clima

close, to, cerrar(ie)

closed, cerrado, -a

cloth, la tela

clothing, la ropa

coffee, el café

cold, frío, -a; It is cold (weather). Hace frío; I am cold. Tengo frío; I have a cold, Tengo catarro.

colour, el color; What is the colour of . . . ? ¿De qué color es . . . ?

come, to, venir

comfortable, cómodo, -a

complete, to, completar

comprehend, to, comprender, entender(ie)

computer, la computadora, el ordenador

concert, el concierto

confess, to, confesar(ie)

congratulate, to, felicitar

consequently, por consiguiente

contain, to, contener

continue, to, continuar, seguir(i)

conversation, la conversación
converse, to, conversar
cooked, cocido, -a
cool, fresco, -a; **It (weather) is cool.** Hace fresco.
copper, el cobre
corn, el maíz
corner, la esquina
correct, correcto, -a
cost, to, costar(ue)
costume, el traje
cotton, el algodón
count, to, contar(ue)
country, el campo, el país (*nation*)
course: of course, por supuesto naturalmente; desde luego; Creo que sí; **Of course not.** Creo que no.
cousin, el primo, la prima
cover, to, cubrir
craftsman, el artesano
cream, la crema
cross, to, cruzar
cry, el grito
cry, to (shout), gritar
culture, la cultura
current, corriente
custom, la costumbre
cut, to, cortar

D

daily, diario, -a
dance, to, bailar
dangerous, peligroso, -a
dark, oscuro, -a
date, la fecha; **What is the date?** ¿Cuál es la fecha?
daughter, la hija
day, el día; **nowadays,** hoy día; **on the following day,** al día siguiente
dear, caro, -a; querido, -a (*beloved*)
death, la muerte
decide, to, decidir
decoration, el adorno
defend, to, defender(ie)
demand, to, demandar
depart, to, partir
descend, to, bajar
describe, to, describir
desire, to, desear; tener ganas
desk, el escritorio
dessert, el postre
die, to, morir(ue); **he died,** murió
different, diferente, distinto, -a
difficult, difícil

diligent, diligente
dine, to, tomar la cena, cenar
dining-room, el comedor
dinner, la comida
dirty, sucio, -a
discover, to, descubrir
dish, el plato
distant, lejano, -a
divide, to, dividir
do, to, hacer
doctor, el médico, el doctor
door, la puerta
doubt, la duda; **without any doubt,** sin duda alguna
doubt, to, dudar
drawing, el dibujo
dress, el vestido
dress, to, vestir(i); **to dress in,** vestirse de
drink, la bebida
drink, to, beber, tomar
drive, conducir, guiar
dry, seco, -a
dry clean, limpiar en seco
during, durante

E

each, cada; **each one,** cada uno
ear, el oído (*hearing*), la oreja
early, temprano
earn, to, ganar
east, el este
eat, to, comer
educate, to, educar
egg, el huevo
employ, to, emplear
employee, el empleado
empty, vacío
end, el fin; **finally,** al fin, finalmente
end, to, terminar, acabar
England, Inglaterra
English, el inglés (*lang.*); **Englishman,** el inglés; **Englishwoman,** la inglesa
enjoy, to, gozar de
enough, basta, bastante
enter, to, entrar en
entire, entero, -a
entrance, la entrada
equal, igual
especially, sobre todo
evening, la tarde
everybody, todo el mundo
everywhere, por (en) todas partes
examination, el examen
examine, to, examinar, revisar (*baggage*)

excellent, excelente
except, excepto, menos
excuse, to, dispensar, perdonar, excusar;
  excuse me, dispénseme, perdón
expect, to, esperar
explain, to, explicar
exporter, el exportador
express, to, expresar
eye, el ojo

F

fable, la fábula
face, la cara
fall, to, caer
fall asleep, to, dormirse(ue)
false, falso, -a
family, la familia
famous, famoso, -a, célebre
far from, lejos de
fare, el pasaje
fast, rápido, -a
fat, gordo, -a
father, el padre
favour, el favor
fear, to, temer, tener miedo
feel, to (well, ill), sentirse (ie)
few, pocos(as)
film, el film, la película
find, to, hallar; to find out, averiguar
fine, fino, -a
finish, to, terminar, acabar
first, primero, -a
fish, el pescado
flight, el vuelo
floor, el suelo; el piso (storey)
flower, la flor
follow, to, seguir(i)
following: on the following day, al día
  siguiente
food, la comida, los alimentos
foot, el pie; on foot, a pie
for, por, para
forget, to, olvidar
fork, el tenedor
form, to, formar
fountain, la fuente
fountain pen, la pluma
French (*lang.*), el francés; **Frenchman**, el
  francés; **Frenchwoman**, la francesa
friend, el amigo, la amiga
from, de; from . . . to, desde . . . hasta
fruit, la fruta
full, lleno, -a

G

game, el juego, el partido
garage, el garaje
garden, el jardín
gentleman (Mr.), el señor
get, to, obtener, conseguir(i); **to get
  (become)**, ponerse; **to get up**, levantarse; **to get on**, subir a; **to get off,**
  salir, bajar de
gift, el regalo
give, to, dar; **to give back**, devolver(ue)
glad, alegre
glass, el vaso (*for drinking*), el vidrio, el
  cristal
glove, el guante
go, to, ir; **to go away**, irse; **to go shopping,**
  ir de compras
gold, el oro
good, bueno, -a
grandfather, el abuelo
grandmother, la abuela
grape, la uva
grapefruit, la toronja, el pomelo
Great Britain, Gran Bretaña
green, verde
greet, to, saludar
greeting, el saludo
grey, gris
group, el grupo
guess, to, adivinar

H

hair, el pelo
half, la mitad; medio, -a
ham, el jamón
hand, la mano; **handmade**, hecho a mano;
  to shake hands, darse la mano
happen, to, pasar
happy, contento, -a, feliz
hard, difícil
hat, el sombrero
have, to, haber (*auxiliary*); tener (*possess*)
head, la cabeza
headache, el dolor de cabeza
healthy, sano, -a; **to be healthy**, tener
  salud
hear, to, oír
heart, el corazón
heavy, pesado, -a
help, la ayuda
help, to, ayudar
here· aquí, acá (*usually after a verb of
  motion*); **Here it is.** Aquí lo tiene Ud.

high, alto, -a
highland, la altiplanicie
holiday, la fiesta
home, en casa; **to go home,** ir a casa
hope, to, esperar; **I hope so.** Espero que
    sí; **I hope not.** Espero que no.
horse, el caballo
hot, caliente; **It (weather) is hot.** Hace
    calor; **I am hot.** Tengo calor.
hour, la hora
house, la casa
how, como, ¿cómo?
how many? ¿cuántos, -as?
how much? ¿cuánto, -a?
hungry: to be hungry, tener hambre
hurry: to be in a hurry, tener prisa
hurry, to, apresurarse
hurt, to, hacer daño a
husband, el esposo

I

ice cream, el helado
if, si
ill, enfermo, -a; malo, -a
imagine, imaginar
immediately, inmediatamente, en seguida
in, en
Indian, el indio
industry, la industria
inform, to, informar, avisar
inhabitant, el habitante
ink, la tinta
inside of, dentro de
instead of, en vez de
intelligent, inteligente
intend, to, pensar + *infin.*
interest, el interés
interest, to, interesar
introduce, to, presentar
invitation, la invitación
invite, to, invitar
Ireland, Irlanda
Irish, irlandés, -esa
iron, el hierro

J

jack, el gato
jar, jug, el jarro
jewel, la joya
jewellery shop, la joyería
juice, el zumo, jugo

K

keep, to, guardar
kill, to, matar
kind, amable
king, el rey
kiss, to, besar
kitchen, la cocina
knife, el cuchillo
know, to, saber; **to know how,** saber;
    to be acquainted with, conocer

L

lady (Mrs.), la señora
lamp, la lámpara
land, la tierra
language, la lengua, el idioma
last, último, -a; **last year,** el año pasado
laugh, la risa
laugh, to, reír(i); **to laugh at,** reírse de
lawyer, el abogado
lazy, perezoso, -a
leader, el caudillo
leaf, la hoja
learn, to, aprender
least, el menos; **at least,** por lo menos
leather, el cuero
leave, to (go out of), salir de
left, izquierdo, -a; **to the left,** a la
    izquierda
lemon, el limón
lend, to, prestar
less, menos
let, to (permit), permitir, dejar
letter, la carta
library, la biblioteca
lie down, to, acostarse(ue)
life, la vida
lift, el ascensor
light, la luz
like, to, gustar; **I like the game.** Me
    gusta el juego.
listen, to, escuchar
little, pequeño, -a; **a little,** un poco
live, to, vivir
lively, vivo, -a
living-room, la sala
load, la carga
long, largo, -a
look at, to, mirar
look for, to, buscar
lose, to, perder(ie)
loud, alto, -a
love, el amor

love, to, querer(ie) a, amar a
low, bajo, -a
luck, la suerte
lucky, afortunado, -a
lunch, el almuerzo

M

magazine, la revista
magnificent, magnífico, -a
maid, la criada
mail, to, echar en el buzón, echar al correo
maintain, to, mantener
majority, la mayor parte, la mayoría
make, to, hacer; **to make a trip,** hacer un viaje
man, el hombre
manner, la manera; **in the same manner,** de la misma manera
many, muchos, -as
market, el mercado
marry, to (someone), casarse con
match, la cerilla, el fósforo
matter, to, importar; **It doesn't matter.** No importa. **What is the matter?** ¿Qué hay? ¿Qué pasa? **What is the matter with you?** ¿Qué tiene Ud.? ¿Qué le pasa?
meal, la comida
mean, to, significar; querer(ie) decir
meanwhile, entretanto
measure, la medida
measure, to, medir(i)
meat, la carne
meet, to (make the acquaintance of), conocer a; **Glad to meet you.** Mucho gusto en conocerle, encantado
meet, to (come together with), encontrar(ue)
melon, el melón
memory, la memoria
menu, la lista, el menú
merchandise, la mercancía
merry, alegre
Mexican, mexicano, -a
Mexico, México
mile, la milla
milk, la leche
million, el millón
Miss (young lady), la señorita
miss, to, echar de menos
mistake, la falta
mistaken (to be), estar equivocado, -a
modern, moderno, -a

money, el dinero, la moneda (*currency*)
month, el mes
moon, la luna
more, más
moreover, además
morning, la mañana; **in the morning,** por la mañana; **a.m.,** de la mañana
most, el(la) más
mother, la madre
motion picture, la película
mountain, la montaña
mouth, la boca
move, to, mover(ue)
much, mucho, -a
music, la música
must (ought to), deber; **(to have to),** tener que; **(probably),** deber de

N

name, el nombre
name, to, nombrar
nature, la naturaleza
near, cerca de (*prep.*)
necessary, necesario, -a; **it is necessary,** es necesario, hay que + *infin.*
necessity, la necesidad
need, to, necesitar
neither, tampoco; **neither ... nor,** ni ... ni
never, nunca, jamás
nevertheless, sin embargo
new, nuevo, -a
news, las noticias
newspaper, el periódico, el diario
next, próximo, -a
nice, bonito, -a, simpático, -a
night, la noche; **at night,** por la noche
nobody, nadie
noise, el ruido
none, no, ninguno, -a
north, el norte
nose, la nariz
nothing, nada
now, ahora
number, el número

O

obey, to, obedecer
object, el objeto
observe, to, observar
obtain, to, obtener, conseguir(i)
occasion, la ocasión
of, de
offer, to, ofrecer

office, la oficina
often, a menudo, muchas veces
old, viejo, -a antiguo, -a
older, mayor
oldest, el(la) mayor
on (top of), encima de
only, sólo, solamente; not only . . . but also, no solamente . . . sino también
open, abierto, -a
open, to, abrir
opportunity, la oportunidad
opposite, frente a
or, o (u *before* o *or* ho)
orange, la naranja
order, to, mandar, pedir(i)
other, otro, -a
ought to, deber
outside of, fuera de
over, sobre
overcoat, el abrigo
owe, to, deber
own, propio, -a

P

pack: to pack a trunk, hacer una maleta
package, el paquete
paint, to, pintar
painter, el pintor
painting, la pintura
paper, el papel
parcel post, el paquete postal
parents, los padres
park, el parque
pass (by), to, pasar
passport, el pasaporte
pavement, la acera
pay, to, pagar
peach, el melocotón
pear, la pera
pen, la pluma
pencil, el lápiz
penny, el penique
people, la gente, las personas
perfectly, perfectamente
permission, el permiso
permit, to, permitir, dejar
person, la persona
petrol, la gasolina; petrol station, la gasolinera; petrol tank, el depósito
pharmacy, la farmacia
pick up, to, coger, recoger
picture, el cuadro
piece, la pieza
pink, rosado, -a

pity, la lástima; What a pity! ¡Qué lástima!
place, el sitio, el lugar
place, to, poner
plain, la llanura
plane, el avión
plateau, la meseta
play, el drama, la comedia
play, to, tocar (*instrument*) jugar(ue) (*game*)
pleasant, agradable
please, por favor; hágame Vd. el favor de; tenga la bondad de
pleasure, el placer, el gusto; with pleasure, con mucho gusto, encantado
pocket, el bolsillo
point out, to, señalar, indicar, mostrar(ue)
policeman, el agente de policía, el policía
poor, pobre
portion, la porción
portrait, el retrato
post, echar al correo
poster, el cartel
possible, posible
post office, el correo
potato, la patata
pottery, la cerámica
pound, la libra
pour, to, echar
practice, to, practicar
prefer, to, preferir(ie)
prepare, to, preparar
present, a, el regalo
present, to, presentar
pretty, bonito, -a
price, el precio
prize, el premio
produce, to, producir
production, la producción
professor, el profesor, la profesora
programme, el programa
progress, to, adelantar
promenade, el paseo
promise, to, prometer
proud, orgulloso, -a
purchase, la compra
purse, la bolsa
put, to, poner; to put on, (*clothing*) ponerse

Q

quantity, la cantidad
question, la pregunta
quickly, de prisa, aprisa

R

radio, la radio
rain, la lluvia
rain, to, llover(ue)
raincoat, el impermeable
rainy, lluvioso, -a
raise, to, levantar
rapid, rápido, -a
rapidly, rápidamente
rare, raro, -a
read, to, leer
ready, listo, -a
really! ¡de veras!
receive, to, recibir
recognize, to, reconocer
recreation, el recreo
red, rojo, -a
regret, to, sentir(ie)
relate, to, contar(ue)
relative, el pariente
remain, to, quedar, quedarse
remember, to, recordar(ue), acordarse
  (ue)
rent, to, alquilar
repeat, to, repetir(i)
reply, to, responder, contestar
representative, el representante
request, to, pedir(i)
resemble, to, parecerse a
reservation, la reserva
resist, to, resistir
respect, el respeto
rest, el descanso
restaurant, el restaurante
return, to, volver(ue) (*to go back*);
  regresar (*to go back*); devolver(ue) (*to
  give back*)
return ticket, el billete de ida y vuelta
rice, el arroz
rich, rico, -a
ride, to, ir (en coche, etc.); to go for a
  ride, pasearse (en coche, etc.), dar un
  paseo (en coche, etc.)
right: to be right, tener razón
right, derecho, -a
river, el río
road, el camino
roll, el panecillo
roof, el tejado
room, el cuarto
round, redondo, -a
row, la fila
run, to, correr

S

salt, la sal
same, mismo, -a; the same thing, lo
  mismo
sandwich, el bocadillo
sash, la faja
sauce, la salsa
say, decir; How does one say? ¿Cómo
  se dice?
scarcely, apenas
school, la escuela
screen, la pantalla
season, la estación
seat, el asiento
seated, sentado, -a
see, to, ver; Let's see. A ver.
seek, to, buscar
seem, to, parecer
sell, to, vender
seller, el vendedor
send, to, mandar,
  enviar
sense, el sentido
sentence, la frase
serve, to, servir(i)
set, to, poner; to set the table, poner la
  mesa
shade, la sombra
shawl, el echarpe
shine, to, brillar
shipment, el envío
shirt, la camisa
shoe, el zapato
short, corto -a, breve
shout, to, gritar
show, to (point out), mostrar(ue),
  enseñar
sick, enfermo, -a; malo, -a
side, el lado; beside, al lado de
sight, la vista
silk, la seda
silver, la plata
silversmith, el platero
similar, semejante
simple, sencillo, -a
since (because), puesto que
sing, to, cantar
sister, la hermana
sit down, to, sentarse(ie); to be sitting,
  estar sentado
size, el tamaño
skirt, la falda
sky, el cielo
sleep, to, dormir(ue)

sleepy: **to be sleepy,** tener sueño
slowly, despacio, lentamente
small, pequeño, -a
smile, to, sonreír(i)
snow, la nieve; **it is snowing,** nieva
so, así; **so much,** tanto, -a; **so that,** para que, de modo que
some, alguno, -a
someone, alguien
something, algo
somewhat, algo
son, el hijo
song, la canción
soon, pronto
sorry: to be sorry, sentir(ie); **I am very sorry.** Lo siento mucho.
soup, la sopa
south, el sur
souvenir, el recuerdo
Spain, España
Spaniard, el español, la española
Spanish (*lang.*), el español, el castellano
speak, to, hablar
spend, to, (*time*) pasar; (*money*) gastar
spicy, picante
spite: in spite of, a pesar de
spoon, la cucharita
spring, la primavera
square, cuadrado, -a
stairway, la escalera
stamp, el sello
stand, el puesto
stand up, to, ponerse en pie; **to be standing,** estar de pie
star, la estrella
state, el estado
station (railway), la estación de ferrocarril
statue, la estatua
steak (beef), el bistec
stenographer, la taquígrafa
step, el paso
sterling, la esterlina
still, todavía
stop, to, parar
store, la tienda
storey, el piso
story, el cuento
straw, la paja
street, la calle
strong, fuerte
student, el(la) estudiante
study, to, estudiar
style, el estilo

subject, el tema
suburb, el suburbio
suit, el traje
suitcase, la maleta; **to pack a suitcase,** hacer una maleta
summer, el verano
sun, el sol; **it is sunny,** hay sol
supper, la cena
surely, de seguro, seguramente, sin duda
surprised, sorprendido
surrounded, rodeado, -a
sweater, jersey
sweet, dulce; **sweets,** los dulces

T

table, la mesa; **to set the table,** poner la mesa
tailor, el sastre
take, to, tomar; **to take away,** llevarse
take out, to, sacar
tall, grande, alto, -a
tank, el depósito
taste, to, probar(ue)
tasty, sabroso, -a
tea, el té
teach, to, enseñar
teacher, el maestro, la maestra; el profesor, la profesora
telephone, el teléfono
telephone, to, llamar por teléfono, telefonear
tell, to, decir
temperate, templado
temperature, la temperatura
textile, el tejido
thankful, agradecido, -a
thanks, gracias
that, ese, -a; aquel, aquella; que (*conj.*)
theatre, el teatro
then, entonces
there, allí, ahí, allá (*usually with a verb of motion*); **there is (are),** hay
therefore, por eso, por lo tanto
these (*adj.*), estos, -as
thick, grueso, -a
thing, la cosa
think, to (believe), creer; **to think of,** pensar en
thirsty: to be thirsty, tener sed
this (*adj.*), este, -a
those (*adj.*), esos, -as, aquellos, -as
through, por
thus, así
ticket window, la taquilla

ticket, el billete, la entrada (*cinema &
theatre*)
ticket-seller, el taquillero
tile, el azulejo
time: What time is it? ¿Qué hora es?
one time, two times, una vez, dos veces,
etc.; on time, a tiempo; to have a good
time, pasar un buen rato
time table, el horario
tin, la hojalata
tip, la propina
tire, to, cansarse
tired, cansado, -a
to, a; in order to, para
toast, la tostada
tobacco, el tabaco
today, hoy
tomato, el tomate
tomorrow morning, mañana por la
mañana
too (also), también
too many, demasiados, -as
too much, demasiado, -a
tooth, el diente
toothache, dolor de muelas
topic, el tema
tourist, el(la) turista
towards, hacia
town, el pueblo
toy, el juguete
train, el tren
tram, el tranvía
travel, to, viajar
traveller, el viajero
tray, la bandeja
tree, el árbol
trip, el viaje; to take a trip, hacer un
viaje
trousers, los pantalones
trunk, el baúl
truth, la verdad
try, to, tratar de; to try on, probar(ue)
turkey, el pavo
typewriter, la máquina de escribir
typical, típico, -a
tyre, el neumático, la llanta

U

umbrella, el paraguas
uncle, el tío
under, debajo de
underground, (railway), el metro
understand, comprender, entender(ie)
unfortunately, desgraciadamente

United States, los Estados Unidos
(*abbreviation*) EE.UU.
university, la universidad
upon, sobre, encima de
use, to, usar, emplear
useful, útil

V

vacation, las vacaciones
valise, la valija
valley, el valle
very, muy
view, la vista
visit, la visita
visit, to, visitar
voice, la voz
voyage, el viaje

W

wait for, to, esperar
waiter, el camarero
waiting-room, la sala de espera
wake up, to, (*somebody*) despertar(ie),
(*oneself*) depertarse
Wales, el País de Gales
walk, to, andar, ir a pie, caminar; to
take a walk, dar un paseo, pasearse
wall, la pared
want, desear, querer(ie)
wash, to, lavar
watch, el reloj
water, el agua (*f*)
way: by the way, a propósito
weak, débil
wear, llevar, vestir(i) de
weather: What's the weather? ¿Qué
tiempo hace?
week, la semana
weigh, to, pesar
well, pues, bien; All right. Está bien.
well known, conocido, -a
Welsh, galés, -esa
when, cuando, ¿cuándo?
where, donde, ¿dónde?
where (whither), ¿a dónde?
whether, si
which, que, ¿qué?
which one (ones)? ¿cuál (cuales)?
while, mientras
white, blanco, -a
who, que, quien, ¿quién?
whom, que ¿á quién?
whose, cuyo, -a, ¿de quién?

why? ¿por qué? ¿para qué?
wide, ancho, -a
wife, la esposa, la mujer
win, to, ganar
wind, el viento; **It is windy.** Hace
  viento.
window, la ventana
winter, el invierno
wise, sabio, -a
wish, el deseo
wish, to, querer(ie), desear
with, con
without, sin
woman, la mujer
wood, la madera
wool, la lana
word, la palabra
work, el trabajo
work, to, trabajar
world, el mundo
worry, to, preocuparse

worse, peor
worth, to be, valer; **It is worth while.**
  Vale la pena.
worthy, digno, -a
write, to, escribir
writer, el escritor
wrong: to be wrong, no tener razón

Y

year, el año; last year, el año pasado;
  next year, el año que viene, el año
  próximo
yellow, amarillo, -a
yesterday, ayer; day before yesterday,
  anteayer
yet, todavía; not yet, todavía no
young, joven
younger, menor
youngest, el menor
youth, el joven

VOCABULARY—SPANISH–ENGLISH

A

a, to, at
abajo, under, below
abierto, -a, open, opened
el abogado, lawyer
el abrigo, overcoat
abril (*m*), April
abrir, to open
acá, here (*usually with a verb of motion*)
acabar, to finish; **acaba de** + *infin.* = to have just
aceptar, to accept
la acera, the pavement
acerca de, about, concerning
acercarse (a), to approach
acompañar, to accompany
aconsejar, to advise
acordarse (ue) (de), to remember
acostarse (ue), to go to bed
acostumbrar, to accustom
el acuerdo, agreement
adelantar, to progress
adelante, straight ahead, forward
además, moreover, also
además de, in addition to
adiós, good-bye
admirar, to admire
aéreo: por correo aéreo, by airmail
el aeropuerto, airport
el aficionado, sport fan
afortunado, -a, lucky
afuera, outside
el agente, agent
agosto, August
agradable, agreeable, pleasant
agradecido, -a, thankful, grateful
el agua (*f*), water
ahí, there
ahora, now
ahorita, just now, in just a minute
el aire, air; **al aire libre**, in the open air
alegrar, to gladden; **alegrarse**, to rejoice, to be glad
alegre, lively, merry
la alfombra, rug, carpet
algo, something; somewhat
el algodón, cotton

alguien, someone, anyone
alguno (algún), -a, someone, any
el alimento, food
el alma (*f*), soul
el almacén, department store
el almuerzo, lunch
alquilar, to rent
alrededor de, around
los alrededores, surrounding area
la altiplanicie, highland
la altura, altitude
el alumno, la alumna, student
allá, there (*usually with a verb of motion*)
allí, there
amable, kind
amar, to love
amarillo, -a, yellow
el amigo, la amiga, friend
el amor, love
ancho, -a, wide
andar, to go, to walk
animado, -a, lively, animated
el ánimo, soul, spirit; courage
anoche, last night
antaño, ancient, of long ago
ante, before, in face of
anteayer, day before yesterday
antes de, before (*refers to time*); **cuanto antes**, as soon as possible
antiguo, -a, old
anunciar, to announce
el año, year; **el año que viene**, next year
el aparador, sideboard
aparecer, to appear
apenas, scarcely
el apetito, appetite
apreciar, to appreciate
aprender (a), to learn (to)
apresurarse, to hurry
aprisa, swiftly, quickly
apropiado, appropriate
aprovecharse de, to take advantage of
aquel, aquella, that
aquél, aquélla, that (one); the former
aquí, here; **Aquí lo tiene Vd.** Here it is.
el árbol, tree
arreglar, to arrange

arriba, above, upstairs
el arroz, rice
el arte (*m* and *f*), art
el artesano, craftsman
el artículo, article
el (la) artista, artist
artístico, artistic
el ascensor, lift
así, thus, so
el asiento, seat
asistir (a), to attend
el aspecto, appearance
atento, attentive
atrás, backwards, behind
atravesar (ie), to cross
aun (aún), even, yet, still
aunque, although
el autobús, bus
la avenida, avenue
averiguar, to find out
el avión, aeroplane
avisar, to inform
¡ay! alas!
ayer, yesterday
la ayuda, aid
ayudar (a), to aid, help (to)
el (la) azúcar, sugar
el azucarero, sugar-bowl
azul, blue
el azulejo, tile

B

bailar, to dance
el baile, dance
bajar (de), to get out (of); to climb (go) down
bajo, low
el balcón, balcony
el banco, bench
la bandeja, tray
bañar, to bathe
el baño, bath; bathtub; bathroom
barato, -a, cheap
¡basta! enough!
bastante, quite, enough
la batalla, battle
el baúl, trunk
beber, to drink
la bebida, drink
bello, -a, beautiful
el beso, kiss
la biblioteca, library
bien, well
bienvenido, -a, welcome
el billete, bill

el billete (de primera) (de segunda), (first-class) (second-class) ticket
blanco, -a, white
la blusa, blouse
la boca, mouth
el bocadillo, sandwich
el bolígrafo, ballpoint pen
la bolsa, purse
el bolsillo, pocket
la bondad, kindness
bonito, -a, pretty, nice
la botella, bottle
el brazo, arm
brillar, to shine
la brisa, breeze
bueno (buen), -a, good
el bulto, bundle
el burro, donkey
buscar, to look for
el buzón, postbox; **echar en el buzón,** to post

C

el caballo, horse
la cabeza, head
cada, each, every
caer, to fall
el café, coffee, café

la caja, box
el calcetín, sock
la calculadora, calculator
caliente, warm, hot
el calor, heat; **hace calor,** it is hot (weather); **tener calor,** to be hot (for persons)
la calle, street
la cama, bed
el camarero, waiter
cambiar, to change, exchange
el cambio, change; **de cambio,** in change
caminar, to go, to travel, to walk
el camino, road
la camisa, shirt
el campesino, peasant
el campo, country
la canasta, basket
la canción, song
cansado, tired
cansarse, to grow weary, tired
cantar, to sing
la cantidad, quantity
la cara, face
la carga, load
el cariño, affection
la carne, meat

la **carnicería,** butcher's shop
caro, -a, expensive, dear
la **carta,** letter
el **cartel,** poster
el **cartero,** postman
la **casa,** house
en **casa,** at home; **volver a casa,** to go home
casarse con, to marry
casi, almost
el **castellano,** Spanish (*language*)
el **catarro,** cold (*med.*); **atrapar un catarro,** catch cold; **tengo catarro,** I have a cold
la **causa,** cause; **a causa de,** because of
la **cebolla,** onion
celebrar, to celebrate
célebre, famous
la **cena,** supper
cenar, to have supper
el **céntimo,** cent
el **centro,** centre
la **cerámica,** pottery
cerca de (*prep.*), near
cercano, nearby
la **cerilla,** wax match
el **cero,** zero
cerrado, -a, closed, shut
cerrar (ie), to close, shut
la **cerveza,** beer
la **cesta,** basket
el **cielo,** sky
el **científico,** scientist
ciento (cien), one hundred; **por ciento,** per cent
cierto, certain, true; **por cierto,** certainly
el **cigarro,** cigar
el **cine,** cinema
el **cinturón,** belt
la **cita,** appointment
citar, to make an appointment with
la **ciudad,** city
claro, -a, clear, light; **¡Claro que sí!** Of course! **¡Claro que no!** Of course not!
la **clase,** class, kind
el **clavel,** carnation
el **cliente,** client
el **clima,** climate
el **cobre,** copper
cocido, cooked, boiled
la **cocina,** kitchen
el **coche,** car
coger, to catch, gather, pick up
el **color,** colour; **¿De qué color es . . .?**

What colour is . . .?
el **comedor,** dining-room
comenzar (ie), to begin
comer, to eat; **comerse,** to 'eat up'
el **comerciante,** businessman
la **comerciante,** businesswoman
la **comida,** meal, food, dinner
como, like, as, how; **¿cómo?** how? **¿cómo no?** of course, why not? **¿cómo se dice?** how do you say?
cómodo, -a, comfortable
el **compañero,** companion
el **compatriota,** countryman
completo, -a, complete
la **compra,** purchase; **ir de compras,** to go shopping
el **comprador,** purchaser
comprar, to buy
comprender, to understand
la **computadora,** computer
común, common
con, with; **conmigo,** with me; **con tal que,** provided that
el **concierto,** concert
condecorado, -a, decorated
conducir, to lead; to conduct
confesar (ie), to confess
conocer, to know, meet, be acquainted with
conocido, -a, well known
conseguir (i), to get, obtain
el **consejo,** advice
consentir (ie), to consent
consiguiente: por consiguiente, consequently
consistir en, to consist of
contar (ue), to count; to relate
contener, to contain
contento, -a, contented, happy
contestar (a), to answer
continuar, to continue
contra, against
conveniente, convenient
conversar, to converse
la **copia,** copy
el **corazón,** heart
la **corbata,** tie
coronado, crowned
correcto, -a, correct
corregir (i), to correct
el **correo,** the mail, the post; **por correo aéreo,** by airmail; **Correos,** the GPO.
correr, to run
la **corrida de toros,** bullfight
corriente, current, popular

cortar, to cut
la cortesía, courtesy
corto, -a, short
la cosa, thing; ¡qué cosa! the idea!
la costa, coast
costar (ue), to cost
la costumbre, custom; es costumbre, it's
the custom
crecer, to grow
creer, to believe, 'think'; Creo que no.
I think not; Creo que sí. I think so;
¡Ya lo creo! Yes indeed; I should say
so!
la criada, maid
el cristal, glass
cruzar, to cross
cuadrado, -a, square
el cuadro, picture
¿cúal? ¿cuáles? which (one, ones)? what?
cualquier, any
cuando, when; ¿cuándo? when?
¿cuánto, -a? how much?
¿cuántos, -as? how many?
el cuarto, room, quarter, fourth
cubierto de, covered (with)
cubrir, to cover
la cuchara, spoon
la cucharita, teaspoon
el cuchillo, knife
la cuenta, bill
el cuento, story
el cuero, leather
el cuerpo, body
¡Cuidado! Take care!
cuidar, to look after; cuidar de, to take
care of
la culpa, guilt, fault
la cultura, culture
el cumpleaños, birthday
cumplir, to fulfil
cuyo, -a, whose

CH

charlar, to chat
chico (a), small
el chico, la chica, boy, girl
la chuleta, chop

D

el daño, harm
dar, to give; dar a, to face (*the street
etc.*); dar las gracias a, to give thanks

to; dar un paseo, to go out walking
or driving; darse la mano, to shake
hands
de, of, from, about
debajo de, under, beneath
deber, ought to, be obliged to, must
débil, weak
decidir, to decide
décimo, tenth
decir (i), to tell, say; es decir, that is to
say
defender, to defend
dejar, to let, to leave, allow; dejar de,
to fail to (do something)
delante de, in front of
demandar, to demand
los demás, the rest
demasiado, -a, too (much), (*pl.*) too
many
dentro (de), inside (of)
el dependiente, clerk
el deporte, sport
el depósito, petrol tank
derecho, -a, right; a la derecha, to the
right; derecho, straight ahead
desaparecer, to disappear
desayunar, desayunarse, to breakfast
el desayuno, breakfast
descansar, to rest
el descanso, rest
describir, to describe
descubrir, to discover
desde, from, since; desde luego, of
course
desear, to wish, want
deseoso, desirous
el desfile, parade, procession
desgraciadamente, unfortunately
el desierto, desert
desocupado, unoccupied
despacio, slowly
despedirse (i) de, to take leave of
despertar (ie), to wake up (*somebody*)
despertarse, to wake up (*oneself*)
despierto, -a, awake
después, afterwards
después de, after
detrás de, behind
devolver (ue), to give back, return
el día, day; al día siguiente, next day;
hoy día, nowadays
diario, -a, daily
el dibujo, drawing
diciembre, December
el diente, tooth

diferente, different
difícil, difficult
digno, worthy
diligente, diligent
el dinero, money
el dios, god
la dirección, address
dirigirse a, to go to, to address (a person)
dispensar, to excuse; dispénseme, excuse me
distinto, different
la diversión, amusement
diverso, -a, varied
divertido, -a, amusing
divertirse (ie), to have a good time, amuse oneself
dividir, to divide
el dolor de cabeza (muelas), (estómago), headache (toothache) (stomachache)
dominar, to dominate
el domingo, Sunday
don (*m*), doña (*f*), title used with first name
donde, where; ¿dónde? where? ¿Por dónde se va a . . .? How does one get to . . .?
dormir (ue), to sleep; dormirse (ue), to fall asleep
el dormitorio, bedroom
el drama, play
la duda, doubt; sin duda alguna, without any doubt
dulce, sweet; los dulces, candy
durante, during
durar, to last
el duro, 5-peseta piece

E

echar, to pour; echarse, to stretch out; echar de menos, to miss
el echarpe, shawl
la edad, age
elevar, to raise; elevarse, to rise
la embajada, embassy
embargo: sin embargo, nevertheless
emocionante, touching, thrilling
empezar (ie) (a), to begin (to)
el empleado, employee
emplear, to use
en, in, on; at; en seguida, at once; en vez de, instead of
encantar, to enchant, charm
encima (de), on top (of)
encontrar (ue), to find, meet

enero, January
enfermo, -a, sick, ill
enfrente de, opposite, facing
enorme, enormous
enseñar, to teach
entender (ie), to understand
entero, whole
entonces, then
la entrada, entrance; ticket (theatre and cinema)
entrar (en), to enter
entre, between
entretanto, meanwhile
enviar, to send
el envío, shipment
el equipaje, baggage
equivocado, -a, mistaken
la escalera, stairway
escocés, -esa, Scottish
Escocia, Scotland
escoger, to choose
escribir, to write
el escritor, writer
el escritorio, desk
escuchar (a), to listen (to)
la escuela, school
ese, -a, that
ése, -a, that (one)
eso, that (*referring to a statement or idea*); a eso de, at about (*time*); por eso, therefore
espacioso, spacious
el español, Spanish (*lang.*)
el español, Spaniard; la española, Spanish woman
el espectador, spectator
esperar, to wait (for), hope, expect; Espero que no. I hope not; Espero que sí. I hope so.
el esposo, husband; la esposa, wife
la esquina, corner
la estación de ferrocarril, railway station
el estado, state
los Estados Unidos, (*abbr.* EE.UU.), the United States
la estantería, shelf, bookcase
estar, to be (*place*); estar en camino, to be on the way; estar para, to be about to
la estatua, statue
el este, east
este, -a, this
éste, -a, this (one)
esterlina, sterling
el estilo, style

esto, this (*referring to a statement or idea*)
estrecho, -a, narrow
la estrella, star
el estudiante, student
el estudio, study
estudiar, to study
el examen, examination
examinar, to examine
excelente, excellent
excepto, except
explicar, to explain
expresar, to express
la expresión, expression
extender (ie), to extend

F

fácil, easy
facilitar, to facilitate
fácilmente, easily
facturar, to check (baggage)
la faja, sash
la falda, skirt
falso, -a, false
la falta, mistake, lack; **Me hace falta,** I lack, I need
faltar, to be lacking, need; **me falta, I** need
la familia, family
famoso, -a, famous
la farmacia, pharmacy
favor: hágame el favor de, please; **Es favor que Vd. me hace,** You flatter me; **por favor,** please
febrero, February
la fecha, date; **¿Cuál es la fecha?** What is the date?
felicitar, to congratulate
feliz, happy
la fiesta, holiday
la fila, row
el fin, end; **al fin,** finally, at last
fino, -a, fine
firmar, to sign
el flan, crème caramel
la flor, flower
la formalidad, formality
la fortuna, fortune
el fósforo, match
el francés, French (*lang.*), Frenchman; **la francesa,** Frenchwoman
la frase, sentence
la frente, front; **en frente de,** in front of; **frente a,** opposite, facing

fresco, cool
frío, cold; **hacer frío,** to be cold (*weather*); **tener frío,** to be cold (*persons*)
la fruta, fruit
el fuego, fire
la fuente, fountain
fuera de, outside of
fuerte, strong
la función, performance

G

Gales, Wales
galés, -esa, Welsh
la gana, desire; **de buena gana,** willingly
ganar, to earn, to win
el garaje, garage
gastar, to spend
el gato, jack (for car); cat
generoso, generous
la gente, people
gordo, -a, fat
gozar (de), to enjoy
gracias, thanks
gracioso, -a, graceful, amusing
grande, large, great
gris, grey
gritar, to shout
el grito, shout, cry
grueso, -a, thick
el grupo, group
el guante, glove
guapo, -a, neat, elegant, handsome
guardar, to keep, guard
la guía, guide book
gustar, to be pleasing to; **me gusta,** I like
el gusto, pleasure; **con mucho gusto,** with much pleasure; **el gusto es mío,** the pleasure is mine; **tanto gusto en conocerle,** very pleased to meet you

H

haber, to have (*auxiliary*)
el habitante, inhabitant
hablador, -a, talkative
hablar, to speak
hacer, to do, make; **hace algún tiempo,** some time ago; **hace calor, frío, etc.,** it is hot, cold, etc. (weather); **hacer daño a,** to hurt; **me hace falta,** I need; **hacer preguntas,** to ask questions
hallar, to find

el hambre (*f*), hunger; tener hambre, to be hungry

hasta, until, to, as far as, even; hasta luego, so long; hasta mañana, until tomorrow; hasta la vista, so long

hay, there is, there are; hay que, it is necessary to, one must; hay (sol) (viento) (polvo) (lodo), it is (sunny) (windy) (dusty) (muddy)

hecho, made; hecho a mano, handmade

el helado, ice cream

el hermano, brother; la hermana, sister

hermoso, -a, beautiful

el héroe, hero

el hierro, iron

el hijo, son; la hija, daughter; los hijos, children

la hoja, leaf, sheet (of paper)

la hojalata, tin

el hombre, man

la hora, hour; time; ¿A qué hora? At what time?

el horario, time table

la hospitalidad, hospitality

hoy, today; hoy día, nowadays

el huevo, egg

huir, to flee

húmedo, wet

I

ida: un billete de ida y vuelta, a return ticket

el idioma, language

la iglesia, church

igual, equal

igualmente, equally, the same to you

imaginar, to imagine

imitar, to imitate

impaciente, impatient

el impermeable, raincoat

imponente, imposing

el importador, importer

importante, important

importar, to matter, to be important; to import; no importa, it does not matter

la impresión, impression

indicar, to point out

indígena, indigenous, native

el indio, -a, Indian

la industria, industry

la información, information; pedir información, to ask for information

informar, to inform

el inglés, English (*lang*.); Englishman; la inglesa, Englishwoman

el iniciador, founder

inmediatamente, immediately

inmenso, -a, immense

inteligente, intelligent

el interés, interest

interesar, to interest

el invierno, winter

invitar, to invite

ir, to go; irse, to go away, leave; ir de compras, to go shopping; ir de paseo, to go out walking or riding

irlandés, -esa, Irish

Irlanda, Ireland

izquierdo, -a, left; a la izquierda, to the left

J

¡ja! ¡ja! ha! ha!

el jabón, soap

jamás, never

el jamón, ham

el jardín, garden

el jarro, jar

el jefe, chief

jira, ir de, to go on a picnic

joven, young

el joven, young man

la joya, jewel

la joyería, jewellery shop, jewellery

el juego, game, set

el jueves, Thursday

el jugador, player, gambler

jugar, to play (*a game*)

el juguete, toy

julio, July

junio, June

juntar, to join, unite

junto a, near, close to; junto con, together with

K

el kilo, kilogramme

el kilómetro, kilometre

L

el labio, lip

labrado, worked, tilled

la laca, lacquer

el lado, side; al lado de, beside

la lámpara, lamp

la lana, wool
el lápiz, pencil
largo, -a, long
la lástima, shame, pity; ¡Qué lástima!
  What a pity!
la lata, tin
lavar, to wash; lavarse, to wash oneself
la lección, lesson
la leche, milk
la lechuga, lettuce
leer, read
la legumbre, vegetable
lejano, -a, far-off
lejos de, far from; a lo lejos, in the distance
lentamente, slowly
levantar, to raise, lift; levantarse, to rise,
  get up
la libra, pound
la librería, bookshop
el libro, book
el líder, leader
ligero, -a, light
la lima, lime
el limón, lemon
limpiar, to clean
la lista, menu
listo, -a, ready
la lotería, lottery
la lucha, struggle
luego, then; hasta luego, so long
el lugar, place
el lujo, luxury
luminoso, -a, bright
la luna, moon
el lunes, Monday
la luz, light

LL

llamar, to call; llamar por teléfono, to
  call up
llamarse, to be called; Me llamo Pablo.
  My name is Paul.
la llanura, plain
la llegada, arrival
llegar, to arrive
llenar, to fill
lleno, -a, full
llevar, to carry; to take, to wear;
  llevarse, to carry (take) away
llover (ue), to rain
la lluvia, rain
lluvioso, -a, rainy

M

la madera, wood
la madre, mother
el madrugador, early riser
el maestro, teacher
magnífico, magnificent
el maíz, corn
el malestar, indisposition
la maleta, suitcase; boot of a car; hacer
  una maleta, to pack a suitcase
malo, -a, bad, sick
la mamá, mummy
mandar, to order, to send
manejar, to drive
la manera, manner; de manera que, so
  that; de (otra) (la misma) manera, in
  (another) (the same) way
la mano, hand; darse la(s) mano(s), to
  shake hands; a mano derecha, on
  the right; a mano izquierda, on the
  left
la manta, blanket
mantener, to maintain
la manzana, apple; block of houses
mañana, tomorrow; hasta mañana, till
  tomorrow
la mañana, morning; por la mañana, in
  the morning
la máquina de escribir, typewriter
el mar, sea
el martes, Tuesday
marzo (m), March
más, more, most; más o menos, more or
  less
la máscara, mask
matar, to kill
las matemáticas, mathematics
mayo (m), May
mayor, older
la mayoría, majority
la media, stocking
el médico, doctor
la medida, measure
medio, -a, half (a, an)
medir (i), to measure

mejor, better; el (la) mejor, best
el melocotón, peach
el melón, melon
la memoria, memory; de memoria, by
  heart
menor, younger; el (la) menor, youngest
menos, less, minus, except; por lo
  menos, at least; echar de menos, to
  miss

menudo: a menudo, often
el mercado, market
la mercancía, merchandise
la merienda, a light supper, 'tea'
la mesa, table
la meseta, plateau
el metro, the underground (railway)
mientras, while; mientras tanto, meanwhile
miércoles, Wednesday
mil, thousand
la milla, mile
el millón, million
mirar, to look (at)
mismo, -a, same; él mismo, he himself; lo mismo, the same thing
la mitad, half
moderno, -a, modern
el modismo, idiom
el modo, way; de este modo, in this way; de todos modos, anyway
mojado, -a, soaked, wet
la moneda, currency, money
la montaña, mountain
el montón, heap, pile
morir (ue), to die
mostrar (ue), to show
el movimiento, movement
el mozo, waiter
el muchacho, boy; la muchacha, girl
mucho, -a, much; muchos, -as, many
mudarse, to move (change house)
la muerte, death
la mujer, woman
el mundo, world; todo el mundo, everybody
murió, he died
el museo, museum
muy, very

N

nacer, to be born
nació, he was born
el nacimiento, birth
nada, nothing, not anything; de nada, you're welcome
nadie, no one, nobody
la naranja, orange
la nariz, nose
la naturaleza, nature
la Navidad, Christmas
necesario, -a, necessary
la necesidad, necessity
necesitar, to need
el negociante, business man

el negocio, business
negro, -a, black
el neumático, tyre
ni . . . ni, neither . . . nor; ni yo tampoco, nor I either, neither do I
la nieve, snow
ninguno, -a, no, none, nobody
el niño, la niña, child
no, not
la noche, night; por la noche, in the evening; esta noche, tonight
nombrar, to name
el nombre, name
el norte, north
el norteamericano, North American (*usually means a person from the U.S.*)
notable, worthy of note
las noticias, news
nuevo, -a, new
el número, number
nunca, never

O

o, or (u *before* o *or* ho)
obedecer, to obey
el objeto, object
observar, to observe
obtener, to obtain
occidental, western
octubre, October
ocupado, -a, busy
el oeste, west
la oficina, office
ofrecer, to offer
el oído, ear (*hearing*)
oír, to hear
el ojo, eye
olvidar, to forget
omitir, to omit
la oportunidad, opportunity
la orden, order
a sus órdenes, at your service
el ordenador, computer
ordinario, -a, ordinary
el orgullo, pride
orgulloso, -a, proud
el oro, gold
oscuro, -a, dark
el otoño, autumn
otro, -a, other, another

P

pacífico, peaceful
el padre, father

pagar, to pay
el país, country
la paja, straw
el pájaro, bird
la palabra, word
el palo, stick
el pan, bread
el panadero, baker
el panecillo, roll
la pantalla, screen
el papá, papa
el papel, paper, role
el paquete, package; **el paquete postal,** parcel post
el par, pair
para, in order to, for; **para que,** in order that
el paraguas, umbrella
parar, to stop
parecer, to seem; **Le parece bien.** It seems all right to him; **parecerse a,** to resemble
la pared, wall
el pariente, relative
el parque, park
la parte, part; **por todas partes,** everywhere
la partida, departure
el partidario, partisan, supporter
partir, to leave
el pasado, past
el pasaje, fare, passage
el pasaporte, passport
pasar, to pass, spend (*time*), happen; **pasar sin,** to get along without; **pasar un buen rato,** to spend a pleasant time; ¿Qué pasa? What is going on?
Pase Vd. Come in: Go ahead.
pasear, to take a walk, to walk about; **pasearse (en coche) (a caballo) (en barco),** to go for a walk or a ride (in a car) (on horseback) (in a boat)
el paseo, promenade
el paso, step
el pastel, cake
la patata, potato
el patio, courtyard
el pato, duck
el pavo, turkey
pedir (i), to ask for
pedir información, to ask for information
la película, motion picture, film
peligroso, -a, dangerous
el pelo, hair

el penique, penny
pensar (ie), to think, to intend to; **pensar en,** to think about
peor, worse
pequeño, -a, small
la pera, pear
perder (ie), to lose
perdonar, to pardon
perezoso, -a, lazy
perfectamente, perfectly
el periódico, newspaper
el permiso, permission; **con su permiso,** allow me
permitir, to permit
pero, but
la persona, person
pesado, -a, heavy
pesar, to weigh; **a pesar de,** in spite of
el pescado, fish
pescar, to fish
el peso, weight
picante, spicy, 'hot' (*of food*)
el pico, peak
el pie, foot
estar de pie, to stand
la piedra, stone
la pierna, leg
la pieza, piece
pintar, to paint
el pintor, painter
pintoresco, -a, picturesque
la pintura, painting
el piso, storey
el placer, pleasure
la plata, silver
el plátano, banana
el platero, silversmith
el platillo, saucer
el plato, dish
la plaza, square
la pluma, pen, fountain pen
pobre, poor
poco, -a, little; **dentro de poco,** in a short time; **pocos, -as,** few
poder (ue), to be able, can, may; **(no) se puede,** one can (not)
el agente de policía, policeman
el pollo, chicken
poner, to put, to place; **poner la mesa,** to set the table; **ponerse,** to put on, to become; **La naturaleza se pone verde.** Nature turns green; **ponerse en marcha,** to start
por, for, in exchange for, by, through,

along; **por cierto,** certainly; **por eso,** therefore; **por lo tanto,** therefore; **por supuesto,** of course; **por todas partes,** everywhere

la porción, portion

¿por qué? why?

porque, because

el portal, arcade

el porvenir, future

posible, possible

postal: el paquete postal, parcel post

el postre, dessert

practicar, to practise

el precio, price

precioso, -a, exquisite, beautiful

precisamente, exactly

preferir (ie), to prefer

la pregunta, question

preguntar, to ask

el premio, prize

preocuparse de, to worry (about)

presentar, to introduce

prestar, to lend

la primavera, spring

primer (o), -a, first

el principio, beginning; **al principio,** at first

prisa: de prisa, fast, quickly; **tener prisa,** to be in a hurry

probablemente, probably

probar (ue), to try, to prove, to taste

el problema, problem

producir, to produce

el profesor, professor

profundo, -a, profound

el programa, programme

prometer, to promise

pronto, soon

la propina, tip

propio, -a, own

proponer, to propose

propósito: a propósito, by the way

proteger, to protect

próximo, -a, next (in time)

el pueblo, town; people

la puerta, door

pues, well, then

el puesto, stand, booth

puesto que, since

el punto, point, period; **en punto,** on the dot (*time*)

Q

que, who, that, which, than; **lo que,** that which, what

¿qué? what, which; **¿Qué tal?** How's everything?

quedar (se), to remain, stay

querer (ie), to wish, want; **querer a,** to love; **¿Qué quiere decir?** What does it mean?

querido, -a, dear, beloved

quien, -es, who

¿quién, -es?, who? ¿a quién, -es? whom? to whom? ¿de quién, -es? whose?

quién sabe, goodness knows

quitar, to remove; **quitarse,** to take off (*clothing*)

R

la radio, radio

rápidamente, rapidly

la rapidez, speed

rápido, -a, rapid, swift

raro, -a, strange, rare

el rato, while; **largo rato,** a long time

razón: tener razón, to be right; **no tener razón,** to be wrong

recibir, to receive

reconocer, to recognize

recordar (ue), to remember

el recreo, recreation

el recuerdo, souvenir

el refresco, soft drink

el regalo, gift

regatear, to bargain

regresar, to return

reír (i), to laugh; **reírse de (i),** to laugh at

el reloj, watch, clock

reluciendo, shining, glittering

repente: de repente, suddenly

repetir (i), to repeat

el representante, representative

requisito, necessary

la reserva, reservation, reserved seat

el resfriado, cold (illness)

resistir, to resist

respecto a, in regard to

el respeto, respect

responder, to answer

la respuesta, answer

el restaurant(e), restaurant

los restos, remains

el retrato, portrait, photograph

revisar, to examine

la revista, magazine

el rey, king

rico, -a, rich
el río, river
la risa, laugh
rodeado, -a, surrounded
rojo, -a, red
romper, to break
la ropa, clothing
rosado, -a, pink
el ruido, noise

S

el sábado, Saturday
saber, to know, to know how
sabroso, -a, tasty, delicious
sacar, to take out
la sala, living-room, hall; la sala de espera, waiting-room
salir de, to leave, to go out of; salir para, to leave for
la salsa, sauce
la salud, health
saludar, to greet
el saludo, greeting
el santo, saint
santo, holy
satisfecho, -a, satisfied
seco, -a, dry
sed: tener sed, to be thirsty
la seda, silk
seguida: en seguida, at once
seguir (i), to continue, to follow
según, according to
segundo, -a, second; el billete de segunda clase, second-class ticket
seguramente, surely
seguro, sure; de seguro, surely
el sello, postage stamp
la semana, week
semejante, similar
sencillo, -a, simple
sentado, -a, seated, sitting down
sentarse (ie), to sit down
el sentido, meaning, sense
sentir (ie), to regret, be sorry; Lo siento mucho, I am very sorry; sentirse (ie), to feel
la señal, signal
señalar, to point out
el señor, gentleman; Mr.
la señora, lady; Mrs.
la señorita, young lady; Miss
septiembre, September
ser, to be
el servicio, service

el servidor, servant
servir (i), to serve; servir para, to serve as; ¿En qué puedo servirle? May I help you?
si, if; whether
sí, yes; certainly
siempre, always
la sierra, mountain range
la siesta, afternoon nap, rest
el siglo, century
significar, to mean
siguiente, following; al día siguiente, the following day
la silla, chair
el sillón, armchair
simpático, pleasant, nice
sin, without (*prep.*); sin que, without (*conj.*)
sino, but (on the contrary)
el sistema, system
el sitio, place
situado, -a, situated
sobre, upon, over
el sol, sun
solamente, only; no solamente . . . sino también, not only . . . but also
solo, -a, alone, only
sólo, only (*adv.*)
la sombra, shade
el sombrero, hat
sonar (ue), to sound, ring
el sonido, sound
sonreír (i), to smile
soñar (ue), to dream
la sopa, soup
sorprendido, surprised
subir, to go up, to climb, to get into (bus, taxi, etc.)
el suburbio, suburb
sucio, -a, dirty
el suelo, floor, ground
el sueño, dream; tener sueño, to be sleepy
la suerte, fate, luck; buena suerte, good luck
el suéter, sweater
sumamente, extremely
supuesto: por supuesto, of course
el sur, south
el surtido, assortment

T

el tabaco, tobacco
tal, such (a); tal vez, maybe

el tamaño, size
también, also
tampoco, neither, either; ni yo tampoco, nor I either
tan, as, so; tan ... como, as ... as
tanto, -a, so much, (*pl.*) so many; tanto ... como, as much ... as, (*pl.*) as many ... as
la taquígrafa, stenographer
la taquilla, ticket window
el taquillero, ticket-seller, booking clerk
la tarde, afternoon; tarde (*adj.*), late
la taza, cup
el té, tea
el teatro, theatre
el tejado, roof
el tejido, textile
la tela, cloth
el teléfono, telephone; llamar por teléfono, to call up
la televisión, television
el tema, theme, subject; temer, to fear
la temperatura, temperature
templado, temperate
temprano, early
el tenedor, fork
tener, to have; tener calor, frío, to be warm, cold (person); tener cuidado, to be careful; tener dolor de (cabeza) (muelas), to have a (head) (tooth) ache; tener ganas de, to have a desire to; tener hambre, sed, to be hungry, thirsty; tener prisa, to be in a hurry; tener que, to have to; tener razón, to be right; tener sueño, to be sleepy; ¿Qué tiene Vd.? What is the matter with you?
teñido, dyed
tercer(o), -a, third
terminar, to end
la ternera, veal
el tiempo, weather; time; a tiempo, on time
la tienda, store
la tierra, land
el timbre, bell
la tinta, ink
el tío, uncle; la tía, aunt
típico, typical
tocar, to play (an instrument); to ring (a bell)
el tocino, bacon, pork
todavía, still, yet; todavía no, not yet
todo, -a, all, every, whole, everything; ante todo, first of all; todo el mundo, everybody; todo el año, all year; todo lo posible, as much as possible; sobre todo, especially
tomar, to take, to eat, drink; tomar la cena, to dine
el tomate, tomato
el torero, bullfighter
el toro, bull
la toronja, grapefruit
la torta, cake
la tortilla, omelette
la tostada, toast
trabajador, -a, hard-working
trabajar, to work
el trabajo, work
traducir, to translate
traer, to bring
el traje, suit, costume
el tranvía, tram
tratar (de), to try (to), deal with
el trigo, wheat
triste, sad
el (la) turista, tourist

U

u, or (*before words beginning with o or ho*)
último, last
unir, to unite; unirse, to join
la universidad, university
usar, to use
el uso, use
útil, useful
la uva, grape

V

la vaca, cow
las vacaciones, vacation
vacío, -a, empty
valer, to be worth; no vale nada, it is not worth anything; valer la pena, to be worth while; más vale tarde que nunca, better late than never
la valija, valise
el valle, valley
la variedad, variety
varios, several
el vaso, glass (*for drinking*)
la velocidad, speed; a toda velocidad, at full speed
el vendedor, seller
vender, to sell

venir, to come
la ventana, window
ver, to see; ¡a ver! let's see!
el verano, summer
veras: ¿de veras? really?
la verdad, truth; ¿verdad? is(n't) that so?
verdaderamente, truly
verde, green
el vestíbulo, hall
el vestido, dress
vestir (i), to dress; vestirse (de), to dress
in
la vez, *pl.* veces, time; a la vez, at the
same time; a veces, sometimes; de
vez en cuando, from time to time;
en vez de, instead of; otra vez, again;
tal vez, perhaps
el viaje, trip; desear buen viaje, to wish
a pleasant journey
la vida, life
el viejecito, little old man
viejo, -a, old
el viento, wind; hace viento, it is windy
el viernes, Friday

la visita, visit, visitor
la vista, view; hasta la vista, so long
vivir, to live; ¡viva! long live!
vivo, -a, lively
volver (ue), to return; volver a casa, to
go home; volver a + *inf.*, to do again
la voz, voice
el vuelo, flight
la vuelta, turn, return; change (money);
a la vuelta, around the corner; un
billete de ida y vuelta, a return ticket

Y

y, and
ya, already, now; ¡Ya lo creo! I should
say so!

Z

la zapatería, shoe shop
el zapatero, shoemaker
el zapato, shoe
el zumo, juice

ANSWERS

Exercise No. 1

1 comerciante
2 quién
3 con
4 padre
5 madre

6 hay
7 se llaman
8 su
9 particular
10 todos los cuartos

11 piso
12 calle
13 grande
14 allí, todo el día
15 ciudad

Exercise No. 2A

1 la
2 una
3 la, los
4 el, la

5 una, un
6 el
7 los, un

8 unos, la, unas, la
9 los, la
10 los, las, la

Exercise No. 2B

1 las calles
2 los comedores
3 los cuartos
4 los señores
5 los dormitorios

6 las cocinas
7 las madres
8 los padres
9 las salas
10 las hijas

11 las ciudades
12 los años
13 las mujeres
14 los hombres
15 los tíos

Exercise No. 2C

1 La señora Adams es inglesa.
2 Vive en Londres.
3 Hay seis personas en la familia.
4 La casa tiene seis cuartos.
5 Es una casa particular.

6 La señora Adams es la madre.
7 El señor Adams es el padre.
8 La oficina está en la calle de Oxford.
9 Va por tren a la ciudad.
10 Allí trabaja todo el día.

Exercise No. 4

1 quién
2 una comerciante de Londres
3 su oficina
4 otros
5 va
6 desea
7 además (también)
8 pero

9 estudia
10 martes, jueves
11 rápidamente
12 muy inteligente
13 español
14 un buen profesor
15 en la primera conversación

Exercise No. 5A

1 es
2 está

3 es
4 está

5 es
6 es

7 está
8 está

9 es
10 es

Exercise No. 5B

1 (d)   2 (f)   3 (a)   4 (b)   5 (c)   6 (e)

313

Exercise No. 5C

1 y	8 por eso	15 gracias
2 en	9 allí	16 grande
3 con	10 aquí	17 pequeño
4 también	11 casi	18 bueno
5 a	12 siempre	19 malo
6 tal vez	13 ¿Cómo está Vd.?	20 rápidamente
7 pero	14 muy bien	

Exercise No. 7

1 está sentado	5 mi esposo	8 están en la mesita
2 hay	6 sobre el piano	9 basta
3 saber	7 un lápiz, un bolígrafo,	10 hasta el jueves
4 Dígame	y unos papeles	

Exercise No. 8A

1 la calle, las calles, street
2 la oficina, las oficinas, office
3 la pared, las paredes, wall
4 la silla, las sillas, chair
5 el señor, los señores, gentleman
6 la mesa, las mesas, table
7 el papel, los papeles, paper
8 la puerta, las puertas, door
9 la estantería, las estanterías, bookcase
10 la ventana, las ventanas, window

Exercise No. 8B

1 debajo de	5 entre	8 detrás de
2 cerca de	6 delante del	9 debajo de
3 encima del	7 alrededor de	10 cerca del
4 sobre		

Exercise No. 8C

1 de la	3 de las	5 a la	7 a los	9 al
2 al	4 del	6 de los	8 a la	10 a las

Exercise No. 9

1 Está sentada en la sala de su casa.
2 El Sr. López está sentado cerca de ella.
3 Sí, hay muchas cosas alrededor de nosotros.
4 Sí, hay muchas cosas en la calle.
5 El esposo de la Sra. Adams toca bien el piano.
6 Está encima del piano.
7 Está sobre el piano.
8 La estantería está delante de una ventana.
9 Está cerca de la puerta.
10 Cerca del escritorio está una silla.
11 Están encima del escritorio.
12 Están en la mesita.

Exercise No. 10

1 (g)	3 (i)	5 (j)	7 (k)	9 (d)	11 (b)
2 (e)	4 (h)	6 (l)	8 (a)	10 (c)	12 (f)

Exercise No. 11

1 todo el día
2 por favor
3 tal vez
4 Buenas tardes
5 con mucho gusto
6 Por eso
7 Cómo
8 Dónde
9 Qué
10 Quién

Exercise No. 12

1 (d)   3 (i)   5 (h)   7 (c)   9 (a)   11 (e)
2 (f)   4 (k)   6 (g)   8 (j)   10 (b)

Exercise No. 13

1 delante de la casa
2 cerca de la puerta
3 alrededor de la ciudad
4 detrás del escritorio
5 encima del piano
6 Los libros del muchacho
7 La madre de las muchachas
8 El hermano de Felipe
9 El padre de María
10 El maestro de los niños

Exercise No. 14A Reading Selection

Mrs. Adams, London Merchant

Mrs. Adams is an English businesswoman who imports art objects from Spain. Therefore she wants to make a trip to Spain in the spring. She wants to talk with her agent and to visit some places of interest in Spain. But she does not know how to speak Spanish.

Mrs. Adams has a good teacher. He is a Spaniard who lives in London, and his name is Mr. López. Tuesdays and Thursdays the teacher goes by train to the house of his student. There Mrs. Adams and Mr. López speak a little in Spanish. Mrs. Adams is very intelligent and learns rapidly. For example, in the first conversation she learns by heart the salutations and farewells. She already knows how to say 'Good day', 'How are you?', 'Good-bye', 'Until tomorrow.' She already knows how to say in Spanish the names of many things which are in her living-room and she knows how to answer well the questions: 'What is this?' and Where is . . .?'

Mr. López is very satisfied with the progress of his student and says: 'Good. Enough for today. Goodbye.'

Exercise No. 15

1 son importantes
2 unos verbos corrientes
3 Por qué
4 Porque, mi
5 con él en español
6 a otros países
7 en tren o en avión
8 Cuánto
9 muy rápidamente
10 Basta por hoy

Exercise No. 16A

1 to listen
2 to want
3 to begin
4 to form, make
5 to expect
6 to converse
7 to practise
8 to travel
9 to ask
10 to answer
11 to begin
12 to study
13 to import
14 to play
15 to visit

Exercise No. 16B

1 Do you speak Spanish?
Yes, I speak Spanish.
What languages does your teacher speak?
He speaks English, Spanish and French.
2 Who plays the piano?
Mary plays the piano.
Don't you play the piano, Rosie?
No, I do not play the piano.

3 Are the students studying the lesson?
No, they are not studying the lesson.
Are they speaking in Spanish?
Yes, they are speaking in Spanish.
4 Do you listen attentively when the teacher is speaking?
Yes, we listen attentively when the teacher is speaking.

Exercise No. 16C

1 no habla
2 estudiamos
3 importa
4 desea

5 espero
6 charlan
7 practican
8 viaja

9 esperamos
10 empiezan

Exercise No. 16D

1 empiezo
2 escucha
3 formas
4 conversa

5 practican
6 ¿pregunta Vd.?
7 contestan
8 ¿estudiamos?

9 desean
10 visito
11 viajo
12 ¿espera Vd.?

Exercise No. 17

1 Están sentados en la sala de la Sra. A.
2 El Sr. L. empieza a hablar.
3 La Sra. Adams escucha con atención.
4 El Sr. L. pregunta.
5 La Sra. A. contesta.
6 Sí, son importantes.
7 Sí, es comerciante.

8 No, no habla español.
9 Porque desea hacer un viaje a España.
or Porque desea hablar con su agente.
10 Espera visitar España, Tenerife, y tal vez a las otras Islas Canarias.
11 Viaja en avión.
12 Aprende rápidamente.

Exercise No. 18

1 abre
2 Pase
3 Buenas tardes, su
4 catarro

5 otros
6 tengo
7 somos
8 años

9 la menor
10 el mayor
11 un rato más
12 al Sr. López

Exercise No. 19A

1 es, Es
2 está, Estoy
3 están, Estamos
4 Es, soy

5 Está, está
6 están, estamos
7 están, Están

8 Son, somos
9 están, están
10 Son, somos

Exercise No. 19B

1 al señor
2 la escuela
3 a su amigo
4 la lección

5 a la señora
6 el tren
7 a Isabel

8 a su agente
9 el parque
10 a José

Exercise No. 19C

1 ¿Cómo está Ud.?
2 Regular, gracias.
3 Mi hija está enferma.
4 Lo siento mucho.
5 Uds. son una familia de seis personas.
6 ¿Van sus niños a la escuela?
7 ¿Habla Ud. español?
8 No, no hablo español.
9 Invito a Carlos a visitar mi casa.
10 Vamos a charlar un rato.
11 Vamos a principiar (comenzar) (empezar)
12 Deseo (quiero) estudiar el español.

Exercise No. 20

1 La criada abre la puerta.
2 El Sr. L. toca el timbre
3 Espera al Sr. L. en la sala.
4 Anita, la hija de la Sra. A. está enferma.
5 Tiene catarro
6 Tiene cuatro hijos.
7 Hay seis personas en su familia.
8 Sus hijos se llaman Felipe, Guillermo, Rosita y Anita.
9 Tiene diez años.
10 Sí, hablan un rato más.
11 La Sra. A. invita al Sr. L. a visitar su oficina.
12 Sí, acepta la invitación.

Exercise No. 21

1 dan a la calle
2 periódicos
3 detrás de su escritorio
4 entra en la oficina
5 Mucho gusto en verle
6 El gusto es mío
7 Me gusta
8 A propósito
9 Veo
10 De qué color
11 De qué color
12 ¡Dios mío!
13 Tengo hambre
14 No lejos de aquí
15 ¡Vámonos!

Exercise No. 22A

1 vivos
2 cómoda
3 rojos
4 verdes
5 altos
6 muchos
7 blancas
8 muchas
9 azul
10 simpática

Exercise No. 22B

1 son
2 está
3 es
4 está
5 estoy
6 están
7 estamos
8 somos
9 son
10 son

Exercise No. 22C

1 La oficina de la Sra. A. es muy bonita.
2 Las ventanas de la oficina son grandes.
3 Muchos papeles están en el suelo.
4 Los tejados de las casas son rojos.
5 El cielo es azul.
6 Las montañas son verdes.
7 El edificio es muy alto.
8 ¿Cómo está Ud., Sra. A?
9 Estoy muy bien, gracias.
10 Los carteles son hermosos.

Exercise No. 23

1 Está en el quinto piso de un edificio alto.
2 No es grande.
3 Sí, es cómoda.
4 En las paredes grises hay algunos carteles.

5 En el escritorio de la Sra. A. hay
   muchos papeles.
6 Está cerca de la puerta.
7 Una mesa larga está entre las dos
   ventanas.
8 La Sra. A. está sentada.
9 Es amarillo.

10 Es negro.
11 Son verdes.
12 Sí, es azul.
13 Son blancas.
14 Sí, son rojos.
15 Es la oficina de la Sra. Adams.

Exercise No. 24

1 sus padres
2 adelanta
3 ¿Qué tal?
4 A propósito, ¿verdad?

5 ¿Cómo no?
6 Aprendo
7 fácil. difícil
8 Estudio, deseo

9 comprendo
10 palabras, diaria
11 las expresiones
12 Me gusta

Exercise No. 25B

1 aprendo
2 toca
3 estudiamos
4 comprenden

5 Leen
6 beben
7 escribe
8 vive

9 bebes
10 quieres
11 viajan
12 abre

Exercise No. 26

1 El Sr. Gómez es un habitante de
   Londres.
2 Sí, habla bien el español.
3 No, son españoles.
4 Sabe que su amiga la Sra. Adams
   aprende el español.
5 Entra en la oficina de la Sra. A.
6 Saluda a la Sra. Adams en español.
7 La Sra. Adams aprende a hablar, a
   leer y a escribir el español.
8 Estudia diligentemente.

9 El Sr. Lopez es su profesor de
   español.
10 Sí, es un buen profesor.
11 Sí, comprende.
12 Aprende las palabras de la vida
   diaria.
13 La Sra. Adams va a hacer un viaje a
   España.
14 Espera ir a España la primavera que
   viene.
15 El Sr. Gómez dice — Buen viaje y
   buena suerte. *or* El Sr. G. lo dice. (He
   says *it*.)

Exercise No. 27

1 civilización
2 reservación
3 instrucción
4 excepción

5 revolución
6 observación
7 invitación

8 elección
9 invención
10 solución

Exercise No. 28

1 Es azul.
2 Hablan español.
3 La Sra. A. tiene hambre.
4 Es blanca y negra.
5 Vivo en Gran Bretaña.

6 Son rojos.
7 Beben leche.
8 Saluda a su amigo.
9 Tengo treinta años.
10 Me llamo . . .

Exercise No. 29

1 (*e*)	3 (*a*)	5 (*b*)	7 (*c*)	9 (*j*)
2 (*g*)	4 (*i*)	6 (*h*)	8 (*d*)	10 (*f*)

Exercise No. 30

1 trabajamos	5 escriben	8 bebe
2 aprenden	6 abres	9 adelantamos
3 empieza	7 permito	10 veo
4 sabe		

Exercise No. 31

1 Sí, aprendo ...	4 Sí, espero ...	7 Sí, comprendo ...
2 Sí, estudio ...	5 Sí, veo ...	8 Sí, acepto ...
3 Sí, trabajo ...	6 Sí, leo ...	9 Sí, visito ...

Exercise No. 32

1 es	6 está	11 son
2 está	7 están	12 eres
3 estoy	8 es	13 es
4 estamos	9 son	14 son
5 es	10 está	15 estoy

Exercise No. 33—Reading Selection 1

Two Friends of Mrs. Adams

Mrs. Adams already knows the names of all the objects in her house. Now she is beginning to study the verbs because she wants to learn to read, to write and to converse in Spanish. She also wants to know the numbers in Spanish. Being a merchant who expects to visit her agent in Spain she needs practice chatting with Spaniards or Spanish-Americans. Fortunately she has two friends who are from Spain and who work near her office in Oxford Street.

One day Mrs. Adams goes to visit these Spaniards. The two gentlemen listen attentively to Mrs. Adams while she speaks with them in Spanish. After ten minutes of conversation the Spaniards ask their friend many questions and are very pleased with her answers.

Exercise No. 34—Reading Selection 2

Mrs. Adams Falls Ill

On Thursday, April 18, at nine o'clock in the morning Mr. López arrives at the house of his pupil, Mrs. Adams. The oldest child, a boy of ten, opens the door and greets Mr. López. They enter the living-room where Mrs. Adams usually awaits her teacher.

But this evening she is not in the living-room. Neither is Mr. Adams there. Mr. López is very surprised and asks the boy: 'Where is your mummy?' The boy answers sadly: 'My mummy is ill and cannot leave her bedroom. She is in bed because she has a severe cold. She also has a headache.'

The teacher becomes very sympathetic and says: 'What a pity! It is not possible to have a lesson today, but next week we are going to study for two hours. Until next Tuesday.'

Exercise No. 35

1 toman	6 para agua	11 muy sencillo
2 dibujos	7 despacio	12 muchas veces
3 por todas partes	8 Tiene que	13 para usarlo
4 cada, propio	9 de todos modos	14 Quiere Ud.
5 para crema	10 tengo	15 No quiere Ud.

Exercise No. 36A

1 aquellas	4 Estas	7 Aquella	10 esta
2 Esta	5 Esas	8 este	11 esa
3 Estos	6 Esos	9 aquellas	12 estos

Exercise No. 36C

1 Estos señores están sentados en el comedor.
2 Estas tazas son de Puebla.
3 Me gustan estos dibujos.
4 Esos platos son de Oaxaca.
5 ¿Trabajan despacio aquellos artistas?
6 ¿Tiene esta familia cinco niños?
7 ¿Tienes hambre, hijito?
8 No, no tengo hambre.
9 ¿Tiene Ud. que escribir una carta, Sra. Adams?
10 Sí, tengo que escribir una carta.

Exercise No. 37

1 Están sentados en el comedor.
2 Toman café y pastas.
3 Dice — ¿Le gustan estas tazas y estos platillos?
4 Es de Puebla.
5 Sí, cada distrito tiene su propio estilo.
6 Es de Oaxaca.
7 Es de Michoacán.
8 Sí, son verdaderos artistas.
9 Trabajan despacio.
10 No tienen prisa.
11 Es difícil obtener un surtido adecuado para el mercado británico.
12 La Sra. Adams ve mucha cerámica de interés artístico.
13 Están en el aparador.
14 Son amarillos y azules.
15 Sí, tiene ejemplares de cerámica corriente, *or* Sí, *los* tiene. (She has *them*.)

Exercise No. 38

1 Sabe Ud.	6 no valen
2 tan importantes como	7 Necesitamos, la fecha
3 Nuestra civilización	8 pasar
4 tiene Ud. razón	9 entretanto, que
5 Puede Ud., que	10 ¿Qué quiere decir . . .?

Exercise No. 39A

1 treinta	5 diez y seis	9 sesenta y dos
2 diez	6 setenta y ocho	10 noventa y siete
3 cincuenta	7 diez y siete	11 ochenta y cuatro
4 cuarenta y nueve	8 quince	12 trece

Exercise No. 39B

cuatro más nueve son trece
ocho más siete son quince
siete por ocho son cincuenta y seis
ocho por tres son veinte y cuatro
diez y nueve menos ocho son once

diez y seis menos tres son trece
cincuenta dividido por diez son cinco
Ochenta dividido por veinte son cuatro

Exercise No. 39C

1 treinta
2 doce
3 siete
4 veinte y cuatro

5 sesenta
6 sesenta
7 setenta y cinco

8 treinta y seis
9 treinta y cinco
10 diez y seis

Exercise No. 39D

1 quiero
2 puedo
3 pensamos
4 piensa Ud.
5 quiere

6 quiere
7 quieren Uds.
8 pueden
9 puedes tú
10 piensan

11 vale
12 cuento
13 tú cuentas
14 cuenta

Exercise No. 40

1 Sí son importantes.
2 Sí son tan importantes como los nombres.
3 Necesitamos números.
4 Piensa en comprar y vender.
5 No valen mucho sin dinero.

6 No es posible comprar y vender sin dinero.
7 Sí, vende y compra.
8 Sí, es comprador y vendedor.
9 La Sra. Adams adelanta día por día.
10 diez, veinte, treinta, cuarenta, cincuenta, ciento.

Exercise No. 41

1 es decir
2 Cuántas veces
3 billetes y comida
4 maletas, tamaños, distancias
5 El sistema monetario

6 cada
7 céntimos
8 Es cierto, de cambio
9 doscientas noventa
10 próxima, este

Exercise No. 41A

1 cuatrocientos
2 trescientos cincuenta
3 quinientos veinte y cinco
4 ochocientos sesenta
5 seiscientos veinte y siete

6 cuatrocientos noventa
7 quinientos sesenta
8 setecientos ochenta
9 doscientos
10 novecientos setenta

Exercise No. 41B

1 Sé los números.
2 ¿Sabe Ud. dónde vive?
3 Sabemos qué desea.
4 No damos el dinero.
5 ¿Dan los billetes?

6 ¿Qué da Juan?
7 Ella no sabe la respuesta.
8 No damos nuestros libros.
9 ¿Sabes las preguntas?
10 No saben quién vive aquí.

Exercise No. 42

1 (400) cuatrocientas pesetas	7 £50 (cincuenta libras)
2 (75) setenta y cinco pesetas	8 No sé
3 (30) treinta pesetas	9 Sí, lo conozco
4 (4) cuatro pesetas	10 Vamos a continuar este tema en
5 (350) trescientas cincuenta pesetas	nuestra próxima conversación.
6 Sí, es millonario.	

Exercise No. 43A

1 nuestros	5 su	8 tu
2 su	6 su	9 mis
3 sus	7 nuestro	10 nuestra
4 mis		

Exercise No. 43B

1 diez, veinte y dos	6 diez y seis, diez
2 veinte, cuarenta y cuatro	7 treinta y dos, veinte
3 treinta, sesenta y seis	8 cuarenta y ocho, treinta
4 cuarenta, ochenta y ocho	9 sesenta y cuatro, cuarenta
5 cincuenta, ciento diez	10 ochenta, cincuenta

Exercise No. 43C

1 digo	6 no ponemos	11 ¿dicen Uds.?
2 hago	7 hacen	12 haces
3 salgo	8 ponen	13 ¿pone Ud.?
4 tengo	9 ¿hace Ud.?	14 pongo
5 decimos	10 ¿salen Uds.?	15 vale

Exercise No. 43D

1 sino	2 sino	3 pero	4 sino	5 pero

Exercise No. 44

1 Cenamos en el restaurante.	6 Se usan kilómetros.
2 Damos al camarero el diez por ciento.	7 La Sra. Adams sabe cambiar
3 La propina es cuarenta y siete pesetas.	kilómetros en millas.
4 Tengo mi maleta pesada en la estación de ferrocarril.	8 Compra dos echarpes, tres corbatas, un sombrero y tres cestas.
5 Pesa treinta kilos. Sesenta y seis libras.	9 El tema es 'la hora'.
	10 Usa el refrán — Más vale tarde que nunca.

Exercise No. 45

1 la película	7 un billete de ida y vuelta
2 la función	8 sale el tren
3 otras preguntas	9 a las nueve de la noche
4 la taquilla	10 Muchas gracias
5 la estación de ferrocarril	11 De nada
6 pide información	12 hago el papel

Exercise No. 46A

1 a las cinco y media de la tarde	6 a las once de la noche
2 a las ocho y cuarto de la tarde	7 a las cuatro y media de la tarde
3 a las diez menos cinco de la mañana	8 a las siete menos diez de la tarde
4 a las once menos diez de la mañana	9 a las diez menos cuarto de la noche
5 a las ocho de la tarde	10 las dos de la tarde

Exercise No. 46B

1 pido	5 comienzo	8 ¿piden Vds.?
2 comenzamos	6 ¿empieza Vd.?	9 repite
3 repiten	7 pides	10 ¿comienza?
4 ¿pide?		

Exercise No. 46C

1 Quiero un billete de ida y vuelta.
2 Pide información.
3 ¿Cuándo sale el tren para Bilbao?
4 ¿Sabe Vd. cuándo llega el tren de Madrid?
5 Llega a las cinco y media de la tarde.
6 ¿A qué hora comienza la primera función?
7 Comienza a las siete y media.
8 ¿Repiten la función?
9 Sí, repiten la función dos veces.
10 Aquí tiene Vd. las entradas.

Exercise No. 47

1 Todo el mundo quiere saber — ¿Qué hora es?
2 La Sra. Adams hace el papel de viajero.
3 El Sr. López hace el papel de taquillero.
4 Quiere comprar un billete de primera clase.
5 Cuesta mil novecientas ocho pesetas.
6 El Sr. L. hace el papel de taquillero de un cine.
7 La Sra. A. pide información.
8 Tiene dos funciones.
9 Compra dos entradas para la segunda función.
10 Paga cien pesetas.

Exercise No. 48

1 Sí pienso ...	5 Sí salgo ...	8 Si, continúo ...
2 Sí, quiero ...	6 Sí, cuento ...	9 Sí, le doy ...
3 Sí, puedo ...	7 Sí, digo ...	10 Sí, sé contar ...
4 Sí, pongo ...		

Exercise No. 49

1 No repetimos ...	5 No venimos ...	8 No tomamos ...
2 No hacemos ...	6 No creemos ...	9 No necesitamos ...
3 No pedimos ...	7 No traemos ...	10 No tenemos ...
4 No tenemos ...		

Exercise No. 50

1 (b)	3 (h)	5 (i)	7 (e)	9 (f)
2 (d)	4 (a)	6 (c)	8 (j)	10 (g)

Exercise No. 51

1 ¿Cuánto cuesta?, tiene que saber
2 pide información, ¿A qué hora?, a las siete y media.
3 tiene hambre, una comida, paga la

cuenta, de cambio, una propina, es decir
4 Piensa, en todas partes, dinero

Exercise No. 52

1 esta	4 esos	7 aquella	10 esas
2 estos	5 este	8 esos	11 aquel
3 ese	6 esa	9 estas	12 aquellas

Exercise No. 53

1 (e)	3 (a)	5 (b)	7 (d)	9 (c)
2 (f)	4 (g)	6 (h)	8 (j)	10 (i)

Exercise No. 54—Reading Selection 1

The Family of Mrs. Adams Comes to Visit Her Office

It is the first time that the Adams family comes to visit Mrs. Adams's office. Mr. Adams and their four children enter a very large building and go up to the fifth floor in the lift. Annie the younger daughter who is only five years old, is very curious and asks her daddy many questions about the office.

When they arrive in the office the mother gets up and says: 'I am very happy to see you all here. What a pleasant surprise!'

The children admire the objects which they see in the office,—the typewriter, the various articles imported from Spain, the Spanish magazines, the many coloured posters. All are very happy.

Philip, the older boy, looks out of the high window and sees the blue sky and the bright sun. Below he sees the cars which pass through the street. From the fifth floor they seem quite small.

After the visit the whole family goes to a restaurant which is not far from the office. They eat with great pleasure, especially the boys, because they are very hungry.

Exercise No. 55—Reading Selection 2

A Modern Fable

Annie, the youngest of Mr. Adams's children, likes the old fables of Aesop very much. She also likes this modern fable which Mr. López has written for her. 'The Fable of the Car and the Donkey' follows:

A car is passing along the road and sees a donkey. The poor donkey is carrying a big, heavy load of wood.

The car stops and says to the donkey: 'Good morning. You are walking very slowly. Do you not want to run fast like me?'

'Yes, yes sir! But tell me how is it possible?'

'It is not difficult,' says the car. 'In my tank there is much petrol. You have to drink a little.'

'No, thank you, petrol is not for me. I prefer fresh grass.'

'How old-fashioned you are!' And the car laughs at the donkey. The car leaves and goes fast. A few kilometres further on the donkey sees the car stopped.

'Good morning, Mr. car. What are you doing stopped here?'

'I have no petrol and I cannot go on,' replies the car.

'Ah, Mr. car,' says the donkey. 'Eat grass. It is perhaps old-fashioned but it is more abundant than petrol.' And the donkey goes slowly on his way while the mocking car remains in the roadway.

Exercise No. 56A

1 los	3 la	5 le	7 la	9 las
2 lo	4 la	6 las	8 los	10 le

Exercise No. 56B

1 La criada la lleva.
2 Los niños lo comen.
3 Los pongo en la mesa.

4 Las digo al estudiante.
5 ¿Por qué no le saluda Ud.?
6 ¿La visitas?

Exercise No. 56C

1 Le veo a Ud., Sra. A.
2 ¿Me ve Ud.?
3 ¿Quién nos ve?
4 El profesor los ve a Uds., muchachos.
5 Vemos la casa. La vemos.
6 Tomo el plato. Lo tomo.

7 Ella escribe los vérbos. Los escribe.
8 Tenemos las sillas. Las tenemos.
9 Las espero a Uds., señoras.
10 Los esperamos a Uds., señores.

Exercise No. 57

1 La Sra. A. sabe pedir información.
2 Prefieren el teatro.
3 Prefieren las películas policíacas.
4 Claro está, las conocen.
5 Vive en los suburbios.

6 Está a cosa de un kilómetro de su casa.
7 Prefieren las filas catorce o quince.
8 Sí, es posible ver y oír bien.
9 Piden ayuda a la acomodadora.
10 Vienen temprano.

Exercise No. 58

1 No saben nada
2 pueden
3 en memoria de, patria
4 más importantes
5 se llama más comúnmente
6 ensayista y filósofo

7 desde el punto de vista
8 del siglo pasado
9 descubrió América
10 Estos nombres
11 caminar, cuyos
12 recordar

Exercise No. 59A

1 de Ud.	3 ellas	5 conmigo	7 ellos, ellos	9 ella
2 nosotros	4 mí	6 contigo	8 usted	10 él

Exercise No. 59B

1 ¿Dónde está su libro (el libro de ella)?
2 ¿Dónde está su libro (el libro de él)?
3 ¿Dónde están sus libros (los libros de ella)?
4 ¿Dónde están sus libros (los libros de él)?
5 ¿Dónde están vuestros padres, muchachos (los padres de vosotros)?

6 ¿Dónde está su casa (la casa de Ud.), Sra. A.?
7 ¿Dónde están sus sillas (las sillas de ellos, *or* ellas)?
8 ¿Dónde está su cuarto (el cuarto de ellos, *or* ellas)?

Exercise No. 60

1 El 26 de julio es la fecha de la fiesta de Santiago.
2 España tiene hoy una monarquía.
3 Juan Carlos es el Rey de España.
4 Se llama más comúnmente la Gran Vía.
5 Prim es el nombre del general.
6 José Ortega y Gasset fue un célebre filósofo y ensayista.
7 Murió en 1955.
8 Núñez de Balboa es el nombre de uno de los conquistadores.
9 Sí, le interesan mucho.
10 Va a recordar las palabras de su maestro y amigo.
11 Hay diez y seis días de fiesta en España.
12 Sí, hay muchos más que en Gran Bretaña.

Exercise No. 61

1 cuyos, recuerdan
2 ciudades españoles
3 más conocidos
4 se encuentran
5 de veras, puede educarse bien y barato
6 a propósito, acerca de
7 recibir
8 más grande
9 más pequeño
10 el más grande y el más largo
11 más alto
12 más altos
13 sus conocimientos
14 Tiene que conocer

Exercise No. 62

1 tan alto como
2 mejor
3 más, que
4 mejor
5 tan, como
6 más nuevo
7 más, que
8 más, que
9 más alta
10 peor
11 mayor
12 más modernos
13 peor
14 tan, como
15 de
16 menor

Exercise No. 63

1 El Amazonas es el río más grande de América del Sur.
2 Londres es la ciudad más grande del mundo.
3 El Aconcagua es el pico más alto de América del Sur.
4 Londres es más grande que Nueva York.
5 Madrid no es tan grande como Londres.
6 Nueva York no es tan antigua como Madrid.
7 Londres es más antigua.
8 Nueva York tiene los edificios más altos del mundo.
9 El Salvador es el país más pequeño de Centro América.
10 (a) El Sr. García es el menor.
   (b) El Sr. Torres es el mayor.
   (c) Sí, el Sr. Rivera es mayor que el Sr. García.
   (d) El Sr. García es el más rico.
   (e) El Sr. Torres es el menos rico.
   (f) El Sr. Torres no es tan rico como el Sr. García.

Exercise No. 64

1 preguntarle a qué hora
2 a las seis y media
3 madrugadora, madrugador
4 temprano
5 estoy lista para salir
6 Leo, dicto

7 un bocadillo con café y tal o cual postre
8 muchas veces, a visitarme
9 a las cinco en punto
10 Las costumbres

Exercise No. 65A

1 At what time do you go to bed?
I go to bed at 11 p.m.
2 At what time do you get up?
I get up at 7 a.m.
3 Do you wash (yourself) before dressing (yourself)?
Yes I wash (myself) before dressing (myself).
4 Where will you be at noon?
I shall be in my office.

5 When do you go from here?
I go from here tomorrow.
6 Do you become ill when you eat too many sweets?
Yes I become ill.
7 In what row do you sit in the cinema?
We sit in the fourteenth or fifteenth row
8 Do you remember our conversations?
Yes, we remember them.

Exercise No. 65B

1 se	3 se, se	5 me	7 se	9 nos
2 se	4 se	6 se	8 se	10 me

Exercise No. 66

1 Se levanta a las seis y media.
2 Se lava y se viste.
3 Se viste en treinta minutos.
4 a eso de las siete se sienta a la mesa.
5 Se levanta temprano.
6 Desayunan juntos.
7 Toma zumo de naranja, café, panecillos y huevos.
8 Toma té en vez de café.
9 A las siete y media está lista para salir.
10 Va en coche a la estación.
11 A eso de las nueve llega a su oficina.
12 Lo toma casi siempre a la una.
13 Toma un bocadillo, con café y tal o cual postre.
14 Muchas veces vienen clientes a visitarle.
15 Termina el trabajo a las cinco en punto.

Exercise No. 67

1 (*i*)	3 (*j*)	5 (*b*)	7 (*h*)	9 (*g*)
2 (*e*)	4 (*d*)	6 (*c*)	8 (*a*)	10 (*f*)

Exercise No. 68

1 Sí, les invito de vez en cuando.
2 No, no lo prefiero.
3 Sí, las conocen bien.
4 Sí, les esperamos a Uds.
5 Las pone en la mesa.
6 No, no le busco a Ud., señor.
7 Me levanto a las ocho.
8 Sí, nos lavamos antes de comer.
9 Se sientan en la fila quince.
10 Mi padre se llama . . .

Exercise No. 69

1 más grande del mundo
2 más grande que
3 mayor que
4 tan alto como
5 la menor de

6 el primer dia
7 el 30 de enero de 1978
8 conmigo
9 sin mí
10 oigo, la recuerdo

Exercise No. 70

1 se dan la mano
2 Tenemos que estudiar
3 Me acuesto
4 hace muchas preguntas
5 Por consiguiente

6 de vez en cuando
7 dar un paseo
8 Vd. debe de estar
9 otra vez
10 a eso de las siete y media de la mañana.

Exercise No. 71—Reading Selection

A Visit to Soho

It is Saturday. Mrs. Adams gets up at eight o'clock, and looks out of the window. The sky is blue. There is a bright sun. She says to her husband: 'Today we are going to visit Soho. It's an international district. There they sell Spanish newspapers and magazines, and there are Spanish shops.'

'Very well,' says her husband.

At nine they get into their car and after a journey of forty-five minutes they reach Soho. They get out of the car and begin to walk through the streets. In a little while they see a group of girls who are standing near a shop, and who are talking quickly in Spanish.

Mrs. Adams greets the girls and begins to chat with them. The conversation follows:

'Good morning, are you Spanish?'

'Yes, madam. I am a student. I am in London to learn English.'

'I am also Spanish. I work in a private house. I help the lady and look after her children.'

'I am English, madam, but I can Speak Spanish well. I have many Spanish girl-friends, and they are my teachers. At home I have some Spanish books and I study a lot. By the way, are you Spanish?'

'No, I am also English, and like you I am studying Spanish. I like the language a lot. It seems that in London there are many people who are studying Spanish. Today I want to buy some bottles of Spanish wine. Tell me, do you know a good shop?'

'Yes, madam. On the corner there is an excellent shop. There they sell a very good Málaga wine.'

'Thank you very much,' she says to the girl. 'Good-bye.'

'Good-bye, madam.'

Mr. and Mrs. Adams go to the shop.

'¡Qué muchacha tan simpático!' says Mrs. Adams to her husband. And then she translates the sentence, because the latter does not understand Spanish: 'What a nice girl!'

'¡Ya lo creo!' replies Mr. Adams smiling, who after all can say a few words in Spanish.

Exercise No. 72

1 ¡Qué tiempo tan lluvioso!
2 Pase, pase, mojado
3 Déme
4 Ponga
5 A cántaros

6 Venga conmigo
7 Tome
8 Permítame
9 Mientras toman
10 Sigue lloviendo

Exercise No. 73A

1 Póngala
2 No la abra
3 Repítalas
4 No lo deje

5 Tráigalos
6 No lo tomen
7 Salúdenlos

8 Cómprenlos
9 Invítenle
10 Háganlo

Exercise No. 73B

1 **escribo** I write   **escriba Ud. escriban Uds.** write
2 **leo** I read   **lea Ud. lean Uds.** read
3 **tengo** I have   **tenga Ud. tengan Uds.** have
4 **veo** I see   **vea Ud. vean Uds.** see
5 **pregunto** I ask   **pregunte Ud. pregunten Uds.** ask
6 **recibo** I receive   **reciba Ud. reciban Uds.** receive
7 **repito** I repeat   **repita Ud. repitan Uds.** repeat
8 **voy** I go   **vaya Ud. vayan Uds.** go
9 **doy** I give   **dé Ud. den Uds.** give
10 **soy** I am   **sea Ud. sean Uds.** be

Exercise No. 74

1 Hace mal tiempo.
2 La criada abre la puerta.
3 Lo pone en el paragüero.
4 Le espera en la sala.
5 Pasan al comedor.
6 Toman té con ron.

7 Pone en la mesa dos tazas y platillos, una tetera, un azucarero y unas cucharitas.
8 Sale del comedor.
9 La Sra. Adams sirve al Sr. López.
10 Echa té con ron en las tazas.

Exercise No. 75

1 está lloviendo
2 están charlando y tomando
3 hace calor, hace frío
4 prefiere Ud.
5 Dígame. Oiga Ud. bien

6 Acabamos de hablar
7 Al atravesar; se sube
8 se elevan
9 más alta de España
10 los Pirineos

Exercise No. 76A

1 Estamos estudiándolas.
2 Carlos está escribiéndola.
3 ¿Estás leyéndolo?
4 La criada está poniéndola.
5 Los señores están tomándolo.

6 Juan y yo estamos contándolo.
7 ¿Están comprándolos Uds.?
8 No estoy leyéndolas.
9 ¿Quién está escribiéndolas?
10 Están vendiéndolos.

Exercise No. 76B

1 No estamos esperándola a Ud., señora.
2 No estamos esperándole a Ud., señor.
3 No están mirándolos a Uds., señores.
4 No están mirándolas a Uds., señoras.
5 ¿Quién está buscándome?
6 Yo estoy buscándote, hijita.
7 El Sr. López está enseñándonos a hablar español.

Exercise No. 76C

1 Estamos estudiando
2 Está poniendo
3 Estamos abriendo
4 ¿Está leyendo Ud.?
5 Está trayendo
6 ¿Quién está esperando?
7 ¿Está tomando Ud.?
8 Estás hablando
9 No estoy escribiendo
10 ¿Está trabajando Maria?
11 Está buscando
12 Están enseñando

Exercise No. 77

1 Están hablando del clima.
2 Hace buen tiempo.
3 No se pone verde en invierno.
4 Ve el gran panorama de sierras y grandes altiplanicies.
5 Está situado en la Meseta Central.
6 Su altura es de 2.200 pies sobre el nivel del mar.
7 El Pico de Mulhacén es la cima más alta de España.
8 Las montañas determinan en gran parte el clima.
9 Hay dos zonas — la zona seca y la zona húmeda.
10 En Andalucía hace mucho calor.

Exercise No. 78

1 seguimos charlando
2 de fuertes contrastes
3 goza de, días sin nubes
4 verse sorprendido por la lluvia
5 Vale la pena
6 Nunca, excepto
7 Tenga cuidado con
8 quedarse, sin
9 acordarme
10 al hacer, a olvidar

Exercise No. 79

1 nada
2 nada
3 nunca
4 Tampoco
5 Nadie
6 nadie
7 nunca
8 nunca
9 Tampoco
10 ni, ni
11 ningún
12 ningún
13 ninguno
14 ninguna
15 nada

Exercise No. 80

1 En el Levante parece que hace primavera todo el año.
2 No, hace gran frío.
3 Los meteorólogos lo dicen.
4 Llueve mucho en Galicia (en el noroeste).
5 Sí, hace frío en invierno.
6 porque a veces hace fresco por la noche.
7 Porque el sol es muy fuerte.
8 No va a olvidar el impermeable.
9 Van a hablar de los alimentos.
10 Sí, le gusta mucho.

Exercise No. 81

1 Se hace, trozos de pollo
2 cocina española
3 de muchas indisposiciones turísticas
4 para acostumbrarme
5 Tenga cuidado
6 platos conocidos
7 ensalada líquida
8 la hacen de huevos
9 lo conozco
10 muy nutritivo
11 Se puede comer fría
12 debe
13 Comemos. No vivimos
14 a olvidar

Exercise No. 82A

1 Se puede
2 Cómo se dice
3 se venden
4 se ven
5 Se dice
6 se habla español
7 Se comen

8 Conoce Ud.
9 No los conozco
10 Sabe Ud.
11 me voy
12 Sabemos
13 se parece
14 dolor de estómago

Exercise No. 82B

1 (*i*)	4 (*k*)	7 (*b*)	10 (*n*)	13 (*j*)	16 (*o*)
2 (*m*)	5 (*a*)	8 (*e*)	11 (*g*)	14 (*p*)	
3 (*f*)	6 (*c*)	9 (*d*)	12 (*h*)	15 (*l*)	

Exercise No. 83

1 La comen en un restaurante español de Londres.
2 El aceite es la base de la cocina española.
3 Causa muchas indisposiciones turísticas.
4 El gazpacho se llama una ensalada líquida.
5 La tortilla mexicana es el pan de México.
6 La hacen de huevos, patatas, cebollas y aceite.
7 No, se puede comer también fría.
8 Comen un dulce, flan o frutas.
9 Porque el estómago británico no se acostumbra rápidamente a los alimentos de España.
10 Cenan a eso de las diez de la noche.

Exercise No. 84

1 (*b*)	3 (*g*)	5 (*j*)	7 (*i*)	9 (*e*)	11 (*c*)
2 (*a*)	4 (*k*)	6 (*h*)	8 (*l*)	10 (*d*)	12 (*f*)

Exercise No. 85

1 Tengo frío
2 Tengo calor
3 Hace buen tiempo
4 Llueve mucho
5 Hace fresco

6 Hace frío
7 Llevo impermeable
8 Llevo abrigo
9 Hay polvo
10 Todas las estaciones

Exercise No. 86

1 (*d*)	3 (*a*)	5 (*c*)	7 (*e*)	9 (*g*)
2 (*f*)	4 (*b*)	6 (*h*)	8 (*j*)	10 (*i*)

Exercise No. 87

1 La abro
2 Los cuento
3 La como
4 La pongo

5 Las repito
6 Los dejamos
7 Las tomamos

8 Las aprendemos
9 Lo escribimos
10 Lo leemos

Exercise No. 88

1 lloviendo	5 pensando	8 contando
2 echando	6 trayendo	9 poniendo
3 pidiendo	7 oyendo	10 haciendo
4 leyendo		

Exercise No. 89—Reading Selection

Philip Does Not Like to Study Arithmetic

One day upon returning from school Philip says to his mother:

'I don't like to study arithmetic. It is so difficult. Why do we need so many exercises and problems nowadays. Is it not a fact that we have adding machines?'

Mrs. Adams looks at her son and says: 'You are wrong, my boy. It is not possible to get along without numbers. For example, one must always change money, calculate distances, and . . . and . . .'

The mother stops speaking on seeing that Philip is not paying attention to what she is saying.

'By the way,' continues the mother with a smile, 'doesn't football interest you either, my son?'

'I should say so, mummy.'

'Well if Chelsea has won thirty games and has lost ten, do you know what percentage of the games it has won?'

On hearing this Philip opens his mouth and exclaims:

'You are right, mother. Numbers, arithmetic and mathematics are very important. I think I'm going to study much more.'

Exercise No. 90

1 hacerle	9 artistas y artesanos
2 acerca del pueblo	10 se ocupan
3 Aquí tiene Ud. Continúe	11 Se ocupan
4 Quiénes	12 cestas y artículos de cuero
5 hoy día	13 Acabo de recibir
6 34 millones de reyes	14 Volveremos a charlar
7 una variedad de productos	15 Que Ud. lo pase bien
8 el producto más importante	

Exercise No. 91B

1 ¿Cuándo vuelven a casa?	6 Acabo de hablar sobre el clima.
2 Vuelven a casa a las diez de la noche.	7 Ella acaba dè volver de la joyería.
3 Los alumnos vuelven a escribir los ejercicios.	8 Acaban de comprar pendientes de plata.
4 Vuelvo a leer la guía de viajero.	9 ¿Acaba de venir Ud. del cine?
5 Acabamos de recibir un envío de mercancía.	10 Acabamos el trabajo.

Exercise No. 92

1 La Sra. Adams va a hacer algunas preguntas.	6 Son el trigo, el arroz, las naranjas y los limones
2 La primera pregunta es— ¿Quiénes son los españoles?	7 El aceite es el producto más importante.
3 Se llaman los íberos.	8 Se ocupan de las artes populares.
4 España tiene 34 milliones de habitantes más.o menos.	9 Hacen artículos artísticos de cuero, de cobre, de hojalata, de plata, etc.
5 El sentido típico es el de la independencia, del honor y del orgullo.	10 La Sra. A. acaba de recibir un envío de España.

Exercise No. 93

1 a ver
2 entretanto, las artes populares
3 de uso diario
4 con bordados sencillos
5 falda larga
6 una camisa blanca
7 es sencillo pero hermoso
8 los colores brillantes, de los gitanos
9 Me gustan
10 de lana o de algodón
11 sirve para proteger
12 Por supuesto, cestas de varios tamaños
13 Tenemos que hablar
14 ¿Le parece bien el martes?
15 Me parece bien.

Exercise No. 94A

1 Visto
2 Me visto
3 visten de
4 Vestimos
5 se visten
6 lleva Vd.
7 Llevo
8 llevan
9 llevan
10 llevamos

Exercise No. 94B

1 Este, ése
2 Estos, ésos
3 Esas, éstas
4 Esta, ésa
5 Aquella, ésta
6 Esta, aquél
7 Esta, aquélla
8 esto, eso
9 Eso
10 Eso

Exercise No. 95

1 La Sra. A. acaba de recibir una caja de mercancía de España.
2 El vestido típico de las regiones les da este aspecto.
3 Los hombres vascos la visten.
4 Están tejidos de lana, de algodón o de seda.
5 Dibujos de pájaros y de animalitos adornan los jarros.
6 Están envueltas en cuero.
7 Sirve para proteger el vidrio.
8 Viene de Talavera y de Manises.
9 Sabe muy poco de las fiestas.
10 Dice — Que Ud. lo pase bien.

Exercise No. 96

1 en un pueblo u otro
2 se celebran
3 Por supuesto
4 Se cantan villancicos
5 también una fiesta mundana
6 Ud. quiere decir
7 se asan
8 del gran sorteo
9 doce días después
10 en el Día Primero de Mayo
11 va de jira
12 Qué lástima
13 ¡Es un deporte magnífico!
14 ver los Toros

Exercise No. 97A

1 primer
2 tercer
3 buen
4 buen
5 gran, grande
6 tercera
7 mal
8 primero
9 buenos
10 algún

Exercise No. 97B

1 Cantan	5 Estoy preparando	8 trata de
2 Celebramos	6 Usa Ud.	9 cogen
3 Visitan	7 contiene	10 llevan (traen)
4 escogen		

Exercise No. 98

1 Se titula—Los días de fiesta.
2 Se celebran con procesiones, ferias, juegos y fuegos artificiales.
3 La corrida de toros es el elemento casi esencial.
4 Celebra el nacimiento de Jesucristo.
5 Se come el pavo tradicional.
6 En la Nochebuena se asan castañas y patatas.
7 Representa la escena de Belén.
8 El gran sorteo se hace en diciembre.
9 Los reciben el Día de Reyes.
10 Se celebra la Fiesta del Trabajo.
11 Las fiestas de Sevilla son las más importantes.
12 Se puede ver el Encierro.

Exercise No. 99

1 Estoy leyendo	9 que es muy imponente
2 Viajaré	10 Mientras estoy en la capital
3 Visitaré	11 No deje Vd. de
4 Veré	12 Vd. hallará
5 Pasaré	13 Sin falta
6 Estoy seguro	14 fuera de los grandes centros
7 al Rastro	15 Tengo ganas
8 En los alrededores	

Exercise No. 100A

1 We shall visit Salamanca.	9 I shall not be cold.
2 I shall spend a week there.	10 He will not come here.
3 I shall be glad to see the university	11 We shall leave at 8 o'clock.
4 Who will travel to Spain?	12 I shall play this role.
5 They will not work hard.	13 They will want to eat.
6 Will you study the lesson?	14 She will put it on the table.
7 Will you have coffee?	15 I shall not be able to go there.
8 Philip will not write the letter.	

Exercise No. 100B

1 Compraré una corbata.	7 Saldré a las ocho de la mañana.
2 Costará cien pesetas.	8 Tomaremos la cena a las siete.
3 Iré al campo.	9 Visitaremos a nuestros amigos.
4 Mi hermano irá conmigo.	10 Estudiaremos nuestras lecciones de
5 Volveré a las nueve de la tarde.	español.
6 Veré a mi amigo Guillermo.	

Exercise No. 100C

1 Aprenderé	7 ¿Verá Juan?	13 Ud. pondrá
2 Escribirá	8 ¿Quién visitará?	14 No querrán
3 Irán	9 No viajaré	15 ¿Saldrá Ud.?
4 Comeremos	10 ¿Estudiarán?	16 Tendré
5 Hablará	11 Haré	17 Estarán aquí.
6 ¿Trabajará Ud.?	12 Vendrá	18 ¿Irán Uds.?

Exercise No. 101

1 ¿Se titula — ¿Qué lugares quiere Ud. visitar, Sra. A?
2 La Sra. A. va a salir pronto.
3 Está leyendo guías de viajero.
4 Viajará en avión.
5 Tomará el centro de la ciudad.
6 Se llama el Parque del Retiro.
7 Pasará al menos un día en el museo.
8 Espera comprar artículos de interés folklórico.
9 Miguel de Cervantes nació en Alcalá de Henares.
10 El rey Felipe Segundo lo hizo construir.
11 Se llama El Alcázar.
12 Dos pueblos célebres por su cerámica son Talavera y Manises.
13 Verá quizás monumentos árabes.
14 El Sr. López tiene ganas de acompañarla.

Exercise No. 102

1 (c)	3 (a)	5 (d)	7 (i)	9 (f)	11 (l)
2 (e)	4 (g)	6 (h)	8 (j)	10 (b)	12 (k)

Exercise No. 103

1 los pantalones	5 la faja	8 la camisa
2 el sombrero	6 los zapatos	9 el vestido
3 el traje	7 los guantes	10 el abrigo
4 la corbata		

Exercise No. 104

1 (c)	2 (e)	3 (b)	4 (f)	5 (d)	6 (a)

Exercise No. 105

1 El panadero, panadería	6 comprador
2 El platero, platería	7 la boca
3 El zapatero, zapatería	8 los oídos
4 El sastre, sastrería	9 los ojos
5 vendedor	10 la cara, la nariz, los labios

Exercise No. 106—Reading Selection

Mrs. Adams's Birthday

It is March 22, the birthday of Mrs. Adams. Today she is 35 years old. In order to celebrate this day the Adams family is going to dine in a fine Spanish restaurant in London.

When they enter the restaurant they see a beautiful basket full of red roses in the centre of the table reserved for the Adamses. Naturally Mrs. Adams is very surprised and gives her dear husband a thousand thanks and kisses.

After a delicious meal, Annie, the younger daughter, says in a low voice to her brothers and sister: 'Now!' and each one of the four children takes out from under the table a pretty little box. They are gifts for the mother.

Anita gives her a silk handkerchief; Rosie, a cotton blouse; William, a pair of gloves; and Philip, a woollen shawl.

The following week Mr. Adams works out the bill for that day, which is as follows:

Supper	£36.70
Tip	3.80
Flowers	12.25
Gifts	36.15
Total	£88.90

Exercise No. 107

1 a leerle
2 Me gustará mucho
3 de informarle
4 le he apreciado
5 Tenga la bondad de, más conveniente
6 muy ocupado
7 Por eso, de antemano
8 de verle a Vd.
9 le mostrará a Vd.
10 en entenderme
11 No hay ninguna
12 darle a Ud. mis gracias más sinceras
13 Ud. es muy bondadoso
14 ¿Me hará Ud. el favor de . . .?

Exercise No. 108A

1 Will you give him the oranges?
2 Bring me the shoes.
3 Kindly read us the letter.
4 As soon as possible I shall write her a letter.
5 Will you teach me the new words?
6 We are not able to send you the money.
7 Who will read the story to us?
8 Tell me: What is Mary doing in the kitchen?
9 I shall not like the bullfight.
10 Does that date seem all right to you?
11 It does not suit me.
12 These things don't matter to me.

Exercise No. 108B

1 le	5 les	9 me	13 Tráiganos
2 nos	6 dígame	10 comprándoles	14 me
3 le	7 les	11 le	15 Nos
4 me	8 les	12 trayéndole	

Exercise No. 109

1 Están sentados en la sala de la Sra. A.
2 Tiene en la mano una copia de la carta a su agente.
3 Va a leerle al Sr. L. la carta.
4 Le gustará mucho oírla al Sr. L.
5 La fecha es — 4 de mayo de 1978.
6 Escribe la carta al Sr. Rufino Carrillo.
7 Usa el saludo — Muy señor mío.
8 La Sra. A. irá de viaje a España.
9 Saldrá de Londres el 31 de mayo.
10 Llegará al aeropuerto de Madrid a la una menos veinte.
11 Permanecerá en la capital dos meses.

12 Hará viajes a lugares de interés en España.
13 Irá a Tenerife, en las Islas Canarias.
14 Ha apreciado los servicios del Sr. Carrillo.
15 Desea conocer personalmente al Sr. Carrillo.

Exercise No. 110

1 una carta en la mano
2 Estoy muy agradecido
3 de informarme
4 Tendré gran placer
5 hablaré
6 Estoy seguro de que
7 felicitarles
8 sin duda alguna, muy simpático
9 Perdóneme, orgulloso
10 por sí misma, muy simpáticos
11 Estoy seguro, podré
12 Lo mejor es
13 Lo peor es
14 Nos
15 unos últimos consejos

Exercise No. 111A

1 Cuánto tiempo
2 Hace seis meses
3 Hace diez años
4 Hace cuarenta y cinco minutos
5 Hace tres días
6 le conozco
7 viven en esta casa
8 están en el cine
9 está en este país
10 estoy aquí

Exercise No. 111B

1 No los pongan Uds. . . .
2 No les escriba Ud. . . .
3 No los traigan . . .
4 No me diga . . .
5 No le mande . . .
6 No me traiga . . .
7 No me dé . . .
8 No me compre . . .
9 No les lean . . .
10 No le venda . . .

Exercise No. 111C

1 Sí, lo visitaré. No, no lo visitaré.
2 Sí, la escribiré. No, no la escribiré.
3 Sí, lo compraré. No, no lo compraré.
4 Sí, los traeré. No, no los traeré.
5 Sí, lo tomaré. No, no lo tomaré.
6 Sí, los pediremos. No, no los pediremos.
7 Sí, la venderemos. No, no la venderemos.
8 Sí, las querremos. No, no las querremos.
9 Sí, los seguiremos. No, no los seguiremos.
10 Sí, las repetiremos. No, no las repetiremos.

Exercise No. 112

1 Acaba de recibir una carta de su agente en España.
2 Estará en la capital durante los meses de junio y julio.
3 Esperará a la Sra. Adams en el aeropuerto.
4 Conversará con ella en español.
5 Está seguro de que la Sra. Adams habla perfectamente el español.
6 Quiere felicitar a la Sra. Adams y a su maestro.
7 El Sr. López está orgulloso de su pueblo.
8 Verá que el Sr. Carrillo es muy simpático, como tantos españoles.
9 Será el martes que viene.
10 Se verán en la oficina de la Sra. Adams.

Exercise No. 113

1 Me alegro de	9 Se dice, Espero que sí
2 Tengo ganas	10 de ir con prisas
3 Por lo menos, darme	11 Ha leído Ud.
4 Eso de la cortesía	12 En cuanto a mí
5 Quiere decir, es digno	13 He gozado
6 Les gusta, acerça de	14 despedirnos
7 conocerse el uno al otro	15 Se dan la mano
8 Como te he dicho	

Exercise No. 114A

1 We have had a good trip.
2 The pencils have fallen on the floor.
3 They have said nothing.
4 What has Paul done with the money?
5 No one has opened the doors.

6 We have not read those newspapers.
7 Have you been at the cinema?
8 Has the child been ill?
9 I have never believed that story.
10 What have they said?

Exercise No. 114B

1 He notado	9 ¿Qué han hecho Uds.?
2 Ha dicho	10 Has abierto
3 No han leído	11 ¿Qué ha dicho Juan?
4 Han sido	12 Ha tomado
5 Hemos estado	13 No he creído
6 No he trabajado	14 Hemos oído
7 ¿Ha enseñado Ud.?	15 ¿Han oído Uds.?
8 ¿Quién no ha escrito?	

Exercise No. 114C

1 El Sr. García venderá . . .	6 Tú no aprenderás . . .
El Sr. García ha vendido . . .	Tu no has aprendido . . .
2 Trabajaré . . .	7 ¿Buscará el niño . . .?
He trabajado . . .	¿Ha buscado el niño . . .?
3 Escribiremos . . .	8 ¿Comprarán Uds. . . .?
Hemos escrito . . .	¿Han comprado Uds. . . .?
4 Leerán . . .	9 Saldré . . .
Han leído . . .	He salido . . .
5 ¿Tomará Ud. . . .?	10 Entrarán . . .
¿Ha tomado Ud. . . .?	Han entrado . . .

Exercise No. 115

1 Se encuentran en la oficina de la Sra. A.
2 Hace calor.
3 Se oyen los ruidos de la calle.
4 La Sra. A. se alegra de irse de la ciudad.
5 El Sr. L. tiene ganas de ir a España.
6 Desgraciadamente, no es posible.
7 Sí, es más formal.
8 Quiere decir que cada hombre es digno de respeto.
9 Ha notado que entre los negociantes hay más formalidades en España que en Gran Bretaña.

10 La Sra. A. está cansada de ir con prisas.
11 La Sra. A. ha leído libros sobre España.
12 El Sr. L. los ha recomendado.
13 Pasará el verano en Londres.
14 Pensará a menudo en su maestro.
15 Sí, le escribirá cartas.

Exercise No. 116

1 Hace cinco meses
2 ha obtenido
3 Por supuesto
4 Al fin
5 a acompañarla
6 no es solamente, sino también
7 está lista
8 ha hecho dos maletas
9 suben al coche
10 Se pone en marcha, a eso de
11 de su equipaje, libras
12 tiene que
13 se despide de
14 A las once en punto
15 La Sra. A. está en camino.

Exercise No. 117A

1 We are beginning the lesson.
2 We have begun the exercise.

3 I do not remember him.
4 I have remembered her.
5 Are they sitting down?
6 Have they sat down?
7 Are you repeating the words?
8 Have you repeated the words?
9 The maid is setting the table.
10 The maid has not set the table.
11 The table is set.
12 She is serving the coffee.
13 She has served the tea.
14 What fruits do you prefer?
15 What fruits have you preferred?
16 The children are going to bed.
17 They have already gone to bed.
18 Are you asking for information?
19 Have you asked for information?
20 The work is not finished.

Exercise No. 117B

1 abierta
2 cerrada
3 despiertos
4 puesta
5 vendida
6 vestidos
7 sentados
8 escritas
9 terminado
10 hecho

Exercise No. 117C

1 Duermo
2 Está durmiendo
3 Duermen
4 ¿Duerme Ud.?
5 Me despido
6 Se despiden
7 No nos despedimos
8 He dormido
9 ¿Ha dormido Ud.?
10 No hemos dormido
11 Me he despedido
12 No se han despedido
13 ¿Se han despedido Uds.?
14 Duerma Ud.
15 No duerman Uds.

Exercise No. 118

1 Hace cinco meses que la Sra. A. estudia el español.
2 Ha pasado muchas horas en conversación con su profesor.
3 Ha aprendido la gramática necesaria.
4 Ha trabajado mucho.

5 Ahora habla español bastante bien.
6 Ha obtenido los billetes para el vuelo.
7 Ha escrito a su agente.
8 Su agente ha prometido recibirla en el aeropuerto.
9 Están despiertos a las cinco de la mañana.
10 Sale a las diez y media de la mañana.
11 Cada pasajero tiene que mostrar su billete.
12 No. La familia no va a acompañarla.
13 Tienen que terminar el año escolar.
14 El señor tiene que quedarse en casa para negocios.

Exercise No. 119

1 (*f*)	3 (*e*)	5 (*d*)	7 (*g*)	9 (*i*)
2 (*c*)	4 (*a*)	6 (*b*)	8 (*h*)	10 (*j*)

Exercise No. 120

1 Dispénseme
2 Hay que
3 Hace algún tiempo
4 Tienen la intención de
5 A menudo
6 tengo prisa
7 Se quedará en casa
8 Por lo menos
9 En cuanto a mí
10 bastante bien

Exercise No. 121

1 (*d*)	3 (*g*)	5 (*a*)	7 (*b*)	9 (*c*)
2 (*e*)	4 (*f*)	6 (*h*)	8 (*j*)	10 (*i*)

Exercise No. 122

1 Me gusta la carta.
2 A ellos les gusta viajar
3 Nos gustan los aviones
4 ¿Le gustan a Ud. las pinturas?
5 A él no le gustan los tomates.
6 No le gusta a ella esta moda.
7 ¿Les gusta a Uds. bailar?
8 ¿No te gusta jugar?
9 Nos parece bien.
10 No me importa

Exercise No. 123

1 cantado	5 hecho	8 dicho
2 vuelto	6 abierto	9 leído
3 llegado	7 recibido	10 despedido
4 puesto		

Exercise No. 124

1 sentadas	5 hechos	8 escrito
2 cubierta	6 escritas	9 acabado
3 abierta	7 puesta	10 abierto
4 cerrados		

Exercise No. 125

1 La he comprado
2 La he abierto
3 Lo he oído
4 Lo he obtenido
5 Los he ayudado

6 Los hemos visto
7 Los hemos vendido
8 Lo hemos completado
9 Las hemos escrito
10 La hemos leído.

Exercise No. 126—Reading Selection

An Extraordinary Programme at the Cinema

This evening Mr. Adams and his wife are going to the cinema. Mr. Adams does not like the majority of Hollywood films, especially those in which the American cowboys fire shots at each other. Neither do the detective pictures interest him.

But this evening an extraordinary programme is being shown in a cinema which is about one kilometre from his house. The film is called: 'A Trip Through Spain.' It is a film about the country which our friend Mrs. Adams is going to visit within a few months and which deals with its history, geography, rivers, mountains, cities, etc., that is to say, a film which ought to interest tourists very much.

The Adamses enter the cinema at 8.30. Almost all the seats are occupied and therefore they have to sit in the third row. Mrs. Adams does not like this, because the movements on the screen hurt her eyes. Fortunately, they are able to change seats after fifteen minutes, and move to the thirteenth row.

The Adamses enjoy this picture very much, and also learn a great deal about the customs of Spain.

On leaving the cinema Mrs. Adams says to her husband:

'Do you know, Charles, I believe that I shall get along very well in Spain. I have understood almost all the words of the actors and actresses in this film.'

Exercise No. 127

1 en la aduana
2 la sala de espera
3 de repente
4 Dispénseme
5 Mucho gusto en conocerle.
6 El gusto es mío
7 El Sr. López está muy equivocado

8 ¿Quién sabe qué más?
9 No tengo prisa
10 Ni yo tampoco
11 da a la plaza
12 ciento cincuenta pesetas al día

Exercise No. 128A

1 entré	2 comí	3 salí	4 vi	5 me senté
entraste	comiste	saliste	viste	te sentaste
entró	comió	salió	vio	se sentó
entramos	comimos	salimos	vimos	nos sentamos
entrasteis	comisteis	salisteis	visteis	os sentasteis
entraron	comieron	salieron	vieron	se sentaron

Exercise No. 128B

1 Who forgot the tickets?
2 Yesterday we received the letters.
3 The man bought a new suit.
4 Last night we did not hear the bell.
5 Did the train arrive on time?

6 They looked for the baggage.
7 The child fell in front of the house.
8 They left the airport in a taxi.
9 Where did Mrs. A. wait for her friend?
10 How much did the raincoat cost?

Exercise No. 128C

1 No compré . . .	6 No pasé . . .
2 No volvimos . . .	7 No oímos . . .
3 No escribí . . .	8 No vendí . . .
4 No llegamos . . .	9 No dejamos . . .
5 No salí . . .	10 No trabajamos . . .

Exercise No. 128D

1 salí	9 salimos
2 llegamos	10 paró
3 examinaron	11 no olvidé
4 oyó	12 gritó
5 Ud. respondió	13 creyeron
6 no pregunté	14 vendimos
7 llamó	15 ¿volvieron Uds.?
8 Uds. desearon	16 ¿leyó?

Exercise No. 129

1 Los aduaneros españoles lo revisaron.
2 Un apuesto señor se acercó a ella.
3 Dijo — Dispénseme ¿Es Ud. la Sra. A?
4 Contestó — soy yo.
5 Pasó a una velocidad espantosa.
6 Deseó decir — Por favor, más despacio.
7 Olvidó el español.
8 Vio autobuses y coches.
9 Gritó — ¡No tengo prisa!
10 Le contestó — Ni yo tampoco.
11 Llegaron al hotel sanos y salvos.
12 Buenos días. ¿Tiene Ud. un cuarto con baño?

Exercise No. 130

1 me llamó por teléfono.
2 a tomar la merienda
3 Al día siguiente
4 Me acerqué
5 me invitó a entrar
6 vino a saludarme
7 Está Ud. en su casa
8 Según la costumbre española
9 Me parece
10 muchas casas semejantes
11 Admiré
12 Me presentó
13 hacerse médico
14 Sintió
15 Nos despedimos, a casa

Exercise No. 131A

1 The maid served us the (late) luncheon.
2 Why did you not wish to invite me?
3 Last night we returned late from the theatre.
4 I wanted to telephone you.
5 What did you do after the meal?
6 They said—'We are not in a hurry.'
7 I repeated all the answers.

8 My friend did not come on time. I was sorry.
9 They asked for information at the information office.
10 They wanted to buy return tickets.

Exercise No. 131B

1 Le dije — Pase Ud.
2 Mi hermano hizo un viaje al Perú.
3 Vine a casa a las siete.
4 Vistieron de falda de algodón.
5 Quiso hacerse médico.

6 Sirvió una taza de chocolate.
7 Pidió información.
8 Quisimos ver la nueva película.
9 El año pasado hicimos un viaje a España.
10 Dijimos — Hasta la vista.

Exercise No. 131C

1 quise
2 no dije
3 hizo
4 vinieron
5 sirvió

6 quisieron
7 repetí
8 hicimos
9 dijeron
10 hicieron

11 ¿Qué dijo?
12 ¿Que dijeron Uds.?
13 no quisimos
14 no vine
15 sintieron

Exercise No. 132

1 El Sr. Carrillo la llamó por teléfono.
2 Llegó a su casa a las cinco de la tarde.
3 Una criada le abrió la puerta.
4 El Sr. Carrillo vino a saludarla.
5 El patio lleno de árboles y flores le encantó.
6 Admiró la fuente de piedra en el centro del patio.
7 Los dos hijos del Sr. Carrillo son serios e inteligentes.
8 Asisten a un Instituto Nacional para Bachillerato.
9 Quiere hacerse médico.
10 Tuvieron que volver a su cuarto.
11 Hablaron de la vida en España, de las costumbres y del arte.
12 Sí, vale la pena de ir allá.
13 La Sra. Adams quiso ir allá.
14 La Sra. Adams y el Sr. Carrillo se despidieron.
15 Volvió a su hotel.

Exercise No. 133

1 ¡Qué hermosa!
2 el centro comercial
3 gastar todo mi dinero
4 Tuve que pensar
5 a través de la historia

6 Ayer
7 cierra
8 está delante del museo.
9 un rato
10 me dormí

Exercise No. 134A

1 At Christmas I gave gifts to all the children.
2 I did not have the opportunity to know you personally.
3 We were not able to pay the whole bill.
4 This house was constructed in the 16th century.
5 On Sunday we took a walk in the Retiro Park.

6 1 was able to converse with him in his beautiful language.
7 He had no difficulty in understanding me.
8 She did not wish to rest much.
9 Mrs. A's family could not accompany her.
10 I put my new hat on my head.

Exercise No. 134B

1 Tuve que estudiar . . .	6 Fuimos al . . .
2 La Sra. A. estuvo . . .	7 Vinieron . . .
3 Los árboles se pusieron . . .	8 No dije nada.
4 Ella dio . . .	9 Uds. no hicieron nada.
5 Fui un estudiante . . .	10 Quisieron Uds. . . .?

Exercise No. 134C

1 tuve	5 puso	8 fui
2 Ud. pudo	6 quisimos	9 Uds. estuvieron
3 fueron	7 dieron	10 nos encontramos
4 dijo		

Exercise No. 135

1 Se titula 'Un paseo por Madrid'.
2 Algunos son del estilo tradicional español, algunos de estilo moderno, y otros una combinación de los dos estilos.
3 Hay tiendas y almacenes elegantes.
4 Se halla en la Plaza de España.
5 Fue a pasearse el domingo.
6 Se junta con la Calle de Alcalá.
7 Los domingos cierra a las dos.
8 Es del siglo 18.
9 Es de Velázquez.
10 Comprendió el orgullo de los españoles en el pasado de su nación.
11 Se sentó en el Parque del Retiro.
12 Sí, es muy interesante.

Exercise No. 136

1 La semana pasada	9 flores, cestas y ropa
2 Vi, que	10 Entre los puestos
3 lleno de gente	11 a divertirse
4 del campo	12 la conversación de las mujeres
5 perderse	13 sobre la vida del campo
6 por una calle de puestos	14 recordaba
7 Vi, de siete u ocho años	15 un día muy divertido
8 Como los demás vendedores	

Exercise No. 137A

1 It was raining buckets when we took leave of the young men.
2 I was thinking of you when I was riding in a car through the streets of Madrid.
3 The tourists and vendors were bargaining and all seemed to be enjoying themselves greatly.
4 I was approaching the door when I met Mr. Carrillo's sons.
5 While we were speaking about the folk arts, Mrs. Carrillo was reading a newspaper.
6 It was very hot when we returned to Seville.
7 When the car was starting, a policeman approached.
8 The aeroplanes were coming and going at all hours.

9 We were tired but we did not want to rest.
10 It was already 4.30 p.m. and we were in a hurry.

Exercise No. 137B

1 yo comía
2 estudiábamos
3 estaba
4 Uds. se despedian
5 se paseaban
6 gritaban
7 bajaba
8 hablábamos
9 iban
10 pasábamos

Exercise No. 137C

1 caminaba
2 iba
3 dijo
4 jugaban
5 cantaron
6 veíamos
7 corrian
8 Ud. perdió
9 vivieron
10 leyó
11 empezó
12 llamaban
13 Uds. no entraron
14 ¿estaba Ud.?
15 éramos
16 oyeron

Exercise No. 138

1 Pasaba por las aldeas.
2 Lavaban ropa.
3 Trabajaban en los campos
4 Era viernes.
5 Venía del campo.
6 Sí, había gente de la ciudad.
7 Porque sabía pedir información en español.
8 Vio a un muchacho de siete u ocho años.
9 Parecía un viejecito.
10 Llevaba un sombrero de ala ancha.
11 Arreglaba su mercancía.
12 Veía el sentido estético de muchos de los vendedores.
13 Una mujer estaba sentada en la acera.
14 Delante de ella había unas pocas cebollas y pimientos.
15 Mientras iba a casa recordaba sus conversaciones con el Sr. L.

Exercise No. 139

1 antes de mi salida, No tenga prisa
2 No he olvidado
3 no descanso
4 tanto que descubrir
5 ayer, al mediodía
6 se venden
7 No pude
8 Nunca me canso de
9 volví a visitar
10 Me gustan mucho, pintores

Exercise No. 140A

1 mío
2 suyos
3 mía, suya
4 mías, suyas
5 mías, suyas
6 míos, suyos
7 mías, suyas
8 suya
9 suyos
10 nuestros

Exercise No. 140B

1 Salía . . .
  Salí . . .
2 Entrábamos . . .
  Entramos . . .

I was leaving . . .
I left . . .
We were entering . . .
We entered . . .

3 Veíamos . . .   We were seeing . . .
  Vimos . . .   We saw . . .
4 Vds. no olvidaban . . .   You were not forgetting . . .
  Vds. no olvidaron . . .   You did not forget . . .
5 El conductor me respondía.   The driver was answering me.
  El conductor me respondió.   The driver answered me.
6 Ellos no aprendían . . .   They were not learning . . .
  Ellos no aprendieron . . .   They did not learn . . .
7 Estaba . . .   I was . . .
  Estuve . . .   I was . . .
8 Los jóvenes iban . . .   The young men were going . . .
  Los jóvenes fueron . . .   The young men went . . .

Exercise No. 141

1 No ha olvidado los consejos del Sr. L.
2 Hay tanto que ver, tanto que oír, etc.
3 Descansaba en un café.
4 Veía las tiendas.
5 Las ha visitado muchas veces.
6 No podía resistir la tentación de volver a visitar las tiendas.
7 Nunca se cansa de mirarlas.
8 Volvió a visitar el Museo de Artes Decorativas.
9 Está a tres manzanas del parque.
10 Le gusta mucho mirarlas.

Exercise No. 142

1 la comida
2 la dificultad
3 hablador
4 divertido
5 viajar
6 segundario
7 la ventanilla
8 el camino
9 la pintura
10 la pregunta
11 la respuesta
12 la llegada
13 fácilmente
14 el campesino

Exercise No. 143

1 he (she) was able, poder
2 I wanted, querer
3 they put, poner
4 I saw, ver
5 they read, leer
6 you said, decir
7 we had, tener
8 I gave, dar
9 he was (went), ser, ir
10 he (she) asked, pedir
11 You did (made) hacer
12 I came, venir
13 he, she made (did), hacer
14 you (*fam. sing.*) had, tener
15 I found out, saber

Exercise No. 144

1 (*j*)   3 (*b*)   5 (*h*)   7 (*d*)   9 (*c*)
2 (*e*)   4 (*g*)   6 (*i*)   8 (*f*)   10 (*a*)

Exercise No. 145

1 recibí, Yesterday I received a package.
2 quedaré, shall remain at home.
3 fuimos, We did not go to the cinema.
4 hacen, Now they are packing the valises.
5 escuchan, The teacher speaks and the students listen.
6 saldrán, Will you leave the city the day after tomorrow?
7 Vio, Did you see him the day before yesterday?
8 Viajaré, Next year I shall travel in Europe.
9 podemos, We are not able to hear him.
10 llegué, I arrived last week.

Exercise No. 146—Reading Selection 1

A Visit to La Granja

On one occasion Mrs. Adams took the sons of Mr. Carrillo on an excursion to the town of La Granja, which is situated some 3,500 feet above sea level, in the Guadarrama mountain range.

The town is not very far from the capital, and our friend arrived without difficulty. On arriving at the town she had a very bright idea. She proposed a lunch in the open air, near the Royal Palace. The boys accepted the project with enthusiasm.

Mrs. Adams entered a grocer's, bought two tins of sardines with tomato sauce. Then she bought some cakes and some buns in a bakery. Finally she bought some oranges and tomatoes at a fruiterer's.

There remained the problem of cold drinks. Now one of the boys had a bright idea. 'Why not buy some bottles of lemonade? There are always lots of cold-drink sellers.' 'Wonderful idea,' commented Mrs. Adams.

Then they began to explore La Granja. King Philip V chose this quiet and beautiful site for his summer residence. He had a palace built. It is said that the palace with its gardens resembles Versailles in miniature. There are fountains and an artificial lake. The old glass-factory interested Mrs. Adams as well. After their stroll, they found a very quiet place. Mrs. Adams opened the tins of sardines and prepared some sandwiches which they ate with the tomatoes. For refreshment they had the lemonade they had bought and finally they had as dessert the delicious oranges. It was a wonderful lunch and the boys were enchanted. They will not forget this experience for many years.

Exercise No. 147—Reading Selection 2

In the Rastro

In all the great cities of the world there is a 'flea market'. In Madrid it is called the Rastro. Do you want to buy a frying-pan or a worn suit of lights of a bullfighter? Here in this picturesque market you will find everything. The Rastro is composed of two parts—in one part they sell antiques, in the other, worn secondhand goods. One Sunday morning Mrs. Adams went to the Rastro and spent a few pleasant and amusing hours there. She looked at all the goods. Some drawings from the 18th century and some articles of pottery from the last century interested her most of all. Of course, she bought all she could. She also saw some antique chairs, but she had no money. Moreover, she thought, they were too big and heavy. On her next visit she will buy them without fail.

Exercise No. 148

1 Every town has a plaza.
2 Everybody goes to the plaza for rest, business, recreation—for everything.
3 Big trees grow on some plazas.
4 In others one sees nothing but dry leaves from some poor little tree.
5 Six kinds of shops in the arcades are: stationery shops, pharmacies, haberdashers, jewellery shops, bookshops, and cafés.
6 They get together in the cafe to chat or read the newspapers.
7 They drink small glasses of wine.
8 They eat tidbits, little slices of fried fish, prawns, sausage or cheese.
9 One sees an old church in the main plaza and perhaps the hotel of the town.
10 During the siesta hours some people rest on the benches, others sleep.
11 The life of the plaza begins again about 4 o'clock.
12 On Sunday afternoons everybody gets together on the plaza for the 'promenade'.
13 The boys walk in one direction and the girls in the opposite direction.
14 At night one sees some travellers who come from the market.

Exercise No. 149

1 El corazón de cada pueblo
2 mientras estaba sentado (a)
3 No se ven más
4 donde se encuentran
5 se reúnen, por la tarde
6 de vino tinto o blanco
7 pinchos, pescado frito o chorizo
8 una iglesia antigua
9 Se ven, cansados
10 Más tarde, que, demasiado pequeños

Exercise No. 150A

1 Duermo
2 No estoy durmiendo
3 ¿Quién duerme?
4 Dormimos
5 ¿Duerme Ud.?
6 Duerma Ud.
7 No duerman Uds.
8 Duerme
9 La niña no está durmiendo
10 ¿Quiénes duermen?
11 duermen
12 está durmiendo

Exercise No. 150B

1 que	3 que	5 que	7 todo lo que	9 de quienes
2 cuyo	4 de que	6 lo que	8 que	10 quien

Exercise No. 151—Test of Reading Comprehension

1 She wanted to take a car trip to the Valley of the Fallen.
2 She invited the sons of Mr. Carrillo to go with her.
3 They met in front of Mrs. A.'s hotel.
4 Mrs. A. had rented a car.
5 They saw nothing but some small houses.
6 They saw the mountains in the distance.
7 They had a puncture.
8 They could not find a jack in the boot.
9 It was noon.
10 A lorry driver stopped, lent them a jack and helped them change the tyre.
11 She thanked him and offered him 100 pesetas.
12 She climbed up slowly, but was nevertheless out of breath.
13 The boys ran up.
14 One can see the whole valley.
15 They felt tired but happy.

Exercise No. 152

1 conmigo en coche
2 los jovenes aceptaron, con alegría
3 Nos encontramos
4 Saqué el coche
5 Lo había alquilado
6 Charlando y riendo
7 De vez en cuando
8 No vimos más que
9 De repente
10 ¿Qué pasó?
11 cambiar la llanta, no había gato
12 a pesar de, paró
13 Nos hace falta un gato
14 y nos ayudó a cambiar el neumático
15 Nos dimos la mano y nos
   despedimos.

Exercise No. 153A

1 habíamos   We had seen the film.
2 había   Had you read many books?

3 había   Who had opened the window?
4 habían   The children had not slept during the night.
5 había   I had not believed the story.
6 habíamos   We had flown over the mountains.
7 habían   They had gone to the theatre.
8 Había   Had you had a good trip?
9 habían   You had said nothing.
10 Habías   Had you eaten the sweets, Johnny?

Exercise No. 153B

1 Él había comprado . . .
2 Yo había visto . . .
3 Habíamos comido . . .
4 ¿Habían recibido . . .?
5 ¿Había puesto Ud. . . .?
6 Uds. no habían oído . . .
7 No habías dormido . . .

8 se había sentado . . .
9 Habían tenido . . .
10 No habíamos dicho . . .
11 ¿Qué había pasado?
12 No habían hallado . . .
13 no habían cambiado
14 se había acercado

Exercise No. 154—Test of Reading Comprehension

1 She had never been a gambler.
2 She had noted that everybody was buying lottery tickets.
3 She was thinking of the possibility of winning one of the lesser prizes or perhaps the first prize.
4 She would take trips all over Spain.
5 She would visit her friends in Spain.
6 She would buy art objects for her house.
7 She bought a ticket from the woman vendor on the corner of the Gran Vía.
8 Next day she was reading the winning numbers in the newspaper.
9 She saw a number with three zeros.
10 She thought she had won a prize of 200,000 pesetas.
11 She was taking trips with her whole family through all Spain.
12 Mrs. A. had the number 25,000.
13 The number 26,000 won the prize.
14 ¿Qué importa? What does it matter?
15 From that moment I was a gambler.

Exercise No. 155

1 llegué, todo el mundo
2 en todas las esquinas
3 el premio gordo
4 volver a visitar
5 a toda la familia
6 soñaba yo

7 con tres ceros
8 qué querían decir los tres ceros
9 Los números que ganaron
10 Busqué
11 Al fin, en un bolsillo
12 había, no había

Exercise No. 156A

1 Iríamos . . .
2 Juan vendería . . .
3 No ganarían . . .
4 Ud. encontraría . . .
5 Leería . . .
6 ¿Llevaría Ud. . . .?

We would go . . .
John would sell . . .
They would not win . . .
You would meet . . .
I would read . . .
Would you take . . .?

7 ¿Les gustarían . . .?	Would you like . . .?
8 Saldría . . .	I would leave . . .
9 No podríamos . . .	We would not be able . . .
10 No dirían . . .	They would say nothing . . .

Exercise No. 156B

1 yo aprendería	6 ¿trabajaría Ud.?	11 yo haría
2 él escribiría	7 ¿vería Juan?	12 él vendría
3 irían	8 ¿quién visitaría?	13 no querrían
4 comeríamos	9 yo no viajaría	14 ¿saldría Vd.?
5 ella hablaría	10 ¿estudiarían?	15 Uds. pondrían

Exercise No. 157—Test of Reading Comprehension

1 An advertisement announcing a bullfight.
2 That bullfighting is most popular for tourists. Most Spaniards prefer football.
3 They are getting more aware of its importance.
4 A heavy polluted atmosphere.
5 Yes, they do now.
6 That man believes he is in the Centre of the Universe but all that is allocated to to him is only a tiny small corner.
7 In October 1969.
8 A Nature Reserve.
9 Fondo mundial para los animales salvajes.
10 In Asturias in the North of Spain.
11 Birds, wild cat, wild boar, foxes, wolves and bears and linxes.
12 Skiing and other Winter sports.
13 In the Sierra del Guadarrama near Madrid and in the Pyrenees in Catalonia.
14 Yes, it is quite popular.

Exercise No. 158

1 Estábamos para salir	7 se cree estar
2 una respuesta inesperada	8 tiene sentido
3 el apoyo tradicional	9 no se acabó aquí
4 en peligro de	10 también se practican
5 fue el primero	11 Quedé muy impresionada
6 Hay mucho que hacer	12 Me ofreció, que ignoraba

Exercise No. 159B

I. 1 The children bring them to me.	II. 1 Carlos me lo da.
2 The students send them to us.	2 Ana nos los presta.
3 They do not sell them to us.	3 El profesor nos lo dice.
4 I give it to you, sonny.	4 Te la damos, niño.

Exercise No. 159C

I. 1 We say it to you.	II. 1 Juan se lo dice a Ud.
2 We bring it to you (pl.)	2 María se la escribe a él.
3 We give them to him.	3 El profesor se los da a Uds.
4 We send them (f.) to them.	4 Se las mandamos a ella.

Exercise No. 159D

I. 1 Tell it to me.
2 Give it to us.
3 Lend them to me.
4 Send them to him.

II. 1 Préstemelos.
2 Mándenoslo.
3 Dígasela a él.
4 Déselos a ella.

Exercise No. 160—Test of Reading Comprehension

1 She had read various interesting books about its history and customs.
2 She was able to describe a little of what she had seen and learned.
3 The people interest her most.
4 Four qualities are: affection, generous hospitality, humour, and their philosophy in face of difficulties.
5 She finds life in Spain more tranquil.
6 She got a different impression in the taxi which brought her to her hotel at fearful speed.
7 She preferred to get a better knowledge of Spain.
8 She will take her whole family with her.
9 She is sure there will be no difficulties.
10 She leaves for Mexico on August 1.
11 She will be glad to write to Mr. L. and give him her impressions of Mexico.
12 She is going to compare Spain and Mexico.

Exercise No. 161A

1 I shall read . . .
2 I had read . . .
3 I have read . . .
4 We have visited . . .
5 We had visited . . .
6 We shall visit . . .
7 I can describe it.
8 I was able to describe it.
9 I shall be able . . .
10 I like your letter . . .
11 I liked your letter.
12 I shall like your letter.
13 They finish . . .
14 They finished . . .
15 They have finished . . .
16 They have much to tell me.
17 They will have . . .
18 They had . . .
19 We shall return home.
20 We returned . . .

Exercise No. 161B

1 sabe
2 Conocemos, no sabemos
3 no puedo
4 conocer
5 se conocen
6 Sé
7 Ud. conoce, Ud. puede
8 Ud. conoce
9 conocerle
10 no pueden

Exercise No. 161C

1 ¿Ha aprendido Ud. mucho sobre España?
2 Sí, he estado allí y he leído muchos libros.
3 ¿Sabe Ud. hablar español?
4 Sí, lo hablo bastante bien.
5 ¿Recuerda Ud. los lugares de que hemos hablado?
6 Los recuerdo bien.
7 ¿Puede Ud. describirlos en español?
8 Sí, puedo describirlos.
9 ¿Qué le gustó más en España?

10 Me gustó sobre todo el pueblo.
11 ¿Es más tranquila la vida de España que la de Londres?
12 En efecto, es más tranquila.
13 ¿Hay mucho que ver en España?
14 Hay mucho que ver, mucho que oír, mucho que hacer y mucho que aprender.
15 Mi viaje está acabado (terminado).

Exercise No. 162

1 Who will ask for information in the railway station?
2 Paul had already eaten lunch when I saw him.
3 Would you want to take a trip to all the countries of Europe?
4 I know that man, but I do not know where he lives.
5 We were writing our letters when the teacher entered the room.
6 Take these papers and put them on my desk.
7 We have bought the newspapers and we have read them.
8 I was not able to describe to them everything I had seen.
9 I came to Spain and they received me with affection.
10 William was speaking all afternoon while I was saying nothing.
11 I did not like the bullfight and therefore I shall not attend another.
12 The fathers (parents) were working while the children were sleeping.
13 We were in the market when it began to rain.
14 It was 8.30 in the morning and still the children were sleeping.
15 They will not come here because they will not have time.
16 Children, won't you play in the yard?
17 My uncle travelled through all the countries of South America.
18 Mrs. Adams liked spicy foods, but she remembered the advice of her teacher and would not eat them.
19 I wanted the toys but Charles would not give them to me.
20 If I find plates with designs of little animals I shall send them to you.
21 He asked for change of a note of 1,000 pesetas and the cashier gave it to him.
22 You have Mary's hat. Return it to her.

Exercise No. 163

1 es una comerciante de Londres
2 un viaje a España para visitar
3 conocerle mejor
4 aprendió a hablar español
5 había leído muchos libros
6 a su amigo y profesor, el Sr. López
7 los lugares de interés histórico
8 la Sra. Adams encontró la vida de España más tranquila que la de Londres
9 en el taxi que la llevó a su hotel
10 la velocidad espantosa del taxi
11 pronto terminó sus negocios
12 no pudo visitar Tenerife
13 tanto que ver, tanto que oír, tanto que hacer, tanto que aprender.
14 volverá a España
15 a toda la familia
16 la última carta de la Sra. Adams
17 Sin duda, y darle sus impresiones de México

Exercise 164—Reading Selection

Toledo

The city of Toledo is situated 44 miles to the south of Madrid, on the right bank of the river Tagus. It is 1,720 feet above sea level, and has some 41,000 inhabitants. It is a very old city and one of the most famous in Spain. It is not only a city, but also a national monument, so that its architecture and character remain and will remain intact.

In the Middle Ages Christians, Arabs and Jews lived in the city. They lived in peace and all contributed to make of Toledo a centre of culture and of a great variety of arts.

The tourist cannot miss visiting the cathedral. Its construction was begun in 1226 and was finished approximately in 1492, the year of the discovery of America. It is worthwhile also to see the Alcázar.

In about 1575 there came to Toledo an immigrant whose name is known in all the world. He came from Crete and was called Domeniko Theotokopouli, but we know him better under the name El Greco. He lived in Toledo until his death in 1614. We can see his paintings in the great museums of the world and in the city of Toledo itself. Indeed, they say that Toledo is one big museum dedicated to El Greco.

Dear reader, don't fail to visit this very beautiful city.

Exercise No. 165

1 She went to Mexico City.
2 Sr. González de las Vega.
3 Among other things she visited the Museum of Anthropology.
4 The University of Mexico, now the National Autonomous University of Mexico.
5 In the square of El Zócalo.
6 Mexicans are very polite and hospitable but more reserved and slower than the Spaniards.
7 One of their main interests is culture.
8 Yes, since the Revolution.
9 A federal republic.
10 Yucatán where the Mayan civilization was.
11 The oil industry is very important.

Exercise No. 166

1 Hace una semana que
2 me esperaba
3 antes de aterrizar
4 a la vez
5 He visitado
6 fue construída
7 una serie de calles estrechas
8 hospitalarios y corteses
9 por todo lo cultural
10 piensa llevarme
11 De regreso
12 todo lo de México

Exercise No. 167A

1 Salgo mañana para México.
2 Quería viajar por Francia.
3 Don Quijote fue escrito por Cervantes.
4 Le di al camarero una propina de diez por ciento.
5 Compró una falda para su madre.

6 Viajo por tren dos veces por semana.
7 El avión estaba para aterrizar.
8 Todos los estudiantes están por el profesor.
9 Le daré quinientas pesetas por este echarpe.
10 La muchacha está leyendo para sí.
11 No puedo ayudarle por el momento.
12 Este libro fue escrito por un padre para sus hijos.

Exercise No. 167B

1 El nino estuvo delante de mí.
2 Es un libro interesante sobre los viajes de un francés.
3 La universidad se encuentra fuera de la ciudad.
4 Sus zapatos están encima de la mesa.
5 Cerca de la plaza hay una catedral antigua.
6 ¿Queda lejos del centro?
7 Antes de almorzar quiero comprar una maleta.
8 Mis padres viven más allá de la plaza principal.
9 Además de la catedral visitamos la universidad.
10 Alrededor del palacio hay jardines bonitos.

1 GALICIA
2 ASTURIAS
3 CANTABRIA
4 PAIS VASCO
5 NAVARRA
6 LA RIOJA
7 ARAGON
8 CATALUÑA
9 PAIS VALENCIANO
10 CASTILLA-LA MANCHA
11 MADRID
12 CASTILLA-LEON
13 EXTREMADURA
14 ANDALUCIA
15 CANARIAS
16 MURCIA
17 BALEARES